T0207190

Lecture Notes in Business Information Processing 479

LNBIP reports state-of-the-art results in areas related to business information systems and industrial application software development – timely, at a high level, and in both printed and electronic form.

The type of material published includes

- Proceedings (published in time for the respective event)
- Postproceedings (consisting of thoroughly revised and/or extended final papers)
- Other edited monographs (such as, for example, project reports or invited volumes)
- Tutorials (coherently integrated collections of lectures given at advanced courses, seminars, schools, etc.)
- Award-winning or exceptional theses

LNBIP is abstracted/indexed in DBLP, EI and Scopus. LNBIP volumes are also submitted for the inclusion in ISI Proceedings.

Han van der Aa · Dominik Bork ·
Henderik A. Proper · Rainer Schmidt
Editors

Enterprise, Business-Process and Information Systems Modeling

24th International Conference, BPMDS 2023
and 28th International Conference, EMMSAD 2023
Zaragoza, Spain, June 12–13, 2023
Proceedings

Editors
Han van der Aa 🄳
University of Mannheim
Mannheim, Germany

Dominik Bork 🄳
TU Wien
Vienna, Austria

Henderik A. Proper 🄳
TU Wien
Vienna, Austria

Rainer Schmidt 🄳
Munich University of Applied Sciences
Munich, Germany

ISSN 1865-1348   ISSN 1865-1356 (electronic)
Lecture Notes in Business Information Processing
ISBN 978-3-031-34240-0   ISBN 978-3-031-34241-7 (eBook)
https://doi.org/10.1007/978-3-031-34241-7

Preface

This book contains the proceedings of two long-running events held alongside the CAiSE conference relating to the areas of enterprise, business-process, and information systems modeling: the 24th International Working Conference on Business Process Modeling, Development, and Support (BPMDS 2023) and the 28th International Working Conference on Exploring Modeling Methods for Systems Analysis and Development (EMMSAD 2023).

The two working conferences had a joint keynote given by Sjaak Brinkkemper, Professor of Software Production, Utrecht University, the Netherlands.

This year both conferences were held in Zaragoza, Spain, during June 12–13, 2023. More information on the individual events and their selection processes can be found on the following pages.

BPMDS 2023

The Business Process Modeling, Development, and Support (BPMDS) working conference has been held for more than two decades, dealing with, and promoting research on BPMDS, and has been a platform for a multitude of influential research papers. In keeping with its tradition, the working conference covers a broad range of theoretical and application-based research. BPMDS started in 1998 as a recurring workshop. During this period, business process analysis and design were recognized as central issues in the area of information systems (IS) engineering. The continued interest in these topics on behalf of the IS community is reflected by the success of recent BPMDS events and the emergence of new conferences and workshops devoted to the theme. In 2011, BPMDS became a two-day working conference attached to CAiSE. The goals, format, and history of BPMDS can be found at www.bpmds.org.

BPMDS 2023 received 26 submissions. Each submission was single-blind reviewed by three members of the Program Committee. Finally, 9 high-quality full papers and 2 short papers were selected. These accepted papers cover a wide spectrum of topics, which we organized under four headers: (1) AI for Business Process Management, (2) Modeling and Transforming Process Data, (3) Decision and Context-Aware Business Process Management, and (4) Modeling Temporal and Behavioral Process Constraints.

We want to thank everyone who submitted papers to BPMDS 2023 for sharing their work with us. Furthermore, we want to thank the members of the BPMDS 2023 Program Committee, who made a remarkable effort in reviewing submissions, the organizers of CAiSE 2023 for their help with the organization of the event, IFIP WG8.1 for its continued support, and Springer for their assistance during the production of the proceedings.

April 2023

Han van der Aa
Rainer Schmidt

EMMSAD 2023

The objective of the EMMSAD conference series is to provide a forum for researchers and practitioners interested in modeling methods for systems analysis and development (SA&D) to meet and exchange research ideas and results. The conference aims to provide a home for a rich variety of modeling paradigms, including software modeling, business process modeling, enterprise modeling, capability modeling, service modeling, ontology modeling, and domain-specific modeling. These important modeling paradigms, and specific methods following them, continue to be enriched with extensions, refinements, and even new languages, to address new challenges. Even with some attempts at standardization, new modeling paradigms and methods are constantly being introduced, especially in order to deal with emerging trends and challenges. Ongoing changes significantly impact the way systems are analyzed and designed in practice. Moreover, they challenge the empirical and analytical evaluation of the modeling methods, which contributes to the knowledge and understanding of their strengths and weaknesses. This knowledge may guide researchers towards the development of the next generation of modeling methods and help practitioners to select the modeling methods most appropriate to their needs.

EMMSAD 2023 accepted papers in the following five tracks that emphasize the variety of EMMSAD topics: (1) Foundations of modeling & method engineering – chaired by Jolita Ralyté and Janis Stirna; (2) Enterprise, business, process, and capability modeling – chaired by Jānis Grabis and Paul Grefen; (3) Information systems and requirements modeling – chaired by Roman Lukyanenko and Marcela Ruiz; (4) Domain-specific and knowledge modeling – chaired by Tiago Prince Sales and Arnon Sturm; and (5) Evaluation of models & modeling approaches – chaired by Renata Guizzardi and Qin Ma. More details on the current and previous editions of EMMSAD can be found at http://www.emmsad.org/.

In total, EMMSAD 2023 attracted 26 submissions. The division of submissions between the tracks was as follows: five related to foundations of modeling and method engineering, six related to enterprise, business, process, and capability modeling, six related to information systems and requirements modeling, four related to domain-specific and knowledge modeling, and five related to evaluation of modeling approaches. Each paper was single-blind reviewed by three members of the program committee and received a meta-review by the track chairs. Finally, 12 high-quality papers, comprising 9 long papers and three short papers, were selected.

We wish to thank all the authors who shared their work with us, as well as the members of the EMMSAD 2023 Program Committee and Track Chairs for their valuable, detailed, and timely reviews. Finally, we thank the organizers of CAiSE 2023 for their help with the organization of the event, IFIP WG 8.1 for its support, and Springer for their continued support.

April 2023

Dominik Bork
Henderik A. Proper

BPMDS 2023 Organization

Program Chairs

Han van der Aa — University of Mannheim, Germany
Rainer Schmidt — Munich University of Applied Sciences, Germany

Han van der Aa	University of Mannheim, Germany
Rainer Schmidt	Munich University of Applied Sciences, Germany

Steering Committee

Ilia Bider	Stockholm University and IbisSoft, Sweden
Selmin Nurcan	University Paris 1 Panthéon Sorbonne, France
Rainer Schmidt	Munich University of Applied Sciences, Germany
Pnina Soffer	University of Haifa, Israel

Program Committee – Senior PC Members

Saïd Assar	Institut Mines-Télécom Business School, France
Judith Barrios Albornoz	University of the Andes, Colombia
Karsten Boehm	FH Kufstein Tirol, Austria
Renata Guizzardi	Universidade Federal do Espirito Santo, Brazil
Dirk Fahland	Eindhoven Univ. of Technology, The Netherlands
Stefan Jablonski	Universität Bayreuth, Germany
Amin Jalali	Stockholm University, Sweden
Paul Johannesson	Royal Institute of Technology, Sweden
Kathrin Kirchner	Technical University of Denmark, Denmark
Agnes Koschmider	Kiel University, Germany
Sander J. J. Leemans	RWTH Aachen, Germany
Henrik Leopold	Kühne Logistics University, Germany
Jan Mendling	Humboldt-Universität zu Berlin, Germany
Michael Möhring	Munich University of Applied Sciences, Germany
Selmin Nurcan	Université Paris 1 Panthéon - Sorbonne, France
Gregor Polančič	University of Maribor, Slovenia
Hajo A. Reijers	Utrecht University, The Netherlands
Colette Rolland	Université Paris 1 Panthéon - Sorbonne, France
Michael Rosemann	Queensland University of Technology, Australia
Pnina Soffer	University of Haifa, Israel
Irene Vanderfeesten	KU Leuven, Belgium

Barbara Weber   University of St. Gallen, Switzerland
Moe Thandar Wynn   Queensland University of Technology, Australia
Alfred Zimmermann   Reutlingen University, Germany

Program Committee – Regular PC Members

Dorina Bano   Hasso Plattner Institute, Germany
Carl Corea   University of Koblenz, Germany
Francesco Tiezzi   University of Camerino, Italy
Francesca Zerbato   University of St. Gallen, Switzerland

Additional Reviewers

Shahrzad Khayatbashi   Linköping University, Sweden
Sara Pettinari   University of Camerino, Italy
Adrian Rebmann   University of Mannheim, Germany
Lorenzo Rossi   University of Camerino, Italy

EMMSAD 2023 Organization

Program Chairs

Dominik Bork	TU Wien, Austria
Henderik A. Proper	TU Wien, Austria

Track Chairs

Jānis Grabis	Riga Technical University, Latvia
Paul Grefen	Eindhoven University of Technology, The Netherlands
Renata Guizzardi	University of Twente, The Netherlands
Roman Lukyanenko	HEC Montreal, Canada
Qin Ma	University of Luxembourg, Luxembourg
Jolita Ralyté	University of Geneva, Switzerland
Marcela Ruiz	Zurich University of Applied Sciences, Switzerland
Tiago Prince Sales	University of Twente, The Netherlands
Janis Stirna	Stockholm University, Sweden
Arnon Sturm	Ben-Gurion University, Israel

Program Committee

Alexander Bock	University of Duisburg-Essen, Germany
Andreas L. Opdahl	University of Bergen, Norway
Arnon Sturm	Ben-Gurion University, Israel
Ben Roelens	Open University of the Netherlands, The Netherlands
Carson Woo	University of British Columbia, Canada
Cesar Gonzalez-Perez	Incipit CSIC, Spain
Christophe Feltus	Luxembourg Institute of Science and Technology, Luxembourg
Claudenir Fonseca	Free University of Bozen-Bolzano, Italy
Drazen Brdjanin	University of Banja Luka, Bosnia and Herzegovina
Elena Kornyshova	CNAM, France

Estefanía Serral	KU Leuven, Belgium
Felix Härer	University of Fribourg, Switzerland
Francisca Pérez	Universidad San Jorge, Spain
Frederik Gailly	Ghent University, Belgium
Geert Poels	Ghent University, Belgium
Georg Grossmann	University of South Australia, Australia
Georgios Koutsopoulos	Stockholm University, Sweden
Giancarlo Guizzardi	University of Twente, The Netherlands
Giuseppe Berio	Université de Bretagne Sud, France
Hans Weigand	Tilburg University, The Netherlands
Hans-Georg Fill	University of Fribourg, Switzerland
Istvan David	University of Montreal, Canada
Jaap Gordijn	Vrije Universiteit Amsterdam, The Netherlands
Janis Stirna	Stockholm University, Sweden
Jennifer Horkoff	Chalmers University of Technology, Sweden
João Paulo Almeida	Federal University of Espirito Santo, Brazil
Jolita Ralyté	University of Geneva, Switzerland
Jordi Cabot	Luxembourg Institute of Science and Technology, Luxembourg
Jose Ignacio Panach Navarrete	Universitat de València, Spain
Juergen Jung	Frankfurt University of Applied Sciences, Germany
Jānis Grabis	Riga Technical University, Latvia
Knut Hinkelmann	University of Applied Sciences Northwestern Switzerland, Switzerland
Kurt Sandkuhl	University of Rostock, Germany
Manfred Jeusfeld	University of Skövde, Sweden
Marcela Ruiz	Zurich University of Applied Sciences, Switzerland
Marne de Vries	University of Pretoria, South Africa
Martin Henkel	Stockholm University, Sweden
Mohamad Gharib	University of Florence, Italy
Monique Snoeck	KU Leuven, Belgium
Pascal Ravesteyn	Utrecht University of Applied Sciences, The Netherlands
Patricia Martin-Rodilla	Institute of Heritage Sciences Spanish National Research Council, Spain
Paul Grefen	Eindhoven University of Technology, The Netherlands
Peter Fettke	German Research Center for Artificial Intelligence (DFKI) and Saarland University, Germany

Qin Ma	University of Luxembourg, Luxembourg
Raian Ali	Hamad Bin Khalifa University, Qatar
Raimundas Matulevicius	University of Tartu, Estonia
Rebecca Deneckere	University of Paris 1 Panthéon – Sorbonne, France
Renata Guizzardi	University of Twente, The Netherlands
Roman Lukyanenko	University of Virginia, USA
Saïd Assar	Institut Mines - Télécom Business School, France
Simon Hacks	Stockholm University, Sweden
Sjaak Brinkkemper	Utrecht University, The Netherlands
Stefan Strecker	University of Hagen, Germany
Stijn Hoppenbrouwers	HAN University of Applied Sciences, The Netherlands
Sybren de Kinderen	Eindhoven University of Technology, The Netherlands
Tiago Prince Sales	University of Twente, The Netherlands
Tong Li	Beijing University of Technology, China
Tony Clark	Aston University, UK
Victoria Döller	University of Vienna, Austria
Victoria Torres	Universitat Politècnica de València, Spain
Yves Wautelet	KU Leuven, Belgium

Additional Reviewers

Achim Reiz	University of Rostock, Germany
Iván Alfonso	Universidad de los Andes, Colombia
Peter Pfeiffer	German Research Center for Artificial Intelligence (DFKI), Germany
Sergio Morales	Universitat Oberta de Catalunya, Spain
Sven Christ	University of Hagen, Germany

Situational AI Engineering for Automated Medical Reporting: Architecting and Experimentation in the Care2Report Research Program (Abstract of Keynote)

Sjaak Brinkkemper ⓘ

Department of Computing and Information Sciences, Utrecht University, Utrecht, The Netherlands
S.Brinkkemper@uu.nl
https://www.uu.nl/staff/SBrinkkemper

Abstract. The emergence of generative pre-trained transformers based on large sets of natural language training data has triggered an abundance of applications ranging from chatbots, essay writing, and poem generation, to text mining. However, at the moment, there is little scientific evidence on the way these AI tools can be integrated into large software applications. AI engineering is the domain of software engineering concerned with the architecting and development of these applications. In this keynote, we will present and discuss the Care2Report research program of Utrecht University that aims to design generic architectures of software applications for the automated reporting of human activity. Innovative interaction and reasoning are now becoming available using off-the-shelf AI technologies: machine learning, language models, speech recognition, action recognition, ontologies, knowledge graph databases, computational linguistics, and several more. We apply this general vision in the healthcare domain due to the societal need in this domain: high administrative burden where administrative duties are reported to take 20 to even 40% of the working time.

We will highlight the system architecture and the experimentation of the research program. We show how networks of architectural pipelines are being deployed to configure the AI technologies into one overall application for the reporting of medical consultations. Prompt engineering plays a significant role in the semantic interpretation of the natural language interaction for the summarization task. The application in the healthcare domain requires proper recognition of anatomic elements, symptoms, observations, diagnosis, and treatment policies. This recognition is configured based on a so-called medical guideline ontology derived from the publicly available guidelines of healthcare professionals. We discuss how prompt scripts can be composed by means of situational reuse of consultation reporting in different medical domains.

We end with an outlook on the future of this exciting, yet challenging, research endeavor.

Keywords: AI engineering · Healthcare informatics · Ontology · System architecture · Prompt engineering

References

1. ElAssy, O., de Vendt, R., Dalpiaz, F., Brinkkemper, S.: A semi-automated method for domain-specific ontology creation from medical guidelines. In: Augusto, A., Gill, A., Bork, D., Nurcan, S., Reinhartz-Berger, I., Schmidt, R. (eds.) BPMDS EMMSAD 2022 2022. LNBIP, vol. 450, pp. 295–309. Springer, Cham (2022). https://doi.org/10.1007/978-3-031-07475-2_20
2. Kwint, E., Zoet, A., Labunets, K., Brinkkemper, S.: How different elements of audio affect the word error rate of transcripts in automated medical reporting. In: Proceedings of BIOSTEC, Volume 5: HEALTHINF, pp. 179–187. SCITEPRESS (2023). https://doi.org/10.5220/0011794100003414
3. Maas, L., et al.: The care2report system: automated medical reporting as an integrated solution to reduce administrative burden in healthcare. In: HICSS, pp. 1–10 (2020)
4. Molenaar, S., Maas, L., Burriel, V., Dalpiaz, F., Brinkkemper, S.: Medical dialogue summarization for automated reporting in healthcare. In: Dupuy-Chessa, S., Proper, H. (eds.) CAiSE 2020. LNBIP, vol. 382, pp. 76–88. Springer, Cham (2020). https://doi.org/10.1007/978-3-030-49165-9_7
5. Molenaar, S., Schiphorst, L., Doyran, M., Salah, A.A., Dalpiaz, F., Brinkkemper, S.: Reference method for the development of domain action recognition classifiers: the case of medical consultations. In: Nurcan, S., Reinhartz-Berger, I., Soffer, P., Zdravkovic, J. (eds.) BPMDS EMMSAD 2020 2020. LNBIP, vol. 387, pp. 375–391. Springer, Cham (2020). https://doi.org/10.1007/978-3-030-49418-6_26
6. Schiphorst, L., Doyran, M., Molenaar, S., Salah, A.A., Brinkkemper, S.: Video2Report: a video database for automatic reporting of medical consultancy sessions. In: 15th IEEE International Conference on Automatic Face and Gesture Recognition, FG 2020, Buenos Aires, Argentina, 16–20 November 2020, pp. 552–556. IEEE (2020). https://doi.org/10.1109/FG47880.2020.00020
7. Wegstapel, J., et al.: Automated identification of yellow flags and their signal terms in physiotherapeutic consultation transcripts. In: Proceedings of the 16th International Joint Conference on Biomedical Engineering Systems and Technologies, BIOSTEC 2023, Volume 5: HEALTHINF, pp. 530–537. SCITEPRESS (2023). https://doi.org/10.5220/0011793800003414

Contents

Foundations and Method Engineering (EMMSAD 2023)

Enterprise Architecture and Transformation (EMMSAD)

Model-Driven Engineering (EMMSAD 2023)

Visualization and Process Modeling (EMMSAD 2023)

AI for Business Process Management
(BPMDS 2023)

Just Tell Me: Prompt Engineering in Business Process Management

Kiran Busch[1]([✉]), Alexander Rochlitzer[1], Diana Sola[2,3], and Henrik Leopold[1]

[1] Kühne Logistics University, Hamburg, Germany
`kiran.busch@the-klu.org`
[2] SAP Signavio, Walldorf, Germany
[3] Data and Web Science Group, University of Mannheim, Mannheim, Germany

Abstract. GPT-3 and several other language models (LMs) can effectively address various natural language processing (NLP) tasks, including machine translation and text summarization. Recently, they have also been successfully employed in the business process management (BPM) domain, e.g., for predictive process monitoring and process extraction from text. This, however, typically requires fine-tuning the employed LM, which, among others, necessitates large amounts of suitable training data. A possible solution to this problem is the use of prompt engineering, which leverages pre-trained LMs without fine-tuning them. Recognizing this, we argue that prompt engineering can help bring the capabilities of LMs to BPM research. We use this position paper to develop a research agenda for the use of prompt engineering for BPM research by identifying the associated potentials and challenges.

1 Introduction

The recent introduction of ChatGPT has dramatically increased public awareness of the capabilities of transformer-based language models (LMs). However, already for a while, LMs are used to address several common natural language processing (NLP) tasks including search, machine translation, and text summarization. Also in the business process management (BPM) community, LMs have been used for tasks such as process extraction from text [2] or activity recommendation [17]. To accomplish this, pre-trained models are typically fine-tuned, which transforms the pre-trained LM into a task-specific model. The performance of fine-tuning, however, is highly dependent on the amount and quality of downstream data available, which is a common issue in BPM practice [2,6].

Recent studies have shown that prompt engineering [8], which leverages pre-trained LMs without fine-tuning them, can effectively address the issue of limited downstream data and yield promising results in various NLP tasks [3,10,20] and in other domains like reasoning [7]. Prompt engineering involves the use of natural language task specifications, known as prompts, which are given to the LM at inference time to provide it with information about the downstream task. For example, when creating a prompt for the extraction of a topic from the text

© The Author(s), under exclusive license to Springer Nature Switzerland AG 2023
H. van der Aa et al. (Eds.): BPMDS 2023/EMMSAD 2023, LNBIP 479, pp. 3–11, 2023.
https://doi.org/10.1007/978-3-031-34241-7_1

"Eliud Kipchoge is a Kenyan long-distance runner", we could append "This text is about ___?" to the text and ask the LM to fill the blank with a topic. Thus, without altering the model itself, prompts provide the context for a downstream task and enable the customization of the outputs and interactions with an LM.

Research towards prompt engineering for BPM tasks is, however, still in its early stages. To our knowledge, only Bellan et al. [2] have conducted research in this field, with the aim of extracting process information from text. While their study demonstrated the potential of using conceptual definitions of business process entities to set the context for the extraction task, the authors acknowledged that providing an LM with the appropriate contextual BPM knowledge via prompts may be a challenging problem that requires further investigation. Against this background, we use this position paper to promote the use of prompt engineering for BPM research. Specifically, we identify potentials and challenges pertaining to the use of prompt engineering for BPM tasks. We believe that prompt engineering has the potential to effectively address a large variety of NLP-related BPM tasks and, hence, reduce the need for highly specialized and use-case specific techniques as well as the need to obtain large training datasets.

2   Background

Recent advances in the NLP field have led to powerful LMs, which have shown remarkable capabilities across a diverse range of tasks such as text summarization [10], machine translation [20], reasoning [7], and many more. The success of applying such models to downstream tasks can be attributed to the transformer architecture [19] and increased model sizes in combination with the computational capacity of modern computer systems, as well as the models' pre-training on massive volumes of unlabeled text. Pre-training an LM enables it to develop general-purpose abilities that can be transferred to downstream tasks [13].

The traditional approach for performing a downstream task with a pre-trained LM is *fine-tuning*, which involves updating the LM's parameters by training it on a large dataset of labeled examples specific to the downstream task [3]. For example, when fine-tuning an LM for the activity-identification task in the context of transforming a text into a process model [1], such a labeled example could be the (input text, activity)-pair ("He ordered the shoes", "order shoes"). However, a major limitation in the fine-tuning paradigm is the need for large task-specific datasets and task-specific training [3], which has two drawbacks. First, the performance of fine-tuning is greatly impacted by the number and quality of examples that are specific to the task, while in practice, the scenarios with sparse data are common. Second, fine-tuning modifies all parameters of the LM, thus requiring a copy of the model to be stored for each task.

Therefore, we are currently observing a paradigm shift from fine-tuning to *prompt engineering* [8], which is driven by the remarkable task-agnostic performance of LMs [3,15]. In the prompt-engineering paradigm, natural language task specifications, referred to as prompts, are provided to the LM at inference time to set the context for a downstream task without changing the LM itself. This approach of "freezing" pre-trained models is particularly attractive, as model sizes

Potentials		Challenges	
Input	1. Effective use of limited data volumes 2. Natural language-based interaction 3. Input optimization via prompt templates	1. Process representation in prompts 2. Limited prompt length	
Model	4. Overcoming task-specificity 5. Improved computational efficiency	3. Choice of pre-trained model 4. Transferability of prompts	
Output	6. Increased explainability	5. Processing the model output 6. Evaluation of prompt templates	

Fig. 1. Potentials and challenges of prompt engineering for BPM

continue to increase. In certain situations, using pre-trained models in combination with prompt engineering has been demonstrated to be competitive with or even better than state-of-the-art fine-tuned models [3,15,16].

Prompt engineering is typically implemented in a zero-shot or few-shot setting, which eliminates the need for large task-specific datasets. While in the zero-shot setting the pre-trained LM is used in combination with a natural language description of the task only, in the few-shot setting, the model additionally receives one or more examples of the task. Both settings rely on the *in-context learning* ability of large LMs, i.e., their ability to perform a downstream task based on a prompt consisting of a natural language instruction and, optionally, a few additional task demonstrations [3]. While in-context learning describes the conditioning of a pre-trained model on a downstream task using a prompt, prompt engineering is concerned with finding effective prompts for in-context learning. Typically, prompt engineering involves the development of task-specific prompt templates, which describe how a prompt should be formulated to enable the pre-trained model to perform the downstream task at hand [8]. Coming back to the activity-identification task in the context of transforming a text to a process model, such a prompt template could include a conceptual definition of "Activity", the task instruction "Identify the activity:", and examples of the task. The development of such templates can be challenging, since the in-context learning performance of an LM is highly sensitive to the prompt format, including examples and the order of these examples [12,22].

3   Potentials

In this section, we discuss the potentials arising from the use of prompt engineering in BPM. Figure 1 provides an overview of the six potentials we identified and whether they relate to the input (i.e., the use of prompts), the LM itself, or the output. In the following paragraphs, we discuss each potential in detail.

1. Effective use of limited data volumes. For many BPM tasks, the acquisition of large labeled datasets is difficult and costly, which can be attributed to several factors. First, annotating data for BPM tasks requires expert or at least domain knowledge [1]. Second, there exists a vast variety of BPM tasks, each requiring separate labeled training datasets. Third, legal aspects limit the availability of data for both organizations and academia, as process-related data can contain sensitive information about the organizations' internal operations. As a result, researchers rarely have access to large amounts of high-quality process data from practice, forcing them to use LMs on small datasets. Applying standard fine-tuning using such small datasets can result in poor performance, as many problems are difficult to grasp from just looking at a few examples [14]. Prompt engineering circumvents these issues by integrating task specifications into the input sequence provided to the LM and has been shown to achieve competitive performance when compared to fine-tuning in low-data regimes [3,15,16]. This indicates a great potential in the BPM field, where limited availability of large task-specific datasets and poor data quality are common issues [2,6].

2. Natural language-based interaction. In recent years, the NLP field has been characterized by a rapid pace of innovation. However, leveraging the breakthrough developments for BPM tasks has usually required specialized knowledge in deep learning. By leveraging natural language task specifications to employ LMs, prompt engineering has the potential to make these ever-more complex models readily accessible and customizable for BPM researchers and practitioners, regardless of their background. In particular, prompts represent an interpretable interface to communicate with LMs [3], which enables incorporating expert knowledge into LMs by simply changing the instruction or examples contained in the prompt. For instance, prompts can provide information about the BPM domain, or, in the context of extracting process information from text, definitions of "Activity", "Participant", and other elements to be extracted [2]. While manually crafting appropriate prompts may still require domain expertise and experience with LMs, research on automated prompt generation [16] can be expected to further lower the barrier to leveraging LMs for BPM.

3. Input optimization via prompt templates. As already discussed, researchers in the BPM field often lack access to high-quality training datasets from practice. This can be problematic when fine-tuning an LM for a downstream task, as training on a dataset containing erroneous samples can lead to undesirable results. To illustrate this, consider the task of next-activity prediction in the context of predictive process monitoring. Now suppose that the training dataset contains process instances with semantic anomalies, e.g., a process instance in which an order is both accepted and rejected. When fine-tuning an LM on such a dataset, it may learn that this is correct process behavior and apply this in prediction tasks. However, in a prompt, we could extend the provided instruction for the prediction task and tell the LM to ignore semantic anomalies in the provided examples. Thus, prompt engineering can help to mitigate issues with erroneous inputs by designing prompts, which enable the LM to use its general-purpose knowledge and correct erroneous examples itself.

4. Overcoming task-specificity. The fine-tuning approach achieves strong performance by transforming a pre-trained LM into a task-specific model using an individual set of annotated samples for every new task. However, the task-specificity of the models is a major limitation, since this means that a new model needs to be trained for each BPM task. As an example, consider the two tasks of transforming a process model into text and predicting the next activity of a running process instance. In the past, these tasks would have been addressed by two completely different, potentially highly specific techniques. Prompt engineering can address this limitation. Given appropriate prompts, a single LM can be used across a wide range of tasks [3]. Thus, prompt engineering can help to use task-agnostic models and develop methods that can be applied across different BPM tasks.

5. Improved computational efficiency. Increasing the size of LMs has been shown to result in performance improvements across a wide range of NLP tasks, particularly in settings that use in-context learning [3]. In recent years, LMs have grown from less than 350 million parameters [4] to more than 175 billion parameters [3]. Fine-tuning such large models requires substantial amounts of time and computational resources, which limits the models' accessibility and results in an immense carbon footprint. Prompt engineering, in contrast, is a fast and more sustainable approach of using a pre-trained model for a downstream task, reducing the cost of tailoring large models to new applications. Prompt engineering can thus help organizations to leverage the general-purpose abilities of a pre-trained LM for the management of their operations in a more timely, cost-effective and sustainable manner.

6. Increased explainability. BPM supports decision-making in organizations, also in critical domains such as healthcare or financial services, which makes it essential to understand the rationale of employed systems. Therefore, the explainability and interpretability of artificial intelligence is becoming a growing area of interest in the BPM field [5]. Prompt engineering can contribute to this emergent research direction in several ways. First, prompts provide an interpretable window into the task-specific behavior of an LM, since they contain all information about a downstream task that the model obtains. In contrast, the quality of the data used for fine-tuning may be less transparent to an LM's user. Second, prompt engineering can help LMs to decompose a task into intermediate steps, which can help to understand how the LM arrived at a particular output. In addition, the decomposition of a task allows for debugging in case of incorrect outputs and can improve the overall performance of an LM [21]. Consequently, prompt engineering has the potential to foster more trust in LMs and increased LM adoption by BPM researchers and practitioners.

4   Challenges

To realize the outlined potentials, various challenges have to be overcome. Figure 1 provides an overview of the challenges we identified and whether they relate to the input (i.e., the use of prompts), the LM itself, or the output.

1. Process representation in prompts. While prompts are task specifications provided in natural language, the input for many BPM tasks is rarely simple text but includes potentially complex representations such as process models or event logs. In addition, many BPM tasks, e.g., process model matching [11], face the challenge of dealing with process data of varying levels of abstraction. This raises the question of how process models or event logs can be expressed in a prompt in such a way that they can be effectively processed by an LM. As an example, consider the task of transforming process models into textual descriptions [1]. We could leverage an LM for this task by representing the process model in a prompt and asking the LM to give a description of the process. Finding such representations for complex process models, which contain sophisticated process structures like gateways or pools, is challenging, as it is not obvious how the non-sequential complexity of process models can be captured in a prompt. The development of prompt templates that are able to incorporate complex process representations and cover a large span of abstraction levels is thus a significant challenge for leveraging LMs for BPM tasks trough prompt engineering.

2. Limited prompt length. The limited input length of an LM restricts the amount of context and instructions that can be provided for a downstream task in a single prompt, making it difficult to include extensive information or numerous task demonstrations. This poses a particular challenge in the BPM field, as process representations often contain a lot of different information, such as resources, responsibilities, or types of activities. Simply using the XML-format of a process model in a prompt, for example, will most likely exceed the input length limitation. When developing prompt templates, it is thus essential to carefully select the pieces of information contained in a process representation that are important for the specific BPM task and need to be provided to the LM via prompt. As an example, consider the process model autocompletion task [11]. When recommending the next modeling step at a user-defined position in a process model, elements close to the given position may be more relevant for this task than other elements appearing in the process model [18]. Thus, when developing prompt templates for BPM tasks under the restriction of limited prompt lengths, such additional considerations need to be taken into account.

3. Choice of pre-trained model. In recent years, a number of pre-trained LMs have been published. Notable examples include BERT [4], GPT-3 [3], and T5 [13]. While several pre-trained LMs have already been employed in the BPM field, there is a lack of systematic comparisons of the existing process knowledge that is contained in these models. Similar to the evaluation of commonsense in pre-trained models [23], it could be beneficial for the selection of a pre-trained model to evaluate the process knowledge contained in different LMs. However, such an evaluation requires benchmarks that are currently not available. Similar benchmarks are also needed for a systematic comparison of the benefits that prompt engineering provides for different pre-trained LMs and BPM tasks.

4. Transferability of prompts. The development of LMs is constantly advancing, with new models, trained on larger datasets or with new training techniques, appearing frequently. Against this background, it is essential to understand the extent to which selected prompts are specific to the LM. A first study that investigates the transferability of prompts for different NLP tasks and unsupervised open-domain question answering has been conducted by Perez et al. [12]. Their study shows that prompt transferability is poor when the model sizes are different. In other words, the same prompt can lead to performances discrepancies between LMs of different sizes. Therefore, similar studies for BPM tasks are needed in order to learn about the transferability of prompts across different LMs in the BPM field and to make prompt engineering efficient in the long run.

5. Processing the model output. When a model is presented with a prompt, it generates an output in response. However, it may be necessary to conduct a post-processing step to convert the model output into a format that is conducive for the BPM task at hand. To illustrate this, consider the translation of process models from a source into a target language [1]. Prompt engineering for this task involves the transformation of a given process model into a textual representation that can be processed by an LM to generate a translation. However, obtaining a translated process model from the translated textual representation requires an additional step. This post-processing step, which addresses the model output, can be challenging as it requires both domain knowledge and an understanding of how the LM generates output.

6. Evaluation of prompt templates. Process representations, such as process models or event logs, can be incorporated into a prompt in many different ways. For example, in the case of an event log, the events could be separated by "," or "then". For more complex process representations, a high number of possible prompt templates can be expected. Taking into account that LMs are highly sensitive to the choice of prompts [22], even similar variants of prompt templates should be evaluated. Therefore, instead of a brute-force trial and error approach with the prompt, it is essential to develop systematic ways for the evaluation of different prompt templates. A complementary approach to systematic evaluations could be the reduction of evaluation effort by disregarding prompt templates that do not adhere to design guidelines for prompt engineering in the BPM field. This would necessitate research on such guidelines, similar to those for prompt engineering for image generation [9]. The evaluation of prompt templates thus represents a challenge for prompt engineering in the BPM field, which can be addressed through different research directions.

5 Conclusion

In this paper, we examined the potentials and challenges of prompt engineering for BPM, providing a research agenda for future work. We demonstrated that the shift *from fine-tuning to prompt engineering* can enhance research efforts in the application of LMs in BPM. While our work should not be seen as prescriptive nor comprehensive, we expect it to help in positioning current research activities and in fostering innovative ideas to address the identified challenges.

References

1. van der Aa, H., Carmona, J., Leopold, H., Mendling, J., Padró, L.: Challenges and opportunities of applying natural language processing in business process management. In: COLING, pp. 2791–2801 (2018)
2. Bellan, P., Dragoni, M., Ghidini, C.: Extracting business process entities and relations from text using pre-trained language models and in-context learning. In: Enterprise Design, Operations, and Computing, pp. 182–199 (2022)
3. Brown, T., et al.: Language models are few-shot learners. NeurIPS **33**, 1877–1901 (2020)
4. Devlin, J., Chang, M.W., Lee, K., Toutanova, K.: BERT: pre-training of deep bidirectional transformers for language understanding. In: NAACL-HLT, pp. 4171–4186 (2019)
5. Galanti, R., Coma-Puig, B., de Leoni, M., Carmona, J., Navarin, N.: Explainable predictive process monitoring. In: ICPM, pp. 1–8 (2020)
6. Käppel, M., Jablonski, S., Schönig, S.: Evaluating predictive business process monitoring approaches on small event logs. In: Paiva, A.C.R., Cavalli, A.R., Ventura Martins, P., Pérez-Castillo, R. (eds.) QUATIC 2021. CCIS, vol. 1439, pp. 167–182. Springer, Cham (2021). https://doi.org/10.1007/978-3-030-85347-1_13
7. Kojima, T., Gu, S.S., Reid, M., Matsuo, Y., Iwasawa, Y.: Large language models are zero-shot reasoners. In: ICML Workshop KRLM (2022)
8. Liu, P., Yuan, W., Fu, J., Jiang, Z., Hayashi, H., Neubig, G.: Pre-train, prompt, and predict: a systematic survey of prompting methods in natural language processing. ACM Comput. Surv. **55**(9), 1–35 (2023)
9. Liu, V., Chilton, L.B.: Design guidelines for prompt engineering text-to-image generative models. In: CHI, pp. 1–23 (2022)
10. Liu, Y., Lapata, M.: Text summarization with pretrained encoders. In: EMNLP-IJCNLP, pp. 3730–3740. Association for Computational Linguistics (2019)
11. Mendling, J., Leopold, H., Pittke, F.: 25 challenges of semantic process modeling. IJISEBC **1**(1), 78–94 (2015)
12. Perez, E., Kiela, D., Cho, K.: True few-shot learning with language models. NeurIPS **34**, 11054–11070 (2021)
13. Raffel, C., et al.: Exploring the limits of transfer learning with a unified text-to-text transformer. J. Mach. Learn. Res. **21**(1), 5485–5551 (2020)
14. Schick, T., Schütze, H.: Exploiting cloze-questions for few-shot text classification and natural language inference. In: EACL, pp. 255–269 (2021)
15. Schick, T., Schütze, H.: It's not just size that matters: small language models are also few-shot learners. In: NAACL-HLT, pp. 2339–2352 (2021)
16. Shin, T., Razeghi, Y., Logan IV, R.L., Wallace, E., Singh, S.: Autoprompt: eliciting knowledge from language models with automatically generated prompts. In: EMNLP, pp. 4222–4235 (2020)
17. Sola, D., van der Aa, H., Meilicke, C., Stuckenschmidt, H.: Activity recommendation for business process modeling with pre-trained language models. In: ESWC. Springer, Cham (2023)
18. Sola, D., Meilicke, C., van der Aa, H., Stuckenschmidt, H.: A rule-based recommendation approach for business process modeling. In: La Rosa, M., Sadiq, S., Teniente, E. (eds.) CAiSE 2021. LNCS, vol. 12751, pp. 328–343. Springer, Cham (2021). https://doi.org/10.1007/978-3-030-79382-1_20
19. Vaswani, A., et al.: Attention is all you need. NeurIPS **30** (2017)

20. Wang, Q., et al.: Learning deep transformer models for machine translation. In: Proceedings of the 57th Annual Meeting of the Association for Computational Linguistics, pp. 1810–1822 (2019)
21. Wei, J., et al.: Chain of thought prompting elicits reasoning in large language models. arXiv preprint arXiv:2201.11903 (2022)
22. Zhao, Z., Wallace, E., Feng, S., Klein, D., Singh, S.: Calibrate before use: improving few-shot performance of language models. In: ICML, pp. 12697–12706 (2021)
23. Zhou, X., Zhang, Y., Cui, L., Huang, D.: Evaluating commonsense in pre-trained language models. In: AAAI, vol. 34, pp. 9733–9740 (2020)

Reinforcement Learning-Supported AB Testing of Business Process Improvements: An Industry Perspective

Aaron Friedrich Kurz[1,2]([∗]) [iD], Timotheus Kampik[2], Luise Pufahl[3],
and Ingo Weber[3,4] [iD]

[1] Technische Universität Berlin, Berlin, Germany
[2] SAP Signavio, Berlin, Germany
{aaron.kurz,timotheus.kampik}@sap.com
[3] Technische Universität München, Munich, Germany
{luise.pufahl,ingo.weber}@tum.de
[4] Fraunhofer Gesellschaft, Munich, Germany

Abstract. In order to better facilitate the need for continuous business process improvement, the application of DevOps principles has been proposed. In particular, the AB-BPM methodology applies AB testing and reinforcement learning to increase the speed and quality of improvement efforts. In this paper, we provide an industry perspective on this approach, assessing requirements, risks, opportunities, and more aspects of the AB-BPM methodology and supporting tools. Our qualitative analysis combines grounded theory with a Delphi study, including semistructured interviews and multiple follow-up surveys with a panel of ten business process management experts. The main findings indicate a need for human control during reinforcement learning-driven experiments, the importance of aligning the methodology culturally and organizationally with the respective setting, and the necessity of an integrated process execution platform.

Keywords: Business Process Improvement · Process Redesign · Reinforcement Learning · AB Testing · Grounded Theory · Delphi Study

1 Introduction

Business processes are crucial for creating value and delivering products and services. Improving these processes is essential for gaining a competitive edge and enhancing value delivery, as well as increasing efficiency and customer satisfaction. This makes business process improvement (BPI) a key aspect of business process management (BPM), which is described as "the art and science of overseeing how work is performed in an organization to ensure consistent outcomes and to take advantage of improvement opportunities" [6].

© The Author(s), under exclusive license to Springer Nature Switzerland AG 2023
H. van der Aa et al. (Eds.): BPMDS 2023/EMMSAD 2023, LNBIP 479, pp. 12–26, 2023.
https://doi.org/10.1007/978-3-031-34241-7_2

DevOps, an integration of development and operations, is "a set of practices intended to reduce the time between committing a change to a system and the change being placed into normal production, while ensuring high quality" [2] and widely applied in the software industry. A new line of research in the field of BPM proposes using DevOps principles, like AB testing, to facilitate continuous BPI with a method called *AB-BPM* [24]. AB testing assesses different software feature versions in the production environment with real users, usually in end user-facing parts of the software. The current version is only retired if the test data supports the improvement hypothesis. Applying such rapid validation of improvements to processes is a departure from the traditional BPM lifecycle, where the possibility of not meeting improvement hypotheses in production is rarely considered, leading to expensive do-overs [7,24]. Going beyond traditional AB testing, AB-BPM proposes the application of reinforcement learning (RL) to utilize performance measurements already while the experiments are conducted by dynamically routing incoming process instantiation requests to the more suitable version.

The AB-BPM method has not yet been systematically analyzed regarding the needs of BPM practitioners. To facilitate applicability, additional research is needed to increase confidence in the proposed approach. Furthermore, BPM practitioners' insights on the AB-BPM methodology can be of value to the wider BPM community, since they can uncover hurdles and possibilities on the path to more automation in the field of process (re-)design. Therefore, this paper presents a qualitative study, with the overarching *research question* being: What do BPM experts think about AB-BPM, and which implications does this have for the further development of the methodology and supporting tools? To this end, we collected data on experts' views regarding the impact, advantages, and challenges of the AB-BPM method in an industry setting. In particular, we study the overall sentiment, perceived risks, potential use cases, technical feasibility, and software support requirements of the AB-BPM method. To obtain the results, a panel of BPM experts from a large enterprise software company was interviewed and participated in follow-up surveys. We applied a mixture of the grounded theory [4] and Delphi [5] research methodologies.

2   Background and Related Work

Organizations of all industries and sizes perform various combinations of activities to achieve desired results, may it be the production of physical goods or the provision of services. These combinations of activities are called business processes [1]. They are often standardized and documented, meaning that each time an organization tries to achieve a particular result, they use a similar combination of activities. Such a standardized business process is often modeled graphically with the Business Process Model and Notation (BPMN) [22]. BPI is a central part of BPM [6], and also a core topic of this study. The traditional BPM lifecycle (see non-blue areas and dotted arrow of Fig. 1) is generally sequential [6] and does not consider failures as "first-class citizens". This means that failures are not considered a necessary part of improvement and evaluated systematically, but rather a nuisance caused by insufficient planning in the redesign phase; and if failure happens, the whole lifecycle has to be repeated.

A more comprehensive approach to assessing the effects of change is AB testing. The main goal of AB testing is to quickly determine whether a particular change to a system component will improve important performance metrics [2]. The initial and the updated version of the component are tested in parallel using randomized experiments in a production environment (A vs B). The new version is often only made available to a select group of consumers, limiting any potential adverse impacts. The method has emerged as a popular approach when updating business-to-consumer software systems [11].

A particularly dynamic approach to AB testing can be facilitated by RL. While supervised learning aims to learn how to label elements from a collection of labeled data, and unsupervised learning tries to find hidden structures in unlabeled data, RL has the goal of optimizing the behavior of a software agent based on a numeric reward in an interactive environment [26]. In RL, the agent is situated in a specific environment and has to decide on an action. This action is then evaluated, and a reward is calculated based on the action's consequence. The goal of the agent is to maximize the total reward it obtains. Learning which choices to make in what situation happens, essentially, through a systematic approach to trial and error [26].

As mentioned above, the sequential approach of the traditional BPI lifecycle fails to rapidly react to improvement hypotheses that are falsified in reality. This is a crucial shortcoming: research on BPI has shown that 75 percent of BPI ideas did not lead to an improvement: half of them had no effect, and a quarter even had detrimental outcomes [7]. This issue can be observed across domains: in a study conducted at Microsoft, only a third of the website improvement ideas actually had a positive impact [12]. Furthermore, comparing process performance before and after the implementation is problematic in and of itself because changing environmental factors may be the primary driver of changes in process performance (or lack thereof). To mitigate these problems, [24] proposes

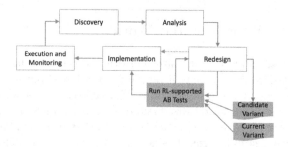

Fig. 1. Traditional BPM/AB-BPM lifecycle, adapted from [6,24]; dotted arrow represents flow in traditional BPI lifecycle, blue areas represent additions in AB-BPM lifecycle.

using AB testing when transitioning from the analysis to the implementation phase. This would mean that the redesigned version is deployed in parallel to the old process version, allowing for a fair comparison. Since AB testing is not traditionally used in such a high-risk and long-running setting as BPM, the authors [24] apply RL to facilitate dynamic testing. With RL algorithms, we can make decisions based on the obtained data faster, by already dynamically routing process instantiation requests to the better-performing version during the experiment itself, thereby minimizing the risk of exposing customers to sub-optimal process versions for too long. Altogether, AB-BPM should also allow for a shorter theoretical analysis of the redesign, in line with the DevOps mantra "fail fast, fail cheap". Figure 1 (including the blue areas, excluding the dotted arrow) presents the improved AB-BPM lifecycle.

In addition to the RL-supported AB testing of improvement hypotheses, the complete AB-BPM method proposes some more test and analysis techniques. Our inquiry focuses on the RL-supported AB testing of process variants: it is at the AB-BPM method's core, whereas the other steps in AB-BPM merely support the design of the RL-supported AB tests. References to AB-BPM in this work solely refer to the RL-supported AB testing of business process variants.

3   Research Method

In order to address the research questions, we apply the grounded theory (GT) research method [4], combined with the Delphi method [17]. The GT research methodology is suitable for building a theory and answering questions about fields where little is known. It has been selected because so far, no research has been conducted on the industry perspective of applying AB testing for BPI. After the initial data collection with semi-structured interviews (*purposive sampling* in GT), we approached the second stage of the GT methodology (also called *theoretical sampling* [4]) as a shortened Delphi method study. The novelty and complexity of the topic and the fact that the experts from the interviews have already been introduced to the AB-BPM method made a follow-up within this group of panelists more suitable than a broader follow-up survey, which would have required training the larger group and led to a more heterogeneous exposure of participant knowledge. The Delphi method has multiple sub-categories, and the version we use is called the ranking-type Delphi method (RTDM). The goal of RTDM is identifying and ranking key issues regarding a certain topic [17]. In the following paragraphs, we describe the research methods used in more detail.

Expert Selection. We have recruited experts from a multi-national software company with more than 100,000 employees. The company develops enterprise software, and the majority of study participants are employees of a sub-unit that specializes in developing BPM software. Due to the study's exploratory nature, the aim was to obtain a perspective from a broad range of experts. For this purpose, we set a number of goals for the selection of the experts: *i)* to include people who develop BPM software as well as people that work in consulting (however, not necessarily both at once); *ii)* to cover various areas of technical skills, e.g., software engineering and data science; *iii)* the study participants should have experience with business process improvement initiatives. The aim was to have a panel with ten experts, in line with standard practice for RTDM studies in Information Systems [17]. After reaching out to eleven people, ten people agreed to take part. Most study participants have a background in software engineering or other product-related roles (e.g., product management). But the panel also includes experts from consulting and a data scientist. The study participants had, on average, 7.6 years (SD = 2.4 years) of full-time industry experience, working in the BPM field for an average of 4.3 years (SD = 1.8 years). Most of the experts (seven) have a degree in the Science/Engineering realm, while some (three) obtained their education in the field of Business/Management. The highest educational degree of five of the study participants is a Ph.D., for four a master's and for one a bachelor's degree. The experts went through three study rounds: the interview, a validation survey and a ranking survey. Regarding participation levels, there was a drop from ten to five in the validation survey, whereas the final ranking survey reached eight people. Since the ranking survey is more important for the final results and included the option to give feedback on the coding as well, the level of participation after the initial interviews can be seen as relatively high.

Interviews. As is common in GT research, we conducted semi-structured qualitative interviews with subject matter experts, aiming to capture a wide range of ideas and thoughts on the complexities of a topic by openly engaging in conversation with subjects and analyzing these interactions [3,21]. Since the order and wording of questions and the follow-up questions are highly flexible in semi-structured interviews, the interview guide is more of a collection of topics to be covered and not a verbatim script. There have also been minor adjustments to the interview guide during the interview phase in response to gained knowledge, in line with standard practice. Such adjustments are considered unproblematic since the goal is not a comparison of different subgroups, to test a hypothesis, or to find out how many people hold certain beliefs, but to find out what kind of beliefs are present [3]. We used the following interview guideline, given in a condensed version: 1. prior experience with BPI, 2. short introduction to AB-BPM (not a question, short presentation; 5–10 minutes), 3. execution of AB tests/feasibility, 4. suitability, 5. prerequisites to adopt the AB-BPM method, 6. risks, 7. tool requirements, 8. open discussion.

Consolidation and Validation. After the interviews, the transcripts were coded, and topics were consolidated (GT phase *initial coding* [4]). After the consolidation, the categories *risks* and *tool features* were selected for further data collection. The selection was motivated by the fact that the experts seemed highly interested in and provided many ideas around these categories; also, the categories can be considered highly relevant for the elicitation of requirements. The item lists were sent to the experts, which then had to validate whether their stance on the issues was properly represented. If not, the experts could give feedback on which items were missing or if some points should be separated and specified more clearly. Note that the narrowing-down phase, which asks the experts to exclude the least important items from each list, was skipped because the lists we presented to the experts had less than 20 items in them, to begin with. This is in accordance with common practice and guidelines [16,17].

Ranking. After validating the relevant points, the ranking phase aims to rank the items – often with respect to the importance of issues. Since our two different lists, i.e., regarding risks and tool features, are topically distinct, we operationalized the ranking metrics differently for each list. Multiple rounds of ranking, as is common in RTDM studies, were outside of the scope of this work due to the extensive interviews and the focus on the exploration of new insights rather than the quantification of known facts. Since *risk* is a complex and hard-to-poll topic, we operationalized it as the product of the perceived likelihood of occurrence and the potential damage if said situation manifests [20]. The participants were asked to rank each the probability and the impact on a Likert scale: very low (1) - low (2) - moderate (3) - high (4) - very high (5). This results in risk scores from 1 to 25. Furthermore, we asked the study participants to rate the importance of possible *tool features* on a Likert scale. The possible choices were: extremely unimportant (1) - somewhat unimportant (2) - neutral (3) - somewhat important (4) - extremely important (5).

4   Results

The main insights from the interviews and questionnaires are outlined below. We present opportunities and challenges that BPM industry experts perceive regarding the AB-BPM method. As software vendor employees, the study participants' answers, to some extent, reflect the experience of the wider industry, i.e., the customers' challenges. Statements of the experts are marked as quotations.

Opportunities. The **sentiment** towards AB-BPM was mainly positive. Multiple consultants brought up that some companies they worked with tried testing new process versions and comparing them with the status quo. However, the tests were mostly unstructured and considered only of a few instances or even no "real" instances (i.e., only tests). This means that any drawn conclusions are not dependable, due to the low number of instances and lack of statistical rigor when it comes to controlling confounding factors. Thus, AB testing provides a useful process improvement method that supports the structured testing of alternative versions.

One question to the study participants was about the **suitability** of the method regarding contextual factors. The study participants were not presented with a list of categories but were free to elaborate on their intuition. More concretely, they were asked for what type of processes and what surrounding circumstances (company, market, industry) they think the methodology would be well- or ill-suited. Their statements were then mapped to the categorization of BPM contexts by [29]. The result can be seen in Table 1. The characteristics in italics present special cases for factors where every characteristic was deemed suitable, which we will outline in the following.

Table 1. Suitability of AB-BPM method regarding BPM context, color coding: green - high suitability , yellow - medium suitability , orange - low suitability . Categorization from [29]. Items in italics present particularly interesting/suitable cases for factors where every characteristic is suitable.

Contextual factors	Characteristics		
Goal-dimension			
Focus	*Exploitation (Improvm., Compl.)*	Exploration (Innovation)	
Process-dimension			
Value contribution	*Core process*	Management process	Support process
Repetitiveness	Repetitive	Non-repetitive	
Knowledge-intensity	Low knowledge-intensity	Medium knowledge-intensity	High knowledge-intensity
Interdependence	Low interdependence	Medium interdependence	High interdependence
Variability	Low variability	Medium variability	High variability
Organization-dimension			
Scope	Intra-organizational process	Inter-organizational process	
Industry	Product industry	Product & service industry	Service industry
Size	Start-up	Small and medium enterprise	Large organization
Culture	Highly supportive of BPM	Medium supportive of BPM	Non-supportive of BPM
Resources	Low organizational resources	Medium organizational resources	High organizational resources
Environmental-dimension			
Competitiveness	Low competitive	Medium competitive	*Highly competitive*
Uncertainty	Low env. uncertainty	Medium env. uncertainty	High env. uncertainty

Focus. No agreement could be reached on whether AB-BPM was suitable for radical changes. [24] present the method primarily for evolutionary changes, while some study participants believe it is suitable for both. However, most consider the method more appropriate for small process changes due to the ease and speed of implementation. AB-BPM would be incompatible with fundamental changes that require "lengthy discussions" and expensive financial obligations, making rapid testing difficult. Somewhat larger changes within the same information system may be feasible, but smaller changes are generally preferred.

Value contribution. Using the AB-BPM method might be especially useful in core processes. This is because other processes are found at many companies and cannot be used for meaningful differentiation. One study participant noted that it is advisable to "differentiate where you differ." They said, "as a sports shoe company, we could strive to have the best finance processes, but that won't make people buy our shoes – we need better shoes and better shoe quality to win in the marketplace." They, therefore, recommended using standard processes for everything but the core processes. This is already common practice and also suggested by academic studies [25]. For core processes, however, experimentation with the AB-BPM method would be highly favorable.

Competitiveness. In general, there were no opinions indicating that any level of market competitiveness would lead to less suitability of the method. Study participants noted, however, that highly competitive markets would increase the need for such a tool to allow for faster process iterations, "to stay competitive."

The elicitation of **requirements** for a tool that executes and supports the AB-BPM method was also part of the study, and the identified feature requirements are presented in the following. First, we present the ranking of the items (see Table 2). Afterward, more details on the items ranked as most important are provided.

The ranking is based on the importance Likert scale presented in Sect. 3. The average importance scores (AVG) are accompanied by the standard deviations (SD) to give an insight into the level of agreement among the experts. Furthermore, the feature requirements have been categorized into presentation, procedure, and support. This categorization has been created after and based on the interviews, during the coding of the interviews (GT phase *intermediate coding* [4]). *Presentation* includes features regarding the presentation of data, or features that are more focused on the front end of the tool in general; *Procedure* are features regarding the underlying technical or methodological procedure; *Support* includes features that already exist in the AB-BPM method but that have not been presented to the study participants during the introduction to AB-BPM (see Sect. 2); they, therefore, support the equivalent suggestions by [24].

Table 2. Item list of desired tool features, in order of perceived importance. Colors in "Code" column depict categories: blue - presentation , pink - procedure , gray - support .

Code	Tool Feature	Imp. AVG	Imp. SD
COM	Communicating process changes efficiently for teaching and enablement of employees	4.75	0.46
DIF	BPMN diff viewer	4.57	0.53
PIB	See potential impact beforehand (amount and business-wise)	4.43	0.79
ETL	Exec. on/with various systems; ETL from various systems for data extraction	4.29	0.95
IAR	Clear insights and action recommendations	4.25	0.71
EES	Emergency exit/stop	4.25	1.04
CPS	Capture process participants sentiments and feedback on process variants	4.13	1.13
DDI	Detailed/drill-down insights	4.13	0.64
IWS	Integrate with simulation	4.13	0.83
BRK	Offer broad range of possible KPIs to take into account	4.00	0.93
EMA	Show analytics embedded in process diagram	4.00	0.58
HID	Use of historical data	4.00	0.58
PSN	Pre-setting stop and notification criteria	3.88	0.83
EXC	Potential exclusion of certain customer groups	3.86	1.07
REC	Randomization/not always choose same employees for test	3.50	0.76
VRC	Result can be different variants for recognized customer patterns	3.50	0.84
MRL	Options for modification of reinforcement learning-based routing	3.43	0.98
XRL	Offer explainable reinforcement learning	3.25	1.28
MTT	Experiment with more than two variants	3.13	1.46

In the following, the three tool features ranked as most important are described in more detail.

See potential impact beforehand (amount and business-wise). According to the study participants, process experts should be able to see estimations on possible impacts beforehand to support an informed decision-making process, e.g., how many customers or what order volume would be affected by the test.

BPMN diff viewer. One study participant emphasized the importance of human experts having a clear understanding of changes in the current initiative. They suggested a "diff viewer for the diagrams" - a graphical representation of changes made to a document from one version to another, commonly used in software engineering. In business process management, this could involve versions of a BPMN diagram, with changes highlighted in different colors. Diff viewers are well-researched and applied in this context, for example in [8,19].

Communicating process changes efficiently for teaching and enablement of employees. The need for process participants to learn how new versions have to be executed was stressed by multiple interviewees. One study participant stated that "one needs to notify the people working on steps in the process of the changes." More "enablement is needed to teach employees the changes," and another study participant noted that "seeing how this [aspect of change management] can be integrated would be an interesting question." This would go beyond just teaching single steps but also create openness and transparency about goals and project setup, allowing for "a lot of change, even in parallel, without people being lost." Similar to the diff viewer, change notification management is a feature that has already received research attention in the context of business process management software [14,30].

Challenges. It is vital to know the core challenges to advance the AB-BPM methodology and adjacent endeavors. Only then can they be addressed and mitigated adequately. The risks and further challenges that the expert panel has voiced are, therefore, outlined below.

A critical goal of this work is to determine the AB-BPM method's principal **risks** since they hinder its usage and implementation in organizations. In the following, we will present the results from the experts' ranking and then give a more detailed outline of the most highly ranked individual risks. The risks, alongside their AVG risk scores and the SD of those scores, can be seen in Table 3. Furthermore, the risks have been categorized as follows. *Culture* are risks regarding the working culture and employees of the company. *Results* include risks regarding results, decisions, and outcomes; *Operations* consists of risks regarding the implementation and execution of the AB-BPM method itself, but also the normal business operations; *Legal* includes risks regarding the cost and loss of income caused by legal uncertainty [27].

Table 3. Item list of risks, in order of perceived risk. Colors in "Code" column describe categories: pink - results , blue - culture , green - operations , gray - legal .

Code	Risk	Risk AVG	Risk SD
CHM	Change management problems during rollout of new variants (cultural)	15.6	4.8
BLE	Blindly following machine-generated analysis results leading to erroneous decisions	15.5	5.7
UVD	Unclear results due to high process variance and process drift	14.4	5.4
IGK	Problems due to improperly set goals/KPIs	14.3	7.0
ESU	Economically or societally undesirable bias	13.6	7.5
TST	Process participants (employees) feeling like test subjects/tracked	11.3	5.8
EPG	Employees purposely acting with a certain goal for the experiment in mind	11.1	4.6
DNO	Disturbance of normal operations	11.1	4.7
DIE	Problems with deploym./impl. and exec. of multiple process variants at same time	11.0	5.6
SEP	Scaling and edge case problems	10.4	6.8
FPI	Failed experimental process instances	10.3	3.5
LRE	Lacking responsibility in case of problems	10.0	8.2
EDA	Employee dissatisfaction due to feeling like one is about to be automated	10.0	3.8
RED	Reputational damage for process provider	9.6	3.1
LCH	Legal challenges due to experiments	9.1	5.4

In the following, details on the three most highly ranked risks are explained in more detail.

Unclear results due to high process variance and process drift. As mentioned before, the execution of business processes can differ from how they were intended to be executed and it is subject to (unintended) changes over time. This phenomenon, called process drift [23], leads to a high variance of executed process versions. This could pose a risk for the AB-BPM method since it is then unclear whether process participants execute the two versions as they are intended. A process participant is a company-internal actor performing tasks of a process [6], i.e., an employee of the organization executing the process. If the process cases vary from the intended way of execution, it is hard to draw conclusions from the results since they might be based on a change that occurred spontaneously instead of the planned process changes. One example might be that "people exchange emails instead of following the steps in the process execution software."

Erroneous machine-generated analysis results are blindly followed. Many interviewees noted that solely relying on the algorithm's interpretation of the data might cause problems. One study participant noted that "such models are always an abstraction of reality [...] and relying on them completely can lead to mistakes." This topic also came up during the discussion of bad prior experiences, when a study participant noted that sometimes wrong decisions were made because of a lack of understanding of data. One potential example is the use of team performance metrics, which are often highly subjective (e.g., workload estimates in some project management methods), without context. Putting data into context and not blindly following statistical calculations is, therefore, a core challenge that needs to be addressed.

Cultural change management problems during variant roll-out.
This risk was added after the validation survey since one study participant remarked that this item was missing. It can be understood as incorporating any other cultural change management issues not yet included in the item list (see blue items in Table 3). The high rating of this item can be seen as an indicator that the human side of the method and adjacent tools must not be left out of research and development efforts. The importance of culture also became very apparent when asked about *prerequisites for the use of the AB-BPM method*. Many study participants noted that the organization would need to have an experiment culture, meaning that they should be open to trying new things and handling failures as learning opportunities. Furthermore, they stated a need for organizational transparency and trust.

The implementation and adoption of AB-BPM as presented in [24] assumes the existence of a Business Process Management System (BPMS) that allows for the direct deployment of BPMN models. A BPMS is an information system that uses an explicit description of an executable process model in the form of a BPMN model to execute business processes and manage relevant resources and data. It presents a centralized, model-driven way of business process execution and intelligence [6]. However, most processes are executed by non-BPMS software, i.e., they are not executed from models directly [9].

Therefore, whether the usage of a BPMS is a requirement for **technical feasibility** is a research question of this study. Altogether, AB testing of business processes seems technologically feasible without a BPMS, one interviewee noted: "I do not think that it is a problem that processes are executed over several IT systems since you only need to be able to start either process version. The route they are going afterward, even if it is ten more systems, is no longer relevant." However, if we want to use live analytics to route incoming process instantiation requests (e.g., as proposed with RL) without a BPMS, we would need an Extract-Transform-Load (ETL) tool. ETL software is responsible for retrieving relevant data from various sources while bringing the data into a suitable format [28]. Relying on a BPMS would not only have the benefit of easier data collection and access, it would also make deploying and executing experimental processes more straightforward. Furthermore, such an ETL tool might also be highly complex due to the many systems processes can potentially touch. One study participant noted that when a BPMS does not exist, "you will have to put a lot of effort into mining performance data; it would be more difficult to get the same data from process mining, covering every path and system." In fact, most study participants did deem a BPMS, or something similar, to be a prerequisite. One study participant stated, however, that while some "central execution platform" would probably be needed, it remains unclear whether these have to be in the shape of current BPMS. Overall, there seemed to be the notion that the integrated, model-driven way of orchestrating and executing business processes offered by BPMS is the direction the industry should move towards.

Besides the risks, the study participants also mentioned **other challenges**. Here, we highlight some of them. Regarding the question of *bad prior experiences* *when conducting BPI initiatives*, some study participants criticized the unclear impact of process improvements during/after BPI projects. This is due to constantly changing environmental factors and the resulting difficulty to compare process data that has been collected at different points in time. This highlights the possible positive impact that AB-BPM could have on BPI efforts, by giving BPM experts a better data basis to evaluate improvement efforts. Regarding the *prerequisites for the use of the AB-BPM method*, on the more technical side, the interviewees noted that many companies would not offer the level of continuous data metrics needed for the dynamic, RL-driven routing during the experiments. This again highlights the need for an integrated process execution (e.g., a BPMS).

5   Discussion

Emerging patterns in the coded items can be brought together to form tool and methodological suggestions. This analysis of patterns in the coded interview data can be seen as an application of the GT phase *advanced coding* [4]. In the following, we present the inferred suggestions and concepts in more detail. These serve as both concrete suggestions and examples of how the requirements can be used when implementing AB-BPM tools.

Integrated Process Model Repository. The idea of integrating the AB-BPM tool with a process model repository (PMR) came up in one interview. It is implicitly supported by statements of most of the other study participants. The main aim of IPMR is to provide a fast and efficient way of introducing new process variants to process participants while allowing them to provide feedback. Once a new business process variant is added, the responsible process expert would need to add additional material to help process participants understand the new version. Suppose a specific process participant is part of an experimental process case (or a new version is permanently rolled out). In that case, they would receive a notification (e.g., via email) with the most important information regarding the process update, with a link to more material. This could be extended with the need for process participants to pass a short test to avoid improvement effort failures due to misunderstanding. They could also provide feedback, which could then be evaluated by the process experts or even considered for the RL experiment.

Instance Recovery Mechanism. The analysis of the interviews made it clear that the danger of failed process instances has to be mitigated in some way. Based on that data, we propose an instance recovery mechanism (IRM). Before starting an experiment, process experts could set thresholds for specific KPIs. The expert would be notified when a process instance reaches such a threshold. They could then intervene in the process execution to make sure that the process consumers still get their desired product or service. The thresholds should be set relatively high, to only intervene in erroneous cases. Otherwise, it could create a bias in the experiment. This is why one also has to consider how such instances are evaluated in calculating the rewards of the RL. Leaving them out of the RL calculations could lead to problems: Imagine only one process version sometimes exceeds the thresholds and has to be salvaged manually. By leaving these instances out, we might misjudge that version. A better approach could include these manually salvaged versions in the model with a certain penalty value. Considering the scientific state-of-the-art, IRM is closely related to the notion of (real-time) business process monitoring, as for example covered in [10,18].

Another pattern that can be observed throughout the interviews is the need for more human control. This can be seen in the perceived risks (e.g., BLE, LRE), as well as in the desired tool features (e.g., EES, CPS, PSN, MRL, XRL). In a previous paper, we have already presented an initial prototype that enhances the AB-BPM methodology with additional features for human control [13].

The presented study has several **limitations**. One possible threat to the validity of results, especially the ranking, is that we employed a shortened RTDM. Usually, there are multiple ranking rounds until the concordance among the experts has reached a satisfactory level. As mentioned above, we decided not to conduct multiple ranking rounds due to the exploratory nature of the study and the extensive interview process, which makes it difficult to be certain in the ranking. Preliminary statistical analysis of the rating differences between the items shows that there is no significant difference between the listed risk items, but there is a significant difference between the ratings of the different feature items. However, given the qualitative nature of the study the rankings should only be seen as rough guidance. The focus of the work is the qualitative elicitation of items. This has been taken into consideration for the discussion and conclusion, meaning that we took all the items into account, not just the most highly ranked.

Another possible threat to the validity of the results is that the participation in the validation round dropped from ten to five. We tried to mitigate validity issues by ensuring higher participation in the ranking round (eight experts participated) and giving study participants the option to also give feedback on the coding in that round. Since no more remarks were made about the coding, we conclude that the coding was satisfactory for all eight study participants of the ranking round.

Furthermore, all study participants are employed by the same company. We tried to attenuate this by selecting experts with extensive experience from various teams and backgrounds. Additionally, the consultants brought in their experience with business process improvement projects from additional companies.

6   Conclusion

The main aim of this study was to obtain practitioners' perspectives on the AB-BPM method. Using mostly qualitative research methods, we shed light on the requirements for the further development of AB-BPM tools and the underlying method. Overall, the study participants perceived the methodology as advantageous in comparison to the status quo. The three main conclusions of the study are: *i)* more possibilities of human intervention, and interaction between the RL agent and the human expert, are a core requirement; *ii)* transparency and features for the participation of process participants are needed to make AB-BPM culturally viable; *iii)* integrated process execution is necessary to facilitate the seamless deployment of parallel process variants and deliver the real-time data needed for dynamic RL and routing. The openness of the semi-structured interviews facilitated the discovery of future research opportunities, e.g., studying companies carrying out unstructured process tests in a production environment, and tool-driven training of process participants. While we focused on a single process improvement method, practitioners' insights on different kinds of business improvement methods [15] could provide insights for studies that compare AB-BPM to other methodologies.

References

1. Aguilar-Savén, R.S.: Business process modelling: review and framework. Int. J. Prod. Econ. **90**(2), 129–149 (2004)
2. Bass, L., Weber, I., Zhu, L.: DevOps: A Software Architect's Perspective, 1st edn. Addison-Wesley, Boston (2015)
3. Brinkmann, S., Kvale, S.: InterViews: Learning the Craft of Qualitative Research Interviewing, 3rd edn. SAGE Publications Inc, Los Angeles (2014)
4. Chun Tie, Y., Birks, M., Francis, K.: Grounded theory research: a design framework for novice researchers. SAGE Open Med. **7**, 205031211882292 (2019)
5. Dalkey, N., Helmer, O.: An experimental application of the DELPHI method to the use of experts. Manage. Sci. **9**(3), 458–467 (1963)
6. Dumas, M., La Rosa, M., Mendling, J., Reijers, H.A.: Fundamentals of Business Process Management. Springer, Berlin (2018)
7. Holland, C.W., Cochran, D.: Breakthrough Business Results With MVT: A Fast, Cost-Free, "Secret Weapon" for Boosting Sales, Cutting Expenses, and Improving Any Business Process, 1st edn. Wiley, Hoboken (2005)
8. Ivanov, S.Y., Kalenkova, A.A.: BPMNDiffViz: a tool for BPMN models comparison. In: Proceedings of the Demo Session of the 13th International Conference on Business Process Management, p. 5 (2015)
9. Kampik, T., Weske, M.: Event log generation: an industry perspective. In: Augusto, A., Gill, A., Bork, D., Nurcan, S., Reinhartz-Berger, I., Schmidt, R. (eds.) Enterprise, Business-Process and Information Systems Modeling, pp. 123–136. Springer International Publishing, Cham (2022)
10. Kang, B., Kim, D., Kang, S.H.: Real-time business process monitoring method for prediction of abnormal termination using KNNI-based LOF prediction. Exp. Syst. Appl. **39**(5), 6061–6068 (2012)
11. Kohavi, R., Longbotham, R.: Online controlled experiments and A/B testing. In: Sammut, C., Webb, G.I. (eds.) Encyclopedia of Machine Learning and Data Mining, pp. 922–929. Springer, US, Boston, MA (2017)
12. Kohavi, R., Longbotham, R., Sommerfield, D., Henne, R.M.: Controlled experiments on the web: survey and practical guide. Data Min. Knowl. Disc. **18**(1), 140–181 (2009)

13. Kurz, A.F., Santelmann, B., Großmann, T., Kampik, T., Pufahl, L., Weber, I.: HITL-AB-BPM: business process improvement with AB testing and human-in-the-loop. In: Proceedings of the Demo Session of the 20th International Conference on Business Process Management (2022)

14. La Rosa, M., et al.: Apromore: an advanced process model repository. Exp. Syst. Appl. **38**(6), 7029–7040 (2011)

15. Malinova, M., Gross, S., Mendling, J.: A study into the contingencies of process improvement methods. Inf. Syst. **104**, 101880 (2022)

16. Okoli, C., Pawlowski, S.D.: The Delphi method as a research tool: an example, design considerations and applications. Inf. Manage. **42**(1), 15–29 (2004)

17. Paré, G., Cameron, A.F., Poba-Nzaou, P., Templier, M.: A systematic assessment of rigor in information systems ranking-type Delphi studies. Inf. Manage. **50**(5), 207–217 (2013)

18. Pedrinaci, C., Lambert, D., Wetzstein, B., van Lessen, T., Cekov, L., Dimitrov, M.: SENTINEL: a semantic business process monitoring tool. In: Proceedings of the First International Workshop on Ontology-Supported Business Intelligence, pp. 1–12. OBI 2008, Association for Computing Machinery, New York (2008)

19. Pietsch, P., Wenzel, S.: Comparison of BPMN2 diagrams. In: Mendling, J., Weidlich, M. (eds.) BPMN 2012. LNBIP, vol. 125, pp. 83–97. Springer, Heidelberg (2012). https://doi.org/10.1007/978-3-642-33155-8_7

20. Renn, O.: Concepts of risk: an interdisciplinary review part 1: disciplinary risk concepts. GAIA - Ecol. Perspect. Sci. Soc. **17**(1), 50–66 (2008)

21. Robson, C.: Real World Research: A Resource for Social Scientists and Practitioner-Researchers. Blackwell, Oxford u.a., reprint. edn (1999)

22. von Rosing, M., White, S., Cummins, F., de Man, H.: Business process model and notation-BPMN. In: von Rosing, M., Scheer, A.W., von Scheel, H. (eds.) The Complete Business Process Handbook, pp. 433–457. Morgan Kaufmann, Boston (Jan (2015)

23. Sato, D.M.V., De Freitas, S.C., Barddal, J.P., Scalabrin, E.E.: A survey on concept drift in process mining. ACM Comput. Surv. **54**(9), 189:1–189:38 (2021)

24. Satyal, S., Weber, I., young Paik, H., Di Ciccio, C., Mendling. J.: Business process improvement with the ab-bpm methodology: Inf. Syst. **84**, 283–298 (2019)

25. Stiehl, V., Danei, M., Elliott, J., Heiler, M., Kerwien, T.: Effectively and efficiently implementing complex business processes: a case study. In: Empirical Studies on the Development of Executable Business Processes, pp. 33–57. Springer, Cham (2019). https://doi.org/10.1007/978-3-030-17666-2_3

26. Sutton, R.S., Barto, A.G.: Reinforcement Learning: An Introduction, 2nd edn. MIT Press, Cambridge (2018)

27. Tsui, T.C.: Experience from the Anti-Monopoly Law Decision in China (Cost and Benefit of Rule of Law) (2013)

28. Vassiliadis, P.: A survey of extract-transform-load technology. Int. J. Data Warehouse. Min. (IJDWM) **5**(3), 1–27 (2009)

29. Vom Brocke, J., Zelt, S., Schmiedel, T.: On the role of context in business process management. Int. J. Inf. Manage. **36**(3), 486–495 (2016)

30. Yan, Z., Dijkman, R., Grefen, P.: Business process model repositories - framework and survey. Inf. Softw. Technol. **54**, 380–395 (2012)

Modeling and Transforming Process Data (BPMDS 2023)

Modelling and Execution of Data-Driven Processes with JSON-Nets

Andreas Fritsch[✉][ID], Selina Schüler[ID], Martin Forell[ID],
and Andreas Oberweis[ID]

Karlsruhe Institute of Technology (KIT), Institute of Applied Informatics and Formal
Description Methods (AIFB), Kaiserstr. 89, 76133 Karlsruhe, Germany
{andreas.fritsch,selina.schueler,martin.forell,andreas.oberweis}@kit.edu

Abstract. Modern business environments are governed by a wide range
of data in various data formats. Despite the importance of integrating
the data and control-flow perspective, existing business process modelling
languages have only limited capability to precisely describe data-driven
processes. In this paper, we propose a new approach called JSON-Nets,
a variant of high-level Petri nets, that utilizes JSON technologies to integrate complex data objects in executable process models. We introduce
JSON-Nets using an illustrative example and provide a formal specification, as well as a prototypical implementation of a modelling tool to
evaluate our conception.

Keywords: Business Process Modeling · Petri nets · JSON

1 Introduction

Established methods for developing information systems largely consider the
process and data perspective as separate, only loosely coupled worlds [28]. This
separation allows for managing the inherent complexity of information systems
and has led to the development of effective and specialized tools [29]. However,
it also creates problems, starting with the simple inability to express certain
phenomena in a conventional process modelling language, to the risk of mismatches between the process layer and the data layer of information system
designs [18,29]. The lack of integration of the data and process perspective was
also identified as a major problem that impedes the uptake of process management systems in practice [29]. Current trends like digitization and automation
further increase the need to integrate the process and data perspective of business
processes. Thus, in recent years, there has been considerable research interest
in this area and several approaches have emerged that tackle the integration
problem under terms like "data-aware", "data-centric" or "data-driven" process
management [23,29].

However, there also exists an older stream of research that addresses the
integration problem by combining various data models (e.g. programming language types [15], relational data [9] or XML [17]) with high-level Petri nets. In

H. van der Aa et al. (Eds.): BPMDS 2023/EMMSAD 2023, LNBIP 479, pp. 29–43, 2023.
https://doi.org/10.1007/978-3-031-34241-7_3

this paper, we present JSON-nets, a new approach that builds upon this tradition and combines the JSON data model [14] with the Petri net formalism. The development of our approach is motivated by the observations, that (1) data integration remains an unsolved problem, (2) Petri nets provide a sound foundation for modelling, analysing and executing processes [16], and (3) that in the recent years, the landscape of data models has changed. For a long time, the relational data model has dominated, but nowadays relational and semi-structured data [1] exist side-by-side in business environments [12]. In particular, the JSON data model has become very popular for data exchange via web services and for databases following the NoSQL paradigm [4].

The work described in this paper follows the guidelines of method engineering, which borrows concepts from "traditional" engineering processes [5]. Starting with a problem statement, existing approaches are analysed regarding their strengths and weaknesses. A new solution, such as an artefact, a method, or a system, is designed and analysed with respect to previously collected requirements. Then the artefact is developed and evaluated in a practical application. Analysis and evaluation might lead to iterations in order to improve a given solution. In our work, the developed artefact is a process modelling language together with a software prototype to support the application of the new language.

We proceed with a brief review of basics regarding business process modelling languages and related high-level Petri nets approaches and introduce an illustrative example in Sect. 2. In Sect. 3 we present our specification of JSON-Nets. Afterwards, in Sect. 4, we show how our specification of JSON-Nets can be implemented using established JSON technologies, and how this implementation can be used to create a feature-rich, yet concise and executable model of our illustrative example. Finally, in Sect. 5, we discuss capabilities and limitations and conclude with an outlook in Sect. 6.

2   Business Process Modeling Languages

Commonly used business process modeling languages, such as BPMN, UML Activity Diagrams, and EPC typically focus on control-flow aspects of business processes [16,28,35]. For data integration, they provide abstract concepts such as "data objects" in BPMN and EPC. UML Activity Diagrams also allow links between process models and data models, but these models are only loosely coupled and they remain essentially independent. In general, the constructs provided in BPMN, EPC and UML lack specific semantics and syntactic rules that are required to explicitly depict data exchange between activities and different data sources [19]. In this paper, we present a Petri nets-based approach to explicitly model the flow of complex data objects through a business process. Therefore, in the following, we briefly present the basic concepts of Petri nets and review other related approaches for integrating Petri nets with data models.

2.1 Petri Nets

Petri nets are a visual formalism that can be used to model dynamic systems [25]. As shown in Definition 1 (based on [25]), Petri nets consist of places and transitions, where transitions model the active components of a system (i.e. the activities in business processes) and are visualized with rectangles. Places model passive components (i.e. business objects) and are visualized with circles. The relations between passive and active components are visually represented with directed arcs.

Definition 1 (Petri net [25]). *A Petri net is a triple $N = (S, T, F)$, where S, T are finite sets, $S \cap T = \emptyset$, $S \cup T \neq \emptyset$, $F \subseteq (S \times T) \cup (T \times S)$. The elements in S are called places, the elements in T transitions, and F is the flow relation. For each transition t, $\bullet t = \{s \in S \mid (s,t) \in F\}$ denotes the pre-set of t and $t\bullet = \{s \in S \mid (t,s) \in F\}$ the post-set.*

In elementary Petri nets, the marking $M \colon S \to \mathbb{N}_0$ assigns each place a number of abstract, indistinguishable *tokens* (represented by black dots). If each place in the pre-set of a transition holds at least one token, the transition is *enabled*. If a transition is enabled, it may *occur*, according to an *occurrence rule*: in the pre-set of the transition, tokens are consumed; and in the post-set of the transition, new tokens are created. Thus, the application of the occurrence rule allows to simulate the flow of tokens through the net.

2.2 High-Level Petri Nets

Petri nets have been combined with different data models in order to model control-flow and data-flow in one single representation. Marked Petri nets, where data values are associated to tokens, are called high-level Petri nets. In general, it is possible to combine such high-level Petri nets with any data or object model, which provides the required filter operations to inscribe the directed arcs in the net. Data model operations are needed to select data from the input places and to specify data which is to be added to the output places of a transition. Data types are assigned to places in a Petri net in order to restrict the set of allowable data values in the respective place. Coloured Petri nets [15] assign data types from programming languages to places. In Predicate/transition-nets [9] relation types from the field of relational databases are assigned to the places, and the marking of each place is given as a relation of the respective type. In NR/T-nets [21], non-first-normal-form relation types are assigned to the places. Non-first-normal-form relation types extend (first-normal-form) relation types by allowing set-valued and tuple-valued attributes. A similar concept is proposed in [13]. Our conception of JSON-Nets is inspired by approaches that work with semi-structured data [1], where the schema for the data stored in tokens is more flexible than in the relational data model. In XML-nets [17] (a variant of SGML-Nets [34]), tokens correspond to XML documents, and places are typed using XML Schema [31] definitions. More recently, [2] has described a similar, but more abstract concept, where tokens are represented by trees whose nodes are labelled with attribute/value pairs.

2.3   Illustrative Example: Foreign Lecture Recognition Process

To motivate and explain our conception of JSON-Nets as a variant of high-level Petri nets, we introduce the example of a (fictional) foreign lecture recognition process at a university. Figure 1 shows a model of the process as an elementary Petri net. The model shows that a student may make a *request* to recognize a lecture he or she has passed at a foreign university during an exchange semester. The request is reviewed by the responsible staff using data from a campus management system about *students* and available *lectures*. If the request is accepted, the *grade* achieved in the foreign lecture is stored in the system. In any case, the student is finally notified about the decision.

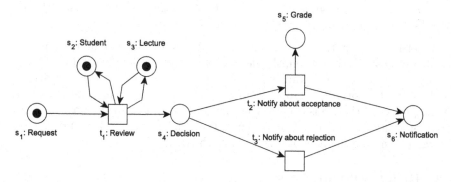

Fig. 1. Illustrative example of a foreign lecture recognition process modelled as an elementary Petri net.

The example shows that a lot of information gets lost when the process is modelled in this concise way using elementary Petri nets: there is no distinction between the situation of different students, or requirements for different lectures at the university. It is also not clear, which path a request will take after a decision has been made, since there is no distinction between a positive or negative decision. In principle, it would be possible to extend the model with further places and transitions to capture these notions. However, as soon as we think about hundreds of different lectures and thousands of different students, this results in a very large and complex model. As a way to deal with such use cases, we introduce JSON-Nets for modeling data-driven processes.

3   Specification of JSON-Nets

In JSON-Nets, places are marked with JSON documents, which allows to model processes that work with complex, semi-structured, and nested data. We first introduce the JSON data model and continue with the definition of the structure and occurrence rule of JSON-Nets.

3.1   JSON Documents

The JSON data model is described in the corresponding standard [8,14] as a lightweight, text-based format for structuring data. JSON specifies four primitive data types, `string`, `number`, `boolean` (`true`, `false`) and `null`. Furthermore, there are two complex data types. `Objects` are represented by two enclosing curly braces ({}) and contain an arbitrary number of key/value pairs. Keys and values are separated by a colon (:) and key/value pairs are separated by commas (,). Every key is a `String` that is unique within the object and a value can be of any JSON type. `Arrays` are represented by two enclosing square brackets ([]) and contain an arbitrary number of JSON values that are separated by commas and may be of different types. Listing 1 shows an example of a JSON document that consists of an `object` with three key/value pairs. The value for the key `"identifier"` is a `number` (12345). The value for the key `"name"` is again an `object` with two key/value pairs, where the values are of type `string`. Finally, the root object has an entry `"lectures"` with a value of type `array` containing two `string` elements. In this listing, one can observe what is called in [4] the "compositional structure" of JSON: every value in the document is itself a valid JSON document (earlier JSON versions only allowed `objects` or `arrays` as valid JSON documents, but in the recent version of the standard this is no longer the case [14]). Furthermore, a combination of objects and arrays allows for arbitrary depth in nested JSON documents.

```
1  {
2    "identifier": 12345,
3    "name": {
4      "first": "Jane",
5      "last": "Doe"
6    },
7    "lectures": ["Software Engineering", "Database Systems"]
8  }
```

Listing 1. Example of a JSON document.

3.2   Structure of JSON-Nets

Compared to elementary Petri nets, JSON-Nets introduce distinguishable, complex structured tokens (JSON documents). When a transition occurs, it consumes the documents in its pre-set and creates new documents in its post-set. Places are interpreted as *document stores* that are typed by a document schema to ensure data integrity. The flow of data is controlled by these schemas, as well as by *document filters* and *check functions*. We further introduce the notion of *read arcs* that only check for the existence of tokens and read the contained data, but don't consume tokens (a similar concept is described e.g. by [30] for elementary Petri nets). First, Definition 2 specifies the structure of a JSON-Net. We will then proceed and explain the mentioned concepts.

Definition 2 (JSON-Net). *A JSON-Net is a tuple*

$$JSN = (S, T, R, C, O, SI, TI, AI, M_0) \tag{1}$$

where

1. S, T *are finite sets,* $S \cap T = \emptyset$, $S \cup T \neq \emptyset$.
2. $R \cup C$ *is the set of input arcs, where* $R \subseteq S \times T$ *is the set of read arcs and* $C \subseteq S \times T$ *is the set of consume arcs, and we always assume* $R \cap C = \emptyset$. *For each transition* $t \in T$,
   - $\bullet t_{read} = \{s \in S \mid (s, t) \in R\}$ *denotes the read-set.*
   - $\bullet t_{consume} = \{s \in S \mid (s, t) \in C\}$ *denotes the consume-set.*
   - $\bullet t = \{s \in S \mid (s, t) \in R \cup C\}$ *denotes the pre-set of the transition.*
3. $O \subseteq T \times S$ *is the set of output arcs and* $t\bullet = \{s \in S \mid (t, s) \in O\}$ *denotes the post-set of a transition* t.
4. *SI assigns to each place* $s \in S$ *a document schema* p_s.
5. *TI assigns to a subset of all transitions* $T' \subseteq T$ *a check function* c_t *with* n *parameters, where* $n = |\bullet t|$ *corresponds to the number of places in the pre-set of the transition.*
6. *AI inscribes*
   - *each arc* $(s, t) \in R \cup C$ *with a filter expression as a document filter* $p_{s,t}$.
   - *each arc* $(t, s) \in O$ *with a document creation function* $q_{t,s}$ *with* n *parameters, where* $n = |\bullet t|$ *corresponds to the number of places in the pre-set of the transition.*
7. M_0 *is a marking of the places in* S *with JSON documents.* $M(s)$ *denotes the set of documents stored in a place* s *under a marking* M.

While *document schemas* and *filter expressions* have different roles in our definition, they essentially have similar functions (as we also discuss later when reviewing JSON technologies in Sect. 4.1): they define restrictions for the structure and individual values of JSON documents. We denote the validity of a document d for the restrictions of a schema or filter expression p with $d \models p$.

The rules defined by a filter expression may be fulfilled by multiple documents in a place. However, when the transition occurs, only one document is selected. This is expressed by introducing the notion of a *filter assignment*. For a given set of documents D and a set of filters P, a mapping of $\beta \colon P \to D$ is called a filter assignment. The vector of documents that results from assigning all documents in the pre-set of a transition t to a filter expression is denoted with $\beta(t)$ as a short form of $(\beta(p_{s_1,t}), \ldots, \beta(p_{s_n,t}))$.

A *document creation function* $q \colon D^n \to D$ creates a JSON document from a given vector of n input documents and a *check function* $c \colon D^n \to \{true, false\}$ maps a vector of n input documents to a boolean value.

3.3   Occurrence Rule for JSON-Nets

Using the concepts and definitions from above, we can now define the occurrence rule for simple JSON-Nets. Definition 3 specifies the conditions for a transition to be enabled.

Definition 3 (Enabled transition in JSON-Nets). *A transition* t *is enabled for a given marking* M *and a filter assignment* $\beta(t)$, *if:*

1. *For each place in the pre-set of the transition, the document filter from the incident arc inscription is assigned with a valid document:* $\forall s \in \bullet t : \exists d_s \in M(s)$, *s.t.* $d_s = \beta(p_{s,t}) \models p_{s,t}$.
2. *For each place in the post-set of the transition, the creation function from the incident arc inscription creates a document that is valid for the document schema of the place inscription:* $\forall s \in t\bullet : q_{t,s}(\beta(t)) \models p_s$.
3. *The check function in the transition inscription is true under the given filter assignment:* $c_t(\beta(t)) = true$.

Therefore, a transition is enabled, (1) if all places in the pre-set of the transition contain at least one document which is valid for the filter expression of the incident arc, (2) all created documents in the post-set are valid for the document schema of the incident places, and (3) the check function evaluates to true. If a transition is enabled, it can occur according to the rule in Definition 4:

Definition 4 (Occurrence rule for JSON-Nets). *An enabled transition in a JSON-Net can occur. The occurrence of a transition* t *under marking* M *yields the marking* M' *with*

$$
M'(s) = \begin{cases} M(s) \setminus \beta(p_{s,t}) & s \in \bullet t_{consume} \wedge s \notin t\bullet \\ M(s) \setminus \beta(p_{s,t}) \cup q_{t,s}(\beta(t)) & s \in \bullet t_{consume} \wedge s \in t\bullet \\ M(s) \cup q_{t,s}(\beta(t)) & s \notin \bullet t_{consume} \wedge s \in t\bullet \\ M(s) & otherwise \end{cases} \tag{2}
$$

When a transition t occurs with an assignment $\beta(t)$, then for each place that is connected with a consume arc ($s \in \bullet t_{consume}$), the document of the assignment $\beta(p_{s,t})$ is removed and for every place $s \in t\bullet$ the document created by the corresponding create function $q_{t,s}(\beta(t))$ is added.

4   Implementation and Evaluation

The above definitions for JSON-Nets do not prescribe a specific syntax for inscriptions. We have underspecified JSON-Nets on purpose, as many different JSON technologies exist that could be used for the inscriptions, and each may have different advantages that are to be explored. In the following, we review existing JSON technologies and motivate our choice of technologies for the prototypical implementation of JSON-Nets.

4.1   Review of JSON Technologies for JSON-Net Inscriptions

In order to specify the syntax for the inscriptions of JSON-Nets the following capabilities are required: (1) For *document schemas* the possibility to specify restrictions for the structure and individual values of documents. (2) For *document filters* the possibility to specify restrictions for the structure and individual values of documents, as well as the possibility to highlight these documents in a set of documents. (3) For *creation and check functions* the possibility to express rules that create JSON documents (or boolean values) based on an input vector of JSON documents.

Due to the popularity of JSON, in particular for data exchange and NoSQL database systems [4], many different JSON technologies exist. Among these, there is no common agreed-upon standard for querying JSON documents and a lack of formalization of core features [4], which makes it difficult to compare the capabilities of JSON technologies. Still, based on [3,4,22] one can distinguish between schema languages, query languages and programming languages to work with JSON data. Additionally, we look at a special case of a template language for JSON. In the following, we provide a description and examples for each technology category. Furthermore, we assess the technologies in each category regarding their capabilities with respect to the three requirements (to restrict, select or create documents). The assessment of the capabilities is also displayed in Table 1 with harvey balls, where ○ expresses that it is not possible to restrict, select or create JSON documents using the technologies in one category and ◑ expresses that it is possible (without further distinguishing possible differences in capabilities within or between categories). ● expresses that the technologies in a category are especially well suited to a corresponding task. Note that this assessment is to a certain extent subjective and based on whether the technology itself is described (in its specification or documentation) as being well-suited for a task. The given list is also not intended as a complete overview, but it captures many popular JSON technologies and provides a structure for discussing the differences in capabilities.

Table 1. Inspection of JSON languages.

Category	Examples	Restrict	Select	Create
Query lang	JSONPath, MongoDB find, XQuery	◑	●	◑
Schema lang	JSON Schema, JSON TypeDef	●	◑	○
Programming lang	JavaScript, Python	◑	◑	◑
Template lang	Jsonnet	◑	◑	●

Query languages are used to access databases of JSON documents and to address nodes in complex structured documents [32,33]. One family of languages within this group is comparable to the XPath standard for XML [32]. They provide powerful features for traversing JSON documents [4]. JSONPath [11] and JMESPath [27] are members of this family, as well as XPath itself, which has added the capability to work with JSON documents in the latest version of the standard [32]. Other examples of query languages are XQuery [33] (an extension of XPath, also with XML and JSON capabilities in its latest version), JSoniq [26] (a JSON-specific query language with syntax similar to XQuery), and

MongoDB-style find functions [20] for accessing NoSQL databases (there exist several NoSQL databases with similar syntax to MongoDB [4]). Many query languages also come with some capabilities to create or manipulate documents, based on previously selected documents. Arguably, some are more limited in this regard, like the projection feature in MongoDB's find function [3], and others are more powerful, as, for example, XQuery's FLOWR expressions can be used to create arbitrary JSON output.

Schema languages have the purpose to constrain the structure of data in a document [3,22]. JSON Schema is a draft for a standardised schema language for JSON documents [36]. It provides features comparable to the XML standard XML Schema [31], like the definition of allowed ranges for values or required and optional object fields. JSON TypeDef is a more lightweight alternative [6]. In general, it is not possible to create documents based on a schema expression, without providing further logic with some additional technology. However, both schema and query languages could be used for restriction, as well as selection tasks: [3] describes a formal logic that captures the capabilities of query languages such as JSONPath, and a formal logic that captures schema languages like JSON Schema and shows that both have similar expressive power.

Since for each JSON type exist equivalents in established *programming languages* [7], they can be used to read and then restrict, filter or create JSON documents. This is particularly easy in weakly typed languages like JavaScript or Python, where JSON documents can be parsed and immediately treated as objects.

A special case is Jsonnet [10] (pronounced "jay sonnet", not to be confused with JSON-Net!), which is described as a *template language* and provides features to dynamically create JSON documents. It is defined as an extension of JSON, so each JSON document is in itself a valid Jsonnet statement. Furthermore, it introduces features from programming languages like variable definitions, functions, and object orientation. Therefore, it is not only capable of describing rules for creating JSON documents, which is its primary feature, but also for restriction and selection.

Ideally, a technology chosen for our implementation should perform well for a specific task, but not be too powerful overall, in order to avoid unnecessary complexity for prospective users [24]. For this reason, our design features (1) *JSONPath* for filter expressions, as it provides powerful features to select documents, but lacks "create" capabilities like XQuery or projection in MongoDB's find function; (2) *JSON Schema* for place typing, as it provides powerful features for restricting the structure of documents, without any capabilities to "create" documents; (3) the template language *Jsonnet* for create and check functions - in terms of expressive power it is arguably as capable as programming languages, but it is specifically designed to describe rules for document creation.

4.2   Software Tool and Example

We provide an implementation of a modelling editor for JSON-Nets which uses JSON Schema for document schemas, JSONPath for filter expressions, and Jsonnet for check- and creation functions under https://github.com/KIT-BIS/json-nets. The complete example of a foreign lecture recognition process, as described in the following, is also available under the link and can be used to apply the occurrence rule to transitions and try different scenarios.

Figure 2 shows the process of our illustrative example as a JSON-Net with arc and transition inscriptions and an exemplary marking. Due to space restrictions, we have omitted the place inscriptions in the figure. However, Listing 2 shows as an example the JSON Schema inscription for the Student place s_2. It describes that a document stored in the place should bear the four fields `studentId`, `level`, `studyProgram` and `email`. The fields `studentId` and `studyProgram` can contain any `string` value. However, the field `level` must be either `"Bachelor"` or `"Master"`, and the field `email` must contain a valid email address.

```
1  {
2    "type": "object",
3    "properties": {
4      "studentId": { "type": "string" },
5      "level": {
6          "type": "string",
7          "enum": ["Bachelor", "Master"]
8      },
9      "studyProgram": { "type": "string" },
10     "email": { "type": "string", "format": "email" },
11   },
12   "required": [ "studentId", "level", "studyProgram",
13     "email"]
14 }
```

Listing 2. JSON Schema inscription of Student place.

The marking in Fig. 2 indicates that there are two requests ($req1$ and $req2$) for recognition of a foreign lecture in place s_1. Furthermore, there are two places that represent databases for student data s_2 and lecture data s_3. These places are connected with read arcs (represented as arcs without arrows). There is no arc inscription shown for (s_1, t_1) which means it is inscribed with an empty JSONPath expression that accepts any document. The inscription of the review transition t_1 is a Jsonnet expression ($Jsonnet_{t_1}$ in Fig. 2) that evaluates to `true` if the `studentId` of a request equals the `studentId` of a selected entry in the student database and the name of the lecture to be recognized (`homeLecture`) equals the `name` of a selected entry in the lecture database. This ensures that the transition only occurs if the required data for a review is available. By convention, we use lowercase-variables in Jsonnet expressions to represent the selected documents from the corresponding places when a transition occurs (i.e. `request`, `lecture`, and `student` for Request, Lecture, and Student, respectively).

When the transition t_1 occurs, the Jsonnet expression $Jsonnet_{t_1, s_4}$ (here in the role of a creation function) inscribed at (t_1, s_4) creates a new JSON document that merges the fields of the selected request document with two new fields (`email` and `accepted`). The value for the `email` field stems from the selected

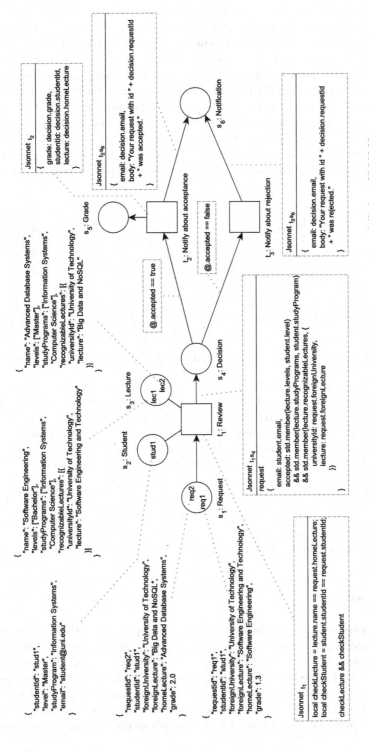

Fig. 2. Illustrative example of a foreign lecture recognition process modelled as JSON-Net.

student document and the value for the `accepted` field evaluates to `true` if: (1) the student applies to recognize a lecture on the level of his or her study program (Bachelor or Master), (2) the student applies to recognize a lecture that is within his or her study program, and (3) the topic of the foreign lecture corresponds to the topic of the home lecture (i.e. it is in the list of `recognizableLectures`). Otherwise it evaluates to `false`. With the given marking, the transition t_1 would be enabled for the assignments β_1: $(req1, stud1, lec1)$ and β_2: $(req2, stud1, lec2)$. When the transition occurs, it removes the selected document from s_1 (req1 or req2) and creates a new document in s_4. The result for β_1 is shown in Listing 3. As can be seen, the request would not be accepted because a Master's student has applied for recognition of a Bachelor's course (for β_2 the request would be accepted).

```
1   {
2       "accepted": false,
3       "email": "student@uni.edu",
4       "foreignLecture": "Software Engineering and Technology",
5       "foreignUniversity": "University of Technology",
6       "grade": 1.3,
7       "homeLecture": "Software Engineering",
8       "requestId": "req1",
9       "studentId": "stud1"
10  }
```

Listing 3. Sample document for a decision based on assignment β_1: $(req1, stud1, lec1)$.

The JSONPath filter inscriptions at the arcs (s_4, t_2) and (s_4, t_3) describe the different paths that a reviewed request can take. If the request was accepted (field `accepted` has value `true`), transition t_2 can occur, and the grade is stored in the database (place s_5). In any case, the student is notified about the acceptance or rejection. Listing 4 provides an example of the document created in s_6 when transition t_3 occurs with the document from Listing 3 assigned to it.

```
1   {
2       "email": "student@uni.edu",
3       "body": "Your request with id req1 was rejected."
4   }
```

Listing 4. Sample document for a notification created by $Jsonnet_{t_2}$.

5   Discussion

The work presented in this paper adds a new approach to the existing body of knowledge regarding data-driven processes. By leveraging two well-known concepts from the process and data domains, we capitalize on their respective strengths. The formality of Petri nets, combined with the JSON data model, provides mechanisms for specifying complex process logic, as well as for ensuring data integrity. It thus enables the modelling, analysis, and simulation of data-driven processes. We argue that a strength of the JSON-nets approach is that it provides extensive capabilities for data-driven processes while remaining (relatively) lightweight and usable, as it inherits the "lightweight spirit" from the JSON data model [4]. Certainly, these claims are yet to be backed with further evaluations, and we lay out our plans for this in the conclusion and outlook section. We focus the rest of the discussion section on the comparison with more closely related high-level Petri net approaches.

Our formal specification of JSON-Nets is comparable with the abstract concept of "Petri nets with data" described in [2]. However, we deviate in several regards, particularly by introducing place and transition inscriptions and introducing a concrete, JSON-specific syntax and implementation. Compared to XML-Nets [17] we provide a new interpretation of the idea of documents with semi-structured data as tokens. As noted before, JSON-Nets inherit the "lightweight spirit" from the JSON data model [4] and can be used with little to no restrictions on data structures for explorative modelling, but also in a very restrictive way if data integrity is paramount for an application scenario. The hierarchical structure of JSON is similar to XML and opens up the opportunity to work with fragments of data (e.g. a transition may consume only a position of an invoice and not the whole invoice). So far, compared to XML-Nets, this feature is missing in our specification, but we consider the specification and implementation presented in this paper as a starting point and intend to iterate upon the concept to further improve and evaluate its capabilities and usability.

6   Conclusion and Outlook

We have presented a formal specification and implementation of JSON-Nets as a modelling language for business processes and have demonstrated how the language can be used to integrate complex, semi-structured, and nested data in an executable process model. For future work, we intend to add the capability to work with fragments of JSON documents, to implement a simulation algorithm for JSON-Nets, and to add more usability features to the modelling editor in order to support users with formulating inscriptions. The planned evaluation includes an evaluation of the expressiveness and an evaluation of the usability of the notation for practical applications. Obviously, usability also depends on the quality of the graphical modelling tool which must support both, Petri net modelling and JSON data modelling. To evaluate the expressiveness we plan to extend and use a pattern-based approach (see workflowpatterns.com). Furthermore, we intend to explore different application scenarios for JSON-Nets, such as digital twins and integrating sustainability data (e.g. carbon emissions) in process models to enable sustainable business process management, and developing a process mining approach that works on existing JSON documents.

Acknowledgements. We wish to thank the anonymous referees for many valuable comments on an earlier version of this paper.

References

1. Abiteboul, S.: Querying semi-structured data. In: International Conference on Database Theory. pp. 1–18. Delphi, Greece (1997). https://doi.org/10.1007/3-540-62222-5_33
2. Badouel, E., Hélouët, L., Morvan, C.: Petri nets with structured data. In: International Conference on Application and Theory of Petri Nets and Concurrency, pp. 212–233. Brussels, Belgium (2015). https://doi.org/10.1007/978-3-319-19488-2_11
3. Bourhis, P., Reutter, J.L., Suárez, F., Vrgoč, D.: JSON: data model, query languages and schema specification. In: ACM SIGACT-SIGMOD-SIGART Symposium on Principles of Database Systems, pp. 123–135. Chicago, United States (2017). https://doi.org/10.1145/3034786.3056120
4. Bourhis, P., Reutter, J.L., Vrgoč, D.: JSON: data model and query languages. Inf. Syst. **89**(3) (2020). https://doi.org/10.1016/j.is.2019.101478
5. Brinkkemper, S.: Method engineering: engineering of information systems development methods and tools. Inf. Softw. Technol. **38**(4), 275–280 (1996). https://doi.org/10.1016/0950-5849(95)01059-9
6. Carion, U.: RFC 8927 JSON Type Definition. https://jsontypedef.com/ (2023)
7. Droettboom, M., et al.: Understanding JSON Schema. Space Telescope Science Institute (2022)
8. ECMA International: The JSON data interchange syntax (2017). http://www.ecma-international.org/publications/standards/Ecma-404.htm
9. Genrich, H.J., Lautenbach, K.: System modelling with high-level Petri nets. Theoret. Comput. Sci. **13**(1), 109–135 (1981). https://doi.org/10.1016/0304-3975(81)90113-4
10. Google: Jsonnet (2023). https://jsonnet.org/
11. Gössner, S.: JSONPath. https://goessner.net/articles/JsonPath/ (2007)
12. Hanine, M., Abdesadik, B., Boutkhoum, O.: Data migration methodology from relational to Nosql databases. Int. J. Inf. Control Comput. Sci. **9**(12) (2016). https://doi.org/10.5281/ZENODO.1339211
13. Hidders, J., Kwasnikowska, N., Sroka, J., Tyszkiewicz, J., Van den Bussche, J.: Petri net + nested relational calculus = dataflow. In: On the Move to Meaningful Internet Systems, pp. 220–237. Agia Napa, Cyprus (2005). https://doi.org/10.1007/11575771_16
14. Internet Engineering Task Force (IETF): The JavaScript object notation (JSON) data interchange format. https://www.rfc-editor.org/info/rfc8259 (2017)
15. Jensen, K.: Coloured petri nets and the invariant-method. Theoret. Comput. Sci. **14**(3), 317–336 (1981). https://doi.org/10.1016/0304-3975(81)90049-9
16. Koschmider, A., Oberweis, A., Stucky, W.: A Petri net-based view on the business process life-cycle. Enterpr. Model. Inf. Syst. Archit. **13**, 47–55 (2018). https://doi.org/10.18417/EMISA.SI.HCM.4
17. Lenz, K., Oberweis, A.: Inter-organizational Business Process Management with XML Nets. In: Ehrig, H., Reisig, W., Rozenberg, G., Weber, H. (eds.) Petri Net Technology for Communication-Based Systems. LNCS, vol. 2472, pp. 243–263. Springer, Heidelberg (2003). https://doi.org/10.1007/978-3-540-40022-6_12
18. Marrella, A., Mecella, M., Russo, A., Steinau, S., Andrews, K., Reichert, M.: Data in business process models, a preliminary empirical study. In: International Conference on Service-Oriented Computing and Applications. Rome, Italy (2015). https://doi.org/10.1109/SOCA.2015.19

19. Meyer, A., Smirnov, S., Weske, M.: Data in business processes. Universitätsverlag Potsdam, Potsdam, Tech. rep. (2011)
20. MongoDB Inc: MongoDB (2023). https://www.mongodb.com/docs/manual/
21. Oberweis, A., Sander, P.: Information system behavior specification by high level Petri nets. ACM Trans. Inf. Syst. **14**(4), 380–420 (1996). https://doi.org/10.1145/237496.237498
22. Pezoa, F., Reutter, J.L., Suarez, F., Ugarte, M., Vrgoč, D.: Foundations of JSON schema. In: International Conference on World Wide Web, pp. 263–273. Montreal, Quebec, Kanada (2016). https://doi.org/10.1145/2872427.2883029
23. Polyvyanyy, A., van der Werf, J.M.E.M., Overbeek, S., Brouwers, R.: Information systems modeling: Language, verification, and tool support. In: International Conference on Advanced Information Systems Engineering. Rome, Italy (2019). https://doi.org/10.1007/978-3-030-21290-2_13
24. Raymond, E.S.: The Art of Unix Programming. Addison-Wesley Professional Computing Series, Pearson Education, Boston (2003)
25. Reisig, W.: Understanding Petri Nets: Modeling Techniques, Analysis Methods, Case Studies. Springer, Berlin, Heidelberg (2013). https://doi.org/10.1007/978-3-642-33278-4
26. Robie, J., Fourny, G., Brantner, M., Florescu, D., Westmann, T., Zaharioudakis, M.: JSONiq (2022).. https://www.jsoniq.org/
27. Saryerwinnie, J.: JMESPath (2015). https://jmespath.org/
28. Snoeck, M., De Smedt, J., De Weerdt, J.: Supporting data-aware processes with MERODE. In: Enterprise, Business-Process and Information Systems Modeling, pp. 131–146. Melbourne, Australia (2021). https://doi.org/10.1007/978-3-030-79186-5_9
29. Steinau, S., Marrella, A., Andrews, K., Leotta, F., Mecella, M., Reichert, M.: DALEC: a framework for the systematic evaluation of data-centric approaches to process management software. Softw. Syst. Model. **18**(4), 2679–2716 (2018). https://doi.org/10.1007/s10270-018-0695-0
30. Vogler, W., Semenov, A., Yakovlev, A.: Unfolding and finite prefix for nets with read arcs. In: Sangiorgi, D., de Simone, R. (eds.) CONCUR 1998. LNCS, vol. 1466, pp. 501–516. Springer, Heidelberg (1998). https://doi.org/10.1007/BFb0055644
31. W3C: W3C XML Schema Definition Language (XSD) 1.1 (2012). https://www.w3.org/TR/2012/REC-xmlschema11-1-20120405/
32. W3C: XPath 3.1. https://www.w3.org/TR/2017/REC-xpath-31-20170321/ (2017)
33. W3C: XQuery 3.1 (2017). https://www.w3.org/TR/2017/REC-xquery-31-20170321/
34. Weitz, W.: SGML nets: integrating document and workflow modeling. In: Hawaii International Conference on System Sciences, pp. 185–194. Kohala Coast, HI, USA (1998). https://doi.org/10.1109/HICSS.1998.651699
35. Weske, M.: Business Process Management: Concepts, Languages, Architectures, 3rd edn. Springer, Berlin (2019). https://doi.org/10.1007/978-3-662-59432-2
36. Wright, A., Andrews, H., Hutton, B., Dennis, G.: JSON Schema: a media type for describing JSON documents (2022). https://json-schema.org/draft/2020-12/json-schema-core.html

Aligning Object-Centric Event Logs with Data-Centric Conceptual Models

Alexandre Goossens(✉) , Charlotte Verbruggen(✉) , Monique Snoeck ,
Johannes De Smedt , and Jan Vanthienen

KU Leuven, Naamsestraat 69, 3000 Leuven, Belgium
{alexandre.goossens,charlotte.verbruggen,monique.snoeck,johannes.smedt,
jan.vanthienen}@kuleuven.be

Abstract. Recently, the consideration of data aspects has seen a surge
in interest both from the perspective of designing processes as from
a model discovery perspective. However, it seems that both research
domains (models for design and model discovery) use different conceptualisations of data/object-aware systems. In an ideal situation, when
(designed) models are implemented, the resulting information systems
are equipped with logging functionalities that allow the rediscovery of
the models based on which the information systems were implemented.
However, there is a lack of guidelines on how to set up logging. From
a logging perspective, logging formats are unclear about the granularity
of events: the logging may be done at the level of entire tasks or at the
level of the operations on individual objects, or a single log may even
contain a mix of events at different granularity levels. The lack of clarity
in this matter complicates the correct interpretation of log information.
The goal of this paper is therefore to investigate how the concepts of
object-centric logging and those for data-aware process modelling may
be better aligned. This will facilitate setting up proper logging at system
implementation time, and facilitate the connection of discovered models
to models-for-design. The investigation resulted in iDOCEM, a meta-
model that aligns the DOCEL and the Merode meta-model. Comparing
iDOCEM to different other logging meta-models demonstrates that the
proposed meta-model is complete enough to capture (more than) existing
logging formats.

Keywords: conceptual modelling · object-centric process logging ·
artefact-centric process modelling · data-aware process modelling ·
object-centric process discovery

1 Introduction

In the business process lifecycle, models are used for two purposes: on the one
hand models are used to create systems (possibly after analysis and redesign),
and on the other hand, models are discovered from logs [6]. These discovered

© The Author(s), under exclusive license to Springer Nature Switzerland AG 2023
H. van der Aa et al. (Eds.): BPMDS 2023/EMMSAD 2023, LNBIP 479, pp. 44–59, 2023.
https://doi.org/10.1007/978-3-031-34241-7_4

models can be the starting point of a new cycle of analysis, redesign, implementation, etc. Especially in case the log is extracted from a black box system, only the data in the log is available to reconstruct the process models. As such the proper logging of implemented processes aligned with the system is a crucial element for process discovery. Recently, the consideration of data aspects has seen a surge in interest, both from a model-for-design as from a model discovery perspective. In particular, recent process mining efforts have revised the task of extracting an event log from the analyzed information system from a single to a multi-object perspective [10]. To serve this purpose, various new efforts have proposed new solutions for object-centric processes including object-centric visualization tools [9], log sampling and filtering techniques [5], and object-centric Petri nets [1]. To enable these analyses and modelling efforts, various object-centric logging formats such as eXtensible Object-Centric (XOC) [18], Object-Centric Behavioral Constraint (OCBC) model [3], Object-Centric Event Logs (OCEL) [10], and more recently Data-aware Object-Centric Event Logs (DOCEL) [12] have been proposed. Likewise, data-aware process modelling has seen a surge in interest as well. Steinau at al. [25] performed an in-depth analysis of no less than 17 different data-aware process management approaches and captured this in the DALEC framework (Data-centric Approach Lightweight Evaluation and Comparison framework).

However, it seems that both research domains (models for design and model discovery) use different conceptualisations of data/object-ware systems. A definition of how the captured event logs are related to the structure of the global system they are extracted from or are trying to discover, is still missing. In an ideal situation, when (designed) models are implemented, the resulting information systems are equipped with logging functionalities that allow the rediscovery of the models based on which the information systems were implemented. One of the conclusions of Steinau et al. [25] is however that while many approaches cover the *design phase* of the business process lifecycle, there remain substantial gaps for the support of next phases of the lifecycle of a business process i.e. *implementation and execution* and *diagnosis and optimization*. To support each phase and the transition from one phase to the next, additional research is needed to define and develop the right instrumentation to provide good support for process monitoring, diagnosis discovery and optimization through proper logging built into information systems at implementation time.

The goal of this paper is therefore to investigate the concepts and terminology used in the different parts of the cycle: the design part, the implementation of the logging and the discovery part, and to propose a meta-model that aligns the DOCEL and the Merode meta-model with a unified terminology.

The rest of this paper is structured as follows: Sect. 2 covers related work on object-centric logging and data-aware process modeling, and revisits the problem. Subsequently, Sect. 3 presents the meta-model iDOCEM that aligns the terminology in different phases of the cycle, and next, Sect. 4 shows how iDOCEM captures all concepts from eXtensible Event Stream (XES), OCEL, DOCEL and the Merode approach. Section 5 provides a discussion of iDOCEM by comparing it to related work and discusses the limitations. Finally, Sect. 6 concludes the paper.

2 Related Work

This section discusses object-centric processes from two angles: the process mining angle (Sect. 2.1) and the data-aware process modelling angle (Sect. 2.2). We conclude with a refinement of the problem statement in Sect. 2.3.

2.1 The Process Mining Angle

The idea that a business process can use and affect multiple objects or can be defined by means of a set of connected subprocesses, each related to an object or artefact, is not new. E.g., Proclets have already been proposed back in 2001, whereby a business process consists of multiple proclets with each proclet being the subprocess of a certain artefact [2]. Since then various object-centric representation formats have been proposed such as Colored Petri Nets (CPN) [16] where each color represents a different object in object-centric Petri Nets [1]. An extension on object-centric Petri Nets was proposed in [11] with Catalogue and Object-aware Nets (COA) where transitions can have guards and data can be directly extracted from databases. Another proposal is Guard-Stage-Milestone (GSM) where the interaction between artefact instances is graphically visualized in a declarative manner [15] and a BPMN extension with the possibility to model data objects to have complex data dependencies was also proposed [19]. More complete overviews can be found in [17,25]. To store object-centric process data, various logging formats have been proposed with the first proposals being eXtensible Object-Centric (XOC) [18] and Object-Centric Behavioral Constraint (OCBC) model [3]. They suffer, however, from scalability issues related to the storage of attributes and object-object relations with each event.

Recently, the more scalable OCEL [10] has been proposed. Certain problems remain with the proposal of OCEL, mainly related to attribute storage. In the case an attribute is updated, according to OCEL, this has to be stored together with the events. This entails however that whenever more than one object participates in an event, this attribute can not be correctly allocated nor to the correct object type nor to the correct individual object. As a result, crucial information related to business process and the data objects is lost. The importance of attributes is acknowledged with the proposal of DOCEL [12] which allows to unambiguously link each updated attribute value to the specific event that updated it and to the object the attribute belongs to.

Next to representing artefact-centric processes, various studies investigated the extraction of artefact-centric knowledge within a process context. How to support many-to-many relations between artefacts in state-based artefact life-cycle models was investigated in [7]. In [21] an algorithm is proposed to automatically discover the object-lifecycle of each data object involved in a business process. When transforming XES logs to OCEL logs, the algorithm developed in [22] is dependent on the correct discovery of artefact-event associations and object-attribute associations. The semi-automatic discovery of datamodels from event logs has been investigated in [4]. The soundness of Data Petri Nets (DPN) with arithmetic conditions using Satisfiability-Modulo-Theory (SMT) technologies has also been studied [8]. These publications, even though not exhaustive, show the interest in artefact-centric knowledge extraction from a process context.

2.2 The Data-Aware Process Modelling Angle

In the field of data-aware process modelling, several frameworks have been proposed to align data modelling and process modelling. In [14], four dimensions are introduced in order to structure artefact-centric process modelling approaches: business artefacts, macro life-cycles, services and associations. Data modelling consists of business artefacts and macro life-cycles, and process modelling consists of services and associations. The services are in essence tasks and associations are links between the services, and between services and macro lifecycles. The paper also lists a number of challenges identified by practitioners at IBM. Interestingly, they already suggest applying process mining techniques in artefact-centric settings. In [17], a set of requirements for the support of data-aware process modelling is presented, followed by a framework detailing the characteristics of data-aware processes. In [25], existing data-aware process modelling approaches are first compared to each other and classified by means of a systematic literature review. The detailed comparison throughout all phases of the business process lifecycle results in a comprehensive set of criteria for full support of data-aware processes. One of the findings of this paper is that tool support mainly focuses on the design phase, but is lacking for the implementation and execution phase, and especially for the diagnosis and optimization phase. Recently, in [24] the gap between the *Design* and *implementation and execution* phase was addressed by developing a formal link between business process modelling and domain modelling and demonstrating how data-aware processes can be co-designed and deployed in combination with a full-fledged domain model and ensuing set of applications services.

2.3 Problem Illustration

The above overview of the related work suggests that the focus lies either on the creation and analysis of the logs, whereby the data modeling formalisms used to create a system from, is disconnected from formalisms for designing models (e.g. BPMN or UML), or, that the focus lies on the formalism used to design and implement a system, but that the logging, and subsequent monitoring, analysis and diagnosis is underdeveloped (cfr. the conclusion of Steinau et al. [25]). To the authors' knowledge, Gonzales et al. [20] is the only related work that focuses on the same problem. They aim to connect the data and process perspective, in order to support process mining in a data-aware setting. They provide a meta-model connecting both perspectives and a detailed description of the developed

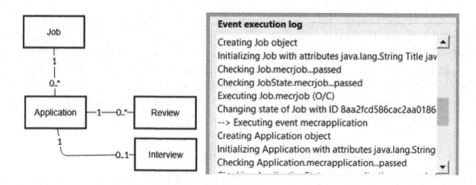

Fig. 1. The log generated by the Merode code generator

tool support applied in several real-world settings. However, the approach is based on the XES specification, a process of a log is still assumed to be dealing with a single object type, and there is no support for object-centric logs nor for an artefact-centric perspective on the global system.

The problems resulting from the mismatch between the definitions of concepts of the metamodels used for system design and those for logging and process mining can be illustrated by means of the concrete case of PhD hiring, orginally described in [17]. Assume that Merode and BPMN are used for system design. As explained in [24], the method addresses the most important elements required for data-aware process modelling. Accordingly, a data model, a set of statecharts defining object behaviour (e.g. the lifecycle of an application) and a set of processes (e.g. the process for obtaining reviews) are defined. The Class Diagram for this example can be found in Fig. 1, left), while the remaining diagrams (state charts and BPMN diagram) can be viewed online[1].

While these models address system design in a satisfactory way, and the generated systems do offer some logging, the way logging is conceived has nevertheless a number of shortcomings from a process mining perspective. On the one hand, the application and its database provide a complete view of the objects created so far, and the logging functionality tracks each attempted triggering of business events, including the failed attempts that result from violating some constraint defined in the models. Figure 1 shows an example of the log of the creation of a vacancy for a job and receiving an application. Even though the log contains information about an action's start, execution, cancellation or completion, the current logging was developed with the aim of providing model-understanding support for modelers, and does not follow any process log format such as XES, OCEL or DOCEL. The Merode log (see Fig. 1, right) is therefore incomplete and not suited for process mining. Reverting to another approach will not solve the issue: in [25], criterion D14 "Support for monitoring" is unsupported by all considered approaches.

---

[1] https://merode.econ.kuleuven.be/MERODExBPMN.html.

When considering the issue from a logging perspective, the main problem is the lack of clarity about what is logged and has to be logged. As DOCEL only contains the notion of "event", such logging does not allow distinguishing whether a logged "event" refers to a user task or a more fine-granular invocation of individual operations on an object. Imagine for example, a user task "Hire Candidate" that invokes an "EVdecideToHire" event that affects the state of the application of the candidate and the job vacancy directly. Possibly, the task also updates the states of the other candidates to "notToHire". Depending on how the logging is set up, the logging may be done at the level of the entire task or at the level of the operations on individual objects, or a single log may even contain a mix of events at different granularity levels. The lack of clarity in this matter complicates the correct interpretation of log information.

Next to that, even though all the object-centric process logging proposals are aimed at storing object-centric processes, none of them include the notion of object lifecycles or states as separate meta-objects within their meta-model. This is mainly due to the fact that data is considered from a pure database perspective, rather than from a domain modelling perspective. As the execution of an event may cause transitions from one state to the next, having information about the states before and after the event execution allows distinguishing between positive and negative events: logging a click on a "submit" button in itself does not provide information about the success or failure of the submission, unless also the resulting state is logged as well. The logging standards do not ensure this information to be logged. For example, XOC starts from the redo logs of databases rather than considering the application logic issuing the database manipulation statements. A domain model may typically contain additional business logic besides the pure data aspects, and logging needs to capture this information properly.

Finally, the lack of a policy on what data to log may mean that not all object relationships are discoverable with the DOCEL log, as typically only objects directly involved in the context of an event are stored. E.g. when submitting a review, typically only the data of the affected review object will be logged, but not necessarily of the related application and job because those objects are not modified by adding a review. This makes that the complete object model behind a process model might not be completely discoverable with a DOCEL log.

The goal of this paper is therefore to investigate how the concepts of object-centric logging and those for data-aware process modelling may be better aligned. This will facilitate setting up proper logging at system implementation time and facilitate the connection of discovered models to models-for-design. Given the large number of formalisms for data-aware modelling on the one hand, and the different formalisms for object-centric modelling on the other hand, we investigate the alignment problem and propose a solution based on the combination of Merode and DOCEL. On the one hand, DOCEL is the better choice as an object-centric format because it systematically unambiguously allocates the right attributes to the right objects and it allows for attributes belonging to objects to change over time and to track this change in contrast to the other object-centric formats that do not support these aspects [12]. On the other hand, Merode is the most recent proposal for data-aware process modelling that satisfies the large majority of the criteria put forward in [17] and is based on state-of-the-art data modelling. The fact that it provides for automatic code generation for the application part, and allows for integration with Camunda, will facilitate further experimentation and development of an adapted DOCEL-compliant log generator.

3   Integrated Data and Object Centric Model (iDOCEM)

The first challenge in aligning object-centric event logs with data-centric conceptual models is unifying the terminology used by both domains. We do this by creating a meta-model based on the Merode meta-model and the DOCEL meta-model [12]. The full Merode meta-model with a description can be found on the Merode website[2]. The complete Merode Approach is described in [23]. The DOCEL meta-model is presented in [12]. The Integrated Data & Object Centric Event Meta-model (iDOCEM) is represented in Fig. 2. In order to maintain the readability of the model, several simplifications were performed:

- Not all attributes are represented. Attributes that were taken from the DOCEL meta-model are mentioned explicitly, but besides that, each class may contain more attributes, such as identifiers.
- The Class 'Data Type' is not included to minimize the number of crossing associations. In the full model[3], the 'Data Type' class is connected to the 'Static Event Attribute', 'Event Parameter', 'Method Parameter' and the 'Object Attribute' class. Data Types represent both basic types such as integer, boolean, float, character, etc. as well as complex types such as string, date, lists. Object Type is a subtype of Data Type as implementing associations results in attributes having the object type as data type.
- The meta-model contains only the elements from the Merode meta-model that are relevant for this problem. For example, the parts related to Inheritance have not been included.

iDOCEM has six zones (shown in Fig. 2). On the one hand, the meta-model is split into an instance level (left) and a model level (right). On the other hand, the meta-model is divided in three areas that deal with data objects, their attributes and their associations (bottom), activities and events (top), and the methods and parameters that connect events to objects (middle). The definitions of the entities used in iDOCEM are provided in Table 1, where the third column provides an illustrative example. The cardinalities at the instance level (on the left) mostly mirror the cardinalities at the model level (on the right). An exception is the association between BUSINESS EVENT and ACTIVITY INSTANCE: while an *event type* can be triggered in multiple *activities* (e.g. the event "submitReview"

---

[2] https://merode.econ.kuleuven.be/merodemetamodel.html.
[3] https://merode.econ.kuleuven.be/iDOCEM.html.

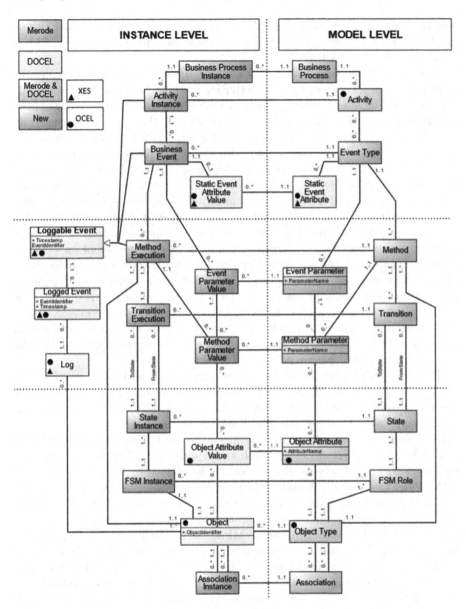

Fig. 2. The iDOCEM meta-model

is triggered both from the professor's task as from the international office's task), a *business event* is always triggered by exactly one *activity instance* (the submission of Monique's review is triggered by Monique's task). The elements that come from the Merode meta-model and the DOCEL meta-model are colored in blue and green, respectively. Elements that appear in both meta-models are colored in orange and new elements are colored in red. Next, elements that appear in XES or in OCEL are indicated with a triangle and circle respectively. This is further discussed in Sect. 4.

The most challenging aspect of combining the meta-models is defining the correspondence between events and activities, as their definitions in the Merode approach (and artefact-centric process modelling in general) differ slightly from the definitions used in process log meta-models. In the Merode approach, an *activity instance* (e.g. hiring Charlotte for the job PhDJob1) in a *business process instance* (Handle vacancy for PhDJob1) can trigger zero, one, or multiple *business events* (trigger EVdecideToHire for Charlotte, and EVdecideNotToHire for all other candidates). The business events in turn trigger *method executions*, affecting the *objects* (MEdecideToHire in object Charlotte + MEdecideToHire in object PhDJob1 + MEdecideNotToHire in all other applications for this job).

As discussed in the problem statement, the concept of an event in artefact-centric process modelling is slightly different from the concept of an event in process log meta-models: an event in an event log either represents the execution of an activity instance, a business event, or even a method execution, depending on the granularity level of logging. In iDOCEM, we manage this disparity by creating LOGGABLE EVENT as an abstract superclass of ACTIVITY INSTANCE, BUSINESS EVENT and METHOD EXECUTION. A *loggable event* can occur several times as a *logged event*. The class LOGGED EVENT captures when a *loggable event* is included in a *log*.

Both in DOCEL and in Merode, object types (e.g. Job, Application, Review) and event types are related in a many-to-many way. In the Merode meta-model, this many-to-many association is reified into the meta-object METHOD. In the Merode approach, an *event type* (e.g. EVdecideToHire) is related to one or multiple *methods*, one for each *object type* that is defined to be affected by the *event type* (EVdecideToHire affects both Job and Application). The *method* captures how an *event type* affects an *object type*, i.e. the *method* may create an instance of the *object type*, change the value of an attribute of the involved object instance and/or perform a transition in the object's lifecycle (e.g. in the class Job, MEdecideToHire moves the object from the state "exists" to the state "Candidate-Hired", and in the class Application MEdecideToHire moves the object from the state "eligible" to the state "CandidateToHire"). Each *object type* is always involved in at least two *event types* (one for the creation of object instances, and one for ending the life of those instances), while each *event type* should always affect at least one *object type* to be considered in scope of a domain model. DOCEL however does not have such a clearly defined policy regarding object and event allocation. Instead the only requirement it has is that it assumes that each *event* directly interacts with the relevant *objects* involved in that *event*. Just like in Merode, each *event* should at least be dealing with one *object* and each *object* should at least be involved in one *event* to be considered in scope of the object-centric process. However, there are no requirements regarding the presence of *events* that create and delete *objects* since a business process can be a snapshot and thus certain *objects* may already have been created before or maybe deleted after the business process snapshot.

The Merode meta-model allows *event types* and *methods* to have attributes (called parameters), but does not define a relationship between the attributes of an *object type* and an *event type* or *method*: it is assumed that this relationship is set in the programming code that defines a *method*'s implementation. For example, the starting date and salary may be parameters of the EVdecideToHire event, and the code inside the methods MEdecideToHire will ensure to write this data in the correct place. In DOCEL on the other hand, *dynamic attributes* of *objects* are also linked to the *event* that changes the value of the attribute. To incorporate this into iDOCEM, EVENT PARAMETER and METHOD PARAMETER are linked, and the latter is linked to the OBJECT ATTRIBUTE class.

4   Aligning the Terminology of Existing Logging Formats

Section 4 aligns iDOCEM's terminology with XES, OCEL, DOCEL, and Merode to explain the differences and equivalences between logging formats and Merode.

XES [13] is a commonly-used business process logging format that logs a process from the perspective of a single object type. Each process execution instance is called a *trace*, which is the execution of a specific case or object of that object type. OCEL [10] is an object-centric event log format allowing to store the logs of object-centric processes and currently the most widely used log format for object-centric processes. Before OCEL, OCBC models [3] were introduced together with the XOC logging format [18] to respectively represent and store object-centric process logs. Both suffer from scalability issues related to the storage of a relevant datamodel and all its attributes with each event [10]. Due to this and the absence of a meta-model in their proposal, OCBC and XOC are not included in the terminology alignment.

The alignment of terminologies between iDOCEM, XES, OCEL, DOCEL and Merode can be found in Table 2. In this table, a cell is colored gray when the meta-model does not contain a class equivalent to the corresponding class in the iDOCEM meta-model. If the meta-model contains a class that has similar but not exactly the same functionality to the corresponding class in iDOCEM, the name of the class is marked with a '*'. If the meta-model contains exactly the same class as the iDOCEM meta-model, the cell is marked with a '='.

Regarding Table 2, a few things should be highlighted. Firstly, iDOCEM is more complete than any of the other meta-models. Second, iDOCEM distinguishes between different kinds of attributes more depending on whether they belong to *objects* or *business events* compared to OCEL and XES. XES only contains the meta-object *Attribute* and *Attribute Type* but these can only be linked to either an *event* or a *trace* which is not always equivalent to an object. OCEL distinguishes between object and event attributes meaning that not all *attributes* associated with an *object* can be changed over time. DOCEL solves this by having both *dynamic* and *static* attributes that belong to an *object* and/or *event*. In domain modelling, all object attributes are dynamic, since the value

Table 1. Terminology used in iDOCEM

Entity	Definition	Example
BUSINESS PROCESS	Model of a business process	BPMN diagram for Handling Vacancy
BUSINESS PROCESS INSTANCE	Occurence of a *business process*	Handling the vacancy for PhDJob1
ACTIVITY	The concept of a task in a business process	User Task Check Write Review
ACTIVITY INSTANCE	Occurrence of an *activity*.	Write a review for Charlotte's application
EVENT TYPE	Type of real-world event that is relevant for the system and may trigger state changes in objects	SubmitReview
BUSINESS EVENT	Occurrence of an *event type*	Monique submits her review of Charlotte's application
STATIC EVENT ATTRIBUTE	Attribute that is inherently linked to an *event type* and cannot be changed, such as the event identifier or timestamp	Time of review submission
STATIC EVENT ATTRIBUTE VALUE	Value of a *static event attribute*.	Time at which Monique submitted her review
METHOD	Procedure according to which the instance of the given *object type* is created, modified or ended as a result of the occurrence of the given *event type*	Code for submitting a review
METHOD EXECUTION	Occurrence of a *method*	Execution of the code when Monique submits her review
LOGGABLE EVENT	The abstract superclass of ACTIVITY INSTANCE, BUSINESS EVENT and METHOD EXECUTION that groups elements that can be logged in an event log	*Abstract classes do not have instances*
LOGGED EVENT	*loggable event* that is included in a *log*	Logging of Monique's submission
LOG	Stored collection of *loggable events*.	Log of Handling Vacancy processes
EVENT PARAMETER	Parameters related to an *event type*, i.e. placeholder for a value that should be supplied when triggering a *business event* and its *methods*, resulting in a change in the *objects*	Parameter "Recommendation" for the EVsubmitReview event type
EVENT PARAMETER VALUE	The value(s) given with each *event parameter*.	"Hire" as value of the recommendation given by Monique
METHOD PARAMETER	Placeholder for a value that should be supplied when invoking the *method*	Parameter "Recommendation" for the MEsubmitReview method in the object type Review
METHOD PARAMETER VALUE	The value(s) given with each *method parameter*.	"Hire" as value of the recommendation given by Monique
OBJECT ATTRIBUTE	Attribute of an *object type* that can be changed throughout the lifecycle of that *object type*	Attribute "Recommendation" in object type Review
OBJECT ATTRIBUTE VALUE	Value(s) given to an *object attribute* by means of a *method execution*	Value of the attribute Recommendation in Monique's review is "Hire"
OBJECT TYPE	Entity/Class in a data model.	Job, Application, Review
OBJECT	Instance of an *object type*.	PhDJob1, Charlotte's application, Monique's review
ASSOCIATION	Relationship between two *object types*	Job has 0..* Applications
ASSOCIATION INSTANCE	Link between two *object instances*	Charlotte's application is linked to PhDJob1
FSM ROLE	*Object types* can have multiple roles in a system. For each role a statechart Machine (*FSM role*) can be defined. An *object type* always has at least one FSM: the default lifecycle	FSM of Review
FSM INSTANCE	Statechart Machine that manages the state of a given *object*.	FSM for Monique's Review
STATE	A *state* exists within the context of a *FSM role* and represents a stage in the lifecycle of an *object type*	state "submitted" in the FSM of Review
STATE INSTANCE	Actual value of a *state* for a given *object* (object being in this state or not)	Value of state "submitted" for Monique's review is "true"
TRANSITION	A *transition* specifies how a *method* causes an *object type* to transition from one *state* to another *state*	transition from "initiated" to "submitted" in the FSM of Review
TRANSITION EXECUTION	Occurrence of a *Transition* where a *method execution* causes an *object* to transition from one *state instance* to another	The execution of the method MEsubmit on Monique's review causes it to transit from the state "exists" to the state "submitted"

Table 2. Terminology Alignment between iDOCEM, OCEL, DOCEL and Merode

iDOCEM	XES	OCEL	DOCEL	Merode
BUSINESS PROCESS				=
BUSINESS PROCESS INSTANCE	Trace*			
ACTIVITY		=	=	IS Supported Task
ACTIVITY INSTANCE	Event*	Event*	Event*	
EVENT TYPE				=
BUSINESS EVENT	Event*	Event*	Event*	
STATIC EVENT ATTRIBUTE	Attribute*	Attribute*	=	
STATIC EVENT ATTRIBUTE VALUE	Value*	Attribute Value*	Attribute Value*	
METHOD				=
METHOD EXECUTION	Event*	Event*	Event*	
LOGGABLE EVENT	Event*	Event*	Event*	
LOGGED EVENT	Event	Event	Event	
LOG	=	=	=	
EVENT PARAMETER	Attribute*	Attribute*	Dynamic Object Attribute*	Event Parameter
EVENT PARAMETER VALUE	Value*	Attribute Value*	Attribute Value*	
METHOD PARAMETER	Attribute*	Attribute*	Dynamic Attribute*	Method Attribute
METHOD PARAMETER VALUE	Value*	Attribute Value*	Attribute Value*	
OBJECT ATTRIBUTE	Attribute*	Attribute*	Dynamic/Static Attribute*	Attribute*
OBJECT ATTRIBUTE VALUE	Value*	Attribute Value*	Attribute Value*	
OBJECT TYPE		=	=	=
OBJECT		=	=	
ASSOCIATION				=
FSM ROLE				=
FSM INSTANCE				=
STATE				=
STATE INSTANCE				=
TRANSITION				=
TRANSITION EXECUTION				=

of an attribute must be set at least once in the life cycle of its object. Hence, iDOCEM does not distinguish between static and dynamic object attributes.

Because iDOCEM links *method executions* to *business events*, which are considered individually or as a group via an *activity instance*, it provides a finer logging granularity that is missing in XES, OCEL or DOCEL, where the results of methods are only represented in *events* and are not linked to specific *activities*. For example, if a customer adds a product to their basket (business event), an *order line* is created and the total amount of the *order* is updated (2 method executions), these two method executions would not necessarily be linked.

Finally, iDOCEM stands apart from XES, OCEL, and DOCEL in its explicit inclusion of multiple object lifecycle meta-objects such as *FSM Role, FSM Instance, State, State Instance, Transition, Transition Execution*, in the meta-model. This makes that iDOCEM is more artefact-centric compared to XES, OCEL, and DOCEL as the inclusion of these object lifecycles is more explicit.

A prime advantage of iDOCEM is that it defines an object-(loggable)event allocation policy. A consistent allocation policy is important because relations between *object types* need to be kept stable across the execution of a business process. If this allocation policy is not consistent or correct, it might not be possible to discover the complete object-centric process since not all objects are linked correctly to the right event, hence missing certain aspects of the process, e.g., with a business event *Ship order* the address of the customer needs to be provided. However if no customer is linked to that event then no address can be provided for that *Ship order* business event. iDOCEM already contains a relationship between OBJECT, METHOD EXECUTION, BUSINESS EVENT and ACTIVITY INSTANCE, defining the allocation of *loggable events* to *objects*. The Merode meta-model(see footnote 2) specifies this relationship even further given that each association must express existence dependency, and object types can acquire methods from their dependents [23]. As such an unambiguous and consistent policy is defined. The second advantage results from iDOCEM containing both an object-centric process storage format and an artefact-centric conceptual model enabling the development of a logging tool for the execution of any artefact-centric conceptual model in a process mining conform format. This opens the door to model simulation of allowed events and non-allowed events and paves the way to further process mining applications regarding describing and analyzing artefact information and business process conformance with the artefact-centric model.

5   Discussion

Section 2.2, introduces the only other publication [20] proposing a meta-model for the same problem. The main differences between both meta-models are:

- While iDOCEM uses two levels of granularity (the model level and the instance level), G. López de Murillas et al. use three levels of granularity by adding the notion of *object versions*. iDOCEM does not contain an OBJECT VERSION class, this is instead captured by an *object* which can have several *object attribute values* for the same *object attribute*. The same applies for *event parameters*, *method parameters* and *static event attributes*. iDOCEM assumes that the data model is kept stable during a process execution leaving out database structure evolution out of scope at this point.
- According to [20], the process and data sides of the meta-model are only connected to each other at the most granular level. In iDOCEM, the connections between the *object types*, *attributes/parameters*, *event types* and *activities* is explicitly modelled on the model level as well, while this is missing in [20].
- In [20] *events* (and *activity instances*) are grouped into *cases*, which are then grouped into *logs*. iDOCEM directly groups *loggable events* into *logs* as the cases can be retrieved using filtering operations on the log.
- Both [20] and iDOCEM include a class (LOGGABLE) EVENT. However, the former defines an event on a more coarse level than the latter. In their meta-model, an *activity instance* can be related to several *events* that define the type of operation (read, write, delete etc.) and/or the lifecycle value of the *activity instance* (start, complete). In iDOCEM, *loggable events* can also represent the trigger of individual *method executions*. Moreover, a *loggable event* can have several *logged events*, each recording a stage in the processing of a *loggable event* (started, completed, ...).

- In [20] only the relationship between ATTRIBUTE and CLASS is modelled, while iDOCEM makes a distinction between different types of attributes (STATIC EVENT ATTRIBUTE, OBJECT ATTRIBUTE, EVENT PARAMETER and METHOD PARAMETER) and how they relate to the other classes.

iDOCEM is based on a specific artefact-centric modelling approach, namely Merode, because the approach has a number of benefits: it is based on popular modelling standards (UML class diagrams and statecharts), it is an event-driven approach, making it an excellent choice to support the generation of event logs, and it is well defined and thoroughly tested and evaluated. In addition, the use of existence dependency in Merode means that object-object relations cannot change. When object-object relationships can change, the associations are reified, thereby explicitly identifying events to set and end object relationships.

iDOCEM does not incorporate the full Merode meta-model, however, it includes all elements that are relevant to the concept of event logs. A main limitation is that the current log format of the applications generated by the Merode prototyper do not yet follow any log storage standard. Furthermore, as the logging only pertains to the application component, tasks in the business process that are executed without support of the application, and tasks that only consult information but do not trigger events, are not logged. This corresponds to logging in information systems that do not make use of process engines. As such, in its present form, the current log format provides only a partial view of the executed processes. The current logging nevertheless demonstrates the feasibility of generating an iDOCEM log from an artefact-centric application generated from a Merode model. By the fact that iDOCEM includes the meta-objects needed to capture the process elements, the format is also capable of describing the logs of a process-aware information system. The use of a process engine would allow to also log the execution of task that do not make use of an application component.

6   Conclusion

This paper starts with the observation that object-centric processes are having to deal with artefact-centric problems some of which artefact-centric approaches have extensive support for. Next to that, it has been highlighted that artefact-centric approaches would benefit from a logging format allowing to store the execution of such models. To solve both issues, this paper aligns the meta-models of the Data-aware Object-Centric Event Log (DOCEL) together with an artefact-centric approach into an Integrated Data & Object Centric Event Meta-model (iDOCEM). iDOCEM includes the concepts present in XES, OCEL and DOCEL and therefore provides a more complete perspective on data-aware process logging with the inclusion of object lifecycles and a wider variety of attributes. While a log generator according to iDOCEM has not yet been fully implemented, the current logging facilities generated by the Merode code generator already demonstrate the feasibility of logging process execution according to this format. Future research will focus on adapting the code generator so as to generate an iDOCEM-compliant log from the applications, as well as expanding the logging to the business process engine level, so as to generate more complete logs including the execution of tasks that do not trigger business events.

References

1. van der Aalst, W., Berti, A.: Discovering object-centric Petri nets. Fundamenta informaticae **175**(1–4), 1–40 (2020)
2. van der Aalst, W.M., Barthelmess, P., Ellis, C.A., Wainer, J.: Proclets: a framework for lightweight interacting workflow processes. Int. J. Cooperat. Inf. Syst. **10**(04), 443–481 (2001)
3. van der Aalst, W.M., Li, G., Montali, M.: Object-centric behavioral constraints. arXiv preprint arXiv:1703.05740 (2017)
4. Maggi, F.M., Dumas, M., García-Bañuelos, L., Montali, M.: Discovering data-aware declarative process models from event logs. In: Daniel, F., Wang, J., Weber, B. (eds.) BPM 2013. LNCS, vol. 8094, pp. 81–96. Springer, Heidelberg (2013). https://doi.org/10.1007/978-3-642-40176-3_8
5. Berti, A.: Filtering and sampling object-centric event logs. arXiv preprint arXiv:2205.01428 (2022)
6. Dumas, M., La Rosa, M., Mendling, J., Reijers, H.A.: Fundamentals of Business Process Management. Springer, Berlin (2013). https://doi.org/10.1007/978-3-662-56509-4
7. van Eck, M.L., Sidorova, N., van der Aalst, W.M.P.: Multi-instance mining: discovering synchronisation in artifact-centric processes. In: Daniel, F., Sheng, Q.Z., Motahari, H. (eds.) BPM 2018. LNBIP, vol. 342, pp. 18–30. Springer, Cham (2019). https://doi.org/10.1007/978-3-030-11641-5_2
8. Felli, P., Montali, M., Winkler, S.: Soundness of data-aware processes with arithmetic conditions. In: CAiSE, pp. 389–406. Springer, Cham (2022). https://doi.org/10.1007/978-3-031-07472-1_23
9. Ghahfarokhi, A.F., van der Aalst, W.: A python tool for object-centric process mining comparison. arXiv preprint arXiv:2202.05709 (2022)
10. Ghahfarokhi, A.F., Park, G., Berti, A., van der Aalst, W.: OCEL standard. Process and Data Science Group, RWTH Aachen University, Tech report 1 (2020)
11. Ghilardi, S., Gianola, A., Montali, M., Rivkin, A.: Petri net-based object-centric processes with read-only data. Inf. Syst. **107**, 102011 (2022)
12. Goossens, A., De Smedt, J., Vanthienen, J., van der Aalst, W.M.: Enhancing data-awareness of object-centric event logs. In: Montali, M., Senderovich, A., Weidlich, M. (eds.) Process Mining Workshops: ICPM 2022 International Workshops. LNBIP, vol. 468, pp. 18–30. Springer, Cham (2023). https://doi.org/10.1007/978-3-031-27815-0_2
13. Günther, C.W., Verbeek, H.M.W.: XES standard definition. IEEE Std. (2014)
14. Hull, R.: Artifact-centric business process models: brief survey of research results and challenges. In: Meersman, R., Tari, Z. (eds.) OTM 2008. LNCS, vol. 5332, pp. 1152–1163. Springer, Heidelberg (2008). https://doi.org/10.1007/978-3-540-88873-4_17
15. Hull, R., et al.: Business artifacts with guard-stage-milestone lifecycles: managing artifact interactions with conditions and events. In: Proceedings of the 5th ACM DEBS, pp. 51–62 (2011)

16. Kleijn, J., Koutny, M., Pietkiewicz-Koutny, M.: Regions of petri nets with a/sync connections. Theoret. Comput. Sci. **454**, 189–198 (2012)

17. Künzle, V., Reichert, M.: Philharmonicflows: towards a framework for object-aware process management. J. Softw. Maint. Evol. Res. Pract. **23**(4), 205–244 (2011)

18. Li, G., de Murillas, E.G.L., de Carvalho, R.M., van der Aalst, W.M.P.: Extracting object-centric event logs to support process mining on databases. In: Mendling, J., Mouratidis, H. (eds.) CAiSE 2018. LNBIP, vol. 317, pp. 182–199. Springer, Cham (2018). https://doi.org/10.1007/978-3-319-92901-9_16

19. Meyer, A., Pufahl, L., Fahland, D., Weske, M.: Modeling and enacting complex data dependencies in business processes. In: Daniel, F., Wang, J., Weber, B. (eds.) BPM 2013. LNCS, vol. 8094, pp. 171–186. Springer, Heidelberg (2013). https://doi.org/10.1007/978-3-642-40176-3_14

20. González López de Murillas, E., Reijers, H.A., Van Der Aalst, W.M.: Connecting databases with process mining: a meta model and toolset. Softw. Syst. Model. **18**(2), 1209–1247 (2019)

21. Nooijen, E.H.J., van Dongen, B.F., Fahland, D.: Automatic discovery of data-centric and artifact-centric processes. In: La Rosa, M., Soffer, P. (eds.) BPM 2012. LNBIP, vol. 132, pp. 316–327. Springer, Heidelberg (2013). https://doi.org/10.1007/978-3-642-36285-9_36

22. Rebmann, A., Rehse, J.R., van der Aa, H.: Uncovering object-centric data in classical event logs for the automated transformation from XES to OCEL. In: Business Process Management-20th International Conference, BPM, pp. 11–16 (2022)

23. Snoeck, M.: Enterprise information systems engineering: The MERODE approach. Springer, Cham (2014). https://doi.org/10.1007/978-3-319-10145-3

24. Snoeck, M., De Smedt, J., De Weerdt, J.: Supporting data-aware processes with MERODE. In: Augusto, A., Gill, A., Nurcan, S., Reinhartz-Berger, I., Schmidt, R., Zdravkovic, J. (eds.) BPMDS/EMMSAD -2021. LNBIP, vol. 421, pp. 131–146. Springer, Cham (2021). https://doi.org/10.1007/978-3-030-79186-5_9

25. Steinau, S., Marrella, A., Andrews, K., Leotta, F., Mecella, M., Reichert, M.: Dalec: a framework for the systematic evaluation of data-centric approaches to process management software. Softw. Syst. Model. **18**(4), 2679–2716 (2019)

From Network Traffic Data
to a Business-Level Event Log

Moshe Hadad[1,2]([✉]) [iD], Gal Engelberg[1,2] [iD], and Pnina Soffer[1] [iD]

[1] University of Haifa, Abba Khoushy Ave 199, 3498838 Haifa, Israel
moshe.hadad@accenture.com
[2] Accenture Labs, Tel Aviv, Israel

Abstract. Event logs are the main source for business process mining techniques. However, not all information systems produce a standard event log. Furthermore, logs may reflect only parts of the process which may span multiple systems. We suggest using network traffic data to fill these gaps. However, traffic data is interleaved and noisy, and there is a conceptual gap between this data and event logs at the business level. This paper proposes a method for producing event logs from network traffic data. The specific challenges addressed are (a) abstracting the low-level data to business-meaningful activities, (b) overcoming the interleaving of low-level events due to concurrency of activities and processes, and (c) associating the abstracted events to cases. The method uses two trained sequence models based on Conditional random fields (CRF), applied to data reflecting interleaved activities. We use simulated traffic data generated by a predefined business process. The data is annotated for sequence learning to produce models which are used for identifying concurrently performed activities and cases to produce an event log. The event log is conformed against the process models with high fitness and precision scores.

Keywords: Event abstraction · Sequence models · Network traffic · Interleaved data

1 Introduction

Business process management (BPM) popularity increased in organizations in recent decades. It allows them to discover, analyse, monitor and continually improve the work being performed [7]. As part of BPM, process mining techniques are used to discover and monitor process models, identify process bottlenecks, detect execution deviations and more. Event logs are the main source for process mining; they are produced by information systems or by recording actions which have been performed as part of process execution. According to the XES standard [10], a log contains traces which describe a process instance execution. A trace is an ordered set of events containing attributes including at least an activity label a timestamp and a case id.

H. van der Aa et al. (Eds.): BPMDS 2023/EMMSAD 2023, LNBIP 479, pp. 60–75, 2023.
https://doi.org/10.1007/978-3-031-34241-7_5

However, standard event logs are not always available, or are available in different forms [11]. Therefore, sources such as databases, machine logs, SOAP messages, and more are analysed to produce standard event logs [11]. For example, [9] extracted event logs from relational databases, and [17] used low-level database logs to discover a process model. Furthermore, processes may span multiple systems or contain activities not covered by the log. We propose to use network traffic data as an additional data source for event log creation.

Network traffic data as a source for process mining has hardly been explored. We believe using it can be beneficial for the following reasons. First, the scope of available event logs might not cover the whole process, as processes may span multiple information systems or include actions which are not logged (e.g., an email exchange). Thus, network traffic data can support a better coverage. Second, some information systems do not produce logs at all, namely, event logs may be unavailable. Network traffic, on the other hand, is used by all kinds of information systems. Third, network traffic data contains information on the physical layer which other sources lack. Adding a link between the physical and the business layer may support additional analysis, such as cyber security risks.

However, attempting to use network traffic data to discover business activities raises substantial challenges. There is a large abstraction gap between the data in network traffic and business activities. Network traffic data is focused on technical network operations. It is generated not only by the business process, but also by many operational network activities, e.g., broadcasting, synchronizing a network session, and more. Its volume is huge and it is composed of small building blocks of various protocols, named packets. A single message may be scattered across multiple packets, or a packet may contain multiple messages. In our data, an average amount of two thousand packets are generated for each process activity. Furthermore, network traffic data is related to multiple activities that are executed concurrently at any moment. Therefore, mapping packets to traces of business activities is extremely challenging. Since network traffic is a stream by nature, the start or the end of each activity instance is unclear.

Building on insights gained in our previous work [8], in this work we deal with more realistic traffic data, where multiple business instances run in parallel. As a result, packets produced by different activities are interleaved, namely, the stream shows packets belonging to different activities in a mixed order. Our goal is to produce a business meaningful event log by identifying which packets represent which activities, and the process cases they belong to. We propose to use a sequence model learning technique. First, we train a model to learn the borderline patterns of an activity (start and end). Then, we train an additional model to learn the full pattern of each specific activity. These models are then used on interleaved network data and classify the packets by activities, which are then assigned case IDs for forming an event log.

The remainder of the paper is structured as follows: Sect. 2 provides background information, Sect. 3 presents the preprocessing required for network traffic data to be used as input for the proposed approach, Sect. 4 presents the event log generation approach, whose evaluation is reported in Sect. 5; Sect. 6 discusses the contribution of the approach with respect to state of the art, while Sect. 7 concludes and indicates future work directions.

2   Background

This section provides the necessary background about TCP/IP communication data and Conditional Random Field (CRF) [15].

TCP/IP Communication Protocols: The communication in a computer network is based on network protocols, responsible for transporting messages as a sequence of packets, encoding, decoding and error corrections. The most used network communication model is the Department of Defense internet architecture model, referred to as the DoD model [6]. The DoD model contains four layers bottom to top: network access layer, internet layer, host-to-host layer and application layer. Each layer encapsulates the layer above it - in a sequence of packets, the inner packets belongs to the top layer, and they are surrounded by packets from the layer below it, and so forth. We are interested in the packets belonging to two layers in particularly: the application layer and the host-to-host layer. The application layer holds packets for protocols that are used by applications for communicating with each other, e.g., HTTP protocol contains a unique resource identifier (URI) and the parameters sent to it. The host-to-host layer holds packets for the transmission protocol where the data is transported. Specifically, it holds the Transmission Control Protocol/ Internet Protocol (TCP/IP), which is a fundamental network protocol, vastly used in many computer networks. TCP is responsible for collecting and reassembling data packets, while IP is responsible for ensuring packets reach the right destination. Consequently, analyzing the TCP/IP protocol can also inform the application layer, since this layer encapsulates the packets of the application layer.

Conditional Random Field: CRF [15] is a machine learning technique which applies to sequential data. It models the probability of a sequence of observations e.g. a sequence of packets, to be originated by an unknown phenomena in our case, by a running activity which here is depicted as sequence of activity labels. More formally, let X be sequence of observations, and let Y be sequence of labels. Then CRF learns the conditional probabilities of $P(Y|X)$ over the training data, namely, the probability of the activity (sequence of labels) given a sequence of packets. $P(Y|X)$ takes the form of:

$$P(Y|X) = \frac{1}{Z(x)} \prod_i^T \exp\{\sum_i^k \theta_k f_k(y_t, y_{t-1}, x_t)\}$$

f_k is a feature function out of k functions. A feature function captures the dependencies between the component of the sequence. θ_k defines the importance of f_k. $Z(x)$ is the normalization factor which normalizes the values to be between zero and one. The input expected by CRF includes the data elements of the sequence, and also a context for each element, in the form of a window to include values that appear before and after it in a predefined range in the sequence.

We propose to use CRF to classify a sequence of packets as activities.

3   Preprocessing of Network Traffic Data and Preparation of a Data Set

Network traffic data is noisy in its nature and huge in its volume. The aim of the preprocessing steps is to remove noise and irrelevant information to obtain a compact, clean, and slightly abstracted data for further analysis. A detailed description of the preprocessing procedure is given in [8].

Network Data Cleaning and Filtering: This step applies the cleaning and filtering method we developed in [8]. In the resulting dataset, each packet is represented as an event in a stream. The data contains all the events that stand for packets in HTTP and SMTP protocols and all the events that stand for packets in the PGSQL protocol whose query type is INSERT or UPDATE (namely, packets that reflect database update operations).

Data Sets Preparation: For the purpose of this research we created two data set. One for training and another for evaluation. Both data sets were created using the simulation environment. While preprocessing should be applied to both training and evaluation data, these two data sets are essentially different. The training data should include a set of labeled sequences, each one represent a known activity. For this purpose, network traffic needs to be recorded in a fully controlled environment, while only one business process is performed in an isolated manner, so the resulting sequence can be tagged by the activity label and serve as a ground truth for training. This implies a designated preparation operation, to be performed in an environment which mimics the actual operational environment of the organization. We note that many organizations have such controlled environments for performing tests and training new employees. The evaluation data set is created by running multiple business processes in parallel. In the resulting data set, the activities' packets are interleaved, thus we call this data set interleaved data set. After training has been accomplished using the training data set, the trained models can be applied to the interleaved data set, which was obtained by the simulated environment but in real-world scenario can be recorded from the operational (production) environment.

4   A Method for Transforming Network Traffic Data to an Event Log

This section describes a method for transforming realistic network data to an event log, whose abstraction level is suitable for process mining analysis. The proposed method, illustrated in Figure 1, includes two stages: (1) Training - where we train models over fully tagged training data, and (2) Event log formation - where we apply the trained models to the interleaved data and transform it to an event log at a business level by identifying activities and case ids.

Training: In this stage we use the training data, which includes separate fully tagged sequences for each activity, to identify case id attributes and to train two kinds of sequence models using CRF.

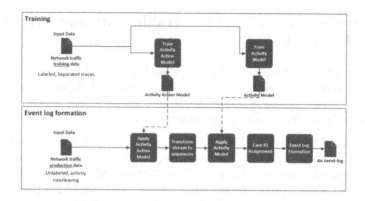

Fig. 1. A method for transforming network data to an event log

Training an Activity Action Model: This model is trained to identify when an activity starts and ends in a given sequence.

Training an Activity Model: This model is trained to identify what activity a given sequence represents (with the highest probability), e.g., whether it is a *Get Job Application* activity or a *Review Application*. Since CRF deals with probabilistic models, the prediction is marked by a probability component. For example, applying the model to a given sequence, the result is of the form *Get Job Application* with a probability of 0.99.

The CRF models perform well on the training data. However, there is a performance variance once the models are applied to the interleaved data. To overcome this, training can be repeated several times, yielding different candidate trained models, from which a best one can be selected.

In addition to training the models, the training phase serves for identifying attributes that can serve as case id indicators. While the training data is tagged with case id, this information is typically not available for interleaved data. Using the training data, the correlation between various attributes and the case id can be calculated. The attributes which have a high correlation with the case id will later on serve as its indicators.

Event Log Formation: In this stage an event log is formed by applying the trained CRF models to the interleaved network data. The details of this process (see Fig. 1) are as follows.

Apply Activity Action Model: The trained activity action model is applied for identifying potential activity actions in the data. The model classifies every event (packet) in the data as an activity start, an activity end, or neither (marked as NoAction). Thus, the start and the end points of activities are marked in the data. Table 1 shows the results of the classification, on an illustrative example, under the column Activity Action.

Transform Stream to Sequences: We create sequences of packets by opening a window for each of the identified start and end events. For a start event the window is in a forward direction, while for the end event its direction is backwards. Figure 2 depicts this process. The size of the window is a hyper parameter which is selected by using the probabilistic feature of CRF, as discussed later.

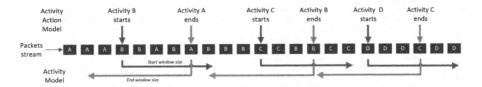

Fig. 2. Forming Sequences

Apply Activity Model: The trained activity model is applied to each sequence, created in the previous step, to identify the specific activity this sequence represents. CRF returns a sequence of tags, i.e., for a sequence of packets, the result is a sequence of activity tags. To get one activity as the answer, we use majority voting regarding the sequence of tags, returning the most frequent activity in the tag sequence. We boost the performance of this classification using Algorithm 1 which is describe later in this paper. Table 1 shows the results of the classification, on an illustrative example, under the column Activity.

These three steps are iterated several times, serving three main purposes. First, to select the best model among the candidate models created at the training phase, iterations are performed, using different combinations of activity action and activity candidate models. For each iteration, the mean probability of the classifications is calculated, so the best performing activity action and activity model can be selected. Second, to determine the window size for the sequences, iterations are performed using different windows for the start activity action and for the end activity action separately. Similarly to the approach for model selection, the window size producing the highest mean probability will be chosen. Window sizes can be set separately for the start activity and for the end activity.

Table 1. An illustrative example of the HR interleaved data set

Request Method Call	Selective File Data	Time Stamp	ActivityAction	Activity	Case Id
version	version	9/18/2020 1:07:22 AM	**Activity Start**	**GenerateJobApplicationActivity**	1
server_version	None	9/18/2020 1:07:22 AM	NoAction	NoAction	
execute_kw	hr.job_search_read	9/18/2020 1:07:22 AM	NoAction	NoAction	
version	version	9/18/2020 1:07:22 AM	**Activity Start**	**GenerateJobApplicationActivity**	2
execute_kw	hr.applicant_create	9/18/2020 1:07:23 AM	NoAction	NoAction	
399	IsNumber	9/18/2020 1:07:23 AM	**Activity End**	**GenerateJobApplicationActivity**	1
version	None	9/18/2020 1:07:29 AM	**Activity Start**	**ResumeReviewActivity**	1

In this table each row represents a packet and its features from the HR interleaved data set.
Only three features are presented here for illustrative reasons the other features were omitted for brevity.

Algorithm 1. improve activity action classification stream index filtering

1: $S \leftarrow$ List of activity action sequences ▷ For each activity action, we create a sequence by opening a window as
   described in 2
2: $CLASSIFICATIONS \leftarrow \emptyset$
3: **for** each sequence s in S **do**
4: $\quad$ $C \leftarrow$ unique stream indices in sequence s
5: $\quad$ **for** each $stream\_index$ in C **do**
6: $\quad\quad$ $s' \leftarrow$ FILTER$(s, stream\_index)$ ▷ Filter out packets with stream_index from s
7: $\quad\quad$ $class', probability' \leftarrow$ CLASSIFY(s')
8: $\quad\quad$ add $class', probability'$ to $CLASSIFICATIONS$
9: $\quad$ **end for**
10: $\quad$ selected_class $\leftarrow$ the class with highest probability appears in $CLASSIFICATIONS$
11: $\quad$ assign selected_class with activity action in sequence s
12: **end for**

Using Stream Index to boost Activity model Performance: To improve the activity model performance we use stream index to reduce the level of noise in the data. We assume the activity model will return a higher probability, for a sequence classification, once we filter events related to other activities which are run in parallel. Stream Index is added by Wireshark[1] for each packet to track protocol streams, it is unique within a TCP connection. This means all events originated from the same TCP connection will share the same stream index. However, many TCP connections can be used in an activity execution, thus there may be many stream indices for an activity. Nevertheless, we iterate over the unique stream_indices in the sequence, use the activity model to identify which stream indices are related with a high probability and filter the unrelated ones. This iteration is depicted in Algorithm 1. The algorithm uses two main functions: (1) Filter: Accepts a sequence of events and a stream index, filters from the sequence events which have the given stream index, returns the filtered sequence (2) Classify: Accepts a sequence and uses the activity model to classify it, returns the classification and its probability.

At the end of this stage, the data is classified as follows: all events in the data are tagged with an activity action i.e. classified as activity start, activity end, or NoAction. The start and end activity actions are also tagged with the activity name identified by applying the activity model, e.g., classified as Get Job Application or Review Application. We now turn to case id assignment.

Case Id Clustering: For case id assignment, attributes which are correlated to case id are identified in the training stage (see Sect. 4). This means there is a one to one, or one to many connection between a case id and attribute values. However, the actual assignment of a case id value is not known since attribute values are different for the training and the interleaved data. Thus we cluster all values linked together in the interleaved data into groups. Each group forms a cluster of values which indicates a specific case id. However, not all values which originated in a specific case id, are linked together in the data. Thus we

---

[1] https://www.wireshark.org/docs/wsug_html_chunked/ChAdvFollowStreamSection.
html.

Algorithm 2. assign a case id to a an activity action using stream index filtering

```
1: S ← List of sequences                                    ▷ The newly formed sequences
2: INDICES ← ∅
3: for each sequence s in S do
4:     class, probability ← original classification of s (based on start forward window)
5:     C ← unique case IDs in sequence s                ▷ The sequence may contains several case IDs
6:     for each case_id in C do
7:         s', stream_indices ← FILTER(s, case_id)      ▷ Get the stream_indices from all packets with the same
       case_id, then filter out all packets with those stream_indices
8:         class', probability' ← CLASSIFY(s')
9:         if class' == class and probability' > probability then    ▷ If the removed events increased the
       probability, we assumed they are unrelated and we add them for removal
10:            add stream_indices to INDICES
11:        end if
12:    end for
13:    filtered sequence ← sequence s filtered by INDICES
14:    selected case id ← first case id appears in filtered sequence
15:    assign selected case id with start and end activities in sequence s
16: end for
```

use a heuristic method based on stream index, data imputing and some domain knowledge to link different values together and group them into clusters.

At the end of this process, we formed clusters of values. Each cluster indicates a process instance. We assign each cluster a number as a case id. We then assign each packet a case id in the following way: We extract the case id attributes' values from the packet (if they exist). We use the clusters to get the case id number for the extracted values and we assign it to the packet. Packets which have no values for the case id attributes are not assigned any case id.

Case Id Assignment: Ideally if all packets classified with an activity are also assigned a case id, we can form an event log. However, this is not necessarily the case. In fact, most packets classified with an activity do not carry the attributes which were identified as case id indicators (Sect. 4) and thus are not assigned a case id. To overcome this, we need to "borrow" a case id from the surrounding packets which do have a case id assignment, and we need to "borrow" it from packets which are part of the same activity sequence. A first step is to form new, more accurate, sequences, which consider the activity classification. The new sequences are formed by matching a start of a specific activity to an end of the same specific activity, following the rule of first in first out, i.e., if two Get Job Application activities started one after another, the first start will get the first end. As opposed to the initial sequences, the newly formed ones are of different lengths. The next step is to use the activity model and stream index for identifying which events in the interleaved data are related with a high probability, so a case id can be inferred from events containing case id indicators to those which lack them, as specified in Algorithm 2. The algorithm uses the Classify function defined for Algorithm 1, but a different Filter function, which accepts a sequence of events and a case id; gets all stream_indices from events in the sequence with the case id, then filters out all events with those stream_indices. It returns the filtered sequence, and the events' indices. Table 1 shows the results of the assignment, on an illustrative example, under the column Case Id.

Producing an Event Log: At this point the data contains events which are identified as a start or an end of a specific activity and are assigned with a case id. Additionally, each event contains an attribute which serves as a time stamp (See example in Table 1). Creating a higher-level event log is now a typical task of representing each activity sequence as an event, whose case id, activity label, and timestamp are according to those of the start activity.

5   Evaluation

The evaluation of the approach had several goals. The main goal was to assess its ability to transform network data to an event log that is suitable for mining analysis in an activity interleaving settings. To this end, we simulated the execution of two different processes and applied the approach to the respective network data. We used conformance checking to measure the fitness and precision of the event logs against the simulated processes. Additional evaluation goals were to assess the effectiveness of the classification of the packets using the two CRF models (activity action model and activity model) with respect to the activities that generated the data. Last, we wanted to assess the contribution of the sequences created by matching start and end events of activities, as compared to the sequences that correspond to either the start or the end of activities. In what follows we describe the settings of the evaluation and the obtained results.

Acquiring and Preparing Network Data: We simulated execution of two business processes, HR Recruitment and Purchase to Pay. The HR Recruitment, as presented in Fig. 3, is a fairly simple process which spans across only the HR lane. The Purchase to Pay, as presented in Fig. 4, is a more complex process, which spans across the sales, purchase, stock, and accounting lanes. We run the business processes over an Enterprise Resource Planning(ERP) web application, ODOO[2]. The simulated environment contained a number of user endpoints, a relational database, a backend, and an email server. Both the business processes and the simulation environment are described in detail in our previous work [8]. We recorded the traffic data, generated by the activities of these processes, using wireshark[3], which is a well known tool for network data capturing.

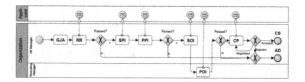

Fig. 3. HR recruitment process

---

[2] https://www.odoo.com.
[3] https://www.wireshark.org.

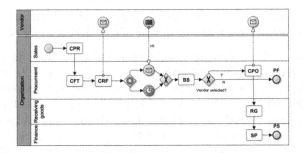

Fig. 4. Purchase-to-pay process

Preprocessing of Network Traffic Data and Preparation of Data Sets: For each business process we created a training dataset and an interleaved evaluation dataset (four datasets in total)[4]. The training datasets were created by running 250 cases of each process, where every activity in every case was recorded in isolation from other cases. The interleaved datasets were created by running 10 cases of each business processes in concurrency settings: each business process case started 10 s after the other. As a result, the data contained cases and activities which were interleaved. For both business processes, different values were stochastically created for each execution e.g. activity participant, time-between activities, and more. We then reduced and cleaned the network data to be usable for analysis as described in Sect. 3. As a result, the data was reduced from 965 packets per activity on average to 42 packets per activity on average.

In the resulting data sets, each packet was represented as an event in a stream. Several columns were kept, e.g., frame.number, as an ordering of the packets, sniff_time, which serves as a timestamp of the packet, and event_with_roles, which captures the source, destination, and message type of the packet. An additional feature engineering step for supporting an effective application of the CRF was performed.

For the training data set we assembled all recorded activities to form one data set, in which InstanceNumber and BusinessActivity features were the indicators of the case id and activity type, respectively. After preprocessing and feature engineering, we formed sequences by using InstanceNumber and BusinessActivity to group the data, so each group corresponded to one activity in one business process case. The first and last events in the sequence were tagged as activity start and activity end, respectively. The rest were tagged as no actions (events that are neither start nor end of an activity).

This, however, was not possible for the interleaved data. We therefore manually inspected this data for evaluation purposes, as ground truth for measuring the performance. We marked the frame where each activity starts and ends, the activity types and case id at those frames and other overlapping activities.

---

[4] https://github.com/HaifaUniversityBPM/traffic-data-to-event-log.

Although some of the events could be traced back to the activity which generated them, many others are left without a distinct association to an activity.

Training: First, we divided the training data set into 70% training data and 30% test data. To identify attributes that would later serve as case id indicators, we ran a correlation analysis and selected attributes which were correlated with the InstanceNumber attribute. We trained the activity action model as well as the activity model, based on the 70% of the data. We used the same CRF setting in both cases - each sequence was fed to the CRF by including each feature's context in a range of 5 events backwards and 10 events forward. We tested the activity action model and the activity model using the remaining 30% of the data. The results for the activity action model classification are highly accurate, F1=1 for both processes, for activity start and NoAction and for the activity end F1=0.91 for the Purchase to Pay process and F1=1 for HR Recruitment process. The results for the activity model show that the classification of events by activity type was highly accurate, yielding F1=1 for all activity types for both processes. We created 150 candidate models in a similar manner, for the best one to be selected later on.

Event Log Formation: We followed the steps of the method as described in Sect. 4. To apply the activity action model and the activity model to the interleaved data, we used the same CRF setting as was defined for the training phase. We validated the results against the manually inspected data. Table 2 depicts the validation results of the activity action model on the interleaved data for the two processes. As seen in the table, the model was able to identify the start and the end of activities with a high accuracy (note the F1 macro avg of 0.96 for HR recruitment and 0.92 for Purchase to Pay). Yet, better results were obtained for the activity start action, with a better accuracy than for the activity end action (F1 of 0.99 vs 0.90, respectively, for the HR recruitment process, and 1.00 vs 0.76 for the Purchase to Pay process).

Table 2. Results of the activity action model for classification of interleaved data

	HR Recruitment				Purchase to Pay			
	precision	recall	f1-score	support	precision	recall	f1-score	support
Activity Start	0.97	1.00	0.99	37	1.00	1.00	1.00	57
NoAction	1.00	0.99	1.00	1224	0.99	1.00	1.00	3591
Activity End	0.84	0.97	0.90	37	0.88	0.67	0.76	57
accuracy			0.99	1298			0.99	3705
macro avg	0.96	0.95	0.96	1298	0.96	0.89	0.92	3705
weighted avg	0.99	0.99	0.99	1298	0.99	0.99	0.99	3705

For transforming the stream to sequences, based on an iterative experimentation, we used the following window sizes: for the HR recruitment process we used a forward window of 41 and a backward window of 7; for the Purchase to

Pay process the forward window was set to 30 and the backward window was of 7 events. Following this, we applied the activity model and inspected the results against the manually tagged data. Table 3 and Table 4 report the results obtained for applying the activity model to the interleaved data of the HR recruitment and the Purchase to Pay processes, respectively. We then assigned a case id to the classified data, to form new sequences based on the identified activities and case id indicators, using the case id assignment Algorithm 2 on the sequences. Eventually, the tagged and classified data was transformed to higher-level event logs for each of the processes.

Table 3. Results of the CRF-trained model for activity classification on the interleaved data for HR Recruitment

	Forward Window for Start Activity				Backward Window for End Activity			
	precision	recall	f1-score	support	precision	recall	f1-score	support
GenerateJobApplication	0.91	1.00	0.95	10	1.00	0.90	0.95	10
ResumeReview	1.00	1.00	1.00	10	1.00	0.50	0.67	10
ScheduleInterviewCall	0.83	1.00	0.91	5	0.83	1.00	0.91	5
PerformInterviewCall	1.00	0.80	0.89	5	0.50	1.00	0.67	5
ScheduleInterviewMeeting	1.00	0.67	0.80	3	1.00	1.00	1.00	3
PerformInterviewMeeting	1.00	1.00	1.00	3	0.67	0.67	0.67	3
ContractProposal	1.00	1.00	1.00	1	0.00	0.00	0.00	1
accuracy			1.00	1257			0.99	1261
macro avg	0.97	0.93	0.94	1257	0.75	0.76	0.73	1261
weighted avg	1.00	1.00	1.00	1257	0.99	0.99	0.99	1261

Evaluating the Higher-Level Event Logs: To evaluate the obtained logs, we used the Pm4Py[5] conformance checking to measure the fitness, precision and F1 against the processes we used to generate the data (see Table 5). As shown in the table, better results were obtained for the HR recruitment than for the Purchase to Pay process, with F1 of 0.93 vs 0.80, respectively. Also note that while precision is high for both processes, the fitness achieved for the Purchase to Pay process is far below that of the HR recruitment one.

We further experimented with different policies for forming sequences. In particular, we wanted to assess whether the sequences that combine start activity with a corresponding end activity for case id assignment outperform sequences that are based on a start activity (with a forward window) or an end activity (with a backward window) only. The results in Table 5 show that better F1 scores are indeed obtained for the start-end sequences for both processes. Additionally, end-activity-based sequences perform better than start-activity-based ones.

---

[5] https://pm4py.fit.fraunhofer.de.

Table 4. Results of the CRF-trained model for activity classification on the interleaved data for Purchase to Pay

	Forward Window for Start Activity				Backward Window for End Activity			
	precision	recall	f1-score	support	precision	recall	f1-score	support
CreatePurchaseRequest	0.82	1.00	0.90	9	1.00	0.89	0.94	9
CreateCallForTender	1.00	0.70	0.82	10	0.90	0.90	0.90	10
CreateRfq	0.73	0.80	0.76	10	0.00	0.00	0.00	10
BidSelection	0.80	0.80	0.80	10	0.64	0.70	0.67	10
CreatePurchaseOrder	0.88	0.88	0.88	8	0.00	0.00	0.00	8
ReceiveGoods	0.78	0.88	0.82	8	1.00	1.00	1.00	8
SubmitPayment	0.86	0.75	0.80	8	1.00	1.00	1.00	8
accuracy			1.00	3649			0.99	3654
macro avg	0.86	0.85	0.85	3649	0.69	0.69	0.69	3654
weighted avg	1.00	1.00	1.00	3649	0.99	0.99	0.99	3654

Table 5. Evaluation of the generated event logs against the simulated business processes

Sequences Type	Hr Recruitment			Purchase to Pay		
	fitness	precision	f1-score[a]	fitness	precision	f1-score[a]
Start-End Sequences	0.92	0.94	0.93	0.69	0.95	0.80
Start Sequences	0.71	0.89	0.79	0.48	0.94	0.63
End Sequences	0.82	1.00	0.90	0.63	0.73	0.68

[a] In this table f1-score is used as a normalization factor based on the fitness and precision

6   Related Work

Discovery of a business-level event-log based on network traffic data is almost unexplored in the context of process mining. In [8] we proposed an approach in that direction that was able to discover business activities based on network traffic data, in settings which exclude coarse-granular event interleaving. In this paper we extend this approach to support transforming a realistic stream of traffic data to a business-level event log.

Van Zelst et al. [19] defined the event abstraction task as a technique that aims to translate instances of fine-granular events into instances of coarse-granular events. A closely related work [16] trained a CRF model based on annotated traces, then used the resulted model to classify unlabeled fine-granular events into coarse-granular events. [1] proposed an event abstraction method for logs which are populated by traffic of a client-server application activity. The method aims to recursively merge similar client-side activities based on their corresponding server-side activities using Pearson correlation coefficient. This is repeated as long as the fitness of a process model, discovered from the log, is below a pre-defined threshold. As opposed to [1], which keeps the technical terminology in the abstracted log, our aim is to bridge the technical gap between network traffic events and business activities and correlate events and cases. Furthermore, we address activity interleaving and concern both server side and application side.

One of the challenges of event log abstraction is to identify the borderlines of the coarse-granular activity in terms of the fine-granular events. [3] identified the borderlines of the activities using different heuristics (as time frame between fine-granular-event instances), which fail as complexity increases. [18] detected the activity borderlines according to changes in the data within the window size. [14] identified activity borderlines by assuming that an entity could be involved in a single interaction simultaneously, and an activity instance is related to a single interaction instance. These assumptions are not valid in our settings.

Another challenge of event log abstraction is to handle concurrency on the coarse-granular level. The literature shows that this challenge could be addressed in various manners. [12] suggested using ontologies to abstract medical actions into medical goals. They utilized a semantic model for goals and actions, employed rule-based reasoning for ancestor selection, and a multilevel abstraction algorithm for interleaved actions. [13] used petri-nets to represent the coarse granular level activities based on behavioral patterns discovered in the fine-granular level. Similarly, [2] expressed the behavioral patterns discovered in the fine-granular level using a declarative process modelling language. We addressed this challenge jointly with the activity borderline detection.

In contrast to the above approaches, we addressed an event-case correlation challenge, due to lack of process case notations in the source data. [5] addressed this challenge by alignment of the log with a given process model. Our proposed stream index filtering algorithm is not supervised by the process model. Similarly, [4] addressed this challenge by analyzing the repetitiveness of event attributes in a network communication log of a distributed system.

Our work contributes to existing literature in the following ways: identifying business-level activities using network traffic data, utilizing sequence model learning techniques for activity borderline detection in concurrent settings, and addressing event-case correlation challenges in network traffic data.

7   Discussion

The approach presented in this paper can facilitate the utilization of network traffic data, which is readily available, for applying process mining in situations where suitable event logs cannot be obtained. By this, it can potentially contribute to expanding the use of process mining. The approach overcomes two main challenges associated with the use of network data for this purpose. One is the noisy and fine granular nature of this data, and second is the interleaving of data generated by many activities that are performed in parallel in enterprises.

As an initial step in the direction of utilizing traffic data for process mining, the work is of a limited scope and has the following limitations. First, it is based on simulated data which might not hold all types of variations as in reality. Furthermore, scalability to the full volume of enterprise operations has not been tested yet. Second, the simulation targets a typical enterprise environment, and does not cover additional communication protocols and behaviors that may exist in more complicated environments, e.g., complex business processes that have parallel activities and encrypted communication. Yet, our results show the possibility and pave a way towards transforming traffic data to an event log that lends itself to business meaningful process mining.

All in all, While the evaluation results reported in the paper show that the approach is capable of handling interleaved data and correctly classifying it to activities, at this point the work can be considered a proof-of-concept. Its application requires much manual work and detailed experimentation, which can span several weeks, for recording and processing the data; and determining parameter values (e.g., window sizes). Yet, by developing the approach we accomplished a break-down of the problem, tackling the related challenges. While much additional work is still needed for developing an applicable and streamlined pipeline the will allow utilizing network traffic data for process mining in a fully automated manner, the proposed method is a substantial step towards this aim.

8   Conclusions

Network traffic data can be useful for process mining, but large conceptual gaps exist between this data and business meaningful event logs that are usable for process mining. In this paper we proposed an approach for producing event log from network traffic data, by addressing the following challenges. First, abstracting the low-level and noisy data to business-meaningful activities. Second, overcoming the interleaving of low-level events due to concurrency of activities and processes. Finally, associating cases to the abstracted events.

The proposed approach addressed these challenges by using two trained sequence models (CRF) to recognize business activities' instances within network traffic stream under activity interleaving settings. Then, grouping together these instances under a case identifier using stream index filtering. Evaluation shows high precision and recall of the activity recognition method, and a promising fitness of the produced event log versus the business level process model.

Future research will develop the method into a scalable and fully automated pipeline, to support process mining based on network traffic data. It will address additional processes, environments, and protocols in more realistic settings. We will develop an end-to-end method that will discover activities in traffic data and will be able to distinguish traffic related to different processes and cases.

Acknowledgement. The work was in collaboration with Accenture Labs, Israel.

References

1. Event Log Abstraction in Client-Server Applications: Online Streaming, – Select a Country –
2. Baier, T., Di Ciccio, C., Mendling, J., Weske, M.: Matching events and activities by integrating behavioral aspects and label analysis. Softw. Syst. Model. **17**(2), 573–598 (2018)
3. Baier, T., Mendling, J., Weske, M.: Bridging abstraction layers in process mining. Inf. Syst. **46**, 123–139 (2014)

4. Bala, S., Mendling, J., Schimak, M., Queteschiner, P.: Case and activity identification for mining process models from middleware. In: Buchmann, R.A., Karagiannis, D., Kirikova, M. (eds.) PoEM 2018. LNBIP, vol. 335, pp. 86–102. Springer, Cham (2018). https://doi.org/10.1007/978-3-030-02302-7_6

5. Bayomie, D., Di Ciccio, C., La Rosa, M., Mendling, J.: A probabilistic approach to event-case correlation for process mining. In: Laender, A.H.F., Pernici, B., Lim, E.-P., de Oliveira, J.P.M. (eds.) ER 2019. LNCS, vol. 11788, pp. 136–152. Springer, Cham (2019). https://doi.org/10.1007/978-3-030-33223-5_12

6. Cerf, V.G., Cain, E.: The DoD internet architecture model. Comput. Netw. (1976) **7**(5), 307–318 (1983)

7. Dumas, M., La Rosa, M., Mendling, J., Reijers, H.A., et al.: Fundamentals of Business Process Management, vol. 1. Springer, Heidelberg (2013). https://doi.org/10.1007/978-3-642-33143-5

8. Engelberg, G., Hadad, M., Soffer, P.: From network traffic data to business activities: a process mining driven conceptualization. In: Augusto, A., Gill, A., Nurcan, S., Reinhartz-Berger, I., Schmidt, R., Zdravkovic, J. (eds.) BPMDS/EMMSAD - 2021. LNBIP, vol. 421, pp. 3–18. Springer, Cham (2021). https://doi.org/10.1007/978-3-030-79186-5_1

9. de Murillas, E.G.L., Reijers, H.A., Van Der Aalst, W.M.: Connecting databases with process mining: a meta model and toolset. Softw. Syst. Model. **18**(2), 1209–1247 (2019)

10. XES Working Group: IEEE standard for extensible event stream (XES) for achieving interoperability in event logs and event streams. IEEE Std **1849**, 1–50 (2016)

11. Huser, V.: Process mining: discovery, conformance and enhancement of business processes (2012)

12. Leonardi, G., Striani, M., Quaglini, S., Cavallini, A., Montani, S.: Towards semantic process mining through knowledge-based trace abstraction. In: Ceravolo, P., van Keulen, M., Stoffel, K. (eds.) SIMPDA 2017. LNBIP, vol. 340, pp. 45–64. Springer, Cham (2019). https://doi.org/10.1007/978-3-030-11638-5_3

13. Mannhardt, F., de Leoni, M., Reijers, H., Aalst, W.V.D., Toussaint, P.: Guided process discovery-a pattern-based approach. Inf. Syst. **76**, 1–18 (2018)

14. Senderovich, A., Rogge-Solti, A., Gal, A., Mendling, J., Mandelbaum, A.: The ROAD from sensor data to process instances via interaction mining. In: Nurcan, S., Soffer, P., Bajec, M., Eder, J. (eds.) CAiSE 2016. LNCS, vol. 9694, pp. 257–273. Springer, Cham (2016). https://doi.org/10.1007/978-3-319-39696-5_16

15. Sutton, C., McCallum, A., et al.: An introduction to conditional random fields. Found. Trends® Mach. Learn. **4**(4), 267–373 (2012)

16. Tax, N., Sidorova, N., Haakma, R., van der Aalst, W.M.P.: Event abstraction for process mining using supervised learning techniques. In: Bi, Y., Kapoor, S., Bhatia, R. (eds.) IntelliSys 2016. LNNS, vol. 15, pp. 251–269. Springer, Cham (2018). https://doi.org/10.1007/978-3-319-56994-9_18

17. Aalst, W.M.P.: Extracting event data from databases to unleash process mining. In: vom Brocke, J., Schmiedel, T. (eds.) BPM - Driving Innovation in a Digital World. MP, pp. 105–128. Springer, Cham (2015). https://doi.org/10.1007/978-3-319-14430-6_8

18. van Eck, M.L., Sidorova, N., van der Aalst, W.M.P.: Enabling process mining on sensor data from smart products. In: 2016 IEEE Tenth International Conference on Research Challenges in Information Science (RCIS), pp. 1–12 (2016)

19. van Zelst, S.J., Mannhardt, F., de Leoni, M., Koschmider, A.: Event abstraction in process mining: literature review and taxonomy. Granul. Comput. **6**(3), 719–736 (2021)

Decision and Context-Aware Business Process Management (BPMDS 2023)

A Novel Decision Mining Method Considering Multiple Model Paths

Pietro Portolani[1,2(✉)], Diego Savoia[1], Andrea Ballarino[2], and Matteo Matteucci[1]

[1] Politecnico di Milano - DEIB, Milan, Italy
{pietro.portolani,diego.savoia,matteo.matteucci}@polimi.it
[2] Consiglio Nazionale delle Ricerche - STIIMA, Milan, Italy
andrea.ballarino@stiima.cnr.it

Abstract. The automatic extraction of a process model from data is one of the main focuses of a Process Mining pipeline. Decision Mining aims at discovering conditions influencing the execution of a given process instance to enhance the original extracted model. In particular, a Petri Net with data is a Petri Net enhanced with guards controlling the transitions firing in correspondence of places with two or more output arcs, called decision points. To automatically extract guards, Decision Mining algorithms fit a classifier for each decision point, indicating what path the case will follow based on event attributes. Retrieving the path followed by the case inside the model is crucial to create each decision point's training dataset. Indeed, due to the presence of invisible activities, having multiple paths coherent with the same trace in the event log is possible. State-of-the-art method consider only the optimal path discarding the other possible ones. Consequently, training sets of related decision points will not contain information on the considered case. This work proposes a depth-first-based method that considers multiple paths possibly followed by a case inside the Petri Net to avoid information loss. We applied the proposed method to a real-life dataset showing its effectiveness and comparing it to the current state of the art.

Keywords: Decision Mining · Process Mining · Decision Trees · Machine Learning

1 Introduction

Process Discovery is one of the fundamental tasks of Process Mining. It aims at extracting a process model automatically from logs recorded by an information system. The discovered model focuses only on the activities' control flow, representing their order relations with frameworks such as Petri Nets or Business Process Model and Notation[1] models. The extracted models can have various purposes, from simulation to conformance checking and process optimisation.

---

[1] https://www.omg.org/spec/BPMN/2.0.2/About-BPMN/.

© The Author(s), under exclusive license to Springer Nature Switzerland AG 2023
H. van der Aa et al. (Eds.): BPMDS 2023/EMMSAD 2023, LNBIP 479, pp. 79–87, 2023.
https://doi.org/10.1007/978-3-031-34241-7_6

Decision Mining, another Process Mining subfield, takes a further step and enhances the process model with information about the decisions influencing its execution. In recent years, the focus on decisions has gained importance as they are among an organisation's most crucial assets [1]. The topic is so relevant that the Object Management Group developed the Decision Model and Notation standard[2], an industrial standard to model decisions.

Decision Points Analysis is a particular type of Decision Mining based on Petri Net models and it uses data to generate information and knowledge to support decision-making processes in the form of annotated decisions [2]. Specifically, it retrieves the decision rules solving a classification problem in every place with two or more output arcs, i.e. a decision point.

Indeed, to create a valid training dataset, it is necessary to know the path the process instance follows inside the process model to locate the crossed decision points correctly. Retrieving such a path is not straightforward, mainly due to invisible activities and loops. Previous approaches developed developed different strategies to select the path, however, current techniques lead to a loss of information considering only one route inside the process model.

In this work, we propose a novel method to consider multiple allowed model paths the case could have taken to go from one activity to the following. The idea is that considering multiple paths will help better characterise the invisible branches of the decision points, resulting in less information loss and, thus, better rules[3].

2   Related Works

Authors in [3] and [4] made major contributions to the Decision Points Analysis field. In [3] the authors propose for the first time to transform every decision point into a classification problem and derive the decision rules from a decision tree used to fit it.

To create the training dataset needed, the authors track the path followed by the case from an activity in the sequence to the following one and assign the related event attributes to the encountered decision points. In case the following activity is an invisible one, the tracking continue until it founds the first next visible activity. It can terminate its search prematurely in correspondence of an ambiguous parts of the net, such as a joint, and consequently it is not able to identify the encountered decision points for that specific trace.

In [4], the authors solve the issue by considering a complete realisation of the net, exploiting the optimal alignment between the Petri Net and the event log introduced in [5]. A downside of this approach, thus, is that the algorithm discards all the suboptimal sequences.

Authors in [6] propose a different but very interesting approach to discover an holistic decision model linking decision to changes in variable.

---

[2] https://www.omg.org/spec/DMN.

[3] code available at https://github.com/piepor/multiple-paths-decision-mining.

In this work, based on [3] and [4], we propose to use multiple possible paths in the model connecting two successive activities in a variant to identify as many decision points affected by the case as possible. Since multiple paths are mainly a consequence of invisible activities, considering more than one path helps to add information about the invisible branches of decision points in their training set. More information allows for better classification and more precise rules.

3   Preliminaries

We briefly describe the problem we want to solve and two entities useful to understand it better.

A *Petri Net* [7] is a bipartite graph composed of a set of places and transitions connected by a set of arcs. Tokens distributed inside the places of the net represent the *state* of a Petri Net, called *marking*. They allow a transition to fire if all its input places contain at least one token. When the transition fires, it removes one token for each input place and gives one to every output place, changing the *state* of the net.

A *Petri Net with data* [8] is a *Petri Net* in which transitions (modeling activities) can *read* and *write* variables [4]. Write operations let firing transitions modify the value of a set of attributes, while read operations enable the use of guards. The latter are additional conditions on the firing of transitions; to be allowed to fire, the guard of a transition must evaluate to true.

The problem a decision mining technique aims to solve is to discover the conditions controlling the behaviour of an examined process. Given a process model in the form of a Petri Net and the related event log, the overall output of the method should be the original model augmented with guards on places with more than one output arc alongside relations between transitions and write operations on attributes, i.e. a Petri Net with data. In particular, we focus on the extraction of the guards' rules.

4   Methods

As already mentioned, our work aims to create the training sets for the decision points classification with the least amount of information loss. Given two subsequent events in a trace, multiple paths in the Petri Net model of the process could be eligible to go from the activity executed in the first event to the next one.

Our method tries to incorporate information from all the allowed paths as much as possible. We use a backward depth-first search to extract the encountered decision points and related targets between two subsequent activities in the trace to achieve this result.

The complete method has two main phases: the decision points extraction and the dataset creation. The first step searches and stores the places with more than one outgoing arc crossed by the allowed paths for every pair of subsequent activities in a variant. When a place is stored, the method also adds the related output transition, i.e. the choice made. Then, for every trace belonging to the variant, the algorithm creates the dataset using the previously extracted decision points.

We used Decision Trees classifiers as in [3] and trained them with the C4.5 algorithm [9] which also describes methods to extract the decision rules.

Algorithm 1. Algorithm to extract the decision points between two activities. Starting from one activity running the backward search on the previous in the trace until a reachable one is found.

function EXTRACTDPs($prevSequence, currTrans$)
    $mapDPs \leftarrow \emptyset$
    $prevSequenceReversed \leftarrow reverseSequence(prevSequence)$
    for $prevAct \in prevSequenceReversed$ **do**
        $mapDPs, found \leftarrow$ BWDDFS($prevAct, currTrans, \emptyset$)
        if $found == True$ **then**
            break
        end if
    end for
    return $mapDPs$
end function

4.1   Decision Points Extraction

As already introduced, our method relies on a backward depth-first search to identify the decision points crossed going from the activity contained in an event to the following one in a trace. Considering a sequence of two activities, $\langle A, B \rangle$, the method starts from the transition B in the Petri Net and searches backwards for the previous activity, A.

In the context of a Petri Net, backwards indicates that the depth-first search follows only the input arcs of every place or transition. In order to consider valid paths, the search is allowed to continue only if the transition encountered is invisible. If the transition considered is visible, whether it is the desired one or not, the search shall stop following that particular path and return the result of the search. If the visible transition is the desired one, the algorithm will add the saved decision points to the ones found on the allowed paths.

Two main issues arise designing the algorithm, namely loops and non-reachable activities. Loops are a problem when considering all the possible paths between two activities: if a loop is composed of only invisible transitions, an infinite number of allowed paths exist. To address this problem, every time an invisible transition is visited, it is added to a list of visited transitions. If the algorithm finds an already visited transition, it will stop the search along that path.

The other issue is related to non-reachable activities. An activity can be non-reachable from another for two main reasons: concurrent activities and not perfectly fitting models. If two transitions, A and B, are on two parallel branches

Algorithm 2. Recursive algorithm to extract decision points and related targets by performing a backward depth-first search of the Petri Net through invisible transitions starting from $currAct$ up to $prevAct$.

---

function BWDDFS($prevAct, currAct, passedActs$)
    $prevActFound = False$
    for $inputArc \in getInputArcs(currAct)$ **do**
        $inPlace \leftarrow getSource(inputArc)$
        $backTrans \leftarrow \emptyset$
        for $innInputArc \in getInputArcs(inPlace)$ **do**
            $transition \leftarrow getSource(innInputArc)$
            $backTrans \leftarrow addTrans(transition, backTrans)$
        end for
        if $prevAct \in backTrans$ **then**
            $prevActFound = True$
            if $isDP(inPlace)$ **then**
                $mapDPs \leftarrow updateDPs(inPlace, currAct, mapDPs)$
            end if
            continue
        end if
        $invActs \leftarrow getInvisibleTransitionsFromInputs(backTrans)$
        for $invAct \in invActs$ **do**
            if $invAct \notin passedActs$ **then**
                $passedArcs \leftarrow addArc(invAct, passedArcs)$
                $mapDPs, found \leftarrow$ BWDDFS($prevAct, invAct, passedActs$)
                $passedArcs \leftarrow removeArc(invAct, passedActs)$
                if $found == True \wedge isDP(inPlace)$ **then**
                    $mapDPs \leftarrow updateDPs(inPlace, invAct, mapDPs)$
                end if
                $prevActFound = prevActFound \vee found$
            end if
        end for
    end for
    return $mapDPs, prevActFound$
end function

---

of the model, it will be impossible for the backward search to find A starting from B. In the same way, if the model does not perfectly represent a variant, two activities may be non-reachable from one another. To solve the non-reachability issue, if the method cannot find the previous activity, it will search for the next previous activity in the sequence. The search will stop when it finds a reachable activity or all the previous activities are non-reachable.

Algorithm 1 reports the overall search algorithm. The search is done for every activity in the sequence, starting from the last and going backwards. The cycle breaks if the backward depth-first search finds the previous activity. Algorithm 2 reports the backward depth-first search algorithm, which has a recursive structure. We remind the reader that every transition in a Petri Net has only input places, and conversely, places have only input transitions.

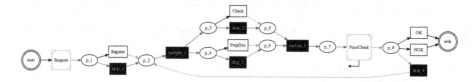

Fig. 1. Petri Net of the running model. The highlighted transitions are the activities used in Sect. 4 to explain the decision points selection. The black arrow indicates the direction and initial transition of the depth-first search. Blue arcs represent valid paths where the recursion will go on. Red ones, instead, track the recursive function until it stops.

Example. To clarify how the algorithm works, consider the variant ⟨*Request, FinalCheck, OK*⟩ and the running model reported in Fig. 1. We want to find decision points crossed by the variant going from activity "*Request*" to "*FinalCheck*". Blue arcs are the valid paths that lead the algorithm to the desired transition while red ones represent paths finding other visible transitions than the target one and, consequently, stopping the search.

The algorithm finds the two valid paths using two recursion lines, one passing through "p_5" and the other through "p_6". When the first recursion finds "*Request*", the function returns a boolean variable indicating the output to the upper levels until "*tauJoint_1*", where the other recursion line will start. Every recursion level has to remove the visited arcs; otherwise, the second recursion line will encounter the input arc of "*tauSplit_1*", marked as already visited, and will stop without reaching the desired transition.

4.2 Training Dataset Creation

The overall algorithm to create the training datasets for the decision trees has two parts. Firstly, for every variant, the method retrieves the data structure relating decision point and targets to every activity contained in the variant, as already explained.

Then, it considers the traces belonging to the variant. For every event in the trace, the algorithm creates a row containing the attributes seen until the previous event and adds it to the decision points mapped in the data structure. If an attribute is repeated multiple times in the sequence of events, the method considers only the most recent one. If an attribute in the row is not present in the dataset, the algorithm adds a column with missing values in previous entries and then adds a new row.

To study the influence of attributes locality on the quality of the classification, we also consider a variation of the method with datasets created considering only the last event in the sequence.

Since every search finds at maximum one visible transition and possibly many invisible ones, the resulting datasets may be unbalanced towards invisible targets. To overcome the problem and balance the data, we use an under-sampling technique, training multiple classifiers with different datasets, each discarding part of the over-represented targets.

5   Results

In this Section we report the results of our method. We use the Road Traffic Fine Management Process [10] to compare our algorithm to the implementation of [4] in the ProM software [11]. We use the F1 score to evaluate and compare the method, which considers the classification's accuracy and precision. Since the classifier predicts the output based on the same splits composing the final rules, better predictions, i.e. higher F1 scores, lead to more precise rules.

We know that more precise rules do not imply better or more meaningful ones, and we use this score for a straightforward comparison with the ProM implementation of the state-of-the-art method that reports this metric.

It is crucial to note that our method does not aim to outperform the state-of-the-art on the classification task but to avoid its information loss. We use the classification performance as a first assessment of our work's validity and leave the analysis of the meaningfulness of the rules and the quality of the resulting model to future studies.

Moreover, since the method aims at discovering decisions inside a process assumed to be static, we are not interested in the classifier's generalisation power and compute the F1 score on the training set without cross-validation.

Table 1. F1 score for the Road Traffic Fine Management Process dataset.

Decision Point	Optimal Alignment	Multiple Paths - Last Event	Multiple Paths
p_1	0.755	0.428	**0.788**
p_2	0.458	0.909	**0.909**
p_3	0.567	0.588	**0.818**
p_5	-	0.259	**0.83**
p_7	-	0.572	**0.893**
p_{12}	0.808	0.727	**0.898**
p_{13}	-	0.11	**0.895**
p_{14}	-	0.766	**0.948**
p_{15}	-	0.649	**0.686**
p_{19}	-	0.872	**0.957**
p_{26}	0.933	0.756	**0.952**

Table 1 reports the F1 score for two different versions of our method compared to the state-of-the-art method based on optimal alignment. To extract the model we used the Inductive Miner [12] with the noise threshold set to 0. As mentioned in Sec. 4.2, we also report the results of our method considering only attributes from the last event in the sequence. The results of our methods are the average across ten different classifiers due to the under-sampling explained in Sec. 4.2.

As expected, the results considering only attributes from the last event in the trace are noticeably worst, with few exceptions like "p_2" and "p_19", meaning that decisions depend on variables written in different parts of the model.

The state-of-the-art method based on optimal alignment cannot discover some of the decision points in the model, while our complete method can find all of them. Considering the decision points discovered by both methods, our has consistently higher F1 scores.

6   Conclusions and Future Works

In this work, we presented a novel method for decision mining on Petri Net that considers multiple possible paths taken by the variant. It can find all the decision points with higher classification quality than the state-of-the-art method.

In future works, we plan to study the quality of the extracted rules and the related model as well as differences with the rules and model retrieved by the state-of-the-art method. We will also test the approach on different datasets, hence different Petri Net sizes, and focus on the influence of the initial Petri Net fitness and complexity on the method's output.

Lastly, we plan to change the method implementation to guarantee that the model's arcs and nodes are visited at maximum once for search.

References

1. Blenko, M.W., Mankins, M.C., Rogers, P.: The decision-driven organization. Harv. Bus. Rev. **88**(6), 54–62 (2010)
2. Leewis, S., Smit, K., Zoet, M.: Putting decision mining into context: a literature study. In: Agrifoglio, R., Lamboglia, R., Mancini, D., Ricciardi, F. (eds.) Digital Business Transformation. LNISO, vol. 38, pp. 31–46. Springer, Cham (2020). https://doi.org/10.1007/978-3-030-47355-6_3
3. Rozinat, A., van der Aalst, W.M.P.: Decision mining in ProM. In: Dustdar, S., Fiadeiro, J.L., Sheth, A.P. (eds.) BPM 2006. LNCS, vol. 4102, pp. 420–425. Springer, Heidelberg (2006). https://doi.org/10.1007/11841760_33
4. de Leoni, M., van der Aalst, W.: Data-Aware Process Mining: Discovering Decisions in Processes Using Alignments, pp. 1454–1461 (2013)
5. Adriansyah, A., van Dongen, B.F., van der Aalst, W.M.P.: Conformance checking using cost-based fitness analysis. In: IEEE 15th International Enterprise Distributed Object Computing Conference (2011)
6. De Smedt, J., Hasić, F., vanden Broucke, S.K., Vanthienen, J.: Holistic discovery of decision models from process execution data. Knowl. Based Syst. **183**, 104866 (2019)
7. Peterson, J.L.: Petri Net Theory and the Modeling of Systems. Prentice Hall. (1981)
8. Sidorova, N., Stahl, C., Trčka, N.: Soundness verification for conceptual workflow nets with data: early detection of errors with the most precision possible. Inf. Syst. **36**, 1026–1043 (2010)
9. Salzberg, S.L.: C4.5: Programs for Machine Learning" by J. Ross Quinlan. Morgan Kaufmann Publishers Inc (1993). (Mach Learn 16, 235–240 (1994))
10. Mannhardt, F., de Leoni, M., Reijers, H.A., et al.: Balanced multi-perspective checking of process conformance. Computing **98**, 407–437 (2016)

11. Eric Verbeek, J.B., van der Aalst, W.M.P.: ProM 6: The Process Mining Toolkit. Eur. J. Oper. Res. (2010)
12. Bogarín, A., Cerezo, R., Romero, C.: Discovering learning processes using inductive miner: a case study with learning management systems (LMSs). Psicothema **30**, 322–329 (2018)

Modeling, Executing and Monitoring IoT-Driven Business Rules

Yusuf Kirikkayis[✉], Florian Gallik, and Manfred Reichert

Institute of Databases and Information Systems, Ulm University, Ulm, Germany
{yusuf.kirikkayis,florian-1.gallik,manfred.reichert}@uni-ulm.de

Abstract. The Internet of Things (IoT) is used in various areas to ease daily life and to make it more efficient. The IoT is a network of physical objects equipped with sensors, actuators, software, and technologies for exchanging the gathered data. In numerous domains, such as healthcare and smart home, IoT devices can be used to enable smart applications. Business Process Management (BPM), in turn, enables the analysis, modeling, implementation, execution, and monitoring of business processes. Extending BPM with IoT capabilities enhances process automation, improves process monitoring, and enables managing IoT-driven business rules. In the context of the latter the aggregation of low-level IoT data into high-level business information is a paramount important step. However, modeling, executing, and monitoring IoT-driven business rules based on BPMN 2.0 and Decision Model and Notation (DMN) might not be the best suited approach. This paper presents a framework that provides an extended BPMN notation for modeling, executing, and monitoring IoT-driven decision processes. The framework is implemented as a proof-of-concept prototype, a real-world scenario is presented to illustrate its use.

Keywords: IoT · Internet of Things · Business Rules · Business Rule Engine · IoT-driven Business Rules

1 Introduction

The interest in the Internet of Things (IoT) has increased continuously in recent years, and the IoT has become one of the most relevant topics in both software industry and computer science [3]. The electronic components built into IoT devices are becoming smaller, cheaper, and more powerful. IoT devices are equipped with sensors, actuators, and various network interfaces. This enables the IoT devices to capture and exchange data as well as to respond to real-world events [2]. While sensors are used to collect data about the state of the physical world (e.g., brightness, GPS, and camera sensors), actuators are used to control the physical world (e.g., watering systems and air conditioning) [6]. The networking of the physical devices enables IoT to digitally transform the dynamic context of the physical world.

© The Author(s), under exclusive license to Springer Nature Switzerland AG 2023
H. van der Aa et al. (Eds.): BPMDS 2023/EMMSAD 2023, LNBIP 479, pp. 88–102, 2023.
https://doi.org/10.1007/978-3-031-34241-7_7

In turn, BPM enables the modeling, implementation, execution, monitoring, and analysis of business processes [2]. In particular, integrating IoT capabilities into BPM systems enhances the real-world awareness of business processes and decision making and, thus, allows for a more comprehensive view on digitized processes. In particular, the interconnection of individual IoT devices enables the specification of complex business rules based on IoT data. Such rules necessitate context aggregation, context awareness, and real-time data [8,9,23]. **Low-level data** are generated by sensing the physical world and then need to be transformed into process-relevant **high-level data** [9,12,23]. Note that historical data from traditional repositories (e.g. databases or data warehouses) are not sufficient to enable IoT-driven decision making in real-time [1]. Instead, corresponding rules necessitate up-to-date high-level IoT data [23]. In the following, we refer to decisions influenced by IoT devices as *IoT-driven business rules*.

Current modeling standards such as Business Process Model and Notation (BPMN) 2.0 and Decision Model and Notation (DMN) do not provide explicit modeling elements for IoT. As a result, the involvement of IoT in the process models does not become apparent. On one hand, this worsens readability and comprehensibility of the models, on the other it increases complexity. Many approaches use BPMN 2.0 to model IoT-driven business processes [6,8,18] and integrate IoT artifacts as resources. As a result, the generated IoT data is directly used (low-level IoT data) without combining it with other IoT data. Consequently, process relevant decisions are hard-coded, like in traditional information systems. Note that this compromises the modeling of meaningful IoT-driven business rules as well as dynamic reactions to events [8]. Moreover, the integration of IoT with business rules is hindered by the lack of a methodological framework that enables connecting IoT infrastructure and BPM systems [8]. To overcome these drawbacks, we present a framework that enables the modeling, execution, and monitoring of IoT-driven business rules bases on an extended BPMN 2.0 notation. The framework aggregates low-level real-time data into high-level business data to which predefined business rules may refer. We extend the BPMN standard with IoT-specific elements, such as *sensor artifact*, *IoT decision container*, and *IoT decision task* to enable IoT-driven business rules with clear semantic.

The remainder of this paper is organized as follows. Section 2 summarizes the issues that emerge when modeling IoT-driven business rules and Sect. 3 describes the particular challenges to be tackled in this context. Section 4 presents our proposal for modeling IoT-driven business rules in BPMN 2.0. Section 5 introduces the system architecture for executing IoT-driven business rules. Section 6 presents the results from a case study in the smart manufacturing domain. Section 7 discusses our findings and Sect. 8 presents related work. Finally, Sect. 9 summarizes the paper.

2   Problem Statement

For modeling IoT-driven business rules, different BPMN 2.0 gateway types may be used, i.e., (I) **exclusive**, (II) **inclusive**, (III) **parallel**, (IV) **complex**, and (V) **event-based** gateways [11].

As the Decision Model and Notation (DMN) standard enables the aggregation of low-level data into high-level information, it may be also used to model IoT-driven business rules [5]. In DMN, the decision requirements are specified with Decision Requirements Diagrams (DRDs). The latter form the requirements between the sub-decisions of a complex decision rule and the data involved in the decision model. The input data of DRDs may be static or dynamic (cf. Fig. 1 (2) and (3)). In turn, the decision logic can be modeled in terms of decision tables [8] [5]. When combining BPMN and DMN, process and decision logic can be modeled separately (cf. Fig. 1 blue area). *Example 1* illustrates the relationship between BPMN and DMN. The described process is shown in Fig. 1.

Example 1: *To identify the severity of Chronic Obstructive Pulmonary Disease (COPD), the patient is equipped with sensors. Patients suffering from COPD have a damaged lung and their airways are restricted. After equipping a patient with sensors, the latter may be queried in parallel. Based on the result, either no treatment, a treatment with an oxygen mask, or a treatment with an inhaler is administered. Finally, the patient record is updated.*

By splitting process and decision logic the complexity of an IoT-driven business rule can be encapsulated in DMN. At runtime, the decision can then be made at the process level by invoking the corresponding business rule task (cf. Fig. 1 blue area). However, due to this separation of concerns at the process level one cannot see how the respective IoT-driven business rules look like. Moreover, there are studies that have proven that an separation of concerns and the required switching between two applications (BPMN and DMN) can lead to a high workload [6]. As another drawback, it is not possible to identify which IoT devices are involved in which IoT-driven business rules. Note that this affects both comprehensibility and transparency. As DMN does not explicitly support the modeling of IoT artifacts, the visual distinction between IoT data (cf. Fig. 1 (2)) and data from a database (cf. Fig. 1 (3)) becomes complicated. Error handling is challenging due to the fact that it is not possible to identify which IoT device is affected. When modeling IoT-driven business rules in BPMN (cf. Fig. 1 purple area), in turn, the complexity increases as more IoT devices and business rules are involved, leading to complex rule nesting. Additionally, the involvement of IoT might not becomes evident in the rules.

2.1   Executing and Monitoring IoT-Driven Business Rules

The execution of IoT-driven business rules modeled either in BPMN or BPMN + DMN can be performed by common workflow engines like Camunda [14]. However, these workflow engines are unaware of the involvement of IoT devices. On one hand, this affects error handling, on the other monitoring the processing of IoT-driven business rules is restricted. Contemporary workflow engines offer various monitoring possibilities (e.g. heatmaps or key performance indicators like throughput time, processing time, and execution time [14]). In contrast, IoT-specific information such as sensor request time, sensor reading, sensor status, or sensor name are not captured. Note that with this approaches IoT-driven business rules cannot be monitored in real-time, which hinders the mapping of the state of the physical world to the digital process.

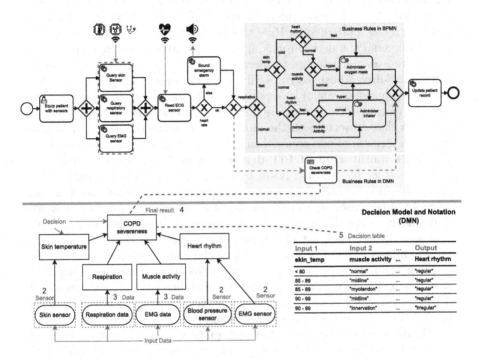

Fig. 1. Relationship between BPMN 2.0 and DMN

3   Challenges

Enhancing BPMN 2.0 with IoT capabilities poses major challenges for the modeling, execution, and monitoring of IoT-driven business rules [1,6,7,12]. In [23], we have identified fundamental challenges to be tackled when in the context of IoT-driven business rules in BPMN 2.0. In this work, we address the following challenges:

C1 Modeling IoT-driven business rules in BPMN 2.0: In Sect. 2, we discussed the current support of BPMN 2.0 for modeling IoT-driven business rules (cf. Fig. 1). When modeling IoT involvement with standard BPMN 2.0 elements, it remains unclear which tasks are IoT-related and which are not. To distinguish between sensors and actuators, the task labels should reflect the involvement of IoT and the process modeler needs to be familiar with IoT characteristics. For modeling IoT-driven business rules, different BPMN 2.0 gateways (e.g., exclusive and complex gateways) may be used. However, this approaches results in complex rule nesting and logic. The complex nesting and ambiguous involvement of IoT makes any extensions or changes difficult.

Therefore, an approach is needed that explicitly enables the modeling of IoT-driven business rules in the context of BPMN 2.0.

C2 Traceability of IoT-driven business rules: When modeling and monitoring IoT-driven business rules, the traceability of the business rules is crucial for process participants. Rule traceability refers to the ability to track and understand the decision-making process. Furthermore, rule traceability enables process participants to identify and address errors or biases in the defined IoT-driven business rules. In order to comprehend and trace back an IoT-driven business rule, it is essential to understand the specifics of how and why the related IoT devices were queried. To tackle this issue, a monitoring approach that presents both the modeled and executed IoT-driven business rules in a structured and comprehensible manner should be implemented.

C3 Fault monitoring of IoT-driven business rules: The failure (e.g., limited battery life and hardware failures) of IoT devices involved in IoT-driven business rules might have consequences. For example, if a non-reachable IoT sensor is queried, no decision can be made, which may lead to deadlocks as the BPMS continuously checks whether or not the IoT-driven business rule is met. Fault monitoring of IoT-driven business rules involves the continuous monitoring and analysis of the system behavior to detect any faults or errors that may arise during the execution of business rules. Note that this process is crucial to ensure the reliability and effectiveness of IoT-driven business rules, as it allows for the early detection and resolution of issues before they can have a significant impact on the process performance.

C4 Real-time monitoring of IoT-driven business rules: Real-time monitoring of IoT-driven business rules enables the continuous monitoring of the involved IoT sensors to ensure that it operates within acceptable parameters and complies with the defined IoT-driven business rule. The real-time monitoring is critical for ensuring the effectiveness and efficiency of the IoT-driven business rules, as it enables to identify and address issues as they occur in real-time.

4 Modeling IoT-Driven Business Rules

This section presents a framework for modeling IoT-driven business rules in BPMN 2.0 (cf. **C1**). As BPMN 2.0 can only facilitate the IoT participation (e.g., different types of activities and events) and the modeling of IoT-driven business rules with workarounds (e.g., gateways and data objects), we opt to extend the BPMN 2.0 meta-model by introducing new modeling elements. The main objectives of this extension are (1) to eliminate ambiguity, (2) explicitly cover IoT involvement, and (3) to ease the modeling of IoT-driven business rules (cf. **C2**). We first describe the extensions based on the meta-model (*Abstract Syntax*) level and then provide an example using that uses the extension for the *Concrete Syntax* (as proposed in [19]).

4.1   IoT Decision Activity

Modeling IoT-driven business rules in BPMN 2.0 constitutes a fundamental challenge. Therefore, we identified the need to extend the BPMN 2.0 meta-model with additional concepts to enable the proper modeling of IoT-driven business rules (cf. **C1**). Figure 2 shows the extension we propose for IoT-driven business rules. more precisely, we extended the *Activity* class with a new subclass called *IoTDecisionActivity*. Each IoT decision activity is associated with one *IoTDecisionContainer* that may contain sub-containers. When activating the IoT decision activity, it triggers the evaluation of both the root container and all sub-containers.

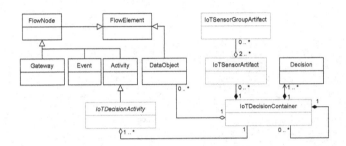

Fig. 2. BPMN 2.0 metal-model extension for IoT-driven Business Rules

4.2   IoT Decision Container

The *IoT decision container* may contain any number of *IoTSensorArtifacts*, which represent physical IoT sensors. *SensorArtifacts* of the same type may combined into an *IoTSensorGroupArtifacts* in order to increase the abstraction level (cf. **C2**). In addition, the container may contain any number of *DataObjects* (i.e., data necessary for decision making, but not originating from IoT devices), and the complete decision logic (cf. Fig. 2). As DMN already provides support for modeling decisions [5], we use the decision meta-model of DMN [10] as a basis for the IoT decision container. The IoT decision activity is associated with one root IoT decision container. Note that the latter may contain sub-containers in a tree-like manner. The tree structure allows the results obtained from the sub-containers to be used in the IoT-driven business rules of all the containers above them.

4.3   Visual Representation of IoT-Driven Business Rules

To visualize the involvement of IoT devices and IoT data in business rules, we extend BPMN 2.0 with the following elements: sensor (group) artifact, IoT decision container, and IoT decision task (cf. Fig. 3). The *COPD severeness* root IoT decision container includes the *Respiration, Skin Temperature, Muscle Activity,* and *Heart Rhythm* IoT decision sub-container. These, in turn, contain sensor artifacts representing various physical IoT devices. Through the IoT decision table, IoT-driven business rules can be defined for each IoT decision (sub-) container based on the physical IoT devices (sensor artifacts). For example, business rule *Pulse < 100 && Heartbeat == regular* is defined in the *HeartRhythm* IoT decision table (cf. Fig. 3). When this business rule becomes satisfied, the *HeartRhythm* IoT decision container returns the result *regular*. The output of the IoT-driven business rules can then be used by the XOR split gateway of the business process based on the IoT decision task to make an IoT-driven decision. After modeling all IoT-driven business rules, the process is deployed on the IoT-enabled business rule engine, which supports the monitoring of the IoT-driven business rules (cf. Challenges **C3** and **C4**).

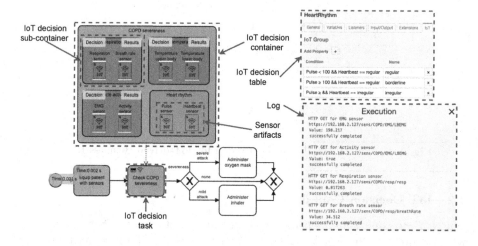

Fig. 3. IoT-driven business rules

5   Executing IoT-Driven Business Rules in BPMN 2.0

The goal of this work is to provide a BPMN 2.0 extension for modeling, execution, and monitoring IoT-driven business rules. The architecture of the framework consists of several components designed to meet the challenges described in Sect. 3. The architecture of the framework is depicted in Fig. 4. It consists of three core components, i.e., (i) Modeler, (ii) IoT-driven business rule engine, and (iii) rule monitoring system (cf. Challenges **C3** and **C4**). The framework is implemented as a web-based software application[1]. For modeling and monitoring IoT-driven business rules, the open-source *bpmn.io*[2] *toolkit* is used. This enables the extension of BPMN 2.0 with individual elements. Communication between the framework and the IoT infrastructure is accomplished by a service invoker,

---

[1] https://github.com/elmurd0r/bpmds_df
[2] https://bpmn.io.

which provides access to external services via protocol-specific adapters such as REST, MQTT, LoRa, and XMP. For each service type, the adapters need to be implemented. To execute the IoT-driven business rules, an open-source BPMN 2.0 engine[3] is used, which is extended with the new elements. In addition, the engine is extended with an element parser, which is aware of the IoT device involvement as well as the specific IoT elements. It further extracts information like custom element type, IoT parameter, and IoT decision table. To determine the structure and order of the decisions, a tree is created in a top-down manner. After parsing and generating the tree, the individual custom IoT elements are executed according to their types and the parsed information. For monitoring, the *bpmn.io* viewer is used with IoT-specific modeling elements. As the monitoring system is directly connected to the IoT-driven business rule engine, it can visualize the rule processing in real-time. Moreover, the execution component is connected to a logging system. The latter records data on IoT device requests, IoT-measured values, IoT device error codes, results of IoT-driven business rules, and decision tables.

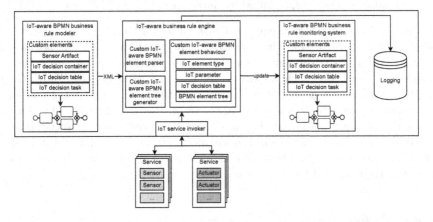

Fig. 4. Architecture for modeling, executing, and monitoring IoT-driven business rules.

6   Demonstration of the Framework

We introduce a sophisticated scenario of a data- and decision-intensive Smart Factory and illustrate the modeling, execution, and monitoring of an IoT-driven business rule by applying the framework in the context of this scenario. In particular, this case study shall investigate the use of the framework in a realistic scenario and check whether it allows for the domain-independent integration of the IoT with business rules. Note that the framework is not limited to specific use cases or processes, but can be applied in many domains and business processes involving IoT-driven business rules.

---

[3] https://github.com/paed01/bpmn-engine.

We use physical simulation models developed by *Fischertechnik*®[4] to emulate the smart factory. The latter simulates a complete production line that consists of two shop floors, which are interconnected to exchange workpieces and to distribute the orders (cf. Fig. 5). Each shop floor comprises 5 stations: (i) high-bay warehouse, (ii) vacuum gripper robot, (iii) oven, (iv) milling machine, and (iv) sorting machine (cf. Fig. 5a). The smart factory is equipped with the following ten types of IoT sensors:

1. Limit switch sensors (represented by red circles and labeled as *LMXX*).
2. Light barrier sensors (represented by yellow circles and labeled as *LBXX*).
3. Compressor sensors (represented by blue circles and labeled as *CRXX*).
4. Temperature sensors (represented by orange circles and labeled as *TSXX*).
5. Encoder sensors (represented by cyan circles and labeled as *ECXX*).
6. Color sensors (represented by purple circles and labeled as *CLXX*).
7. Vibration sensors (represented by pink circles and labeled as *VRXX*).
8. Brightness sensors (represented by green circles and labeled as *BNXX*).
9. Humidity sensors (represented by neon green circles and labeled as *HDXX*).
10. Air quality sensors (represented by dark red circles and labeled as *AQXX*).

In total, the Smart Factory is equipped with 70 sensors (cf. Fig. 5b). First, there are 16 light barrier sensors that detect the interruption of a light beam and display it as an electrical signal. Second, 20 limit switch sensors are actuated by the movement of a machine part or the presence of an object. Third, the 6 compressor sensors measure the overpressure of the suction and the 2 temperature sensors deliver the temperature in the oven. Fourth, the 8 encoder sensors output the current position of the motor and the 2 color sensors recognize the color of a particular workpiece in the sorting machine. Finally, 4 vibration sensors, 4 brightness sensors, 4 humidity sensors, and 4 air quality sensors are used to ensure the quality of the workpieces.

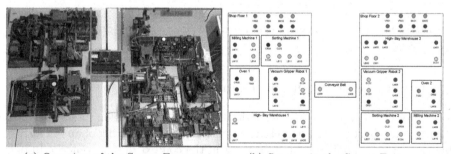

(a) Overview of the Smart Factory.   (b) Sensors in the Smart Factory.

Fig. 5. Smart Factory.

---

[4] https://www.fischertechnik.de/en/simulating/industry-4-0.

Figure 6 illustrates the IoT-driven business rule modeler introduced in Sect. 4. Depending on the result of the IoT decision container *Smart Factory*, either Shop Floor 1 or Shop Floor 2 is selected. In this context, IoT sensors are used whose values are aggregated or combined within the IoT decision container. This way, the physical state of the Smart Factory is transformed into its digital twin and the decision can be made based on the sensor measurements and the IoT-driven business rules. For example, in Fig. 6, the IoT decision task *Select Shop Floor* is connected to the *Smart Factory* root decision container. This decision container, in turn, contains six IoT decision sub-containers resulting in a tree structure. Note that each decision container may comprise n IoT decision sub-containers and n sensor artifacts. Each individual IoT decision container has an IoT decision table, which is part of the properties panel.

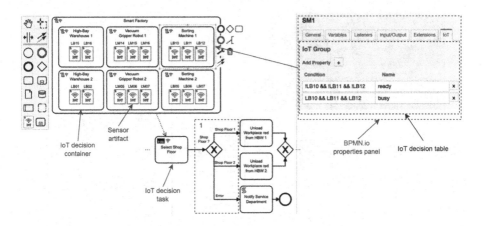

Fig. 6. IoT-driven business rule modeler.

All sensors required for checking business rule *Select Store Floor* can be placed within the IoT decision containers via drag and drop. Required information such as sensor name and REST or MQTT path can be configured with the modeler for each individual sensor artifact. First, the IoT-driven business rules are defined in the IoT decision table. Figure 6 shows the IoT-driven business rules of the IoT decision sub-container *Sorting Machine 1*. For example, it is defined that *Sorting Machine 1* returns *ready* if sensors LB10, LB11, and LB12 are true. In turn, the individual results of the IoT decision sub-containers may be used by the root IoT decision container *Smart Factory* to define other IoT-driven business rules. Figure 7 shows examples of these IoT-driven business rules of the root IoT decision container.

To execute the process fragment from Fig. 6, it is stored in an XML file, which is then deployed to the IoT-driven business rule engine (cf. Fig. 4). The latter parses the XML file and executes the process fragment. As soon as the rule engine recognizes a task of type *iotDecisionTask*, all sensors of the IoT decision container are queried in parallel. The technical information needed for this is contained in the XML file as well. After retrieving the measured values of all sensors, the business rules defined in the IoT decision tables are processed inside out, i.e., the innermost IoT decision container is processed first. Note that this becomes necessary as the results of the IoT sub-decision containers are needed for evaluating the rule in the root decision container. The resulting output of the IoT-driven business rule can then be used, for example, at a corresponding XOR split gateway to make an IoT-driven decision (cf. Fig. 6, (1)).

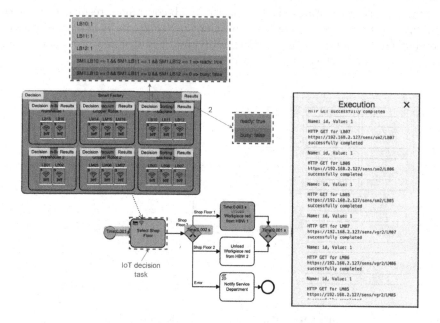

Fig. 7. Monitoring IoT-driven business rules in real-time.

As the monitoring system is directly connected to the IoT-driven business rule engine (cf. Fig. 4), the instance of the decision processes can be monitored in real-time (cf. C4). Successfully queried sensors that provide a measured value are colored in green. If sensors do not provide a measured value within a specified timeout or cannot be reached, they will be colored in red. Before, the sensors are colored in orange. Note that the latter indicates that the sensors are currently queried or processed. Moreover, these color patterns are used for the IoT decision containers as well. Besides this visual representation, the individual queries of the sensors can be tracked via a log (cf. Fig. 7), which allows for detailed analysis in the case of errors (cf. C3). Furthermore, each individual IoT decision container has the *Decision* and *Result* labels in the respective upper corner. Hovering the mouse over *Decision* (cf. Fig. 7, (1)) displays all IoT-driven business rules in the table (cf. C2). The measured values of the sensors have background color blue, whereas the IoT-driven business rule fulfilling the condition is colored in green. Finally, the IoT-driven business rule that does not fulfill the condition is colored in red. Label *Results* displays all possible outcomes defined by the IoT decision container using the IoT decision table. The final decision resulting from the IoT decision container has background color green, all other results have color red (cf. Fig. 7, (2)). During rule monitoring, the entire IoT decision container may be expanded or collapsed by clicking on the WLAN icon (cf. Fig. 7 (3)).

A video showing the processing of an IoT-driven business rule based on our framework can be viewed on YouTube[5]. It shows the decision engine, the monitoring component, and the behavior of the smart factory in real-time.

7 Discussion

Regarding the case study we were able to model, execute, and monitor IoT-driven business rules of the presented Smart Factory scenario based on the proposed framework. Note that we also successfully applied the framework in other domains, including smart home, smart logistics, and smart healthcare scenarios. As a benefit, the involvement of IoT devices and the composition structure of the IoT-driven business rules becomes explicit in BPMN 2.0 processes (cf. C1). In addition, IoT-driven business rules as well as their outcome can be monitored and tracked during runtime (cf. C2). If an error occurs, its source can be easily identified. Various color patterns as well as a real-time log are used for this purpose (cf. C3 and **C4**). As the specified IoT-driven business rules can be exported as an XML file, the IoT decision containers and the sensor artifacts that reside inside these containers can be reused. Further note that rule complexity is split across multiple IoT decision containers of which each has its own IoT decision table. Finally, the componentized architecture allows for the easy introduction of new communication protocols and sensor types (cf. Fig. 4).

8 Related Work

Several approaches and extensions for covering IoT aspects in BPMN 2.0 have been proposed in literature [7,16,17,20]. However, these approaches do not utilize IoT data for decision making and context reasoning [17,23]. As shown in Sect. 2, the modeling of IoT-driven business rules based on BPMN 2.0 itself becomes confusing with increasing number of involved IoT devices. Furthermore, the complexity and, thus, the comprehensibility of business rules might be affected [23]. Another proposed approach is to apply Complex Event Processing (CEP) for sensor data aggregation [13,15,24]. While CEP is a promising approach for transforming low-level IoT data to high-level process-relevant data, usually, its implementation uses a specific event processing language and external tools.

[6] presents an approach that enables the interdisciplinary specification of IoT-enhanced business processes. Three primary aspects are taken into consideration for modeling: (1) business processes, (2) IoT devices, and (3) sensors processing. [6] argues that a separation of concerns is advantageous with respect to

---

[5] https://youtu.be/juIuIZhxPHk.

the diverse responsibilities of modelers. Nonetheless, their findings also indicate that the use of three distinct modeling languages might result in a considerable workload for modelers tasked with multiple aspects, as they now need to be familiar with each language.

[21] introduces a framework for bridging the gap between IoT infrastructure and BPM systems by integrating IoT devices into context ontologies. The goal of this integration is to improve business process decision making. An ecosystem with the four components contextual process models, contextual models, decision models, and contextual process execution is proposed. This framework does not allow modeling and monitoring IoT-driven decisions, as decisions are treated separately from the process control flow. In [22], a process model for logistics management based on RFID sensors is proposed. The values sensed by the RFID sensors are analyzed to improve decision making. The presented process model enables the detection of inconsistencies based on IoT-driven decisions. However, the presented process model is specific to logistics management and cannot be used in other domains. In addition, the business rules are hard-coded in the process model.

[5] studies the modeling of IoT-aware processes and compares BPMN 2.0 and the combination of BPMN and DMN in this context. Three different cases with increasing needs for IoT data aggregation are modeled. The study results have shown that BPMN+DMN offers advantages for complex aggregation. However, relevant aspects are not covered, including the explicit representation of involved IoT devices, rule traceability, fault monitoring, and real-time monitoring (See the challenges in Sect. 3). [4] uses BPMN 2.0 conditional events to integrate decisions into business processes. The collection of IoT data is performed by an integrated communication architecture for IoT and BPM system. However, the logic defined behind the conditional events does not become apparent in the business process as it relies on an external modeling tool (*Node-RED*). In turn, this makes it difficult to identify and trace errors in the business process. In [13], the authors annotate BPMN 2.0 modeling elements (e.g., activities) to enable subscriptions to IoT events. The proposed approach allows to aggregate low-level data into high-level data. Again, neither the involvement of IoT devices nor the composition of the defined business rules become apparent.

[7] extends BPMN 2.0 with IoT-specific artifacts and events to highlight the involvement of IoT devices. The artifacts and events allow polling physical IoT devices in real-time. A corresponding architecture is provided for this purpose. In turn, the collected IoT data can be used for decision making based on gateways. The approach only enables the use of low-level IoT data for decision making, but does not consider their aggregation to high-level data.

Altogether, none of the discussed approaches provides a complete solution for modeling, execution, and monitoring IoT-driven business rules. Most works extend BPMN with IoT-related elements to enable the participation of IoT, or they use external CEP approaches making neither the involvement of IoT devices nor the composition structure of IoT-driven business rules explicit. In addition, to the best of our knowledge, no BPMN 2.0 engine for executing IoT-driven business rules in real time exists. Another missing aspect concerns the monitoring of IoT-driven decisions. During the execution of the business rules it is crucial to be able to monitor the current business rule state as well as to track back possible errors.

9 Summary and Outlook

We presented a BPMN 2.0 extension for modeling, execution, and monitoring IoT-driven business rules as well as a corresponding architecture taking the defined challenges into account. For modeling IoT-driven business rules, we extended BPMN 2.0 with the elements *IoT decision container*, *sensor artifact*, and *IoT decision task*. Based on this extension, the involvement of IoT devices and the composition structure of IoT-driven business rules become apparent. The sensor artifacts serve as input of the IoT decision container. IoT-driven business rules can be executed by the IoT-driven rule engine of the framework. As the monitoring system is directly connected to this engine, it can visualize the rule processing in real-time. During monitoring, all processed IoT-driven business rules and IoT-measured data values are displayed. In addition, different processing states can be visually distinguished with different colors. To detect possible errors (e.g. defective or non-reachable IoT devices) the engine tracks every single event and generates a log entry. We applied the framework in a case study and successfully integrated IoT-driven decisions into an activity-centric approach. Altogether, we consider our work as an important contribution to enhance BPM systems with IoT capabilities.

In future work we will equip the framework with additional services. While the current framework can detect unreachable sensors and monitor them in the IoT-driven business rule engine and monitoring system, we plan to add features for identifying and handling errors such as outliers and erroneous sensor values. Furthermore, we will conduct a study to evaluate the usability of the concept.

References

1. Janiesch, C., et al.: The Internet of Things meets business process management: a manifesto. In: Systems, Man, and Cybernetics Magazine (2020)
2. Kirikkayis, Y., Gallik, F., Reichert, M.: Towards a comprehensive BPMN extension for modeling IoT-aware processes in business process models. In: 16th International Conference on Research Challenges in Information Science (RCIS), (2022)
3. Chang, C., Srirama, S.N., Buyya, R.: Mobile cloud business process management systems for the internet of things: a survey. In: Computing Surveys (CSUR) (2016)
4. Schönig, S., Achermann, L., Jablonski, S., Ermer, A.: IoT meets BPM: a bidirectional communication architecture for IoT-aware process execution. Softw. Syst. Model **19**, 1443–1459 (2020)
5. Hasić, F., Serral, E., Snoeck, M.: Comparing BPMN to BPMN + DMN for IoT process modelling: a case-based inquiry. In: Symposium on Applied Computing (2020)
6. Valderas, P., Torres, V., Serral, E.: Modelling and Executing IoT-enhanced business processes through BPMN and microservices. Syst. Softw. **184** (2022)

7. Kirikkayis, Y., Gallik, F., Winter, M., Reichert, M.: BPMNE4IoT: a framework for modeling, executing and monitoring IoT-driven processes. In: Fut. Internet **15** (2023)

8. Song, R., Vanthienen, J., Cui, W., Wang, Y., Huang, L.: Context-aware BPM using IoT-integrated context ontologies and IoT-enhanced decision models. In: 2019 IEEE 21st Conference on Commerce and Enterprise Computing (2019)

9. Koschmider, A., Mannhardt, F., Heuser, T.: On the contextualization of event-activity mappings. In: Daniel, F., Sheng, Q.Z., Motahari, H. (eds.) BPM 2018. LNBIP, vol. 342, pp. 445–457. Springer, Cham (2019). https://doi.org/10.1007/978-3-030-11641-5_35

10. OMG: Decision Model and Notation (DMN) 1.2, (2018)

11. OMG: Business Process Model and Notation (BPMN) 2.0, (2010)

12. Hasić, F., Serral, E.: Executing IoT Processes in BPMN 2.0: Current Support and Remaining Challenges. In: 2019 13th International Conference on Service Science (2019)

13. Baumgraß, A., et al.: Towards a Methodology for the engineering of event-driven process applications. In: Reichert, M., Reijers, H.A. (eds.) BPM 2015. LNBIP, vol. 256, pp. 501–514. Springer, Cham (2016). https://doi.org/10.1007/978-3-319-42887-1_40

14. Camunda: Process Engine. https://docs.camunda.org/manual/7.8/user-guide/process-engine/. Accessed 5 Apr 2022

15. Soffer, F.N., et al.: From event streams to process models and back: challenges and opportunities. Inf. Syst. **81**, 181–200 (2019)

16. Sungur, C.T., et al.: Extending BPMN for wireless sensor networks. In: 2013 IEEE 15th Conference on Business Informatics (2013)

17. Meyer, S., Ruppen, A., Hilty, L.: The Things of the Internet of Things in BPMN. In: Persson, A., Stirna, J. (eds.) CAiSE 2015. LNBIP, vol. 215, pp. 285–297. Springer, Cham (2015). https://doi.org/10.1007/978-3-319-19243-7_27

18. Vanhoorelbeke, F., Snoeck, M., Serral, E.: Identifying the challenges and requirements of enterprise architecture frameworks for iot systems. In: Dalpiaz, F., Zdravkovic, J., Loucopoulos, P. (eds.) RCIS 2020. LNBIP, vol. 385, pp. 576–581. Springer, Cham (2020). https://doi.org/10.1007/978-3-030-50316-1_41

19. Braun, R., Esswein, W.: Towards an integrated method for the extension of MOF-based modeling languages. In: Bellatreche, L., Manolopoulos, Y. (eds.) MEDI 2015. LNCS, vol. 9344, pp. 103–115. Springer, Cham (2015). https://doi.org/10.1007/978-3-319-23781-7_9

20. Petrasch, R., Hentschke, R.: Process modeling for industry 4.0 applications towards an industry 4.0 process modeling language and method. In: 13th International Joint Conference on Computer Science and Software Engineering (JCSSE) (2016)

21. Song, R., Vanthienen, J., Cui, W., Wang, Y., Huang, L: Context-aware BPM using IoT-integrated context ontologies and IoT-enhanced decision models, In: Conference on Commerce and Enterprise Computing, July 2019

22. Oliveira, R., et al.: An intelligent model for logistics management based on geofencing algorithms and RFID technology. Expert Syst. Appl. **42**, 6082–6097 (2015)

23. Kirikkayis Y., Gallik, F., Reichert M.: Modeling, executing and monitoring iot-driven business rules with bpmn and dmn: current support and challenges. In: Enterprise Design, Operations, and Computing, (2022). https://doi.org/10.1007/978-3-031-17604-3_7

24. Seiger, R., Huber, S., Schlegel, T.: Toward an execution system for self-healing workflows in cyber-physical systems. In: Softw Syst Model, **17**(2), 551–572 (2018)

A Generic Approach Towards Location-Aware Business Process Execution

Leo Poss[✉] and Stefan Schönig

University of Regensburg, Regensburg, Germany
{leo.poss,stefan.schoenig}@ur.de
https://go.ur.de/iot

Abstract. Locally distributed processes include several process participants working on tasks at different locations, e.g., craftspeople working on construction sites. Compared to classical IT environments, new challenges emerge due to the spatial context of a process. Real-time location data from Internet of Things (IoT) devices consumed through BPM technology can help businesses to implement more efficient and effective processes.

Those advantages, however, have only been touched by small parts of existing research, while the architecture and implementation of executable location-aware processes area only ever been vaguely considered. Therefore, we introduce and present a non-exhaustive list of concepts for the use of location data for BPM as well as a location-aware approach for process execution and present a multi-layer system architecture based on standard BPM technology.

Keywords: Process execution · Location-awareness · Distributed processes

1 Introduction

Business Process Management (BPM) is a managing approach to goal-driven design, and the optimization of diverse and cross-organizational business processes using methods and tools to support the design, execution, management, and analysis of processes [10]. Mobile and locally distributed processes typically include several process participants working on subsequent tasks at different locations, e.g., a craft business employing multiple actors working on different construction sites.

Those kinds of processes encounter different challenges that have to be solved: While processes in classical IT environments mostly do not consider the spatial context, because the distances between places of fulfillment are quite small and thus might be neglectable [8], the enhancement of process execution using the inherent location distributions make up a big part of possible improvements.

The Internet of Things (IoT) describes a world where every object can connect to a data network having its own digital identity [13]. IoT devices are a

H. van der Aa et al. (Eds.): BPMDS 2023/EMMSAD 2023, LNBIP 479, pp. 103–118, 2023.
https://doi.org/10.1007/978-3-031-34241-7_8

fundamental technology to deliver contextual and location data, that can be used within different phases of BPM [18]. Data gained from IoT devices representing different locations of involved entities describe the entity's location conditions and circumstances [1,17]. Real-time location data from IoT devices consumed through BPM technology helps businesses to implement more efficient and effective processes.

Consider, e.g., a mobile distributed business process from a crafts enterprise, where workers drive to customers to replace broken heaters. Here, location data can be used, to allocate the repair order instance and the corresponding tasks to the person closest to the customer's location. However, in the area of BPM, most research has touched only aspects of location awareness, such as process adaptation, process modeling, and mining [3,11], or managerial aspects of context-aware processes [15,26]. The description and implementation of an executable system to capture and process location data for business processes are either neglected, only vaguely contained, or described for a closed environment scenario, for example, of a smart factory [36]. In particular, to the best of the authors' knowledge, the allocation of concrete actors to tasks based on location data and reordering the task lists of multiple process instances based on the distance is still an open research issue. The described research gap poses the following research question: *What are possible concepts for the use of the location context of actors and entities in BPM and how can they be used during process execution?*

We fill this gap in the following sections by introducing concepts for the use of IoT-based location information in BPM as well as an implementation of an executable and well-defined location-aware approach for process execution. More detailed, we present a multi-layer system architecture based on standard BPM technology implementing an extensive set of location-aware concepts based on a real-world use case enhancing mobile distributed processes: *(i)* location-based task allocation, *(ii)* location-based automated start, and termination of tasks and process instances as well as location-event based dispatching of tasks, and *(iii)* location-based reordering of tasks. The presented approach has been implemented and evaluated using a common real-life distributed process from several craft businesses, combining the potential of the use of location data with an executable implementation to adapt to other real-life processes.

The remainder of this paper is structured as follows: In Sect. 2 we present the background and related work w.r.t. location-aware BPM as well as our research methodology. Section 3 describes the underlying location-aware example process. In Sect. 4, we present our concepts for location-aware process execution. Section 5 describes implementation details, and the paper is finally concluded in Sect. 6.

2 Theoretical Background and Related Work

2.1 Background on Context- and Location-Aware Business Processes

Business Process Management. A business process is a set of activities that are performed to achieve a business result [10]. *Business Process Management*

(BPM) is a managing approach to goal-driven design, and the optimization of diverse and cross-organizational business processes using methods and tools to support the design, execution, management, and analysis of business processes. Using BPM, businesses can take advantage of improvement opportunities and align their processes to the needs of clients and their own goals. While the inherent standardization might seem like a good idea initially, the over-standardization impedes handling external influences, which might work for a production line, but hinders the optimization of mobile workloads ("the management of processes should fit the process nature" [5]). For a production line, external data might be less relevant from a process perspective and thus disregarded, while mobile processes are very much dependent on different locations.

IoT-Aware BPM. The *Internet of Things (IoT)* describes a world where every object can connect to a data network having its own digital identity [13], where electronic hardware can be used to remotely communicate with physical objects. The existing gap between human actors and electronic devices can be bridged by using tightly integrated systems that use data gained from IoT devices to improve efficiency and effectiveness and enable data-driven work. IoT data is a fundamental technology to deliver context information and data, that can be used in BPMS. Process execution, monitoring, and analysis based on IoT big data can enable a more comprehensive view of processes. Embedding intelligence by way of real-time data gathering from devices and sensors and consuming them through BPM technology helps businesses with adding value by saving costs and improving efficiency.

Context-Aware BPM. Data gained from IoT devices representing different locations of involved entities describes the entity's conditions and circumstances, thus being part of the *process context* [1]. In Human-Computer Interaction (HCI), the concept of context has been part of research for many years, leading to different definitions, with the relationship as the distinguishing factor. In HCI, the relationship between an actor and a system gets contextualized, while we are contextualizing the entity included within a BPMS, i.e., using the context of an actor or a task within the execution of a process instance. Schilit et al. [28] define a *context-aware system* as a system that has the ability to discover and react to changes in the environment while Huebscher and McCann [17] define *context-awareness* itself as the ability of an application to adapt to the context of its users, and the *user's context* as the circumstances or situations in which a computing task takes place. Küpper [21] describes *location-based services* without the connection to business processes and before practical use of IoT, as being a part of context-aware services based on two levels of context, the *primary context* like time, location, identity, and activity that are based on sensors and a *secondary context* level comprised of personal, technical, social, physical and spatial context which can be derived by combination, deduction, or filtering of primary context data.

Location-Aware BPM. Küpper [21] defines *spatial locations* as based on well-defined reference systems that subdivide a geographical area into units of a common shape and size, most commonly specified as a numerical explicit representation in a coordinate system (e.g., latitude and longitude), while in the real world, we commonly use street names and numbers (addresses) for defining a location of an entity. Both formats can be converted into each other using geocoding, and while addresses are more human-readable, they are often less accurate – considering both, timeliness and accuracy – and prevent numerical calculations on location information. Following the earlier differentiation of primary and secondary context, in this work *IoT-data* will refer to all data gained from IoT devices, which can be *location data* (data to represent a location, primary context), while *spatial data* includes the location of an entity as well as other information based on the location of an entity (secondary context, e.g., the distance between two entities).

In the context of *Complex Event Processing* (CEP), Etzion [12] distinguishes between different types of context: temporal, state-oriented, segmentation oriented, and spatial. For this research, only the spatial classification is important, which gets further divided into three different parts, where spatial information can be used as part of the generation of events [12]: (i) *Fixed location*: Describes a fixed location like the position of a customer or the company's office, (ii) *Entity distance location*: Represents locations within a certain radius of an entity, e.g., geofencing, (iii) *Event distance location*: Similar to entity distance location, but describes the radius drawn around an event happening (e.g. an accident) as the basis to include subsequent events. Another differentiation that has to be made for the location information of entities is the basic difference between *dynamic* and *static locations*, while the latter remains the same, the first can change over time.

Even though the concepts and goals of CEP and BPM have been focused on different application areas, within the context of IoT, they share various similarities, and both approaches can be combined [30]. In comparison to other research focusing on using context information during the modeling of a process like Hallerbach et al. [15] and Brocke et al. [4] and Janiesch et al. [18] focusing on the overall architecture and possible benefits, this papers' focus lies on the actual execution of business processes and how they can benefit through the use of location data and IoT. Finally, we define the term *mobile distributed process* as a process that includes several actors, working on subsequent tasks at different locations, *implicitly constraining* the task's execution to a specific location, e.g., a craft business employing multiple workers working on different construction sites. This leads to a distinct set of problems compared to classical (IT) environments of business processes, where the spatial context of a process is less important or the distances between places of fulfillment are quite small and might be negligible.

2.2 Related Work

We give a list of related work in Table 1, presenting an overview of the corresponding problem definition, as well as the goal, the chosen approach, and the result – independent of their original application domain. The individual approaches can be classified into four non-exclusive categories, namely: *graphical modeling extensions* where the spatial perspective aims to explicitly model locations in business processes, *conceptual modeling extensions* where new use cases are presented (mainly the location-based restriction of the execution of tasks e.g. in [9,32] as well as research considering the *architecture of BPMSs* and the *use of spatial information to derive new functionality*, e.g. the use of location data from event logs to get an overview of task locations [3] or the visualization of work items and resources [22]). Note that even if the approach of Stürzel [32] is conceptually defined and executable, the author and others like Decker et al. [9] and Tchemeube et al. [34] only consider location constraints as use for spatial information during process modeling or execution. On the other hand, Compagnucci et al. [8] give an overview of related work for the combination of IoT and BPM, but not specifically for location data or the use of context information. They determine that most extensions avoid handling data, thus disregarding the core of the connection between location and their use for business processes.

2.3   Research Methodology

The following sections follow the basic course of the well-established *Design Science Research Methodology* (DSRM) which has the basic goal of creating useful artifacts within the information systems discipline [16]. Methodologically the current procedure model of Johannesson and Perjons [20] divides the research process into six iterative phases: (i) *explicate problem*, (ii) *define requirements*, (iii) *design and develop artifact*, (iv) *demonstrate artifact* and finally (vi) *evaluate artifact*. While the problem and requirements for a solution have already been outlined in Sects. 1 and 2, the following Sect. 4 explain the different concepts of the use of spatial information with BPM, Sect. 5 is going the last step and providing a prototypical implementation for the previously presented concepts, combining the demonstration and evaluation of the concepts.

3   Location-Aware Business Process Application

In the following sections, we present different possibilities for the use of spatial information within executed business processes, relying on BPMN [23] as the de-facto standard for business process modeling. Driven by a real-life application, we explain the use of spatial information within a mobile distributed business process from craft businesses, where workers drive to customers to replace broken heaters. The BPMN model of the process is depicted in Fig. 1.

The process starts with an incoming job, including the customer's location, before the option of instantly executing the job is checked. After allocating a certain actor to the job, provided the system knows the current location of all workers, they drive to the customer, replace the heater, and drive back to the depot to replenish their stock. The final step of the process is the generation of an invoice for the customer. The given process model highlights various opportunities where location-based data can contribute to more effective and efficient execution of the process.

Table 1. Related work concept matrix following Webster and Watson [35]

	Goal	Approach/Procedure	Outcome	Drawback	Notation	Executable?	Graphical	Conceptual	Architectural	New functionality
[19]	Develop a system, to effectively handle constraints of network connectivity and mobility of workflow resources	Two-level approach: Global level: Dynamic assignment of activities based on e.g. resource location. Local level: Additional resource attributes to prioritize activities for participants	Resource management by custom work list handler, supporting late and dynamic binding to location-dependent activities. Integration of map view	Dated approach focusing on constraints in mobile connectivity, only worklist reordering	–	●	○	○	●	●
[2]	Modelling location-aware business processes based on architectural primitives	Business-rule driven architecture with semantic coordination and location primitives. Process flow: Business rules restricting the execution of an activity	Influence of location laws on activities based on predefined location	Not executable, handles only location constraints	–	○	○	○	○	○
[9]	Include location constraints in BPM	Location constraints on activities at design time and dynamic constraints during run time. Graphical symbols and extension of the BPMN meta-model	Extension of the BPMN meta-model	Not executable, handles only location constraints	B	○	●	●	○	○
[31]	System architecture for location information in process optimization within a factory of things	Focus on the provision of location information to location-aware client applications. Externalize location rules from the source code into a knowledge base. System architecture handling aggregation, mapping, and allocation of location information	Conceptual idea to location-aware application architecture	Not executable, processes event logs to gain insights of execution locations	–	○	●	○	●	○
[14]	Comparison of business process notations regarding location aspects	Comparison of adaptations of notations, attempt to create notation for mobile information systems from scratch	Suggestion on the visual appearance (color-fill, icon, etc.) of location aspects of existing notations	Not executable, graphical representations only	B/P	○	●	○	○	○
[22]	Decision support for choosing next work task	Map metaphor and distance notions to visualize work items and resources. Distance notions for priority of work items based on different factors, e.g. location. Visualization is split into work items and resource layers	Work list visualization framework based on maps and distance notions implemented as YAWL component	Decision support system for worklist reordering, location only	–	●	●	○	●	●
[34]	Shorten wait times in the cardiac care process	Combination of location system and BPM by complex event processing (CEP)	Abstract location-aware BPM system architecture. Implementation prototype of architecture	Different application area, CEP for process improvement, fixed process	B	●	○	○	●	●
[29]	Modelling location-aware business processes. Location-aware extension of process execution system	Declarative language for modeling business processes. Provision of additional modeling elements for location dependencies in DPIL. Description of how elements could be executed by business process execution engine	Concept and prototype of declarative location-aware process execution engine. Location-dependent task assignment and process progression	Only declarative modeling, no implementation, worklist reordering	B	◉	○	●	●	○
[38]	Identify and conceptualize location-dependencies in process modeling	Pattern-based approach to identify location-dependency in process models	Location dependent task symbol, location dependent condition	Only graphical, influence control flow with location data	B	○	○	●	○	○
[6]	BPMN event extension for IoT	Create new BPMN events with an extended event definition (includes location event)	Start, intermediate, and end event and extended event definition for location, fault tolerance, and quality of information	Retrospective event processing based on location (and other IoT) data	B	○	○	●	○	○
[37]	Constrain control flow and process behavior based on location	Petri net modeling extension, mapping to colored Petri nets. Usage of location constraints using geospatial relationships	Modelling technique can specify how location impacts the basic control flow	Only Location constraints	P	●	●	○	○	○
[11]	Extend BPMN to enable the modeling of mobile context-aware business processes	Sensor modeling for the dependencies of context information. Context marker, context event, and context expression language by extending the BPMN meta-model	Context4BPMN extension with context-aware BPMN elements and a modeling guideline	Focus on general modeling general context events, no implementation	B	○	○	●	○	○
[32]	Integration of an executable location constraint annotation into business process modeling languages	Integration of an executable location annotation in Petri nets and BPMN. Petri nets: Introduction of new constructs. BPMN: Usage of artifacts and associations	Extension of graphical and formal representation of Petri nets and BPMN by location constraints	Only location constraints during modeling	B/P	◉	●	●	○	○
[3]	Include location in process modeling and process mining	Geospatial information in event logs, process mining: Nodes represent geographic locations, and transitions represent the activities. Process model is visualized on a map	Location aspects of business processes are treated as "first class" modeling entities. Activity flow is secondary	Location data for process mining, process model from enhanced event logs	–	◉	○	●	○	●

Notation: **B**: BPMN, **P**: (colored) Petri nets, –: other/not specified; Categories: ○ only conceptual, ◉ description of implementation, ● actual implementation

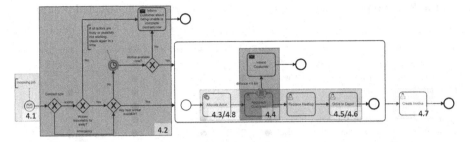

Fig. 1. Exemplary Real-life process from a craft business enhanced with location data

4   Concepts for Location-Aware Business Process Execution

In this section, we explain the different identified conceptual ways location-based data from IoT systems can influence executable mobile distributed processes. Table 2 shows a non-exhaustive list of the identified conceptual uses for location-aware business processes together with a classification of BPMN concepts that we will explain in more detail in the following sections. The following table also differentiates between single-instance and multi-instance, the first including concepts that can be used on a single execution instance of a process, whereas the latter implies the existence of at least two process instances (multi-instance).

4.1   Location-Based Automatic Start of Process Instances

Location data can be used to automatically start process instances, e.g. an even more specific assembly task starting on arrival at the customer. Primary context information, i.e., the single location of a entity alone, is not sufficient to start a process instance. Only when the location of at least one other entity or a different location for the same entity is available, metrics can be calculated to initiate a process instance, e.g. the event distance location with the place of fulfillment for the job being the event. Fundamental to that is the availability of location data outside the bound process instance for all involved entities.

Depending on the calculation of the used metric, logic is required to be included within an event start (conditional start event), meaning the calculation has to happen "outside" of the process instance's lifecycle, implying the start of the process instance is not bound to the BPMS but gets triggered externally. Depending on the viewpoint and the modeling choice, the triggering event of a process could also be modeled as part of a message start event, thus losing semantic information during the modeling. Coming back to the presented context levels of Küpper [21]: spatial information of the involved entities are primary data, as they are gained from sensors (or more specifically mobile IoT devices), and can not be used by themselves, whereas the distance between two entities is derived, thus secondary context, and can be used to start a process instance.

Table 2. Concepts for the use of location-based information in executed processes

Conceptual use	Involved BPMN concept				
	Task	Gateway	Boundary event	Single-instance	Multi-instance
Automatic start of process instances	○	○	○	●	○
Decision making through location-based data	○	●	○	●	○
Location-based task allocation	●	○	○	●	●
Location-based monitoring of tasks	●	○	●	●	●
Location-based event dispatching	●	○	●	●	○
Location-based automatic completion of tasks	●	○	●	●	○
Location-based automation of tasks	●	○	○	●	●
Location-based worklist reordering	●	○	○	●	●

4.2 Decision Making Through Location-Based Data

Decisions are a basic part of any modeling language and enable the structuring of the process by influencing the process flow [10]. Depending on the frequency of the location data available and needed, decisions can be implemented in all parts of the system architecture, from using an expression that gets evaluated directly within the BPMS, to using lifecycle hooks and execution listeners attached to the BPMS or deferring decisions to the middleware or possibly processing them as a stream using CEP, closing the abstraction gap between IoT data and human executable processes while including all three spatial context classifications. While location data could be collected with a sub-second frequency, the information gain and usefulness of that amount of redundant data is questionable and depends on the application area, but as we are using execution times for invoicing (see Sect. 4.7), the granularity of the data cannot be too coarse.

Other approaches for location-constrained tasks or processes also fall in this category, as, conceptually, location constraints describe the restriction or sole permission for the execution location of a task in regards to an earlier one. This means, that one task is only allowed to be executed at a different location than before (e.g., quality control, where the same station is not allowed to control itself) or the organizational efforts of synchronizing transport between multiple different places of fulfillment (branches).

4.3 Location-Based Task Allocation

The allocation of a task to a process participant specifies the responsibility for a single task or a group of tasks to a concrete user. During process modeling, tasks can get assigned to a certain user group whose members are candidates for execution, meaning the allocation happens deferred during the process execution [10,27]. While earlier approaches considered the use of location data for process models (cf. Sect. 2.2), the research gap of allocating concrete users to tasks based on location data has been neglected.

The realization of a location-based task allocation is primarily a task of a smart cross-system implementation. Let us explain this directly using the example application scenario: After all preliminary checks, the subprocess of concrete manual work starts with the allocation of the current process instance to exactly one worker. The start of the tasks triggers the calculation as well as the allocation itself. Because the BPMS itself does not store real-time data and because of the separation of the backend and the data-handling middleware, the BPMS has to either actively get the information or delegate the task to the middleware. Depending on the actual need, both possibilities are feasible. And even more, we then can either try to get the current location of all possible entities by directly querying the sensor and use the most current stored data as a fallback or solely rely on the most current known location. After calculation, a list of distances with unique identifiers for the corresponding actors is returned that needs to be sorted and then finally used for the allocation. Based on the different locations and the application area, different logical expressions could be included outside of the "closest to the target location" used in the real-world example.

Ultimately, the allocation gets sent to the BPMS, including the current distance to the target location, which can then be further used for supporting the actors and increasing transparency of the allocation process. Internally, after calculation, the task is finished, and the execution engine proceeds to the following task(s) (here: the nearest worker receives the task *Approach customer* to her interface and is assumed to start driving to the customer). As with Decision Model and Notation (DMN), where the goal is a decision between multiple process flows [33], the allocation of a single actor to a task based on location data can be understood as the boolean decision for one and against all other actors.

4.4 Location-Based Event Dispatching

The supervision of tasks in BPMN is conceptualized with the use of boundary events, where different reactions to events occurring during the execution of a single task can be modeled [10]. Those events can split the process flow during the execution of a single task or subprocess. BPMN defines conditional non-interrupting boundary events to trigger a separate flow based on a condition happening while one task is executed [23], which can be enriched by spatial data. Following the classification of spatial context data of Etzion [12], we can divide all occurring events into three classes, which can be modeled into the model based on their impact.

Within the application, as soon as the task *Approach customer* starts, meaning that the allocated worker is on their way to the customer, the actors' location can further be monitored to automatically dispatch the *Inform customer* task. As soon as the worker is within a radius of 5 km of the customer, a non-interrupting conditional boundary event is triggered which starts a send task – a service task used to model explicitly sending information – informing the customer about the imminent arrival of the worker.

4.5   Monitoring Process Execution

The inclusion of spatial information also eases the monitoring of process execution improving transparency by displaying all involved entities on a map, visualizing the physical environment where tasks are going to be performed including temporal properties of the process instance [22]. Furthermore, for multiple instances running in parallel, the inclusion of current and historic data could be used for the calculation of the median execution time of a single task or a group of tasks or the maximum distance traveled to a customer among the most recent n jobs.

Conceptually, the middleware has to keep calculating the distance of the allocated actor to the customer's location in the background and push the result as a process variable to the BPMS. Depending on the needs of the company, a fitting granularity of updates has to be chosen.

4.6   Location-Based Automatic Completion of Tasks

The process flow defines the basic order of all parts of a process model, where each element (excluding start and end events) has at least one predecessor and one successor [10]. Upon the completion of an element, all directly connected elements of the model are triggered, a process which can also be automated using location-based data. Both, the update frequency and the accuracy of location information are influencing the precision of automatically completing the current and proceeding into the following flows. Another factor to be noted is the fact that user tasks are not automatically executable in a BPMS and thus do not implement any logic [10]. Nevertheless, BPMSs typically provide lifecycle hooks as listeners that can be used to execute logic when certain states of the task's lifecycle, like *create*, *assignment*, or *complete* are reached.

Let us face the real-world application again. Arriving within 200 m of the customer's location, the active task is automatically terminated and the task *Replace heating* is started, i.e., the process models' control flow is actively influenced by location data. Conceptually, as soon as the allocated user enters the radius, the middleware sends an event to the provided endpoint of the BPMS to proceed with the process, again within the context of the entity distance location. After successfully finishing the job at the customer, the actor leaves the perimeter again, triggering the termination of the task within the BPMS, and gets removed from the current process instance.

4.7   Location-Based Automation of Tasks

Location data can be used for enhancing the execution of service tasks in BPMN to automate non-value-adding tasks like the documentation of work, as well as supporting tasks for value-adding processes. Due to the simple fact that most BPMS normally save records of historic execution data, this information can be used on a multi-instance basis to calculate and verify metrics like start and finish time, as well as custom location-specific data of tasks like comments made by field workers for specific entity locations (Imagine a heating engineer storing location specific information assigned to one customer). These comments can be used as supporting location-based information for future projects. And within our running example, the last task is creating an invoice, that can be automated or supported using the execution times of the current process instace tasks split into time driving and working on-site at the customer, simplifying and automating the billing process, while removing non-value-adding documentary work.

4.8 Location-Based Worklist Reordering

Taking a step back from a single executed process instance, location-based information can also be used to reorder the work list of an actor based on location information, e.g., the actual distance of a process participant to a point of interest like a customer location, i.e. entity and possibly event distance location. In contrast to the concept of work list reordering in Pflug et al. [25], who investigate the influence of randomly reordering tasks on the overall temporal performance, Petter et al. [24] use recommender systems in combination with BPM to use event logs to construct recommendations for the next task to get executed by a human actor. Following this approach, any metric calculated based on the location of an actor or a combination with other metrics can be used to rearrange the tasks within a work list of a certain user. Jeng et al. [19] already touched the topic within their local resource management, adding the work preferences of human resources and application-specific resource types and states to a decision matrix while also differentiating between filtering possible tasks or prioritizing them. Within the running example, imagine multiple open jobs, i.e., tasks from different process instances, at different customers not yet allocated to a single actor. Each of the available actors gets a list of those tasks on their mobile user interface sorted by distance to the corresponding jobs, and can then choose their next task based on this information.

5   Implementation

Our goal is to provide a system-based, fully executable location-based approach based on existing standard process management technology. In this section, we outline the BPM-based system architecture as well as the involved frameworks for a prototypical implementation.[1] Furthermore, we demonstrate the enactment of a typical mobile distributed process of a craft business.

Figure 2 summarizes the different tools and technologies used to execute the process. *Node-RED*[2] is a graphical programming tool used to collect, process, and simulate IoT data. It serves as the connecting part between the world of IoT and BPM by providing access to different nodes for, e.g., MQTT handling and basic HTTP. On the other side, the *Camunda Platform* (v7.18)[3] is used in

---

[1] https://github.com/LeoPoss/location-aware_bpm.
[2] https://nodered.org.
[3] https://camunda.com/en/platform.

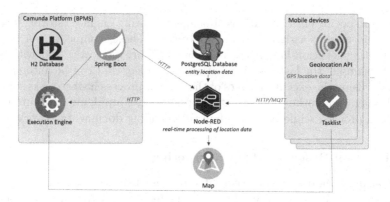

Fig. 2. System architecture for the presented implementation

combination with a *SpringBoot*[4] application to implement the BPMS, as well as the backend and frontend part. The Camunda platform comprises the execution engine and two frontend components that provide an overview of deployed processes and a user-based task list.

As described in Sect. 2 location-aware processes primarily depend on *fixed locations* as well as *entity and event distances* (the distances between two entities or between an entity and an event) that need to be calculated before treating the result similar to other data. Before being able to calculate the distance between two entities using for example the Haversine-Formula (see [7]) or third-party providers for navigation data like driving- or arrival time, depending on the actual use, we have to use geocoding to translate street names into numerical coordinates to calculate with. Still, on an environment or system level, the following preconditions have to be fulfilled to successfully use the implemented process: *(i)* all users that should participate in the process must have access to the BPMS (own account and mobile device for access); *(ii)* all actors have access to a mobile device that can determine their position; *(iii)* all field workers are assigned to the same user group within the BPMS; *(iv)* the BPMS has to implement and expose all needed endpoints for external integration.

The implementation adheres to the well-established data patterns of Russell et al. [27] explaining the usage and exchange of data in implementations of process models – a fundamental part bridging the abstraction between conceptual solutions and reasoned prototypical implementations. For this implementation approach, events generated by the data-handling middleware are actively pushed to the BPMS (immediately forwarding important information), whereas calculations made within the BPMS are actively pulling current location data. The exact interaction between pull- and push communication, data patterns, and appliances remain an open question, as they seem to be bound to the implementation and the decisions themselves, rather than the concepts.

---

[4] https://spring.io/projects/spring-boot.

6   Conclusion and Future Work

As seen in the related works, the idea of using spatial information to facilitate locally distributed work within a factory hall, or even mobile work, is not new and has been part of research for nearly 20 years. Neither is the combination of spatial information and business processes. Whereas using IoT devices as an enabler and coming from a real-world application rooted in an executable process at its base, this paper closes the gap between conceptual approaches for the use of location in BPM and the real world.

In this work, we summarize different ways of using contextual location information for the process based on the location of different entities, facilitating process execution and enabling further automation of process execution. Compared to earlier approaches, the process is efficiently executable using Camunda as the BPMS and can be easily extended because of the strict separation between the different systems. All main parts of single processes can be enriched using the location as contextual information during execution, from simply using the distance between two locations in an expression for logic gateways or start and end events (starting and finishing a process) and tasks (allocating a task to the user closest to an entity) up to terminating tasks based on the spatial information and dispatching events based on an entities location or the distance between two entities. Considering multiple concurrently running process instances, we can use location data to intelligently reorder the task list of all actors, use multiple different actors as candidates for the allocation of tasks or gain insights through monitoring their execution. The presented list of possibilities shows the upcoming potential of the combination of IoT and BPM by using contextual information in BPM to improve efficiency and improve the workflow of workers working within mobile distributed processes.

The remaining limitations for the prototypical implementation are, on the one hand, the missing synchronization between BPMS and middleware – during the process execution, values like user groups and included users have to be actively made available from the BPMS to the middleware – and on the other hand, the synchronization of busy states or different handling overall, as currently, the middleware keeps track of the occupancy of all workers (The simple allocation of an actor to a task does not imply them working on the task). In future work we will further conceptualize the use of contextual information for BPM with different processes and start reintroducing logic outsourced to the middleware back into BPM by extending the elements, making sure the decision logic is visible at all times and not encapsulated and hidden away from the process model. On the other hand, we will present formal descriptions for different location-based operators and their calculations and quantitatively validate the improvements made through the combination of IoT and BPM w.r.t throughput and cycle times.

Acknowledgement. This work is funded by the "Bayrische Forschungsstiftung (BFS)" within the project *IoT-basiertes Daten- und Prozessmanagement im Handwerk (TRADEmark)*.

References

1. Abowd, G.D., Dey, A.K., Brown, P.J., Davies, N., Smith, M., Steggles, P.: Towards a better understanding of context and context-awareness. In: Gellersen, H.-W. (ed.) HUC 1999. LNCS, vol. 1707, pp. 304–307. Springer, Heidelberg (1999). https://doi.org/10.1007/3-540-48157-5_29
2. Aoumeur, N., Fiadeiro, J., Oliveira, C.: Towards an architectural approach to location-aware business process. In: 13th IEEE International Workshops on Enabling Technologies: Infrastructure for Collaborative Enterprises. IEEE Computer Society (2004)
3. Behkamal, B., Pourmasoumi, A., Rastaghi, M.A., et al.: Geo-enabled business process modeling. In: 18th International Conference on Business Process Management (2020)
4. vom Brocke, J., Baier, M.-S., Schmiedel, T., Stelzl, K., Röglinger, M., Wehking, C.: Context-aware business process management. Bus. Inf. Syst. Eng. **63**(5), 533–550 (2021). https://doi.org/10.1007/s12599-021-00685-0
5. vom Brocke, J., Zelt, S., Schmiedel, T.: On the role of context in business process management. Int. J. Inf. Manag. **36**(3), 486–495 (2016)
6. Chiu, H.H., Wang, M.S.: Extending event elements of business process model for Internet of Things. In: 2015 IEEE International Conference on Computer and Information Technology; Ubiquitous Computing and Communications; Dependable, Autonomic and Secure Computing; Pervasive Intelligence and Computing. IEEE (2015)
7. Chopde, N.R., Nichat, M.: Landmark based shortest path detection by using A* and haversine formula. Int. J. Innov. Res. Comput. Commun. Eng. **1**(2), 298–302 (2013)
8. Compagnucci, I., Corradini, F., Fornari, F., Polini, A., Re, B., Tiezzi, F.: Modelling notations for IoT-aware business processes: a systematic literature review. In: Del Río Ortega, A., Leopold, H., Santoro, F.M. (eds.) BPM 2020. LNBIP, vol. 397, pp. 108–121. Springer, Cham (2020). https://doi.org/10.1007/978-3-030-66498-5_9
9. Decker, M., Che, H., Oberweis, A., et al.: Modeling mobile workflows with BPMN. In: 2010 Ninth International Conference on Mobile Business and 2010 Ninth Global Mobility Roundtable (ICMB-GMR). IEEE (2010)
10. Dumas, M., La Rosa, M., Mendling, J., et al.: Fundamentals of Business Process Management. Springer, Heidelberg (2018). https://doi.org/10.1007/978-3-662-56509-4
11. Dörndorfer, J., Seel, C.: A framework to model and implement mobile context-aware business applications. In: Schaefer, I., Karagiannis, D., Vogelsang, A., Méndez, D., Seidl, C. (eds.) Modellierung 2018. Gesellschaft für Informatik e.V., Bonn (2018)
12. Etzion, O.: Event Processing in Action. Manning (2011)
13. Gershenfeld, N., Krikorian, R., Cohen, D.: The Internet of Things. Sci. Am. **291**(4), 76–81 (2004)
14. Gopalakrishnan, S., Sindre, G.: Diagram notations for mobile work processes. In: Johannesson, P., Krogstie, J., Opdahl, A.L. (eds.) PoEM 2011. LNBIP, vol. 92, pp. 52–66. Springer, Heidelberg (2011). https://doi.org/10.1007/978-3-642-24849-8_5
15. Hallerbach, A., Bauer, T., Reichert, M.: Context-based configuration of process variants. In: 3rd International Workshop on Technologies for Context-Aware Business Process Management (TCoB 2008) (2008)

16. Hevner, A.R., March, S.T., Park, J., et al.: Design science in information systems research. MIS Q. **28**(1), 6 (2004)
17. Huebscher, M.C., McCann, J.A.: Adaptive middleware for context-aware applications in smart-homes. In: Proceedings of the 2nd Workshop on Middleware for Pervasive and Ad-Hoc Computing. ACM Press (2004)
18. Janiesch, C., Koschmider, A., Mecella, M., et al.: The Internet of Things meets business process management: a manifesto. IEEE Syst. Man Cybern. Mag. **6**(4), 34–44 (2020)
19. Jeng, J., Huff, K., Hurwitz, B., et al.: WHAM: supporting mobile workforce and applications in workflow environments. In: Proceedings Tenth International Workshop on Research Issues in Data Engineering. RIDE 2000. IEEE Computer Society (2000)
20. Johannesson, P., Perjons, E.: An Introduction to Design Science. Springer, Cham (2021). https://doi.org/10.1007/978-3-319-10632-8
21. Küpper, A.: Location-Based Services - Fundamentals and Operation. Wiley, Hoboken (2005)
22. de Leoni, M., Adams, M., van der Aalst, W.M., et al.: Visual support for work assignment in process-aware information systems: framework formalisation and implementation. Decis. Support Syst. **54**(1), 345–361 (2012)
23. OMG: Business Process Model and Notation (BPMN), Version 2.0.2 (2011). http://www.omg.org/spec/BPMN/2.0.2/
24. Petter, S., Fichtner, M., Schönig, S., et al.: Content-based filtering for worklist reordering to improve user satisfaction: a position paper. In: Proceedings of the 24th International Conference on Enterprise Information Systems. SCITEPRESS (2022)
25. Pflug, J., Rinderle-Ma, S.: Analyzing the effects of reordering work list items for selected control flow patterns. In: 2015 IEEE 19th International Enterprise Distributed Object Computing Workshop. IEEE (2015)
26. Rosemann, M., Recker, J., Flender, C.: Contextualisation of business processes. Int. J. Bus. Process. Integr. Manag. **3**(1), 47–60 (2008)
27. Russell, N., Van Der Aalst, W.M.P., Hofstede, A.T.: Workflow Patterns - The Definitive Guide. MIT Press, Cambridge (2015)
28. Schilit, B., Theimer, M.: Disseminating active map information to mobile hosts. IEEE Netw. **8**(5), 22–32 (1994)
29. Schönig, S., Zeising, M., Jablonski, S.: Towards location-aware declarative business process management. In: Abramowicz, W., Kokkinaki, A. (eds.) BIS 2014. LNBIP, vol. 183, pp. 40–51. Springer, Cham (2014). https://doi.org/10.1007/978-3-319-11460-6_4
30. Soffer, P., Hinze, A., Koschmider, A., et al.: From event streams to process models and back: challenges and opportunities. Inf. Syst. **81**, 181–200 (2019)
31. Stephan, P.: System architecture for using location information for process optimization within a factory of things. In: Proceedings of the 3rd International Workshop on Location and the Web - LocWeb 2010. ACM Press (2010)
32. Stürzel, P.: Modellierung und Ausführung von Workflows unter Berücksichtigung mobiler Kontextinformationen. KIT Scientific Publishing, Karlsruhe (2018)
33. Taylor, J., Fish, A., Vanthienen, J., et al.: Emerging standards in decision modeling. In: Intelligent BPM Systems: Impact and Opportunity. iBPMS Expo, Chicago (2013)
34. Tchemeube, R.B., Amyot, D., Mouttham, A.: Location-aware business process management for real-time monitoring of a cardiac care process. In: CASCON, vol. 13 (2013)

35. Webster, J., Watson, R.T.: Analyzing the past to prepare for the future: writing a literature review. MIS Q. **26**(2), xiii–xxiii (2002)
36. Wieland, M., Kopp, O., Nicklas, D., et al.: Towards context-aware workflows. In: CAiSE 2007 Proceedings of the Workshops and Doctoral Consortium, vol. 2, no. 25 (2007)
37. Zhu, X., Vanden Broucke, S., Zhu, G., et al.: Enabling flexible location-aware business process modeling and execution. Decis. Support Syst. **83**, 1–9 (2016)
38. Zhu, X., Recker, J., Zhu, G., et al.: Exploring location-dependency in process modeling. Bus. Process. Manag. J. **20**(6), 794–815 (2014)

Modeling Temporal and Behavioral Process Constraints (BPMDS 2023)

A Time-Aware Model for Legal Smart Contracts

Josef Lubas$^{(\boxtimes)}$ and Johann Eder

Department of Informatics-Systems, Universität Klagenfurt,
Klagenfurt am Wörthersee, Austria
{josef.lubas,johann.eder}@aau.at

Abstract. Smart Contracts that embody real world legal contracts require not only a sound and secure implementation but also a careful analysis of the underlying contractual commitments. Temporal clauses are abundant in contracts, requiring permissions and obligations to be executed in temporal relationships with observed events. Before signing a contract a thorough analysis, whether breaches of temporal clauses are imminent, whether all temporal obligations can be fulfilled are inevitable to avoid the cost of violating temporal commitments. We present a contract model that focuses on modeling temporal commitments explicitly. And we present techniques based on these contract models to analyze the temporal properties of contracts, in particular, whether a party can guarantee to fulfill all temporal commitments under all foreseeable circumstances. We present a framework that supports the development and negotiation of contracts precluding the risk of violating temporal clauses.

Keywords: Smart Contract · temporal clauses · controllability

1 Introduction

Formal modeling of contracts has a long tradition [16,18] and received renewed attention with the development of the concept of Smart Contracts exploiting the potential of blockchains and distributed ledgers [3,7,28]. *Legal Smart Contracts* [13] embody legally binding agreements between contracting parties by precisely encoding contract clauses as computer programs that perform certain actions in response to contract relevant events recorded on a blockchain.

There are still many open research questions for developing, designing, and deploying Smart Contracts [27,31]. As Smart Contract code is immutable once deployed on the blockchain, a major concern is the establishment and verification of its correctness and security at design-time. Events in recent years showed that vulnerable Smart Contract implementations can cause serious financial damage (the infamous DAO-hack [22]). Thus, extensive work on formal methods for assuring correctness and security of Smart Contract implementations has been conducted in recent years [7,28].

While verifying correctness and security of the implementation of Smart Contracts is a necessary step to facilitate Smart Contract adoption, another major

© The Author(s), under exclusive license to Springer Nature Switzerland AG 2023
H. van der Aa et al. (Eds.): BPMDS 2023/EMMSAD 2023, LNBIP 479, pp. 121–135, 2023.
https://doi.org/10.1007/978-3-031-34241-7_9

problem remains: A correct and secure implementation of a poorly designed contract or agreement may still lead to unforeseeable issues at run time. For example there could be unavoidable contract breaches due to conflicting (temporal) requirements. Therefore, prior work on the formalisation and analysis of traditional contracts and e-Contracts now also gained importance in the field of Smart Contracts [12,13].

Contracts and also Smart Contracts [4] typically contain temporal commitments, temporally constrained permissions and obligations (cancellation of a reservation until a certain deadline, guaranteed delivery date, duration of a lease contract, etc.). Surprisingly, the modeling and analysis of temporal commitments within Smart Contracts and the possibility of their fulfilment by the contracting parties did not receive much attention in research with the exception of a few approaches, e.g. the early attempt addressing temporal clauses in contracts proposed in [20].

The aim of the research present here is to support the development of contracts with temporal commitments. This requires a formal contract model that allows the modelling of temporal conditions. In addition, it also requires techniques to check the temporal properties of contracts, in particular to analyze whether the temporal conditions are conflicting and whether contract parties have the capability to act according to the contract without violating any temporal obligation. And last but not least, it requires tools which help the parties to design and negotiate temporal clauses for contracts such that the resulting contract is agreeable by all parties.

2   Running Example

We use the following simplified contract between a customer, a construction company, a supplier, and a sub-contracting company as a running example to illustrate the problem we address in this paper and also to demonstrate the solution we are proposing. This example shows a generic interaction between contract parties with special focus on temporal commitments and serves as a basis for introducing our model informally.

After the customer (A) commissions the construction company (D) the following terms apply:

1. D commissions company B to perform construction work.
2. D is obliged to commission a supplier C to deliver required materials to the construction side.
3. B guarantees to start construction work within 7 days after required materials are delivered to the construction side.
4. B guarantees to finish construction work within 2 weeks.
5. C guarantees delivery within 3–5 days.
6. After materials are delivered, D is obliged to inform A at least 7 days in advance about the start of the construction work.

Our example contains 6 clauses defining obligations, permissions and prohibitions between the contracting parties. In this example the contracting parties make certain temporal commitments where the fulfillment of these commitments is mutually dependent. For example clause 6 requires D to perform some action in advance of another parties action. However, the actual time at which the other party performs this action is unknown at design time of the contract. Thus, D is required to react to the observed circumstances at run-time. This scenario gives rise to the central question: "Can a contracting party (D) guarantee to fulfill its temporal obligation under all foreseeable circumstances?".

In order to support automated temporal contract analysis and based on that the negotiation of temporal commitments, we introduce a time-aware contact model. Further, we propose a framework for the detection of unavoidable contract breaches and for computing admissible temporal commitments.

3   A Time-Aware Contract Model

The necessity to reason about Smart Contracts on a more generic or abstract level than its implementation in source code, leads to the development of contract models inspired by models for choreographies and orchestrations [10], e.g. [17] describes contracts as choreography diagrams using tasks for representing the actions governed by the contract. We follow here a similar approach, however, focusing on events rather than tasks, as events are the items recorded on the blockchain when a Smart Contract is executed. We can view the entries in the blockchain created by the Smart Contract as an event log documenting the enactment of a Smart Contract instance. And in this view, a Smart Contract is some piece of code stored on the blockchain, implementing an automaton that sets actions depending on the sequence of events stored on the blockchain.

The mission of a model for a Smart Contract in this perspective is to define admissible sequences of events. In addition we provide means to express temporal clauses in a declarative way, i.e. to define which conditions on the time-stamps of the events are required to hold in the event log. This approach has the benefit that we are able to express contracts on a conceptual level independent from its implementation (e.g. in contrast to referring to timer events [17]).

We define a contract model in form of a special kind of process model consisting of nodes representing either events or control-flow structures (start/end of the contract, parallel-split/join and exclusive-split/join in order to express sequential, parallel- and conditional control flow, respectively) and edges between the nodes denoting precedence relationships between the nodes representing which sequences of events are admissible by the contract. Each event node is associated with a contract-party which may or must set this event. We call this party the controller of the event.

In addition the model features temporal constraints between events: lower-bound constraints require a minimal time span between events, while upper-bound constraint denote the maximum allowed time span between events. Duration constraints are combinations of upper- and lower-bound constraints and denote the admissible time-interval between events. Precedence constraints and duration constraints are redundant in the model but turned out to be quite convenient for modelers to express and comprehend temporal constraints. Each temporal constraint has a controller, the party which has to comply with this temporal constraint. These temporal constraints restrict when a party of the contract may or has to perform activities leading to the registration of the events.

Event nodes and temporal constraints may be contingent or non-contingent. It is in the sole discretion of the controller, when to set a non-contingent event. For an example: When a costumer may cancel an order within 14 days then it is under the control of the customer, when to execute the cancellation. Contingent events and durations, on the other hand, are not under full control of the controller, but may depend on circumstances of the environment (third parties external to the contract). For an example, if the compensation for a cancelled order has to be received by the customer within 8 days after the order is cancelled, the provider is limited by the fact that a transfer of funds may take between 1 and 4 days by the banking system.

Definition 1 (Time-Aware Contract Model). *A time-aware contract TC is a tuple (P, N, E, C), where:*

- *P is a set of contract parties with $ex \in P$ representing a universal external party.*
- *N is a set of nodes n with $n.type \in \{start, event, xor\text{-}split, xor\text{-}join, par\text{-}split, par\text{-}join, end\}$. Each $n \in N$ with $n.type = event$ is associated with a controlling party $n.x = p$ with $p \in P$ and a contingency indicator $n.i \in nc, cont$ for non-contingent events, contingent events resp. Each $n \in N$ is associated with an execution time point $n.t \in \mathbb{N}$.*
- *E is a set of edges $e = (n_1, n_2)$ with controller $e.x = n_2.x$ defining precedence constraints requiring that $n_2.t > n_1.t$.*
- *C is a set of temporal constraints with each $c \in C$ associated with a responsible party $c.x = p$ with $p \in P$ as controller, and a contingency indicator $c.i \in nc, cont$; We consider three types of temporal constraints between nodes $a, b \in N$ with $n.type = event|start|end$, and a distance $\delta \in \mathbb{N}$:*
  - *upper-bound constraints $ubc_p(a, b, \delta)$, requiring that $b.t \leq a.t + \delta$;*
  - *lower-bound constraints $lbc_p(a, b, \delta)$, requiring that $b.t \geq a.t + \delta$.*
  - *duration constraints $d_p(a, b, \delta_{min}, \delta_{max})$, requiring $a.t + \delta_{min} \leq b.t \leq a.t + \delta_{max}$*
- *All constraints between 2 nodes have the same controller and the same contingency indicator.*
- *The controller of a constraint between the nodes a and b has to be the controller of a or of b.*

With the techniques presented in the next section, we can analyze temporal properties of a temporal contract model, in particular, whether the contract model contains conflicts, which may necessarily result in the violation of temporal constraints. This notion of "free of conflicts" can formally be represented as dynamic controllability [9].

Besides this general analysis, we argue that it is also necessary to analyze the contract from the viewpoint of a particular party of the contract. The notion of contingency of the nodes and constraints of a contract depends on the view point, i.e. the flexibility of one party to decide when to set a non-contingent event, on the other hand is an uncertainty, and hence, a contingent event and time-span for the other party. In a contract view for a particular party p, all nodes and constraints not controlled by p are contingent.

Definition 2. *A time-aware contract* $TC = (P, N, E, C)$, *is a contract view for the party* $p \in P$, *iff for all nodes* $n \in N$ *with* $n.x = p : n.i = nc$, *for all* $c \in C$ *with* $c.x \neq p : c.i = cont$.

From a contract TC we can easily derive the contract view TC_p for a party p by setting the contingency indicators of all nodes and constraints not controlled by p to *contingent*. For our running example presented in Sect. 2 we derive TC_D, the view of party D with representation shown in Fig. 1:

- $P =$ {Customer A, Company B, Supplier C, Construction Company D, ex}
- $N =$ {(Start, start), (P1s, split),($MaterialOrdered_D$, event, nc)
  ($MaterialDelivered_C$, event, cont), ($CustomerInformed_D$, event, nc), (P1j, join), ($ConstructionWorkStarted_B$, event, cont),
  ($ConstructionWorkFinished_B$, event, cont), (End, end)}
- $E =$ {$(Start, MaterialOrdered_D)$,
  $(MaterialOrdered_D, MaterialDelivered_C)$, $(MaterialDelivered_C, P1s)$,
  $(P1s, CustomerInformed_D)$,
  $(P1s, ConstructionWorkStarted_B)$, $(CustomerInformed_D, P1j)$,
  $(ConstructionWorkStarted_B, ConstructionWorkFinished_B)$,
  $(ConstructionWorkFinished_B, P1j)$, $(P1j, end)$}
- $C = $ {$d_C(MaterialOrdered_D, MaterialDelivered_C, 3, 5, cont)$,
  $ubc_B(MaterialDelivered_C, ConstructionWorkStarted_B, 1, 7, cont)$,
  $lbc_D(CustomerInformed_D, ConstructionWorkStarted_B, 7, nc)$,
  $ubc_B(ConstructionWorkStarted_B, ConstructionWorkFinished_B, 14, cont)$
  }

The model includes 5 distinct parties, a set of nodes consisting of events governed by the contract (e.g. $MaterialDelivered_C$, etc.) and control-flow elements (e.g. 'Start', 'Split', etc.). C is the set of all temporal constraints derived from temporal clauses given by the contract. Since in this example we examine the contract in the view of D we define temporal constraints controlled by parties other than D to be contingent. For example from clause 3 we derive $ubc_B(MaterialDelivered_C, ConstructionWorkStarted_B, 7, cont)$ an upper-bound constraint requiring that B is responsible for starting construction work at most 7 days after materials are delivered by C, which is contingent from the view of D.

4   Temporal Feasibility of Contracts

Before signing a contract, it is important for a party to analyze, whether the temporal constraints are conflicting, whether it is possible to obey all the temporal obligations written down in the contract. This property of feasibility, we

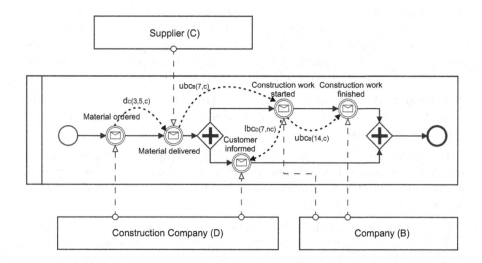

Fig. 1. Graphical representation of the contract model described in Sect. 3

are aiming here, is that a contract is dynamically controllable, which corresponds to the notion that the temporal requirements are not conflicting [9].

4.1 Dynamic Controllability

Controllability is stricter than satisfiability. To employ the notion of controllability (or dynamic controllability) is necessary. Satisfiability is too weak to guarantee that it is possible to execute the contract without violating a temporal constraint, as satisfiability only states that there exists an assignment of time points to events such that all temporal constraints are satisfied. This notion, however, ignores that some of the time-points cannot be controlled by a particular party. Controllability and dynamic controllability guarantee that all temporal obligations can be fulfilled in all (foreseeable) circumstances. For an example, a provider has to be able to fulfill the temporal obligation whenever a client invokes her permission of cancelling the order within the permitted cancellation period. The constraints, however, are still satisfiable, if the provider can only fulfill the obligation for a particular date. In an analogy, satisfiability corresponds to a winning situation in a one person game, while controllability corresponds to a winning situation in a two person game.

Dynamic controllability is well established for temporal constraint networks (TCN) and for temporally constrained process models. For process models the notion of dynamic controllability is considered to be the most relaxed criterion which still guarantees that the process controller is able to steer a process instance in a way, such that no temporal constraint is violated despite the uncertainties arising from contingent activity durations. Dynamic controllability requires that an execution strategy exists, where the controller is able to assign time-points to activities in response to observed durations of contingent activities. We transfer the notion of dynamic controllability here to the particularities of the time-aware contract model.

Definition 3 (Dynamic Controllability (DC)). *A contract-view TC_p of a contract $TC(P, N, E, C)$ is dynamically controllable for a contract party p, iff p is able to dynamically assign time points to every $n \in N$ it controls ($n.x = p$), such that no temporal constraint $c \in C$ is violated.*

The verification of temporal characteristics like consistency, satisfiability, or controllability is predominantly based on the formalism of Timed-Game Automata [30] or Temporal Constraint Networks (TCN) [6,15,24]. Especially Simple Temporal Networks with Uncertainty (STNU) [29] have been shown to be well suited for verifying dynamic controllability of process models [8].

A TCN is a graph-based formalism for reasoning on temporal constraints, consisting of nodes that represent time-points and edges expressing temporal constraints. Efficient sound and complete algorithms for verifying dynamic controllability of STNUS have been developed in the last years [14,15,24].

A STNU $S(\mathcal{T}, \mathcal{L}, \mathcal{C})$ is a graph where nodes (set $\mathcal{T}$) represent time points, and edges (set $\mathcal{L} \cup \mathcal{C}$) represent binary constraints between time points. The special node $Z \in \mathcal{T}$ represents the *zero* time point. Edges can be of type non-contingent (set $\mathcal{C}$) or contingent (set $\mathcal{L}$). Non-contingent edges (A, B, δ) between two time points A and B represent the requirement that the executor must assign a value to B such that $B \leq A + \delta$ is satisfied. A contingent edge (A^C, l, u, C) between two time points A^C and C states, that the value of C cannot be assigned by the executor but is guaranteed to be between l and u after the value of A^C. The value of the activation time point A^C must be assigned by the executor.

Approaches for checking dynamic controllability of process models require a mapping into an equivalent STNU, such that the resulting STNU is a complete representation of all elements occurring in the temporal model of the process. The mapping is based on applying a set of mapping rules [8].

4.2 Preparation Step

In a preparation step, we map a given contract into an equivalent STNU, similar to the approach for process models. And since we argue that a contract has to be feasible for each contracting party, it is required to perform this preparation step for each viewpoint of the contracting parties.

Thus, we first generate all the views from the contract model according to Definition 2. In order to map each view into an equivalent STNU, we introduce a normalization procedure in the next step. Through normalization we derive $TC_p \rightarrow TC_p*$, an equivalent contract view but all contingent upper-bound and lower-bound constraints are transformed into contingent duration constraints.

Definition 4 (Normalization). *Let $TC_p(P, N, E, C)$ be a time-aware contract model. TC_p* is a normalized TC_p such that: $\forall c \in C \in TC_p$ with contingency indicator $c.i = cont$:*

1. $\forall \ ubc(a, b, \delta), lbc(a.b.\delta') : \exists d(a, b, \delta', \delta) \in C \in TC_{p}*$
2. $\forall \ ubc(a, b, \delta), \nexists lbc(a, b, \delta') : \exists d(a, b, 1, \delta) \in C \in TC_{p}*$
3. $\forall \ lbc(a, b, \delta), \nexists ubc(a, b, \delta') : \exists d(a, b, \delta, \infty) \in C \in TC_{p}*$

The final preparation step is the mapping. In the following we describe a set of rules that transform a normalized contract view into an equivalent STNU.

Definition 5 (STNU-mapping). *Let $TC(P, N, E, C)$ be a time-aware contract model. The STNU $S(\mathcal{T}, \mathcal{L}, \mathcal{C})$ equivalent to TC is derived by applying the following rules:*

1. *The start node of the process is mapped into the STNU Z time point; the end node of the process is mapped into an end time point;*
2. *$\forall \ n \in N$ with n.type = event: n is mapped into a corresponding time point $n.t \in \mathcal{T}$;*
3. *$\forall \ (n1, n2) \in E$, a corresponding non-contingent edge $(n2, n1, 0)$ is in $\mathcal{C}$;*
4. *$\forall \ d(a, b, n_{min}, n_{max}) \in C$ with c.i = nc: is mapped into a corresponding non-contingent edge for the minimum duration $(b, a, -n_{min})$ and a non-contingent edge for the maximum duration $(a, b, n_{max}) \in \mathcal{C}$;*
5. *$\forall \ d(a, b, n_{min}, n_{max}) \in C$ with c.i = cont:*
   (a) *iff a.i = nc: $\exists$ a corresponding contingent link $(a, n_{min}, n_{max}, b) \in \mathcal{L}$;*
   (b) *iff a.i = cont: $\exists$ dummy time point n such that:*
       − *$\exists$ 2 non-contingent edges $(a, n, 0), (n, a, 0) \in \mathcal{C}$*
       − *and $\exists$ a contingent link $(n, n_{min}, n_{max}, b) \in \mathcal{L}$;*
6. *$\forall c \in C$ with contingency indicator c.i = nc:*
   (a) *$\forall \ ubc(a, b, \delta): \exists$ non-contingent edge $(a, b, \delta) \in \mathcal{C}$;*
   (b) *$\forall \ lbc(a, b, \delta): \exists$ non-contingent edge $(b, a, -\delta) \in \mathcal{C}$;*

The application of the mapping rules in Definition 5 transforms all events and control-flow elements of the contract into STNU nodes with the start node being transformed into the special Z time point. By applying rule 3, each precedence constraint is mapped into a non-contingent STNU edge. Non-contingent duration constraints are mapped to two STNU edges, one for expressing the minimum and one expressing the maximum duration bounds for the node duration (rule 4). Contingent duration constraints are mapped to a special contingent link (rule 5). If a duration constraint exists between two contingent nodes, we introduce a dummy time point between them. This is only a technical requirement and does not affect the semantic of the STNU. Any other temporal constraint is mapped into non-contingent STNU edges (rule 6).

By applying the above mapping, we derive a STNU encoding of the example contract model shown in Fig. 2. We used the common STNU notation with contingent edges dashed, inverted w.r.t. non-contingent edges, and labeled them with the contingent time point name. For a more compact presentation, in the figure we abbreviate event names $MaterialOrdered(MO)$, $ConstructionWorkStarted$ (CWS), $ConstructionWorkFinished$ (CWF), $MaterialDelivered(MD)$, $CustomerInformed(CI)$ and omit nodes resulting from the mapping of the par-split and par-join.

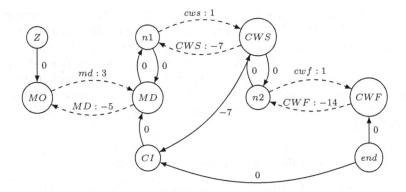

Fig. 2. STNU derived from the example contract shown in Sect. 2

4.3   Checking Dynamic Controllability

In order to check dynamic controllability of STNUs we rely on a sound and complete constraint propagation system called RUL [2]. In essence, the RUL system is a set of inference rules that are applied to derive additional temporal constraints from existing ones. By repeatedly applying these rules on a given STNU one of two events will happen eventually (1) no more additional temporal constraints can be derived, then the STNU is DC or (2) derived temporal constraints form a negative cycle indicating a contradiction.

For example a STNU with nodes A, B and a constraint C stating that B has to happen at most 5 time units after A (edge $A \xrightarrow{5} B$). Suppose that by applying one of the rules another constraint can be derived that requires A to happen at least 6 time units before B. This results in the following set of edges: $A \xrightarrow{5} B \xrightarrow{-6} A$, a negative cycle, meaning that the STNU is not DC.

Since such a contradiction ultimately means that at least one temporal constraint derived from temporal commitments of a contract cannot be satisfied without violating another, we can say that a STNU encoding of contract that has shown not to be contracting, also implies that the contract itself represents no contradiction and thus, is dynamically controllable.

5   Supporting the Design of Contracts

While checking temporal correctness is a necessary first step, it is arguably not sufficient to support the design of temporally correct contracts. We believe that contracting parties also need to know which temporal constraints are in conflict and how to resolve such conflicts, as basis for negotiating temporal commitments that all contracting parties are able to satisfy.

We constructed our example from Sect. 2 intentionally such that it is not DC. The RUL system applied on the STNU representation of that example correctly computes that the STNU is not DC. But what can we do with that information?

Which actions are necessary to remove the conflict? The RUL system itself does not provide a list of the conflicting constraints causing contract parties to manually reason about the origin of the conflict, probably using an approach based on trial and error. In our opinion (and in analogy to the approach described in [19]) a better approach is to exploit the RUL system. Since initially existing constraints represent temporal commitments in the contract, we can analyze how those additional temporal constraints, that led to a negative cycle, derived from the existing ones.

5.1 Identifying Conflicting Clauses in Contracts

The RUL system contains rules that generate additional STNU edges. In general, each rule applies to three STNU nodes X, Y, Z connected to each other through constraints $C1$ and $C2$ ($X \xrightarrow{C1} Y \xrightarrow{C2} Z$). The particular rule determines whether an additional constraint $C3$ ($X \xrightarrow{C1+C2} Z$) can be derived through transitivity. Such derivations are called *triangular reductions*.

For a given STNU that is not DC, the RUL system will derive a negative cycle. If we keep a history of all triangular reductions that led to the negative cycle, we are able to determine its origin (i.e. the set of initial constraints that are in conflict). The history of each constraint can be represented as binary tree, with internal nodes representing derived constraints and leaf nodes representing initial constraints. Traversing the tree structure from a node to its children represents the node provenance.

Considering Fig. 3 with $C6$ representing a negative cycle for a given STNU. The tree shows that $C6$ is derived by $C0$ and $C5$., with $C5$ itself being derived by $C4$ and $C3$ ($C0$ has no children, thus representing an initial constraint). Traversing the tree along the edges eventually gives a set of leaf nodes that represent the set of conflicting constraints from which the negative cycle derived ($C0, C1, C2, C3$).

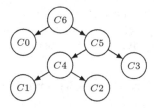

Fig. 3. History of $C5$ in the form of a binary tree.

5.2 Computing Acceptable Temporal Commitments

With the information about the set of conflicting constraints given, the natural subsequent question is how to re-design a contract such that it entails no conflicts instead. Since conflicting constraints originate in poorly designed contractual commitments that are unacceptable for at least one party, we argue that it lies within the interest of the affected parties to negotiate. Our ultimate goal in this work is therefore to support this negotiation between the affected parties by providing information about which temporal commitments are acceptable and which not. We can do that by computing the most restrictive bound that does not violate dynamic controllability.

Definition 6 (Most Restrictive Constraint). *Let $S(\mathcal{T}, \mathcal{L}, \mathcal{C})$ be an STNU. Let $A, B \in \mathcal{T}$ be two STNU nodes. The most restrictive non-contingent constraint between A and B is $A - B \leq \delta$, with δ the minimum value such that $S(\mathcal{T}, \mathcal{L}, \mathcal{C} \cup \{A - B \leq \delta\})$ is DC, and for any $\delta' < \delta$ $S(\mathcal{T}, \mathcal{L}, \mathcal{C} \cup \{A - B \leq \delta'\})$ is not DC.*

From Definition 6 follows that the most restrictive constraint bound for an arbitrary non-contingent STNU edge is the minimum value such that the respective STNU is DC. Increasing the computed value therefore means relaxing the given constraint. In terms of a contract, the most restrictive constraint value can e.g. be interpreted as the fastest delivery that can be guaranteed, the longest possible delay acceptable, the shortest deadline etc. Computing these values for given temporal commitments can be especially useful during the contract design phase as it provides the basis for negotiation.

The computation of the most restrictive constraint can be realized by a binary search [19]: Given a STNU edge $C = (A, B, \delta) \in$ STNU S, we compute the most restrictive value for δ by adding C to S, check whether S is DC and then iteratively either increase the value of δ if S is not DC, or decrease δ if S is DC until δ is the extremal value for which S is DC. Preliminary experiments showed that this approach is fast enough for the contracts we analyzed (cf. Sect. 5.4)

5.3 Tool Support

To show the feasibility of our approach we implement a tool as proof-of-concept prototype based on a temporal process designer tool [19] that applies the RUL system in order to check for conflicts in process models while keeping the history of all derived constraints. The tool[1] is also capable of identifying the subset of constraints that led to a conflict. In addition it is also possible to compute the most restrictive constraint that can be added to the process model without violating dynamic controllability. In the following we describe how this tool can be used to support the design of temporally correct contracts based on the running example introduced in Sect. 2.

The first task is to model the contract and subsequently transform it into an equivalent STNU (as described in the previous section). Once the corresponding STNU is derived, the tool performs the DC-check and provides a set of conflicting constraints by highlighting them in red (see Fig. 4). Note that the mapping rules, strictly seen, do not require that *CustomerInformed* is transformed into

---

[1] The GitLab repository for the designer tool is available under https://git-isys.aau.at/ics/Papers/temporal-process-designer.

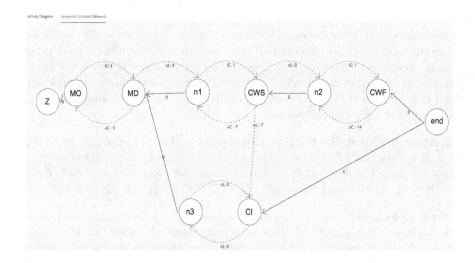

Fig. 4. Tool snippet: Conflict detection (Color figure online)

2 STNU nodes. This however is a technical requirement of our implementation and does not influence the correctness of the computation.

From the tool output we can identify a set of 4 conflicting constraints: $C1(MD, n1, 0)$, $C2(n1, CWS, 1)$, $C3(CWS, CIe, -7)$, $C4(CIe, n3, 0)$. Since $C1$ and $C2$ do not represent contractual commitments, we can reduce this set to $C2$ and $C3$ only since both originate from clause 3 and 6 of the contract, respectively.

This means that it is simply not possible for D to guarantee to inform the customer 7 days in advance of construction work. Which makes sense since D cannot control the actual start of construction work. Instead, it is possible that if B starts construction work only 1 day after the delivery happened, D will not be able to inform the customer in time and thus breach the contract.

After identifying the source of conflict, we may use the tool to compute time spans that would allow D to guarantee the fulfillment of the commitment instead. The user chooses one of the conflicting constraints (in our example we choose $C3$) and the tool computes the most restrictive constraint value (which is -1 in our example). The result means that D can always guarantee to inform the customer 1 day in advance of the start of construction work no matter when B will actually do so. With that information at hand, the contractual commitments could be re-negotiated.

5.4   Evaluation of Feasibility

To evaluate the approach we implemented a rather straightforward procedure for checking dynamic controllability - iteratively applying the rules until a fixpoint is reached or a negative cycle is detected. We measured an average computation time on a standard laptop with i7 CPU (2.6 GHz) and 16 GB RAM for a set of

randomly generated STNUs with 50 nodes and 10 constraints around 0.5 s. So
we can conclude that the approach is feasible for typical problem sizes. Applying an optimized algorithm for checking dynamic controllability such as [14]
will significantly enhance the performance of our approach. We plan to perform
evaluations based on real world contract data in follow-up publications.

6   Related Work

Formal analysis of Smart Contracts is predominantly performed on the implementation aspect of Smart Contracts (see [28] for an overview). Thus, a rich
body of research is focusing on general properties of software such as saftey and
liveness [26] as well as Smart Contract specific considerations such as liquidity
[1]. There are also research efforts generating correct-by-design Smart Contracts
based on finite-state-machines [21] and petri-nets [32]. However, none of these
approaches considers the particularities of representing and checking temporal
clauses.

Techniques from the research area of traditional contract analysis are considered relevant for our research purpose. Previous work by Hvitved [16] explores
different existing approaches for formalizing traditional contracts. Contracts in
general can be expressed in terms of petri nets [5,18], finite-state machines
[12,23] or in different types of logic such as dynamic and defeasible logic [11,13].

The contribution of the work presented here is to focus on the representation
of temporal clauses in Smart Contracts and to make recent results for temporal
reasoning in various types of temporal constraint networks usable for analyzing
temporal properties of contracts to avoid concluding a contract with conflicting
temporal obligations. The representation of temporal clauses will lead to the
generation of time aware implementations of Smart Contracts in analogy to [25]
for web-service orchestrations.

7   Conclusion

Designing correct Smart Contracts requires a thorough analysis of temporal
commitments to check whether each of the contracting parties is able to guarantee their fulfillment. We, therefore, developed a time-aware contract model
that sets the focus on temporal commitments of Smart Contracts. Based on
this model we were able to define temporal feasibility of contracts based on
the notion of dynamic controllability. For verifying whether a given contract is
dynamically controllable, we present a set of rules that can be applied for transforming time-aware Smart Contract models into temporally equivalent temporal
constraint networks STNUs. The formalism of STNUs allows us to apply well
established constraint propagation algorithms to check for dynamic controllability. Furthermore, we do not only check, but also identify which subset of the
temporal constraints are in conflict. We also support the incremental development or negotiation of temporal clauses in contracts by computing the strongest
temporal constraint which can be inserted without causing conflicts. Finally, we

showed the feasibility of our approach by implementing a tool as a proof-of-concept prototype. With this tool users can design time-aware contract models while making sure the contract is dynamically controllable and thus receive support for the negotiation of temporal commitments.

References

1. Bartoletti, M., Zunino, R.: Verifying liquidity of bitcoin contracts. In: Nielson, F., Sands, D. (eds.) POST 2019. LNCS, vol. 11426, pp. 222–247. Springer, Cham (2019). https://doi.org/10.1007/978-3-030-17138-4_10
2. Cairo, M., Rizzi, R.: Dynamic controllability of simple temporal networks with uncertainty: simple rules and fast real-time execution. Theor. Comput. Sci. **797**, 2–16 (2019)
3. Clack, C.D.: Smart contract templates: legal semantics and code validation. J. Digit. Bank. **2**(4), 338–352 (2018)
4. Clack, C.D., Vanca, G.: Temporal aspects of smart contracts for financial derivatives. In: Margaria, T., Steffen, B. (eds.) ISoLA 2018. LNCS, vol. 11247, pp. 339–355. Springer, Cham (2018). https://doi.org/10.1007/978-3-030-03427-6_26
5. Daskalopulu, A.: Model checking contractual protocols. arXiv cs/0106009 (2001)
6. Dechter, R., Meiri, I., Pearl, J.: Temporal constraint networks. Artif. Intell. **49**(1–3), 61–95 (1991)
7. Dixit, A., Deval, V., Dwivedi, V., Norta, A., Draheim, D.: Towards user-centered and legally relevant smart-contract development: a systematic literature review. J. Ind. Inf. Integr. **26**, 100314 (2022)
8. Eder, J., Franceschetti, M., Köpke, J.: Controllability of business processes with temporal variables. In: Proceedings of the 34th ACM/SIGAPP Symposium on Applied Computing, pp. 40–47 (2019)
9. Eder, J., Franceschetti, M., Lubas, J.: Time and processes: towards engineering temporal requirements. In: Proceedings of the 16th International Conference on Software Technologies - ICSOFT, pp. 9–16. INSTICC, SciTePress (2021). https://doi.org/10.5220/0010625400090016
10. Eder, J., Lehmann, M., Tahamtan, A.: Choreographies as federations of choreographies and orchestrations. In: Roddick, J.F., et al. (eds.) ER 2006. LNCS, vol. 4231, pp. 183–192. Springer, Heidelberg (2006). https://doi.org/10.1007/11908883_22
11. Fenech, S., Pace, G.J., Schneider, G.: Automatic conflict detection on contracts. In: Leucker, M., Morgan, C. (eds.) ICTAC 2009. LNCS, vol. 5684, pp. 200–214. Springer, Heidelberg (2009). https://doi.org/10.1007/978-3-642-03466-4_13
12. Flood, M.D., Goodenough, O.R.: Contract as automaton: representing a simple financial agreement in computational form. Artif. Intell. Law **30**, 391–416 (2022). https://doi.org/10.1007/s10506-021-09300-9
13. Governatori, G., Idelberger, F., Milosevic, Z., Riveret, R., Sartor, G., Xu, X.: On legal contracts, imperative and declarative smart contracts, and blockchain systems. Artif. Intell. Law **26**(4), 377–409 (2018). https://doi.org/10.1007/s10506-018-9223-3
14. Hunsberger, L., Posenato, R.: Speeding up the RUL⁻ dynamic-controllability-checking algorithm for simple temporal networks with uncertainty. In: Proceedings of the AAAI Conference on Artificial Intelligence, vol. 36, pp. 9776–9785 (2022)
15. Hunsberger, L., Posenato, R., Combi, C.: A sound-and-complete propagation-based algorithm for checking the dynamic consistency of conditional simple temporal networks. In: 2015 22nd International Symposium on Temporal Representation and Reasoning (TIME), pp. 4–18 (2015). https://doi.org/10.1109/TIME.2015.26

16. Hvitved, T.: Contract formalisation and modular implementation of domain-specific languages. Ph.D. thesis, Citeseer (2011)
17. Ladleif, J., Weske, M.: A legal interpretation of choreography models. In: Di Francescomarino, C., Dijkman, R., Zdun, U. (eds.) BPM 2019. LNBIP, vol. 362, pp. 651–663. Springer, Cham (2019). https://doi.org/10.1007/978-3-030-37453-2_52
18. Lee, R.M.: A logic model for electronic contracting. Decis. Support Syst. **4**(1), 27–44 (1988)
19. Lubas, J., Franceschetti, M., Eder, J.: Resolving conflicts in process models with temporal constraints. In: Proceedings of the ER Forum and PhD Symposium 2022. CEUR Workshop Proceedings, vol. 3211. CEUR-WS.org (2022). http://ceur-ws.org/Vol-3211/CR_103.pdf
20. Marjanovic, O., Milosevic, Z.: Towards formal modeling of e-contracts. In: Proceedings Fifth IEEE International Enterprise Distributed Object Computing Conference, pp. 59–68. IEEE (2001)
21. Mavridou, A., Laszka, A., Stachtiari, E., Dubey, A.: VeriSolid: correct-by-design smart contracts for Ethereum. In: Goldberg, I., Moore, T. (eds.) FC 2019. LNCS, vol. 11598, pp. 446–465. Springer, Cham (2019). https://doi.org/10.1007/978-3-030-32101-7_27
22. Mehar, M.I., et al.: Understanding a revolutionary and flawed grand experiment in blockchain: the DAO attack. J. Cases Inf. Technol. (JCIT) **21**(1), 19–32 (2019)
23. Molina-Jimenez, C., Shrivastava, S., Solaiman, E., Warne, J.: Run-time monitoring and enforcement of electronic contracts. Electron. Commer. Res. Appl. **3**(2), 108–125 (2004). https://doi.org/10.1016/j.elerap.2004.02.003
24. Morris, P.H., Muscettola, N.: Temporal dynamic controllability revisited. In: Proceedings of the AAAI, pp. 1193–1198 (2005)
25. Pichler, H., Wenger, M., Eder, J.: Composing time-aware web service orchestrations. In: van Eck, P., Gordijn, J., Wieringa, R. (eds.) CAiSE 2009. LNCS, vol. 5565, pp. 349–363. Springer, Heidelberg (2009). https://doi.org/10.1007/978-3-642-02144-2_29
26. Sergey, I., Kumar, A., Hobor, A.: Temporal properties of smart contracts. In: Margaria, T., Steffen, B. (eds.) ISoLA 2018. LNCS, vol. 11247, pp. 323–338. Springer, Cham (2018). https://doi.org/10.1007/978-3-030-03427-6_25
27. Singh, A., Parizi, R.M., Zhang, Q., Choo, K.K.R., Dehghantanha, A.: Blockchain smart contracts formalization: approaches and challenges to address vulnerabilities. Comput. Secur. **88**, 101654 (2020)
28. Tolmach, P., Li, Y., Lin, S.W., Liu, Y., Li, Z.: A survey of smart contract formal specification and verification. ACM Comput. Surv. **54**(7), 1–38 (2021). https://doi.org/10.1145/3464421
29. Vidal, T., Fargier, H.: Contingent durations in temporal CSPs: from consistency to controllabilities. In: Proceedings of TIME 1997: 4th International Workshop on Temporal Representation and Reasoning, pp. 78–85 (1997)
30. Zavatteri, M., Viganò, L.: Conditional simple temporal networks with uncertainty and decisions. Theor. Comput. Sci. **797**, 77–101 (2019)
31. Zheng, Z., et al.: An overview on smart contracts: Challenges, advances and platforms. Future Gener. Comput. Syst. **105**, 475–491 (2020)
32. Zupan, N., Kasinathan, P., Cuellar, J., Sauer, M.: Secure smart contract generation based on petri nets. In: Rosa Righi, R., Alberti, A.M., Singh, M. (eds.) Blockchain Technology for Industry 4.0. BT, pp. 73–98. Springer, Singapore (2020). https://doi.org/10.1007/978-981-15-1137-0_4

Efficient Computation of Behavioral Changes in Declarative Process Models

Nicolai Schützenmeier[1]([✉]), Carl Corea[2], Patrick Delfmann[2],
and Stefan Jablonski[1]

[1] Institute for Computer Science, University of Bayreuth, Bayreuth, Germany
{nicolai.schuetzenmeier,stefan.jablonski}@uni-bayreuth.de
[2] Institute for IS Research, University of Koblenz, Koblenz, Germany
{ccorea,delfmann}@uni-koblenz.de

Abstract. Modelling processes with *declarative process models*, i.e. sets of constraints, allows for a great degree of flexibility in process execution. However, having behavior specified by means of symbolic (textual) constraints comes along with the problem that it is often hard for humans to understand which exact behavior is allowed, and which is not (think for example of checking relationships between constraints). This becomes especially problematic when modellers need to carry out *changes* to a model. For example, a modeller must make sure that any alteration to a model does not introduce any unwanted or non-compliant behavior. As this is often difficult for humans, editing declarative process models currently bears the risk of (accidentally) inducing unforeseen compliance breaches due to some overlooked changes in behavior. In this work, we therefore present an approach to efficiently compute the behavioral changes between a declarative process model M and a corresponding (edited) model M'. This supports modellers in understanding the behavioral changes induced by an alteration to the constraints. We implement our approach and show that behavioral changes can be computed within milliseconds even for real-life data-sets.

Keywords: Behavioral Changes · Declare · Re-Modelling Support

1 Introduction

In the field of business process management, modelling processes with *declarative process models* – as opposed to using imperative (flow-chart-like) process models – is receiving increased attention [8,19]. In essence, declarative process models allow for a definition of business processes as sets of declarative constraints, where any behavior within these constraints is allowed [15].

While this bears many advantages in regard to flexibility, a disadvantage of declarative process models is that they are often-times harder to understand [10,14], i.e., the modeller has to fully understand all constraints and their inter-relations to assess which sequences of activities are allowed, and which are not. This becomes increasingly challenging when modellers need to make *changes* to

H. van der Aa et al. (Eds.): BPMDS 2023/EMMSAD 2023, LNBIP 479, pp. 136–151, 2023.
https://doi.org/10.1007/978-3-031-34241-7_10

a model, e.g., deleting some constraints. In such cases, a modeller needs to fully understand the *behavioral changes* induced by changing the model, in order to ensure that no non-compliant behavior accidentally becomes allowed due to the change (or vice-versa, that no important behavior becomes unsupported).

To support modellers in this task during re-modelling, we present an approach for computing behavioral changes between a declarative process model M and a second model M' (where M' is derived from M by any number of changes to M). This can prove to be useful for a) understanding behavioral changes induced by any alteration, and b) leveraging such insights for comparing change operations (e.g., deciding which constraint to delete). Here, our contributions are as follows:

- We present an approach for computing the behavioral changes between two declarative process models – in the following denoted M and M' – (Sect. 4). To this aim, we utilize automata representations of the original declarative process models and compute difference automata. Based on this representation, we show how behavioral changes can be computed by generating admissible traces (up to user-defined lengths) over the difference automata.
- We implement our approach and conduct an evaluation with real-life data-sets (Sect. 5). We show how our approach and implementation can be used to efficiently compute and visualize behavioral changes within (milli)seconds.

As we build on the notion of automata representations of declarative process models, we present an initial foundational discussion on the relation between behavioral changes and automata theory in Sect. 3. Here, we also propose results for concretely verifying hierarchical relations (e.g., subsumption) between declarative constraint-sets. Our discussion is based on the preliminaries presented in Sect. 2 and is concluded in Sect. 6.

2   Motivation and Prerequisites

In this paper, we will consider the DECLARE [15] standard as a concrete language for declarative process models. DECLARE comes with a set of predefined constraint types that allow end-users to define constraints over company activities. For example, the constraint RESPONSE(a, b) states that each activity a must eventually be followed by an activity b. We will formalize the syntax and semantics of DECLARE in Sect. 2.2.

2.1   Motivation and Related Work

The setting of this work is that companies might have a declarative process model M which may have to be changed over time, because, for example, relevant regulations have changed. This change will result in an altered process model M'. A change operation σ is one of the following functions (i) $a(\phi) = M \cup \phi$ *(Adding)*, or (ii) $d(\phi) = M \setminus \phi$ *(Deletion)* applied to a set of constraints M. We write $M' = \sigma(M)$ for the constraint-set obtained by applying σ to the original model M. Note that "updating" can be achieved via a combination of the above.

Original Model M	Altered Model M'	Allowed Behavior (Examples)
Response(a, b)	Response(a, b)	Behavior in M:
Response(b, c)	Response(b, c)	✓abxc ✓bcx ✗aebdc ...
Response(d, e)	~~Response(d, e)~~	Behavior in M':
	Response(a, e) *(NEW)*	✗abxc ✓bcx ✓aebdc ...

Fig. 1. Declarative process model M, corresponding (altered) process model M', and examples of accepted (✓) and violating (✗) traces.

Motivational Example. Consider the example shown in Fig. 1. The exemplary model M (left) originally contains three RESPONSE-constraints. As a motivational example, assume the original model M is altered by both deleting one constraint and adding another, resulting in M' (cf. Figure 1 (middle)). As can be seen in the most right column, this results in direct *behavioral changes*. For example, the sequence abxc is not allowed anymore (as in M' the activity a should be followed eventually be an activity e), and the sequence aebdc is now allowed (which was not allowed before). For long-term model management, understanding these changes is of utmost importance, as modellers need to be aware whether the alteration to the process model yielded any non-compliant behavior (or vice-versa, whether important behavior becomes unsupported) [22]. However, even in such small examples, manually considering all possible changes may be unfeasible, as it would require humans to consider all interrelations between constraints. Here, approaches are needed that support modellers in understanding behavioral changes during re-modelling. Thus, the aim of this work is to develop an approach for computing the behavioral changes, i.e., a concrete set of traces, between an original model M and an altered version M'.

Related Work. At the core, this work is related to *comparing* declarative process models, respectively, their languages and behaviors. The idea of verifying *hierarchical* relations between declarative process models has been introduced in works such as [13]. That work, or the approaches in [18,19], offer techniques to verify the *equivalence* of two specifications. However, the setting of this work is a different one: Here, we are trying to understand *differences* between the specifications. Understanding such differences, e.g., in the scope of (re-)modelling, is crucial to ensure any changes to the model do not result in any unwanted behavior, or to consider a trade-off between different change operations (e.g., deciding which constraint to delete). However, to the best of our knowledge, this topic of *understanding* behavioral changes during (re-)modelling – although being directly motivated from the long-term management of declarative specifications – has been given little attention. To clarify, there is a variety of works investigating the behavioral comparison of process models and languages, e.g., based on behavioral profiles [16], language quotients or the notion of process entropy [17]. Those works allow to *measure* notions related to precision [1,20], or language extension [17], by means of a numerical value (mostly between 0 and 1). However, those works do not allow to concretely *identify* the set of traces that is different between the models. This would however be vital for experts to inspect this set of traces - it is clear that behavior is "different" in a re-modelling setting; what is not clear is whether there are any *unwanted* changes in the behavior, which is not possible to determine only by means of a value. As a result, this work extends the existing body of knowledge by presenting techniques to identify the concrete set of traces corresponding to behavioral changes between two specifications. This allows the modeller to comprehend the exact changes in behavior. The authors in [21] investigate the effects of manual changes to declarative models, which is closely related to the problem related in our work.

The idea of behavioral changes between two specifications has initially been discussed in a previous work [5]. However, a limitation of that work is that a set of traces (to be compared) has to be provided. So either, a company has to provide a concrete set of traces, or, all possible traces up to a certain length have to be considered (which is not feasible, as this would scale exponentially). In this work, we solve this problem by computing difference automata of M and M', and utilizing these difference automata as input for a novel trace generation algorithm. As we will show, our proposed approach performs very well also for real-life data-sets (in the range of (milli)seconds), and therefore allows for a feasible and efficient computation of behavioral changes.

2.2 Declarative Process Models

The previous section has informally introduced declarative process models. The formal definition follows:

Definition 1 (Declarative Process Model). *A declarative process model is a tuple $M = (A, T, C)$, where A is a set of propositions, T is a set of templates (i.e., constraint types), and C is the set of constraints, which instantiate the template elements in T with activities in A. For readability, we will denote declarative process models as a set of constraints (C).*

In DECLARE, next to the introduced RESPONSE constraint-type, many other predefined templates are available. For example, CHAINRESPONSE(a, b) states that an activity a must *directly* be followed by an activity b. Negations are also available; for example, NOTRESPONSE(a, b) states that any activity a must never be followed by an activity b. For further constraint types, please refer to [15].

For all DECLARE constraints, the semantics are traditionally defined with linear temporal logic on finite traces (LTL$_f$) [6]. The underlying idea is that time is represented as a linear sequence $T = \langle t_1, \ldots, t_m \rangle$, where t_1 is the designated starting point. LTL$_f$ formulas can then be used to specify properties that must hold over this sequence. LTL$_f$ formulas are built from a set of symbols $\mathcal{A}$ and are closed under the Boolean connectives, the unary operator $\mathbf{X}$ (*next*), and the binary operator $\mathbf{U}$ (*until*). An LTL$_f$ formula φ is then built via the grammar

$$\varphi ::= a | (\neg\varphi) | (\varphi_1 \wedge \varphi_2) | (\varphi_1 \vee \varphi_2) | (\mathbf{X}\varphi) | (\varphi_1 \mathbf{U} \varphi_2).$$

with $a \in \mathcal{A}$. Intuitively, $\mathbf{X}\varphi$ denotes that φ will hold at the next point in the sequence, and $(\varphi_1 \mathbf{U} \varphi_2)$ denotes that φ_1 will hold until the point in the sequence when φ_2 holds. From these basic operators, the operators $\mathbf{F}$ and $\mathbf{G}$ can be derived: $\mathbf{F}\varphi$ (defined as $\top\mathbf{U}\varphi$) denotes that φ will hold (eventually) in the future. $\mathbf{G}\varphi$ (defined as $\neg\mathbf{F}\neg\varphi$) denotes that φ will hold for all following states. As an example, the semantics of RESPONSE(a,b) are defined as $\mathbf{G}(A \rightarrow \mathbf{F}(B))$. Likewise, NOTRESPONSE(a,b) is defined as $\mathbf{G}(A \rightarrow \neg\mathbf{F}(B))$.

For any LTL$_f$ formula (or constraint) φ, we say that t satisfies φ, denoted $t \models \varphi$, if φ holds in t_1. For a DECLARE process model, given its set of constraints C, a trace t satisfies C if t satisfies all $c \in C$.

The set of traces that satisfy the declarative model is also referred to as its *language*. Given a declarative model $M = (A, T, C)$, we define the function $\epsilon : \mathcal{U}_\mathcal{M} \times A^* \rightarrow \{\top, \bot\}$ via

$$\epsilon(M, t) = \begin{cases} \top \text{ if for all } c \in C : t \text{ satisfies } c \\ \bot \text{ otherwise} \end{cases}$$

where $\mathcal{U}_\mathcal{M}$ denotes the universe of all declarative process models. This function takes as input a declarative process model and a trace $t \in A^*$, and returns $\top$ if the trace satisfies the declarative process model (and $\bot$ otherwise). In turn, we define the *language* $\mathcal{L}$ of a model M as follows.

Definition 2 (Language). *Given a declarative process model M, the language $\mathcal{L}$ w.r.t. M is defined via $\mathcal{L}(M) = \{t \in A^* \mid \epsilon(M, t) = \top\}$.*

2.3 Automata Theory

The approach presented in this work exploits the research line of representing declarative specifications as finite state automata [7]. In the following, we briefly introduce the basic concepts and algorithms of automata theory.

Definition 3. (FSA, [12]). *A **deterministic finite-state automaton (FSA)** is a quintuple $D = (\Sigma, S, s_0, \delta, F)$ where Σ is a finite (non-empty) set of symbols, S is a finite (non-empty) set of states, $s_0 \in S$ is an initial state, $\delta : S \times \Sigma \rightarrow S$ is the state-transition function (which, given a state s and a symbol σ, specifies the state $s' = \delta(s, \sigma)$ that is reached), and $F \subseteq S$ is the set of final states.*

A *run* of an FSA D as above is a finite sequence $\rho = s_0\sigma_0 s_1\sigma_1 \ldots \sigma_{n-1}s_n$, alternating states and labels, s.t. $s_{i+1} = \delta(s_i, \sigma_i)$ for all $0 \leq i < n$ and $s_n \in F$. Given ρ as above, its corresponding *trace* $\sigma_0 \ldots \sigma_n$, denoted by $\lambda(\rho)$. Let $R^n(D)$ denote the set of all runs of length n for an FSA D. The **language** $\mathcal{L}$ w.r.t. D is then defined via $\mathcal{L}(D) = \{\lambda(\rho) \mid \rho \in R^n(D), n \geq 0\}$ [8].

Note that in this work, we assume an automaton to be minimized [12].

2.4 Transformation of Declarative Process Models to Finite State Automata

As noted in [7], the language of any declarative process model M is *regular*, i.e., by definition, it can be expressed by means of a finite state automaton

D [4] (s.t. $\mathcal{L}(D) = \mathcal{L}(M)$). To generate an FSA-representation of a DECLARE model $M = (A, T, C)$, each DECLARE constraint $\tau \in C$ is transformed to an individual finite state automaton D_τ. For every D_τ, the alphabet consists of the activities of the process and the accepted words are exactly those whose corresponding traces are not forbidden by the corresponding constraint, i.e., $\omega \in \mathcal{L}(D_\tau) \iff \omega$ is not forbidden by τ. To consider the DECLARE model with all of its constraints, we have to construct an automaton that represents the conjunction of all constraints. For a declarative process model $M = (A, T, C)$, this can be achieved by computing the *product automaton* [7] of all automata D_τ (for all $\tau \in C$).

We denote the universe of all possible declarative process models as $\mathcal{U}_\mathcal{M}$, and the universe of all possible deterministic FSAs as $\mathcal{U}_\mathcal{D}$. Then, we define the transformation of a declarative model to an FSA as follows.

Definition 4. ([8]). *The transformation function D for a declarative process model M is defined as a function $D\colon \mathcal{U}_\mathcal{M} \to \mathcal{U}_\mathcal{D}$, which transforms M into the corresponding FSA $\in \mathcal{U}_\mathcal{D}$. In the following, for a declarative process model M, we refer to its automaton as its "corresponding automaton D", instead of $D(M)$.*

Example 1. Fig. 2 shows the corresponding finite state automata D and D' for the DECLARE process models M and M' introduced in Fig. 1.

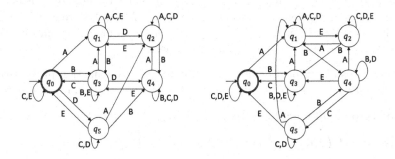

Fig. 2. Automata D and D' for DECLARE models M (left) and M' (right).

3   Foreword: Difference Automata

A *difference automaton* $\mathrm{Diff}_{D,D'} = D \setminus D'$ is an automaton that represents all traces that are accepted by an automaton D but not by D'. As we will show, using difference automata allows to compute the exact behavioral changes between two declarative process specifications (cf. Sect. 4). The use of difference automata however also allows to verify *general* properties for hierarchical relations (e.g., inheritance), which we discuss first in this section. Details on difference automaton construction will be provided in Sect. 4.1.

Following the terminology in [13], we say that a declarative process model M' specializes M, if the set of traces accepted by M' is a subset of the set of traces accepted by M. Vice versa, we say that M' generalizes M for the other direction. Importantly, these notions of inheritance are *purely semantic* - specialization and generalization are defined over language subsumptions. In other words, we do not check whether the *set of constraints* is a subset of the other, but whether a *language* is contained in another. To do so, we exploit that the transformation from M to its corresponding automaton D is language preserving, and propose to apply difference automata for inheritance verification.

Let two declarative process models M, M', and corresponding automata D, D' as before. Then, consider the union $\mathbf{U}$ of both difference automata, i.e., $\mathbf{U}(D, D') = (D \setminus D') \cup (D' \setminus D)$. Consider as reference the areas of the Venn-diagram in Fig. 3. Then, for $\mathbf{U}$, one of the following four conditions must hold[1]:

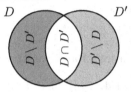

Fig. 3. Reference Venn-diagram.

1. The area $D \setminus D'$ (●) is empty, meaning there is no trace accepted by M which is *not* accepted by M'. Hence, M' generalizes M.
2. The area $D' \setminus D$ (○) is empty, meaning that, analogously, M' specializes M.
3. Both areas in $\mathbf{U}$ are empty (●,○), meaning there is no trace which is not also accepted by the other. As a result, this means M and M' are equivalent.
4. Neither area ● or ○ is empty, so, the two languages are incomparable, as no set of accepted traces is a subset of the other.

These cases allow for a definition of the following verification properties for hierarchies. Proofs follow directly from the definition of the symmetric difference.

Proposition 1 (Generalization). $\mathcal{L}(M) \subseteq \mathcal{L}(M')$ *iff* $D \setminus D' = \emptyset$.

Proposition 2 (Specialization). $\mathcal{L}(M') \subseteq \mathcal{L}(M)$ *iff* $D' \setminus D = \emptyset$.

Proposition 3 (Equivalence). $\mathcal{L}(M) = \mathcal{L}(M')$ *iff* $D \setminus D' = D' \setminus D = \emptyset$.

These technical results provide new means for the verification of hierarchies between declarative specifications, and extend the results in [13] with concrete means for hierarchy verification based on difference automata. Note that as mentioned, it follows that if both $D \setminus D'$ and $D' \setminus D$ are non-empty, then M and M' are incomparable (i.e., neither $\mathcal{L}(M') \subseteq \mathcal{L}(M)$ nor $\mathcal{L}(M) \subseteq \mathcal{L}(M')$ hold).

4   Computation of Behavioral Changes

We now introduce our approach for computing the behavioral changes between an original declarative process model M and an altered version M'. Figure 4

---

[1] Note that we assume both D and D' to be satisfiable.

shows our approach overview. Our approach takes as input two declarative process models M and M' and computes the set of traces (up to a user-defined trace-length) that are only accepted in exactly one of the models (but not the other). We refer to these traces as the *behavioral differences*, or changes, between M and M'. These traces can be provided to the expert, in order to inspect whether the alteration from M to M' introduced any unwanted behavioral changes. Our approach is divided into four steps (cf. Fig. 4). As a first step

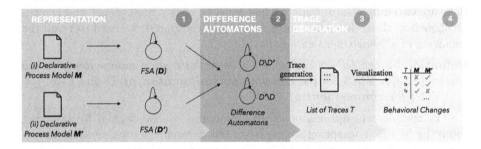

Fig. 4. Approach overview for computing behavioral changes.

(1), we transform both models M and M' to finite state automata, denoted D and D' (see Sect. 2.4). This allows us to perform needed operations, in particular, computing the difference automata, in step two (2). Based on the difference automata, as step three (3), we compute all traces (up to a length defined by the user) which are only allowed in one declarative process model (but not the other). Concretely, traces are computed by considering the difference automata and generating all corresponding, admissible runs (traces) up to the predefined trace-length via a breadth-first search. The result of this step is a set of traces (w.r.t. the user-defined trace-length) that corresponds to any behavioral changes. As a final step (4), these insights can then be presented for inspection, e.g., *Was any (unexpected/unwanted) behavior lost due to the model alteration?*, or *is any (unexpected/unwanted) behavior now allowed after the model alteration?*. In this work, we show as an example a concrete visualization techniques based on the trace sampling approach presented in [3]. However, the insights gained in step (3) can also be plugged in to any other form of (mining) tool.

A clear advantage of our approach is that there is no need for verifying traces against models (which would be a bigger computational burden). Instead, we exploit the difference automata, which directly encode all behavior changes in our setting. Any behavior outside the difference automata will automatically be the same for M and M', so it can be disregarded during the analysis of behavioral changes. As a result, our approach only computes the needed traces (as opposed to computing all possible traces up to a certain length and then verifying which traces are accepted). As we will show, this allows us to efficiently compute behavioral changes even for real-life data-sets (cf. Sect. 5).

In the following, we will present the individual steps of our approach in detail. As a running example, we will often refer to M, M' from Fig. 1.

4.1   (Steps 1+2) Computing Difference Automata

We recall that the input of our approach is two declarative process models M and M'. These models are initially transformed into corresponding finite state automata, denoted D and D' (Step (1), cf. Sect. 2.4). Subsequently, in step two (2), we compute the two difference automata $D \setminus D'$ and $D' \setminus D$. Importantly, there are **two** difference automata which must be constructed ($D \setminus D'$ and $D' \setminus D$). To show how these difference automata can be computed, we need to recall the definition of a *complement automaton* [12]:

Definition 5. *Let* $D = (\Sigma, S, s_0, \delta, F)$ *be a finite state automaton. We call* $D^C := (\Sigma, S, s_0, \delta, S \setminus F)$ *the* **complement automaton of** D *and* $\mathcal{L}(D^C) = \Sigma^* \setminus \mathcal{L}(D)$ *the* **complement of** $\mathcal{L}(D)$.

The complement automaton of an automaton can be derived by swapping accepting and non-accepting states. Now, the *difference automaton* [12] can be defined by using the construct of the complement automaton:

Definition 6. *Let* D *and* D' *be two FSAs. Then, the automata* $\mathrm{Diff}_{D,D'} := D \times D'^C$ *and* $\mathrm{Diff}_{D',D} := D' \times D^C$ *are called the* **difference automata**.

We recall the two automata D and D' from Fig. 2, which represent the two DECLARE constraint-sets M and M' introduced in Fig. 1. The first difference automaton $\mathrm{Diff}_{D,D'}$ is illustrated in Fig. 5. The language $\mathcal{L}(\mathrm{Diff}_{D,D'})$ consists of all words which are accepted by D but not by D'. Hence, it represents all traces, which were lost by transforming process model M into process model M' (cf. Figure 1).

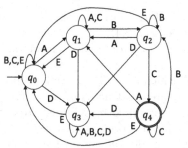

Fig. 5. Difference automaton $\mathrm{Diff}_{D,D'}$.

The second difference automaton $\mathrm{Diff}_{D',D}$ is analogous and represents all traces which are accepted by D' and not by D. Note that $\mathcal{L}(\mathrm{Diff}_{D',D})$ represents the set of all new traces, which where added by the transformation of model M into M'. For reasons of space, the second automaton $\mathrm{Diff}_{D',D}$ is not shown.

4.2   (Step 3) Trace Generation

As a next step in our approach (3), we generate all accepted traces (up to a user-defined length) over the difference automata from step (2). We generate all traces via a breadth-first search on the FSA graph structure, i.e., for each difference automaton, we begin in the initial state and generate all admissible runs up to the user-defined length by iteratively traversing through the FSA, storing only paths (= traces) ending in an accepting state.

Example 2. We recall the difference automaton $\text{Diff}_{D,D'}$ shown in Fig. 5. Recall that this difference automaton encodes all behavioral changes that are <u>not</u> allowed anymore after changing the underlying declarative constraint-set M to M' (cf. Fig. 1). Here, for a user-defined trace-length of 4, the set of all traces (...that are not allowed anymore after the model change) are *abc, babc ,cabc, eabc, aabc, acbc, abbc, abcc.* A second set of traces for $\text{Diff}_{D',D}$ can be computed analogously (There are 85 traces for $\text{Diff}_{D',D}$ with max. trace-length 4).

As a result, using the described trace generation method, we can obtain two sets of traces: traces (i.e., the behavior) which are not allowed anymore after the model change, and traces, which are now newly added after the model change. We acknowledge that the subscripts in "$\text{Diff}_{D,D'}$" (and always getting the "direction" of the difference automaton right) might be cumbersome or confusing for modellers. Therefore, we introduce the following auxiliary notation.

Definition 7. *Consider a user-defined trace-length l. Furthermore, let two automata D, D', and the two corresponding difference automata $\text{Diff}_{D,D'}, \text{Diff}_{D',D}$. Then, define the sets of traces T_{lost}^l and T_{added}^l via*

$$T_{lost}^l = \{L \in \mathcal{L}(\text{Diff}_{D,D'}) \mid |L| \le l\}, \quad T_{added}^l = \{L \in \mathcal{L}(\text{Diff}_{D',D}) \mid |L| \le l\}.$$

In other words, T_{lost}^l denotes the set of traces (w.r.t. a trace-length l) that corresponds to *lost* behavior (behavior not allowed anymore after the model change), and T_{added}^l denotes the set of traces w.r.t. l that corresponds to behavior that was added with the model change (not possible before). It is easy to see that the concrete sets can be obtained via the proposed trace generation approach.

4.3 (Step 4) Presentation of Behavioral Changes

The obtained sets of traces T_{lost}^l and T_{added}^l can now be presented to the user, s.t. the expert can assess whether the alteration to the declarative process model induces any unwanted behavioral changes.

An example of how this could be presented to the user is shown in Fig. 6 (a). Here, for the two models M and M' from our running example (cf. Fig. 1) and a trace-length of 4, all corresponding traces from T_{lost}^l and T_{added}^l are listed, with an indication in which declarative model (M or M') the corresponding behavior is allowed. An overview such as the one in Fig. 6 (a) allows to quickly check the behavioral changes (in the form of traces). Arguably, if the user-defined trace-length parameter is set to larger values, the actual sizes of the sets T_{lost}^l and T_{added}^l may be too large as to show *all* traces in such a "list" overview. For instance, in the running example from Fig. 1, setting the trace-length parameter to 8 yields around 22k traces that would need to be considered. Processing such a high number of traces is likely unfeasible for humans. Here, we propose to build on the approach for selecting *representative traces*, proposed in [3]. Using different methods from sampling, that approach allows to pass a set of traces and returns a (much) smaller set of "representative" traces from that set [3]. This allows to present the expert a much smaller list of representative traces, i.e., a collection of traces that are representative for the behavioral changes. An example of this is shown in Fig. 6 (b), which shows the representative traces for our running example with a user-defined trace-length of 8 (>22k total traces). As can be seen, the lost behavior includes many traces that end with the activity c. The user can therefore verify whether this is an important behavior that should be kept (in that case requiring further re-modelling). Likewise, there is a lot of added behavior (traces) that allow to end with an activity b, without the activity c occurring. The user can leverage this insight to check whether this is compliant, or if c in fact must occur in the trace.

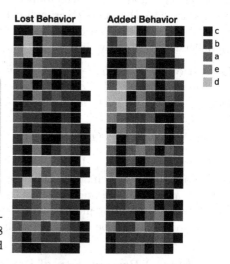

Traces	M	M'
abc	✓	✗
aabc	✓	✗
...	✓	✗
d	✗	✓
dbc	✗	✓
...	✗	✓

(a) List overview of behavioral changes between M, M', for a trace-length of 4 (8 traces lost in total and 85 traces added through model change).

(b) Representative traces of the behavioral changes between M, M', for a trace-length of 8 (roughly $22k$ different traces in total), using the visualization approach from [3].

Fig. 6. Two different visualization methods for presenting behavioral changes: List view (left) for smaller trace sizes, and representative sample trace visualization (right) for larger trace sizes.

To further provide users with more high-level insights (e.g., to help when the concrete set of traces is too large to be inspected manually), we also propose the two following baseline measures. For this, define $\#T^l_{lost} = |T^l_{lost}|$ and $\#T^l_{added} = |T^l_{added}|$, which describe the cardinality of behavioral changes.

Such measures are useful in general to assess the "magnitude" of an alteration to the original declarative process model, i.e. *"how severe is the behavioral change?"*. Importantly, this also plays an important role for comparing *different* viable change operations. For example, assuming there are multiple viable change operations (e.g., different constraints that could be deleted individually), the above measures can be used to rank these change operations by their magnitude w.r.t. the induced behavioral change. For this, an original M has to be altered by all viable change operations $\sigma_1, ...\sigma_n$, yielding models $\sigma_1(M), ..., \sigma_n(M)$. Then the behavioral change between M and all $\sigma_x(M)$ can be computed, in order to obtain the corresponding metrics (e.g., $\#T_{lost}^l$). This allows to rank change operations by their degree of induced behavioral change, e.g., the modeller could then opt to perform the change operation which induces the least behavioral change to the declarative specification. Please see [17] for an overview of further related metrics, e.g., language extension or language coverage.

5   Tool Support and Evaluation

We implemented our approach in Java.[2] Our implementation takes as input two DECLARE models (in text form) and a user-defined length, and can compute the behavioral changes (in form of traces) as proposed by our approach. To evaluate the feasibility of our approach, we conducted run-time experiments with the real-life data-sets of the Business Process Intelligence Challenge (BPIC).[3] From these data-sets (event logs), it is possible to *mine* DECLARE constraint-sets [2,9].

For our evaluation, we used the available BPIC data-sets of the last 5 years, i.e., the log of the BPIC 2017 (financial industry), BPIC 2018 (fund process), BPIC 2019 (purchase process) and the BPIC 2020 (reimbursement process). The data-set of the BPIC'20 contains sub-logs, which are marked accordingly. For each log, we mined a DECLARE constraint-set. As mining parameters, we selected mining parameters as suggested in [7], namely a support factor of 75% (minimum number of cases a rule has to be fulfilled in), as well as confidence and interest factors of 75% (support scaled by the ratio of cases in which the activation occurs, resp. support scaled by the ratio of cases both the activation and reaction occur). An exception was made for the BPI 2017 log, as these parameters yielded too many (hundreds) of constraints here - instead the parameters of 95%, 95%, 95% were chosen here. The table in Fig. 7 (a) shows the sizes of the resulting constraint-sets. All obtained constraint-sets can be found online.(see footnote 2)

For the mined constraint-sets, we then tested our approach. For this, we took each constraint-set and randomly deleted 25% of all constraints. This is meant to emulate a modeller modifying the specification by 25%. For the original and the altered constraint-sets, we then computed the difference automata. Last, we used our trace generation method to compute all traces corresponding to a behavioral change (i.e., we computed T_{lost}^l and T_{added}^l) for a trace-length of 10. The experiments were run on Mac OS with 3GHz processor and 16 GB RAM.

The needed runtimes to compute these traces (behavioral changes) are shown in Fig. 7 (b). As can be seen, most computations could be performed in under 1 s. The longest computation took around 41s, which still seems feasible in our

---

[2] https://github.com/NicolaiSchuetzenmeier/Computation-Behavioral-Changes.
[3] https://data.4tu.nl.

dataset	constraints
BPI 2017	154
BPI 2018	178
BPI 2019	14
BPI'20(domestic)	32
BPI'20(int.)	116
BPI'20(permits)	70
BPI'20(requests)	32

(a) Overview of considered data-sets.

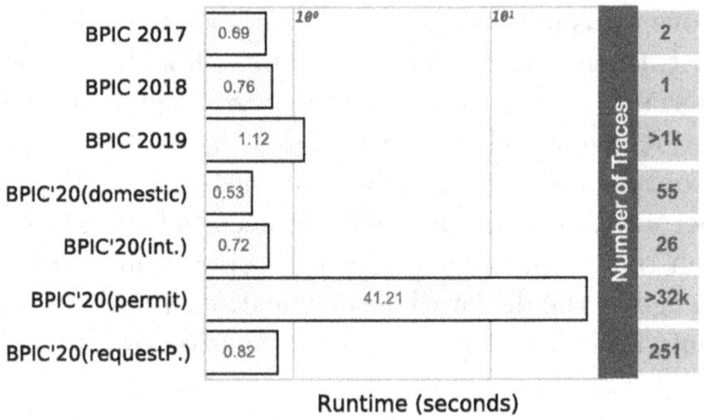

	Runtime (seconds)	Number of Traces
BPIC 2017	0.69	2
BPIC 2018	0.76	1
BPIC 2019	1.12	>1k
BPIC'20(domestic)	0.53	55
BPIC'20(int.)	0.72	26
BPIC'20(permit)	41.21	>32k
BPIC'20(requestP.)	0.82	251

(b) Runtimes for computing behavioral changes between the constraint-sets and the respective modified versions (modified by 25%) for a trace-length of 10.

Fig. 7. Run-time experiments details.

opinion. This indicates that for the considered data-sets, it is possible to compute behavioral changes in a "live" setting, e.g., during re-modelling.

To gain further understanding on the scalability of our approach, we repeated the experiments with a trace-length in the range from $2, 4, ..., 16$, and multiple modification percentages in the range from $10\%, 20\%, ..., 50\%$. Figure 8 shows the results of this evaluation for the example of the BPIC 2019 log. As can be seen, the performance is clearly affected by the user-defined trace-length. On the contrary, the actual percentage of modifications does not seem to have a strong impact on runtime (observe that there is no large slope in the direction of the x-axis [%]). Figure 8 quite nicely shows the limitations of our approach, but also the actual use-cases for our approach: Our approach is not geared to compute behavioral changes (traces) for extremely long trace-lengths. Rather, it performs best in settings were modellers want to understand smaller fragments in behavioral change (e.g., up to a trace-length of 10). This is actually also much in line with the actual trace-lengths that can be observed in the analyzed data-sets, e.g., the average trace-length in the shown BPIC 2019 data-set was 6.33. This makes it seem plausible that considering behavioral changes up to a trace-length of around 10 can provide valuable insights. Also, as there was some (minor) impact on run-time relative to the modification %, it is questionable whether our approach can be used to efficiently compare arbitrary declarative process models. However, our approach performs very well in re-modelling settings, where only a smaller percentage of constraints are modified.

Figure 7 (b) also shows the number of traces within the behavioral changes (w.r.t. a trace-length of 10). As can be seen, there are cases where the number of behavioral differences relates to 1 or 2 traces only. In such cases, it is plausible for the expert to manually inspect these traces. For the BPIC'20(permit) data-set, there were however over 32k traces that behaved differently between the original constraint-set and its altered version. In this case, the introduced visualization technique from [3] can be used to present a representative set of traces for these 32k traces. An example of this is shown in Fig. 9, which depicts the representative traces for all mentioned 32k traces. Such a visualization allows experts to easily obtain an overview of the behavioral changes induced by the changes. For example, in the second row, it can be seen that some traces are now allowed where the declaration is approved twice at the end of the process. This might be unwanted behavior, requiring a reconsideration of the changes made.

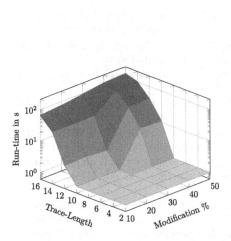

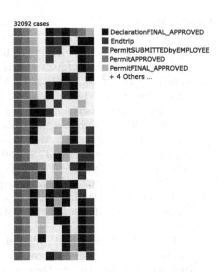

Fig. 8. Run-time results for computing behavioral changes on the BPIC'19 data-set - with different parameter settings regarding the considered trace-length and the modification percentage (fraction of deletions).

Fig. 9. Visualization of representative behavioral changes for the BPIC'20 (permit) data-set, for a trace-length of 10 (> 32k traces in total).

6   Conclusion and Future Work

In this paper, we present an efficient approach for computing behavioral changes - in the form of traces - between a declarative process model M and its altered version M'. While there are approaches to measure the similarity of declarative specifications, those approaches do not present the concrete traces that behave differently. Here, our approach supports modellers by facilitating to inspect the concrete set of traces that behave differently in the modified process model. Such insights are of utmost importance from the perspective of re-modelling, among other things to ensure that a modified process model does not yield any non-compliant behavior.

In future work, we aim to extend our approach to other declarative process modelling languages, e.g., DCR graphs [11] and HiDec [13]. Also, we aim to conduct eye-tracking experiments with end-users to investigate the cognitive effects of our introduced approach.

Acknowledgements. We thank Gaël Bernard and colleagues for help and access to their tool for selecting representative sample traces [3].

References

1. Fouda, E.: Data science in action. In: Learn Data Science Using SAS Studio, pp. 3–21. Apress, Berkeley (2020). https://doi.org/10.1007/978-1-4842-6237-5_1
2. Alman, A., Di Ciccio, C., Haas, D., Maggi, F.M., Nolte, A.: Rule mining with rum. In: 2nd International Conference on Process Mining, Italy (2020)
3. Bernard, G., Andritsos, P.: Selecting representative sample traces from large event logs. In: ICPM, Eindhoven, Netherlands. IEEE (2021)
4. Ceccherini-Silberstein, T., Machi, A., Scarabotti, F.: On the entropy of regular languages. Theoret. Comput. Sci. **307**(1), 93–102 (2003)
5. Polyvyanyy, A., Wynn, M.T., Van Looy, A., Reichert, M. (eds.) BPM 2021. LNBIP, vol. 427. Springer, Cham (2021). https://doi.org/10.1007/978-3-030-85440-9
6. De Giacomo, G., De Masellis, R., Montali, M.: Reasoning on LTL on finite traces: insensitivity to infiniteness. In: 28th AAAI Conference on AI, Canada. AAAI (2014)
7. Di Ciccio, C., Maggi, F.M., Montali, M., Mendling, J.: Resolving inconsistencies and redundancies in declarative process models. Inf. Syst. **64**, 425–446 (2017)
8. Di Ciccio, C., Montali, M.: Declarative process specifications: reasoning, discovery, monitoring. In: van der Aalst, W.M.P., Carmona, J. (eds.) Process Mining Handbook. LNBIP, vol. 448, 108–152. Springer, Cham (2022). https://doi.org/10.1007/978-3-031-08848-3_4
9. Di Ciccio, C., Schouten, M.H., de Leoni, M., Mendling, J.: Declarative process discovery with minerful in prom. In: BPM (Demos). CEUR-WS (2015)
10. Haisjackl, C., et al.: Understanding declare models: strategies, pitfalls, empirical results. SoSym **15**(2), 352 (2016)
11. Hildebrandt, T.T., Mukkamala, R.R., Slaats, T., Zanitti, F.: Contracts for cross-organizational workflows as timed dynamic condition response graphs. J. Log. Algebr. Program. **82**(5–7), 164–185 (2013)
12. Hopcroft, J., Motwani, R., Ullman, J.: Introduction to Automata Theory, Languages, and Computation. Pearson/Addison Wesley (2007)
13. De Masellis, R., Di Francescomarino, C., Ghidini, C., Maggi, F.M.: Declarative process models: different ways to be hierarchical. In: Sheng, Q.Z., Stroulia, E., Tata, S., Bhiri, S. (eds.) ICSOC 2016. LNCS, vol. 9936, pp. 104–119. Springer, Cham (2016). https://doi.org/10.1007/978-3-319-46295-0_7
14. Nagel, S., Delfmann, P.: Investigating inconsistency understanding to support interactive inconsistency resolution in decl. process models. In: ECIS. AISel (2021)
15. Pesic, M., Schonenberg, H., Van der Aalst, W.M.P.: Declare: full support for loosely-structured processes. In: 11th EDOC, Annapolis. IEEE (2007)
16. Polyvyanyy, A., Armas-Cervantes, A., Dumas, M., García-Bañuelos, L.: On the expressive power of behavioral profiles. Formal Aspects Comput. **28**(4), 597–613 (2016). https://doi.org/10.1007/s00165-016-0372-4

17. Polyvyanyy, A., Solti, A., Weidlich, M., Di Ciccio, C., Mendling, J.: Monotone precision and recall measures for comparing executions and specifications of dynamic systems. ACM Trans. Softw. Eng. Methodol. **29**, 1–41 (2020)
18. Schützenmeier, N., Käppel, M., Ackermann, L., Jablonski, S., Petter, S.: Automaton-based comparison of declare process models. SoSym **22**(2), 667–685 (2023)
19. Schützenmeier, N., Käppel, M., Petter, S., Jablonski, S.: Upper-bounded model checking for declarative process models. In: Serral, E., Stirna, J., Ralyté, J., Grabis, J. (eds.) PoEM 2021. LNBIP, vol. 432, pp. 195–211. Springer, Cham (2021). https://doi.org/10.1007/978-3-030-91279-6_14
20. Tax, N., Lu, X., Sidorova, N., Fahland, D., van der Aalst, W.M.P.: The imprecisions of precision measures in process mining. Inf. Process. Lett. **135**, 1–8 (2018)
21. Zugal, S., Pinggera, J., Weber, B.: The impact of testcases on the maintainability of declarative process models. In: Enterprise, Business-Process and Information Systems Modeling, vol. 81 (2011)
22. Zugal, S., Pinggera, J., Weber, B.: Toward enhanced life-cycle support for declarative processes. J. Softw. Evol. Process **24**(3), 285–302 (2012)

Beyond Temporal Dependency: An Ontology-Based Approach to Modeling Causal Structures in Business Processes

Kerstin Andree[1], Dorina Bano[2(✉)], and Mathias Weske[2]

[1] Technical University of Munich, Heilbronn, Germany
kerstin.andree@tum.de
[2] Hasso Plattner Institute, University of Potsdam, Potsdam, Germany
{dorina.bano,mathias.weske}@hpi.de

Abstract. Causality is an ubiquitous but elusive concept describing the relationship between cause and effect. In the context of business processes, it defines ontological, i.e., existential, and temporal dependencies between activities. Modeling languages define types of constraints and dependencies between activities. However, they mainly focus on the representation of the business process and the activity execution order without addressing the nature and type of activity interrelationships, i.e., its ontological profile. This paper proposes a new way of understanding activity relations through the fundamental distinction between temporal and ontological dependencies. Ten general types of activity interrelationships are derived covering all possible relationships between two activities in loop-free processes. They can be used as an aid in process redesign tasks, compliance checking, and to compare and analyze existing modeling approaches.

Keywords: Causality · Business Process Modeling · Ontological Dependence · Activity Interrelationships

1 Introduction

The knowledge of cause and effect relationships serves as a foundation to understand, analyze and improve business processes. Business process models define such relationships between activities using modeling languages [22] such as *Business Process Model and Notation* (BPMN) [15]. However, the concept of causality is poorly addressed in business process modeling [1] and, additionally, varies between different modeling approaches [1,11,12]. In particular its ontological component, i.e., the existential dependency in a cause-effect relationship between activities, is not addressed. As a consequence, different types of causal dependence cannot be differentiated. Similar to the fact that causality observed in nature, i.e., laws of nature, differ from causal dependencies proven by probabilistic approaches, it is true that different types of causal dependency can be observed in business processes. They differ in their type of ontological dependence.

© The Author(s), under exclusive license to Springer Nature Switzerland AG 2023
H. van der Aa et al. (Eds.): BPMDS 2023/EMMSAD 2023, LNBIP 479, pp. 152–166, 2023.
https://doi.org/10.1007/978-3-031-34241-7_11

The importance of incorporating an ontological-based perspective on relationships between activities in business process models is shown by Adamo et al. [2]. Process comprehension and redesign can be significantly improved. This paper, therefore, researches activity interrelationships from an ontological-based perspective and explores the notion of causality in the context of business process modeling. We present an approach for defining activity interrelationships based on the differentiation into two types of activity dependency, namely ontological dependence and temporal dependence. Ten general types of activity interrelationships are derived that allow for an explicit specification of any dependency between any pair of process activities including long-term dependencies. The resulting adjacency matrix can be used as a prescriptive process model that not only illustrates the causal dependencies within the process, but also streamlines process redesign and compliance evaluations. Furthermore, the proposed differentiation of types of relationships offers great potential in comparing modeling approaches and improving process discovery algorithms.

This paper is organized as follows, preliminaries are introduced in Sect. 2. Section 3 explains how to define business processes from an ontological-based perspective. Related work is discussed in Sect. 4. Section 5 introduces two application scenarios that benefit from our approach for process representation. Finally, Sect. 6 concludes.

2   Preliminaries

In this section, we introduce the essential terminology required to comprehend this paper and provide a brief overview of causality and ontological dependence.

2.1   Business Processes and Relations

Business processes are defined through *activity interrelationships* that encode dependencies between two different activities, which are determined by the overall business goal [22]. Formally, we define $\mathscr{A}$ as the set of process activities and $S_R \subseteq (\mathscr{A} \times \mathscr{A})$ as the set of activity interrelationships.

Activity interrelationships are initiated and influenced by various artifacts in the process environment, such as events and rationales. As a result, processes are constantly interacting with their environment, and must adhere to laws and standards. Figure 1 shows an overview of the relationships between activities and the process environment. It is inspired by the insights observed by Galton [9], Adamo et al. [2], and Correia [8].

Activities are typically closely tied to process states, which represent system knowledge about previous actions [12]. These states are triggered and terminated by activities or events. As it is illustrated in Fig. 1, along with states and events, other factors such as rationales, exist in the process environment. These can include norms, laws of nature, and business rules that define particular process behavior and must be complied with.

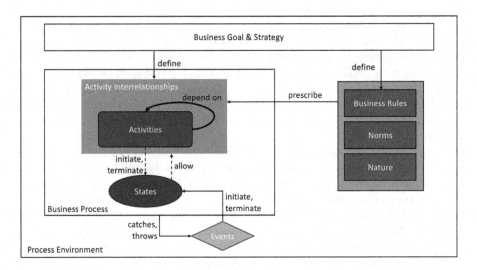

Fig. 1. Overview of activity dependencies in the context of business processes.

Incorporating states into the analysis of activity interrelationships provides a more accurate representation of a process. However, it also increases the complexity of the process behavior. Therefore, in this paper, we have chosen to initially focus on a thorough examination and definition of activity interrelationships without considering states, events, and rationales, in order to simplify the analysis.

2.2   Causality and Ontological Dependence

Causality is a concept that has been studied for thousands of years [16]. In contrast to *causation* defining a relation between two specific events, causality corresponds to a law-like relation between types of events [13]. Despite its long history of study, defining causality is a challenging task due to its complexity.

Although there exist different approaches to explain causal dependency, but none are able to capture all forms of it. To illustrate this, let us consider two examples from real life:

(1) Smoking causes lung cancer.
(2) Letting go of a previously held apple causes it to fall to the ground.

Both statements describe a cause-effect relationship between two events. For statement (1) it is not true that smoking *always* causes lung cancer. There might be other causes for people to have lung cancer. Based on data, the *probabilistic approach* identifies such cause-effect relations by proving that the probability of getting lung cancer is higher for people who smoke, compared to those who do not.

In contrast, *counterfactual assumptions* explain causation by stating that an event A is a cause of another event B if B does not occur in an environment that is identical to the natural environment except that A does not occur [10]. For example, the concrete object (apple) would not fall if it had not been let go (cf. statement (2)). However, the counterfactual assumption fails to identify causal relationships in situations that may have varying results, such as when someone gets lung cancer despite not smoking. Thus, subtle differences between causal dependencies make it challenging to provide an universal definition of causality.

This paper examines causality in business processes from an ontology-based perspective. Since we do not rely on event data we do not use the probabilistic approach. Based on a differentiation between different types of activity dependency we propose a prescriptive model to define general and causal relationships. Thereby, the notion of *ontological dependence* is utilized. Ontological dependence, originating from philosophy, describes a family of properties and relations [8]. It is assumed that every object has an ontological profile, meaning that its existence can be deduced from other facts. Therefore, causal dependence implies an ontological dependence of the considered events [9]. For example, letting go of an apple causes it to fall due to the force of gravity, which is its origin.

3   Activity Interrelationships

Activity interrelationships define relations expressing "dependencies among activities" [14]. We distinguish between two types of *activity dependence*: an ontological dependence (d_o) and a temporal dependence (d_t). Thus, each type of activity interrelationships is composed of a tuple of activity dependencies (d_t, d_o). As shown in Fig. 1, a state s may allow activity interrelationships whereas a rational r explains the origin and motivation of activity dependencies. Therefore, we define a relationship between two different activities including secondary dependencies such as states and environmental factors as the quadruple $(r, s, (d_t, d_o))$. Figure 2 puts this definition in relation to Fig. 1. Note that the color scheme corresponds to the elements in Fig. 1. If there is an ontological and temporal dependence between two activities B, C that depend on state s, it is true that s has been initialized before B and C being started, e.g., through an activity A. Additionally, s is only terminated after B and C being terminated. Rationales, however, are defined for explanatory reasons without indicating any activity constraints. They are used for process redesign. The type of an (causal) activity interrelationships is mainly defined through the tuple of activity dependencies.

The introduced definition allows to specify any dependency between any pair of activities of a process. In this paper, we focus on the different types of activity dependencies without considering states and explanatory rationales. To provide initial insights into the applicability of the proposed analysis of relationships, we apply it to declarative process modeling. The so-called *activity interrelationships matrix* used for business process representation contains each activity dependency tuple for any pair of activities. It is a prescriptive process model

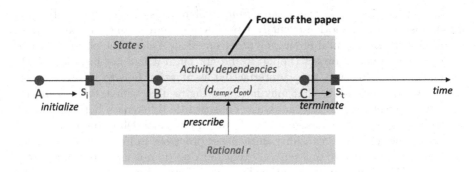

Fig. 2. Activity interrelationship between activities B and C that is allowed through the initialization of state s and prescribed by rationale r.

with the intent to answer the questions of when which activity can or should be executed. For each activity it explicitly specifies which relations must hold, i.e., which dependencies to other activities exist, in order to enable this activity. Note that we exclude cyclic and alternating behavior due to reasons of complexity. Activity multi instances would need to be addressed as well as their influence on long-term dependencies throughout the process. Moreover, types of activity dependence, especially the ontological dependency, significantly increases in complexity since existential relationships cannot be explicitly identified in complex loops containing optional behavior.

This section explains the two types of activity dependence. Based on a discussion of causality in the context of business processes, we derive a definition for causal dependence in business process models. Finally, ten types of activity interrelationships are introduced each representing one combination of activity dependency types.

3.1   Activity Dependence

Temporal dependence is defined as a relative order of a pair of activities in a process. For example, in a process P with two activities A, B temporal activity dependence indicates that activity A happens before B in P or vice versa. Such type of ordering is commonly used in modeling languages such as BPMN [15]. They define activity execution orders by specifying the enablement of an activity in relation to a termination of another one. It does not indicate an exact occurrence in time as it is known from traces in event log data but provides a relative position of the activities in a process.

We further distinguish between a *direct* and an *eventual* temporal dependence. In contrast to the latter, the first does not allow for any other activity to be executed in between.

Definition 1 (Temporal Dependence). *Given a set of process activities $\mathscr{A}$ and two process activities $A, B \in \mathscr{A}$ with $A \neq B$. $A \prec B$ defines a temporal* *dependence between A and B, iff for each case it is true that A needs to terminate in order to enable B.*

We distinguish between a direct temporal dependence $A \prec_d B$, i.e., a termination of A directly leads to the beginning of B, and eventual temporal dependence $A \prec_e B$, i.e., B eventually follows A meaning that there may be other activities before B begins.

The ontological dependency of an activity A is also specified in relation to another activity B but focuses on their existential dependence rather than their temporal ordering. If A implies B ontologically, it means that there is an existential relationship between them. The reason for the existential dependence may relate to the contextual information of both activities, such as one activity causing the other, or to the overall business goal, indicating that these activities happen together in a process. Besides the ontological implication, there are other types that are summarized in the following definition:

Definition 2 (Ontological Dependence). *Given a set of process activities $\mathscr{A}$ and two process activities $A, B \in \mathscr{A}$ with $A \neq B$. An ontological dependence between A and B provides information about the occurrence of the two activities. We differentiate into different types of ontological dependence formalized through Boolean algebra:*

- *$A \Rightarrow B$ defines an ontological implication between A and B. Whenever A happens, B must happen or must have happened.*
- *$A \Leftrightarrow B$ defines an ontological equivalence between A and B, iff $A \Rightarrow B$ and $B \Rightarrow A$.*
- *$A \nLeftrightarrow B$ defines a negated ontological equivalence between A and B. Either A or B occurs.*
- *$A \barwedge B$ defines an ontological NAND between A and B. An occurrence of A excludes the occurrence of B and vice versa, or neither A nor B occur.*
- *$A \vee B$ defines an ontological OR between A and B. At least one of the two activities must occur.*
- *If none of the above ontological dependencies apply to two activities A, B, then A and B are ontologically independent of each other.*

To understand the differences between temporal and ontological dependence, we refer to the activity lifecycle [12]. A temporal dependence between two activities A, B, e.g., $A \prec B$, defines that B can only be enabled when A has been closed (cf. Fig. 3). It does not matter whether A was terminated or skipped because a temporal dependence only indicates the relative position of the two activities. Considering the Fig. 3b, $A \prec B$ is still true. If an ontological dependence exists between A and B, for example $A \Rightarrow B$, this means that once activity A begins, B will begin or has begun too. Note that a pure ontological dependence between A and B does not provide any information about the relative order of the two activities which is the reason why $A \Rightarrow B$ holds for Fig. 3a and Fig. 3c. B is not dependent on A from an ontological point, so B can also start without A being enabled. However, once A begins, B cannot be in state skipped. Otherwise, the ontological dependence is violated.

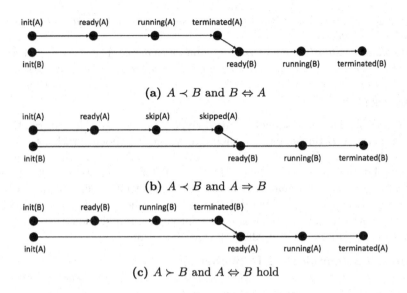

(a) $A \prec B$ and $B \Leftrightarrow A$

(b) $A \prec B$ and $A \Rightarrow B$

(c) $A \succ B$ and $A \Leftrightarrow B$ hold

Fig. 3. Ontological and temporal dependency in the context of the activity lifecycle.

3.2 Causality in Business Processes

Considering causal relationships in daily life such as an apple that falls because someone let it go, we recognize both a temporal and an ontological dependence between the events *"let go an apple"* and *"apple falls"*: If the apple would not have been let go, it would not have fallen. This observation also applies to causality in the context of business process representation. In business processes, we consider two activities to be causally dependent if they are temporally and ontologically dependent on each other. A pure ontological dependence between two activities A, B does not necessarily mean that A causes B or vice versa (cf. common cause principle [3]). There may be a third activity C that causes A and B. Similarly, a pure temporal dependence does not imply that there is a contextual and existential relation between the two activities that is required for causality.

The differences in each type of activity dependence result in different types of causality that can be recognized in business processes. However, not every type of ontological dependency is compatible with a temporal one, e.g., a NAND relation requires that two activities do not both occur in one case, so there is no temporal dependency. The types of temporal and ontological dependencies that can be combined and the (causal) types of activity relationships that can be generally defined are explained in the next section.

3.3 Types of Activity Interrelationships

An activity interrelationship combines a temporal dependence with a type of ontological dependence resulting in ten different types of activity interrelationships (cf. Table 1). An activity interrelationship (A, B) is read from left to right.

$(A, B) = (\prec, \Rightarrow)$, for example, equals the following activity dependencies: $A \prec B$ and $A \Rightarrow B$. Temporal or ontological independence are marked with a dash $(-)$, respectively. Note that we refer to activity interrelationships as the combination of activity dependencies (d_t, d_o), since we exclude states and rationales in this paper.

Table 1. Meaning and notation of activity interrelationships for two process activities A, B with $A \neq B$.

	$A \prec B \ (A \prec_d B)$	$B \prec A \ (B \prec_d A)$	Temporal Independence
$A \Rightarrow B$	A (directly) leads-to B $(A, B) = (\prec, \Rightarrow)$	B (directly) precedes A $(A, B) = (\succ, \Rightarrow)$	A implies B $(A, B) = (-, \Rightarrow)$
$B \Rightarrow A$	A (directly) precedes B $(A, B) = (\prec, \Leftarrow)$	B (directly) leads-to A $(A, B) = (\succ, \Leftarrow)$	B implies A $(A, B) = (-, \Leftarrow)$
$A \Leftrightarrow B$	A is in (direct) ordered co-occurrence with B $(A, B) = (\prec, \Leftrightarrow)$	B is in (direct) ordered co-occurrence with A $(A, B) = (\succ, \Leftrightarrow)$	A co-occurs with B $(A, B) = (-, \Leftrightarrow)$
$An \Leftrightarrow B$	-	-	A does'nt co-occur with B $(A, B) = (-, \nLeftrightarrow)$
$A \barwedge B$	-	-	A NAND B $(A, B) = (-, \bar{\wedge})$
$A \vee B$	-	-	A OR B $(A, B) = (-, \vee)$
Ontological Independence	A (directly) before B $(A, B) = (\prec, -)$	B (directly) before A $(A, B) = (\succ, -)$	A and B are independent $(A, B) = (-, -)$

Between two process activities A, B with $A \neq B$, one out of ten different types of activity interrelationships can hold depending on the respective types of activity dependence. First, consider the temporal dependence $A \prec B$. If, additionally, $A \Rightarrow B$, the relation is called *leads-to*, i.e., the occurrence of A implies the occurrence of B. We formally express such a relation as $(A, B) = (\prec, \Rightarrow)$. Note that a *leads-to* relationship is also true if $A \succ B$ and $A \Leftarrow B$. In this case, however, it is B that *leads-to* A. If $B \Rightarrow A$, the execution of B depends on the existence of A. The relation is then described as A *precedes* B or *directly precedes* if $A \prec_d B$, indicated by the tuple $(A, B) = (\prec, \Leftarrow)$ or $(A, B) = (\prec_d, \Leftarrow)$, respectively. In case the activities are mutually ontologically dependent, we refer to the combination of $A \prec B \ (A \prec_d B)$ and $A \Leftrightarrow B$ as *(direct) ordered co-occurrence*. Accordingly, these relations also apply for $B \prec A \ (A \prec_d A)$. Again, please note that the relationships *precedes* and *ordered co-occurrence* are listed twice in Table 1.

If A and B are not temporally dependent on each other, e.g., in case of parallelism, but $A \Leftrightarrow B$, the relation indicates a *co-occurrence* between A and B represented through $(A, B) = (-, \Leftrightarrow)$. Having two activities A, B being temporally independent, but in exclusion, we define the activity interrelationship as a *non-co-occurrence*. Note that $A \nLeftrightarrow B$ implies that one of the two activities A, B must occur. If it is additionally allowed for A, B to happen both, we speak of an *OR* relationship. In contrast, a *NAND* relationship does allow for neither A nor B to occur. An ontological implication $A \Rightarrow B$ indicates that an occurrence of A implies an occurrence of B without defining their temporal order.

If there is no ontological dependence, but the activities are temporally dependent on each other, we define such an activity interrelationship as a pure temporal dependence. Assume $A \prec B$ ($A \prec_d B$) but no ontological dependence applies, the relationship is then defined as A *(directly) before* B. Finally, we speak of *activity independence* if neither a temporal nor an ontological dependence hold $((A, B) = (-, -))$.

Specifying activity interrelationships for one given process with $|\mathscr{A}| = n$ and $\mathscr{A}$ being the set of process activities results in a $n \times n$ matrix called *activity interrelationships matrix*. It is a declarative approach to define business processes by specifying the relationship of each pair of process activities. Used as a prescriptive model, it contains both temporal and ontological dependencies between each pair of activities formalized using the tuple notation introduced above. This allows for a complete overview of all (long-term) dependencies and relations that must hold in order to enable an activity of the process. Note that only causal and pure temporal dependencies force a relative execution order of related activities. Pairs of activities that only ontologically depend on each other only have an existential relationship and can be executed whenever it fits best. Moreover, the matrix representation indicates causal dependence explicitly. We can identify three types of causal dependence among the ten types of activity interrelationships introduced in this paper: *leads-to*, *precedes*, and *ordered co-occurrence*. In addition, the activity interrelationships matrix provides an overview of *all* dependencies an activity has instead of its nearest neighbours. The adjacency matrix is read from left to right so that each cell indicates exactly one relationship between two activities. For its creation, an information source is required, e.g., domain experts or normative process models, that provide all required information about activity dependencies that hold between any pair of process activities.

4   Related Work

Declarative modeling languages such as Dynamic Condition Response (DCR) Graphs [11] define the causality relation as a partial order indicating prerequisites for a given event. However, causality is neither differentiated into different types of activity dependencies nor into different types of causal dependence. Similar to BPMN [15], the constraint-based modeling language ConDec [17] that was created using the DECLARE system [18] does not differentiate into different types of activity dependencies. This is because it was originally designed for process representation and capturing different behavior of knowledge-intensive processes rather than analyzing differences in activity interrelationships from a foundation-oriented point of view. It is true that the ConDec relation constraints can be mapped to the types of activity interrelationships introduced in this paper. In contrast to DECLARE, however, we do not aim at process modeling, but offer a way to think about dependencies between activities by providing a foundational framework to compare and analyse modeling approaches, e.g., in terms of causality.

The limitations of declarative modeling approaches were also shown by Soffer [20]. While the languages focus on constraints on activity interrelationships, the influence and dependencies of states and especially contextual information is neglected. This is the reason why we propose a definition of activity interrelationships not only based on activity dependencies but on environmental rationales and states of affairs. In contrast to Soffer, we differentiate into two types of activity dependency instead of separating the intended change of an activity execution from the actual one. We believe that explicitly distinguishing temporal from ontological dependence provides a more profound understanding of activity interrelationships in general. The inclusion of states and contextual information, however, needs to be addressed in future work.

Declarative modeling languages often rely on linear temporal logic instead of an ontology-based perspective on expressing activity interrelationships. Temporal logic is a logical formalism used to describe relations between activities, which is defined as a logical formalism for describing a rich set of activity execution constraints in business processes [6]. Temporal modalities are combined with Boolean connectives to define formulae representing relationships and constraints. However, because of its non-intuitive notation, temporal logic is difficult for usage by end users [7]. Therefore, graphical notations such as *BPMN-Q* [4] have been presented that provide behavioral patterns that can be easily translated to such formulae but are less complex to comprehend. Temporal logic focuses on temporal sequences. However, in this paper, we also consider activity interrelationships from an ontological point of view. Therefore, we use Boolean algebra instead of temporal logic for formalization.

Looking at philosophy, Galton [9] explains relationships and dependencies by differentiating between causal and causal-like dependencies. He recognized that states and processes[1] passively influence causal relationships, while events that cause or act on something must be active in some way. The approach describes relationships on a general level that are also relevant to business processes. Thus, the insights from Galton's analysis help to classify and define activity interrelationships in processes. Moreover, it highlights the relevance of states regarding causal dependencies and motivates for future work in this area.

A similar analysis to [9] is presented by Lehmann et al. [13]. The authors studied the impact that different types of constraints in dependencies have on causal relations. Furthermore, they distinguish between *causality* as "a law-like relation between types of events" and *causation*, "the actual causal relation that holds between individual events". This paper focuses on a causality-based analysis of relationships since it provides generic types of activity interrelationships instead of specific dependencies between concrete activity instances.

The link between philosophical studies and business process management is established by Adamo et al. [1]. They analyze activity relationships for process models represented as BPMN based on ontological dependence and introduce a relation type called *causal dependency*. In addition, the authors identify three

---

[1] Note that the *process* term in this case does not refer to business processes. It is rather an action that continues constantly.

different rationales of ontological dependence to motivate and explain relationships between activities. In [2], Adamo et al. introduce a graphical notation to extend BPMN models so that (1) for each control flow relationship between activities, it is indicated what type of relationship it is and (2) on which rationale this relationship is based. An evaluation of the approach confirmed that an explicit representation of ontological dependencies in process models improves the quality of process comprehension and redesign outcomes. This paper also analyses activity interrelationships from an ontological point of view. However, we propose a more formal, foundation-oriented framework to classify different types of relationships.

5   Application Scenarios

Business processes are often redesigned due to changing regulations or internal procedures [1,5]. Therefore, compliance checking and process redesign are constant tasks in business process management. Both can benefit from a ontology-based definition for business processes. This section explains the advantages of using an activity interrelationship matrix and what we can learn from it.

5.1   Process Redesign

To explain the application scenario of process redesign we use a process example taken from the hotel industry [21]. Due to space reasons we use an excerpt of it dealing with the cancellation of reservations. If the hotel receives a cancellation message, it will always try to rent the room. However, if this does not succeed by the end of the day, the guest must pay the fee for the first night. In case of a success, the hotel management decides whether the guest has to pay the rent for the first night or not. Finally, the reservation needs to be marked as cancelled in the system.

The described process can be defined through the activity interrelationships matrix shown in Table 2. Based on the text above we identified four activities: "Rent Room" (RR), "Contact Management" (CM), "Charge Rent" (CT), and "Cancel Reservation" (CR). Please note, that we use abbreviations in the activity interrelationships matrix for each activity. The relations of each pair of activities was manually derived of which one is causal: A successfully completion of activity "Rent Room" causes, i.e., precedes, activity "Contact Management". The ontological implication indicates that an occurrence of "Contact Management" implies the occurrence of "Rent Room" whereas the temporal dependence adds the relative order so that "Rent Room" terminates before "Contact Management" may begin. We also notice that activity "Cancel Reservation" must occur because there exists an ontological equivalence between it and each activity listed but there is no relative position in the process defined.

Table 2. Activity interrelationships matrix of the cancellation process example.

	RR	CM	CT	CR
RR	-	$(\prec, \Leftarrow)$	$(-, \Leftarrow)$	$(-, \Leftrightarrow)$
CM	$(\succ, \Rightarrow)$	-	$(\prec, -)$	$(-, \Leftrightarrow)$
CT	$(-, \Rightarrow)$	$(\succ, -)$	-	$(-, \Leftrightarrow)$
CR	$(-, \Leftrightarrow)$	$(-, \Leftarrow)$	$(-, \Leftarrow)$	-

Now suppose the hotel manager has recruited a business analyst to analyze the process that is currently implemented as shown in Fig. 4. The analyst observes that the "Rent Room" activity has a long execution time and is often not completed but interrupted due to the specified time (end of the day). This is due to an error in the system. Since the reservation is marked as cancelled in the last step of the process, the actually free room does not appear among the available rooms for arriving guests. The analyst decides to perform a resequencing of activity "Cancel Reservation". It is moved to the beginning of the process so that "Cancel Reservation" occurs before "Rent Room". By analyzing the activity interrelationships matrix shown in Table 2, the analyst notices that "Cancel Reservation" is not temporally dependent on another activity which is why it can be moved to any position. The analyst's proposed solution can thus be implemented.

5.2   Compliance Checking

Whether standards, rules, and special routines specified by domain experts or norms are adhered to while process execution can be answered by compliance checking [12]. Several approaches have been presented to support compliance checking by introducing techniques that rely on formalization such as Petrinets [19] and temporal logic [4, 7]. However, none of them includes a causality-based representation of compliance rules.

Besides for process representation, the activity interrelationships matrix introduced in this paper can also be used as a normative model, prescribing compliance rules. Boolean algebra allows us to use truth tables to express when a relation holds and when it does not. Moreover it allows for efficient compliance checking since the formalization is machine-readable. Having event log data containing a finite set of traces, we are able to analyze whether the prescribed logical expressions of both dependencies hold for them. Traces provide information about activity occurrences. Given the set of all process activities $\mathscr{A}$ that may occur in a case, we can specify for each activity $A \in \mathscr{A}$ if it was executed (1) or not (0) in the trace under consideration. To analyze whether an activity interrelationship holds in a given trace, we evaluate each logical expression provided by the matrix with the activity truth values of the trace inserted.

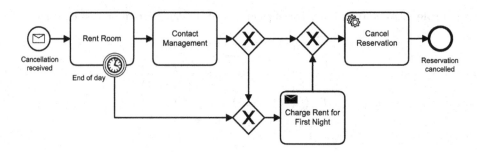

Fig. 4. Cancellation of a hotel reservation request (Rent Room-RR, Contact Management-CM, Charge Rent for First Night-CT, Cancel Reservation-CR).

Table 3. Evaluation of truth values for compliance checking.

Trace	A	B	$A \Leftrightarrow B$	$A \prec B$	Violation
t_1	1	1	1	1	0
t_2	0	1	0	1	1

Suppose the activity interrelationship $(A, B) = (\prec, \Leftrightarrow)$ and the following set of two traces assuming $\mathscr{A} = \{A, B\}$:

$$t_1 = \langle A, B \rangle, t_2 = \langle B \rangle$$

Trace t_1 does not violate the activity interrelationship (A, B). However, t_2 does. To check the traces for compliance, we first evaluate the ontological dependence $A \Leftrightarrow B$. To do so, we compute the truth value of the dependence with the truth values for A, B inserted. For t_1, the logical expression $A \Leftrightarrow B \equiv 1 \Leftrightarrow 1$ is true. Additionally, $A \prec B$ is also true. $A \Leftrightarrow B \equiv 0 \Leftrightarrow 1$, however, is false (cf. Table 3).

6   Conclusion and Future Work

Causal relations are omnipresent in this world, and business processes are no exception. Besides the temporal dependence of related activities in a cause-effect relation, the different types of ontological dependence allows to distinguish different types of causality and activity interrelationships. Although related work recognizes the importance of incorporating the ontological-based perspective on activity interrelationships in process modeling, a profound understanding of the interplay of different types of activity dependencies is missing.

This paper addresses this gap by presenting an approach to analyze activity interrelationships based on distinguishing between different types of activity dependencies. We define ten general activity interrelationships as the combination of temporal and ontological dependence between a pair of unequal process activities. By utilizing Boolean algebra for formalization, our approach enables an explicit yet intuitive specification of relationships in processes. The approach has great potential for supporting process redesign tasks and compliance checking. We also see an applicability for the comparison of different modeling languages and the further development of process discovery algorithms. This needs to be researched in future work.

The presented ontology-based definition of activity interrelationships forms the basis for a comprehensive and explainable specification of activity dependencies. However, states and explanatory rationales need to be further researched to complete the introduced notion of activity interrelationships as a quadruple. Additionally, the presented approach is currently limited to loop-free processes and lacks an evaluation proving the additional support for domain experts when performing process redesign tasks and compliance checking. Due to the relevance of cyclic behavior in business processes, this needs to be addressed in future work.

References

1. Adamo, G., Borgo, S., Di Francescomarino, C., Ghidini, C., Guarino, N., Sanfilippo, E.M.: Business process activity relationships: is there anything beyond arrows? In: Weske, M., Montali, M., Weber, I., vom Brocke, J. (eds.) BPM 2018. LNBIP, vol. 329, pp. 53–70. Springer, Cham (2018). https://doi.org/10.1007/978-3-319-98651-7_4
2. Adamo, G., Francescomarino, C.D., Ghidini, C., Maggi, F.M.: Beyond arrows in process models: a user study on activity dependences and their rationales. Inf. Syst. **100**, 101762 (2021). https://doi.org/10.1016/j.is.2021.101762
3. Arntzenius, F., Hitchcock, C., Rédei, M.: Reichenbach's common cause principle. In: The Stanford Encyclopedia of Philosophy, Winter 2019 edn. Metaphysics Research Lab, Stanford University (2019)
4. Awad, A.: BPMN-Q: a language to query business processes. In: Enterprise Modelling and Information Systems Architectures - Concepts and Applications, Proceedings of the 2nd International Workshop on Enterprise Modelling and Information Systems Architectures (EMISA 2007). LNI, Germany, vol. P-119, pp. 115–128. GI (2007)
5. Awad, A., Decker, G., Weske, M.: Efficient compliance checking using BPMN-Q and temporal logic. In: Dumas, M., Reichert, M., Shan, M.-C. (eds.) BPM 2008. LNCS, vol. 5240, pp. 326–341. Springer, Heidelberg (2008). https://doi.org/10.1007/978-3-540-85758-7_24
6. Baier, C., Katoen, J.: Principles of Model Checking. MIT Press, Cambridge (2008)
7. Caron, F., Vanthienen, J., Baesens, B.: Comprehensive rule-based compliance checking and risk management with process mining. Decis. Support Syst. **54**(3), 1357–1369 (2013). https://doi.org/10.1016/j.dss.2012.12.012
8. Correia, F.: Ontological dependence. Philos Compass **3**(5), 1013–1032 (2008)
9. Galton, A.: States, processes and events, and the ontology of causal relations. In: Formal Ontology in Information Systems - Proceedings of the Seventh International Conference, FOIS 2012. Frontiers in Artificial Intelligence and Applications, vol. 239, pp. 279–292, Austria. IOS Press (2012). https://doi.org/10.3233/978-1-61499-084-0-279
10. Halpern, J.Y.: Actual Causality. MIT Press, Cambridge (2016)

11. Hildebrandt, T.T., Mukkamala, R.R.: Declarative event-based workflow as distributed dynamic condition response graphs. In: Proceedings Third Workshop on Programming Language Approaches to Concurrency and Communication-Centric Software, PLACES 2010. EPTCS, Cyprus, vol. 69, pp. 59–73 (2010). https://doi.org/10.4204/EPTCS.69.5

12. Kunze, M., Weske, M.: Behavioural Models - From Modelling Finite Automata to Analysing Business Processes. Springer, Cham (2016). https://doi.org/10.1007/978-3-319-44960-9

13. Lehmann, J., Borgo, S., Masolo, C., Gangemi, A.: Causality and causation in DOLCE. In: Formal Ontology in Information Systems, Proceedings of the International Conference FOIS, pp. 273–284 (2004)

14. Montali, M.: The ConDec language. In: Specification and Verification of Declarative Open Interaction Models. LNBIP, vol. 56, pp. 47–75. Springer, Heidelberg (2010). https://doi.org/10.1007/978-3-642-14538-4_3

15. OMG: Business Process Model and Notation (BPMN), version 2.0.2. Technical report, Object Management Group (2014). https://www.omg.org/spec/BPMN/2.0.2/PDF

16. Pearl, J., Mackenzie, D.: The Book of Why: The New Science of Cause and Effect. Basic Books (2018)

17. Pesic, M., van der Aalst, W.M.P.: A declarative approach for flexible business processes management. In: Eder, J., Dustdar, S. (eds.) BPM 2006. LNCS, vol. 4103, pp. 169–180. Springer, Heidelberg (2006). https://doi.org/10.1007/11837862_18

18. Pesic, M., Schonenberg, H., Van der Aalst, W.M.: DECLARE: full support for loosely-structured processes. In: 11th IEEE International Enterprise Distributed Object Computing Conference (EDOC 2007), pp. 287–287. IEEE (2007)

19. Ramezani, E., Fahland, D., van der Aalst, W.M.P.: Where did i misbehave? Diagnostic information in compliance checking. In: Barros, A., Gal, A., Kindler, E. (eds.) BPM 2012. LNCS, vol. 7481, pp. 262–278. Springer, Heidelberg (2012). https://doi.org/10.1007/978-3-642-32885-5_21

20. Soffer, P.: A state-based intention driven declarative process model. Int. J. Inf. Syst. Model. Des. 4(2), 44–64 (2013). https://doi.org/10.4018/jismd.2013040103

21. Sowa, J.F.: Knowledge Representation: Logical, Philosophical and Computational Foundations. Brooks/Cole Publishing Co. (1999)

22. Weske, M.: Business Process Management - Concepts, Languages, Architectures, 3rd edn. Springer, Heidelberg (2019). https://doi.org/10.1007/978-3-662-59432-2

Foundations and Method Engineering (EMMSAD 2023)

Principles of Universal Conceptual Modeling

Roman Lukyanenko[1]([⊠]) (iD), Jeffrey Parsons[2], Veda C. Storey[3], Binny M. Samuel[4] (iD),
and Oscar Pastor[5]

[1] University of Virginia, Charlottesville, VA 22903, USA
romanl@virginia.edu
[2] Memorial University of Newfoundland, St. John's, NL A1B 3X5, Canada
jeffreyp@mun.ca
[3] Georgia State University, Atlanta, GA 30302, USA
vstorey@gsu.edu
[4] University of Cincinnati, Cincinnati, OH 45040, USA
samuelby@uc.edu
[5] Universitat Politécnica de València, València, Spain
opastor@dsic.upv.es

Abstract. The paper proposes a new frontier for conceptual modeling – *universal conceptual modeling* (UCM) – defined as conceptual modeling that is general-purpose and accessible to anyone. For the purposes of the discussion, we envision a non-existent, hypothetical universal conceptual modeling language, which we call *Datish* (as in English or Spanish for data). We focus on the need for a universal conceptual data model to explain the expected benefits of UCM. Datish can facilitate the design of many different applications, including relational databases, NoSQL databases, data lakes, and artificial intelligence systems, and enable use by a broad range of users. To pave the way for rigorous development of such a language, we provide a theoretical basis for Datish in the form of a set of universal conceptual modeling principles: flexibility, accessibility, ubiquity, minimalism, primitivism, and modularity. We apply these principles to illustrate their usefulness and to identify future research opportunities.

Keywords: Universal Conceptual Modeling · Conceptual Modeling · Conceptual Modeling Foundations · Universal Data Modeling Language · Datish

1 Introduction

The paper proposes a new frontier for conceptual modeling - *universal conceptual modeling* (UCM) – defined as conceptual modeling that is general-purpose (i.e., able to model any domain) *and* accessible to anyone (i.e., able to be used and understood by the broadest audiences possible). Universal conceptual modeling can be instantiated in several specific artifacts, such as a universal modeling language, a universal approach for requirements elicitation, and corresponding modeling tools, all of which should be usable by as many people as possible.

© The Author(s), under exclusive license to Springer Nature Switzerland AG 2023
H. van der Aa et al. (Eds.): BPMDS 2023/EMMSAD 2023, LNBIP 479, pp. 169–183, 2023.
https://doi.org/10.1007/978-3-031-34241-7_12

To explain the benefits of UCM, we focus on the need for universal conceptual *data* modeling – modeling of form and structure of a domain to facilitate data management, including data collection, storage, retrieval, and interpretation [12]. Conceptual data models, (or data models, for short), such as ER or UML class diagrams, are particularly valuable at the initial phases of IT development, especially (but not only) for relational database design [42, 46, 52, 61]. Data models are also used to support communication and understanding and provide documentation for a variety of IT development projects. In addition, data models are becoming increasingly useful for understanding existing data sources, and information systems [31].

For the purposes of the paper, we envision a non-existent, hypothetical universal data modeling language *Datish* (as in English or Spanish for data). Modeling with Datish amounts to following the *grammar* of Datish – a set of constructs and rules for representing the form and structure of a domain of interest [52, 58, 61]. In the form of design principles, UCM provides theoretical guidance and rationale for the design of the constructs and rules of Datish such that this language can be "spoken" by anyone, anywhere. This means the ability to produce, interpret and use the diagrams (or scripts) in Datish. This language can be used on its own or together with existing (more specialized) conceptual modeling languages.

Many past efforts are relevant for UCM and Datish. Some existing conceptual modeling languages have been widely adopted, but do not meet our concept of "universal." Notably, the entity-relationship diagrams (ERDs) and the Unified Modeling Language (UML) are widely used for database design and software engineering, respectively. There have been extensions of these languages to make their semantics more precise, yet more accessible (e.g., ConML, [24]). Other relevant efforts include domain modeling, such as Domain Modelling [3], ArchiMate [2] or SysML [35]. These languages are indeed suitable for broad applications, but not for everyone. Some (e.g., [3]) explicitly require advanced technical skills. All are complex (having dozens of constructs), making the learning and use curve quite steep for non-experts in modeling. In addition, nearly all of these languages carry assumptions that make them inadequate for some applications. For example, a common assumption is that of inherent classification [49], whereby objects are assumed to be members of predefined entity types or classes. This makes it especially challenging to use these languages for supporting more flexible modeling common in artificial intelligence, analytics, social media, and NoSQL contexts [1, 19, 39, 41].

There are ongoing efforts to develop a common language for specific contexts, such as big data [6, 9, 10]. There are also highly flexible, generic modeling frameworks, such as RDF, Petri nets, graph models and their extensions (e.g., HERAKLIT [20]). These approaches, while flexible and applicable to many applications, do not consider broad audiences and cater to seasoned developers. Although the notion of a "universal data language" emerged in industry [62], it seeks to support the development of services, rather than being ready for any use by anyone. In general, developments in practice are motivated by specific problems (e.g., semantic interoperability), and not grounded in underlying theories, making it difficult to understand why a solution is effective and why it is expected to work beyond a specific setting.

Because there is an unbounded range of design choices, theoretical foundations in the form of design principles must be established to ensure Datish implements effective designs. Design principles are recognized as vital, but overlooked, design contributions [25]. As Moody [44] warns, relying on common sense when making design decisions "is unreliable as effects of graphic design choices are often counterintuitive." Equipped with theoretically sound design principles, artifacts (here, the constructs and rules of Datish) can be developed in a more rigorous manner and with greater transparency, thereby increasing confidence in the usability and expressive power of Datish.

Prior work has also considered some properties relevant for UCM. Notably, when developing visual notations Moody [44] proposed several principles, including semiotic clarity, perceptual discriminability, semantic transparency, complexity management, cognitive integration, visual expressiveness, dual coding, graphical economy, and cognitive fit. As these principles are instrumental in building scientifically grounded effective visualizations, they are relevant to Datish. However, they do not specifically consider the design of UCM. For example, they do not identify universal shapes, construct names, or constructs. Likewise, some of these ideas do not apply to UCM. For example, minimality, rather than expressiveness, appears to be a key feature of universal systems. There is thus a need to develop specific principles tailored to universal conceptual modeling. Before developing UCM design principles, we first describe the expected benefits of a universal data language.

2   The Benefits of Universal Conceptual Modeling

Universal conceptual modeling is a broad concept, and is expected to bring benefits in data management, process engineering, software development, and other contexts where conceptual modeling is used. In data management applications, using a UCM-based languages such as Datish is expected to resolve several growing challenges faced by data modelers, IT developers and, increasingly, non-data-professionals who use data for their work. We describe these challenges below.

Proliferation of modeling languages poses new challenges. Since 1970s hundreds, if not thousands, of modeling languages have been proposed [51, 63]. To some extent, this situation was mitigated when in 1980s popular languages emerged for important classes of applications, such as the ER model and the UML class diagram model for relational database design. Yet, as the scope of data tasks continued to expand, new languages emerged. Now, there is a deluge of conceptual modeling languages (e.g., SysUML for modeling systems, ArchiMate for modeling enterprises). UML itself has multiple diagram types that can be used to model data (e.g., Class, Object, Activity, Profile). Highly niche and boutique languages have been developed, such as Formalized Administrative Notation (FAN) designed to support administrative workers in Argentina [32]. Practitioners lament the proliferation of languages, suggesting a "universal data language" can eliminate the modern Tower of Babel-like confusion [62].

Increased Complexity and Sophistication of Modeling Languages and Non-expert Users. In addition to the development of new languages, existing languages continue to expand, seeking greater expressiveness. For example, UML contains 13 different types of diagrams, each with specialized elements. As studies show, practitioners utilize only a fraction of these elements. However, other than through statistical analysis of usage patterns [14, 45] and in passing interest [58], little effort has been undertaken to theoretically distil a "universal core" of conceptual modeling. Having this core is important, given that ordinary people, such as functional employees or members of the general public, are beginning to conduct conceptual modeling. It is unreasonable to expect them to be able to filter out non-core elements in a complex language. The presence of more advanced features (e.g., participation cardinality) has been shown to impede domain understanding by non-experts [31]. This is consistent with the findings on negative impacts of technologies with too many features or *bloatware* [18]. For novices, many modeling languages might appear bloated.

Modeling Challenges for Emerging Technologies. Despite the proliferation of languages, existing languages struggle to support many emerging technologies and applications. In developing artificial intelligence systems, social media systems, NoSQL databases (e.g., MongoDB), data lakes, and in agile or DevOps contexts, conceptual modeling languages struggle to remain relevant [5, 34]. For example, given the choices available in database technology (e.g., relational, key-value pair, graph-based, columnar), a pressing practical challenge is how to select an appropriate storage technology before using modeling specific to it (e.g., using DataVault [22]). A generic modeling language can help understand the general patterns in a domain (e.g., prevalence of unique objects vs highly similar objects) and suggest the right storage approach.

Supporting Data Analytics. An emerging need is to use conceptual models in support of data exploration, business analytics, and data mining. Common to many of these applications is the idea that modeling does not need to be extensive, and that some form of quick, "lightweight" modeling would be helpful [8, 34]. This suggests the value of a language with few, but fundamental, elements.

Facilitating Broader and Deeper Integration. Whereas many traditional conceptual modeling languages assume development of a particular system, modern systems involve a variety of data sources and technologies. For example, a data lake may ingest data from social media, enterprise systems, suppliers, data warehouses and reports. Even though there are approaches for modeling such systems, they all eschew the complexity of having to represent data in its full diversity. A final, unified view is shown instead (e.g., DataVault approach) [22]. Having a universal language might make it possible to model individual data sources and their interconnections simultaneously using a single notation. This would help to better support the development and use of integrated technologies and promote broader understanding of data and systems in the entire enterprise.

Overcoming the above challenges will be beneficial for data management. Benefits of a universal language are well-known in computing. In the database field, SQL served as a universal query language until the rise of NoSQL and NewSQL databases. Indeed, the universality of SQL, which is based on another general-purpose foundation, relational algebra, has been a partial reason for the success of relational databases. It is not surprising that some NoSQL databases also use flavors of SQL, such as Google's Big-Query or the SQL interfaces for NoSQL engines (e.g., PartiQL for DynamoDB, Atlas SQL for MongoDB). Even greater benefits accrue from the universal use of binary and first-order logic in computing. It is, thus, reasonable to expect significant benefits from a universal conceptual modeling language for data management.

3   Design Principles for Universal Conceptual Modeling

We conducted a literature review on topics that could provide a basis for principles of UCM, focusing on data modeling and Datish. Considering the role of conceptual modeling in representation, communication, problem solving and design [7, 27, 30, 42, 46, 50, 58], we assembled relevant search keywords. Using Google Scholar, we searched for terms such as "universal language", "general purpose language", "universal cognition", "universal sign system", "universal forms", and "universal design", as well as their reasonable combinations and related terms (e.g., "ontological primitives"). This was an iterative process, because reviewing this literature was useful in identifying other relevant sources mentioned by these works (e.g., the theory of generative design [64]).

The results of this review are diverse and highly interdisciplinary – ranging from universal art forms and music to studies of mathematics, culture, design, natural and artificial languages. Next, we reviewed the results with the aim to ascertain the potential of these works to constrain or motivate principles *behind* these universal concepts. At the end of this process, several themes emerged, originating mainly from the disciplines of anthropology, linguistics, semiotics, psychology, philosophy, and design. We draw primarily on theories from these disciplines.

In addition to the source of the principles, the review attested to the *possibility* of creating a unified data modeling language. Diverse interdisciplinary investigations suggest much universality and commonality among the elements that make up conceptual models or make them effective. Studies discuss "universal cognitive structures", "cultural universals" [e.g., 57], "cognitive universals" [e.g., 4], "semantic universals" [e.g., 23], universal "ontological primitives" (note, the concept of universals has a different meaning in ontology) [e.g., 33], and "universal design" [47] in addition to a variety of taxonomies and ontologies of these elements [e.g., 15, 36]. These suggest that tapping into these ideas could offer design guidance for Datish.

We distil the following principles of Universal Conceptual Modeling (UCM) representations based on the literature we found.

Flexibility. A prominent group of linguistics led by Chomsky holds that underlying all natural languages is so-called *universal grammar* (UG) – the innate principles that appear in all languages and are simply being instantiated when a speaker learns a particular language [11]. The UG sets general principles and parameters (e.g., that every word can be identified with a linguistic category), which then become instantiated into specific languages. Although the UG theory describes a universal meta-language, it suggests that a language aspiring to be general should permit *large variation* of expressions based on *few* principles and parameters. However, none of the principles and parameters are strictly binding, in that a given linguistic expression can deviate from them. Among other things, these flexible principles and parameters allow for great cultural diversity of human languages, and permit for language evolution – all desirable characteristics for a language such as Datish.

Flexibility has also been suggested by other theories. For example, the theory of tailorable design suggests for tailorable technologies (flexible systems that can be modified by a user in the context of use), to be based on the notions of dual design perspective (building some design functionalities, but allowing significant design choices to be defined by the user) [21]. Norman [47] argues that "[t]he best solution to the problem of designing for everyone is *flexibility*: flexibility in the size of images and computer screens, in the sizes, heights and angle of tables and chairs. Allow people to adjust their own seats, tables and working devices" (emphasis added). These ideas inform the following general principle:

Principle 1 (Flexibility): A UCM language is creative and flexible, based on few general parameters; local interpretation, adaptation and evolution of the language is expected and encouraged.

Principle 1 stands in opposition to the common "closed world" assumption underlying many computing languages (programming, conceptual), where rules of the language are explicitly established and are strictly binding. Diagrams (or scripts) that do not conform to the grammar or meta-model of a given language are deemed "invalid." In contrast, we encourage flexible and creative use, adaptation, and evolution of Datish. As with UG and universal design, such openness and flexibility are key to ensure Datish can cover a broad range of uses and is accessible to the widest audiences.

Accessibility. Research shows that universal systems are those that can be described using highly accessible and intuitive language. In psychology, research on basic level categories suggests that there is a small list of universal concepts (e.g., "bird", "tree") [54]. These concepts are "universal" in so far as they are present in virtually every culture. Furthermore, they are invariant to language proficiency and domain expertise: both experts and novices understand the meaning of these categories and can use them effectively. Basic level categories have already been considered in conceptual modeling research [8].

Related to the notion of conceptual accessibility is the theory of "universal design" [47], which states that design needs to be maximally inclusive and sensitive to all potential users. This means designs should address the requirement of marginalized communities on the notion that, if the design works for them, it should also work for others [47]. There are indeed many groups that are not considered as prototypical designers and users of conceptual models, such as IT novices [31], people with cognitive limitations due to age or illness, and visually impaired people (most models are visual in nature). Although we cannot guarantee Datish can fully support these populations, we make explicit the aspiration to do so.

Considering the notions of basic level categories, universal design theory and the aspiration of modeling for everyone, we propose:

Principle 2 (Accessibility): The UCM language components (e.g., modeling constructs, rules, symbols) should be maximally accessible to the broadest possible modelers and users.

Accessibility is important for several reasons. First, it supports wider adoption of the language. With non-experts in information technology increasingly engaging in design, the concepts underlying Datish need to be understandable and familiar to everyone. Second, the accessible elements of Datish signal to modelers that accessibility is an important virtue in modeling, which can encourage modelers to choose more accessible concepts for their respective domains. Hence, accessibility is the capability of making everyone confident that they can access, understand, and tailor Datish to fit their purpose in a "friendly" way, so they can conclude that it is worthy of use.

Ubiquity. In addition to accessibility, the constructs, visual notation, and rules used in a universal language should be ubiquitous; that is frequently used by different people, in different situations and settings.

For example, there is a small set of symbols nearly universally shared across cultures. In particular, "shapes found across many cultures include lines, circles, spirals, zigzags, squares and squares of circles" [53]. These shapes have a relatively stable and common general and contextualized understanding (e.g., a circle in the night sky is commonly assumed to be a moon). Furthermore, the manner in which the symbols are drawn exhibit strong regularity across cultures and within cultures (e.g., by different age groups). For example, parallel sides and right angles are considered basic compositional forms for graphical elements, known as the "geometric regularity effect," a recent discovery in neuroscience [16, 55, 56].

Principle 3 (Ubiquity): The UCM language components should be ubiquitous, shared across people from different backgrounds and having different levels of expertise.

Minimalism. An important consideration in developing universal representations is the scope and coverage of Datish. Conceptual modeling research has traditionally privileged language expressiveness, under the assumption that all relevant constructs from the real world should be present in the language; otherwise "construct deficit" occurs, in which case some relevant facts cannot be modeled [44, 60]. However, while these ideas are relevant for developing complete representations in the context of traditional information systems development (typically by professionals for well-defined modeling purposes, such as database design), they are detrimental for a universal language. It is simply impossible to exhaust all of the possible kinds of real-world objects and events and predetermine the requisite constructs in a universal language. This problem has been studied previously within the context of *generative systems* (e.g., the number system, the Internet) with the capacity to produce both expected and unexpected variation as a result of open and fundamentally unpredictable use [59, 64].

According to the theory of generative systems, the single most important principle of a generative system design is *minimalism* or "procrastination" [64]. The idea is to only endow a generative system with absolutely essential features for functioning, and permit these features to evolve or be extended by its users. This principle has a strong rationale: the presence of too many choices may create high cognitive load and impede the adoption and use of a universal system, especially by novice designers.

Psychology research suggests humans are capable of operating with and memorizing seven, plus or minus two, chunks of information [43]. Hence, seeking to limit the essential number of constructs to between five and seven (or less) can facilitate better learning and use of a universal language. This results in the next principle:

Principle 4 (Minimalism): Limit the components of a UCM language to the essential few.

Primitivism. Conceptual modeling languages seek to represent concepts about the world. As already implied by the minimalism principle, universal models should be based on an absolutely minimum set of constructs. This means that the ontological notions about reality should be the most basic, primitive ones. The idea of "ontological primitivism" can be found in a number of philosophical theories about reality [26, 28, 38, 60], as "every theory of nature needs to identify at least one ontological primitive, since we cannot keep on explaining one thing in terms of another forever" [33]. However, there is considerable debate about what these principles are. Hence, rather than strictly suggesting that a UCM be implemented in terms of ontological primitives, we offer an open-ended call:

Principle 5 (Primitivism): The UCM language components should consist of common ontological primitives.

Modularity. Design research on extensible, generative technologies, converge on an important principle of universal, flexible and accessible systems – modularity of system components [21, 64]. Modularity is the property of having multiple self-contained components that can be combined in a flexible way. Modularity allows systems to be combined and recombined, based on evolving and individual needs. It also permits the management of complexity, which can still be a challenge, even when the number of design choices are intentionally minimized. We propose the following principle:

Principle 6 (Modularity): The UCM language components should be modular and combinable in flexible, unrestricted ways.

The six principles – flexibility, accessibility, ubiquity, minimalism, primitivism, and modularity – constitute the theoretical basis of universal conceptual modeling. These principles are based on ideas from several disciplines and theories that have grappled with the notion of universality. Note that the principles of UCM are not independent. Although each brings its own angle to UCM, there is notable convergence in their guidance. For example, primitivism supports minimalism and modularity makes a language more flexible. We note further that many of the principles explicitly consider the challenges faced by novice designers. For example, minimalism, accessibility, and ubiquity are directly informed by the needs of novice users.

At the same time, there can be some tension among the principles. For example, the concepts that philosophy deems primitive might not be seen as accessible to broad audiences, such as the ontological concept of 'perdurant.' Indeed, our version of Microsoft Word does not even include this word in its dictionary. Likewise, linguistic accessibility (e.g., specific concepts of "bird", "tree") may not correspond to constructs deemed ontological primitives (e.g., object, time, space, relationship, basic level category in general) [17, 27, 54].

By articulating these principles, we are able to adopt converging interdisciplinary knowledge on universal systems. Equipped with this knowledge, we next sketch the paths from these principles to the universal conceptual modeling language Datish. A complete language design is beyond the scope of this paper because our focus is on the UCM. Rather, this brief exposition illustrates the application of the principles to assist in communicating their generative power and utility.

4   Implementing Universal Conceptual Modeling

An overarching implementation strategy is considering all principles together. Many principles converge; others may conflict. A design choice consistent with one principle can be strengthened or attenuated based on corroboration or conflict from the other principles. The aim is to select language components that satisfy as many principles as possible.

The first principle, *flexibility*, suggests that creating a language of considerable flexibility supports local interpretation, adaptation, and evolution. This principle can guide Datish design and be repeated at different points of the language description and instruction for learning. Flexibility also means that a local interpretation of this language is not only permissible, but consistent with the design philosophy and, therefore, should be encouraged. It is a novel and counterintuitive principle, so it is important to clearly signal this unusual design feature to users.

Flexibility can factor in many ways in the Datish design. The constructs of the language can be used in any order, in any variation. For example, the language can permit representing only individuals, irrespective of what categories they belong, or only categories. The representations of individuals do not necessarily have to agree with the templates defined by the categories.

The *accessibility* principle involves, among other considerations, paying special attention to marginalized communities, including analysts with special needs (e.g., due to cognitive impairments), modeling novices and members of the public. Here, some guidance has already been developed by the conceptual modeling community. These include semiotic clarity and semantic transparency by Moody [44]. Another example is provided by Castellanos et al. [8] who synthesized psychology research on basic level categories and provided actionable guidelines for selecting basic classes. These procedures can be employed in the choice of concepts for Datish. For example, concepts such as *attribute* and *relationship* are among the basic terms that would be elements of a universal language. In addition, Datish can break away from the common assumption of conceptual models as static 2-dimensional diagrams. Modern IT allows users to present content as images, videos, sounds, embedded virtual reality or augmented reality. The research community needs to explore these avenues more actively to continue democratizing modeling and removing barriers on those who engage with conceptual modeling.

Ubiquity suggests selecting graphic representations from the basic repertoire of shapes (i.e., lines, circles, squares). These shapes can be articulated based on geometric regularity (i.e., using parallel sides and right angles). Hence, for example, a square should have straight corners.

Minimalism can be implemented by choosing only constructs that are indispensable for capturing key domain semantics. Here, guidance can come from a review of broad practitioner and academic literature on data modeling. For example, many conceptual modeling projects use concepts such as entities, objects, attributes, or roles. In specific applications, such as data storage, constructs such as *aggregate* [6] or *relation* [13] are central. Such a review can identify the recurring patterns in the use of modeling constructs with the aim to distil the most essential ones. Yet, such guidance needs to be considered critically, because conceptual modeling languages have been historically dominated by assumptions, such as representation by abstraction, that might be unhelpful in a universal language design. Other guidelines can also be used to resolve some of the choices among concepts (e.g., ontological primitivism, conceptual accessibility).

Note that philosophy does not have a monopoly over ontological primitives. Valuable addition guidance can come from psychology, as well as other disciplines, including art and design. This is especially valuable when considering all of the UCM principles together, as the acceptance by other areas of the ontological primitives can signal a good candidate for a universal construct [e.g., 29].

Underlying all the design choices is the notion of *modular design*. The universal language needs to use identifiable and clearly separable components. These would permit language users to utilize different components based on their needs, as well as build upon the components and extend the language to more specific uses. For example, a specific component can deal with specialized constructs (e.g., system [40]).

The tension among these principles can be lessened if we assume there is a certain logic in the order in which these principles need to be realized and we can identify which among these principles is the most essential. Flexibility, accessibility, ubiquity, and modularity all deal with the way in which a language is presented to a user and is used. In contrast, minimalism, primitivism, and modularity mainly deal with what semantics the language can convey. However, all principles contribute to promoting representation or learning and usage in their own way. Table 1 summarizes the principles and explains how each contributes to either representation or language usage.

Table 1. Principles of UCM and their core benefit (highlighted)

Principle	Representation and Semantics	Learning and usage
Flexibility	Allows language extensions and improvisations in language use	Allows diverse expressions and makes it more inclusive
Accessibility	Constrains representations to those which are accessible	Makes the language potentially usable to broadest audiences
Ubiquity	Constrains representations to those which are most common, frequently used	Makes the language potentially usable to broadest audiences
Minimalism	Focuses on very small number of constructs and rules	Makes the language easier to learn and use
Primitivism	Focuses on only basic, fundamental constructs	Makes the language more intuitive, as well as general
Modularity	Allows the selection of modules based on representational needs	Makes the language easier to learn and use

From the perspective of promoting representation or learning and usage, we suggest Datish should ensure it has a solid ability to represent essential domain semantics (following Minimalism and Primitivism), while striving for a flexible, accessible, common, and module presentation to make it easier to learn and use.

5 Discussion and Conclusion

This research reviewed important limitations in current modeling practices, along with new modeling opportunities and applications, to identify a promising direction of universal conceptual modeling (UCM). To support this type of modeling with sound theory, we proposed design principles for creating a universal conceptual modeling language, *Datish*. The principles are derived from a literature review across multiple disciplines dealing with universal design, cognition, signs, and forms.

While our objective has been to develop foundations for a universal conceptual modeling language, our work can also be useful for existing conceptual modeling languages. First, some existing conceptual modeling languages, while not universal, are widely used, notably, the popular ER model and UML. The principles of UCM are derived from relevant references to the design and use of these existing conceptual modeling languages. For example, the notion of geometric regularity can be applied to the constructs of these languages to assess the general accessibility of these shapes. We anticipate that shapes inconsistent with the geometric regularity principle would be more difficult to learn, especially for novices.

Notably, many conceptual modeling languages already use ubiquitous shapes, but without theoretical justification. Moody [44], for example, laments that even such important and standard language as "UML does not provide design rationale for any of its graphical conventions [such as using a rectangle for the class construct]". In addition to guiding Datish, the UCM principles can be used to evaluate the choices made "intuitively" by language designers in the past (after all, geometric regularity and symbol universality effects were expected to influence these decisions).

An important direction for future research is the actual development of Datish based on our outline of the design process involved in this language construction. Among other things, this would entail articulating the relevant primitive modeling constructs and creating a new notation consistent with the design principles, with an emphasis on justifying specific design choices.

Once that language has been developed, it should be evaluated empirically to ensure its efficacy in practice and to refine the language (especially shedding light on the trade-offs amongst the principles). Asking practitioners to create models or read models created by Datish could be beneficial. Empirical work could include both qualitative (e.g., semi-structured interviews, focus groups) and quantitative methods (e.g., experiments, surveys). These design decisions could be evaluated using an artifact sampling approach [37] to ensure the design choices do not have unintended effects on understanding and use.

With respect to reading Datish diagrams, using the models for understandability (e.g., domain knowledge) might be an initial evaluation that should be followed up with the use of the model for querying data; that is, the tasks of the models are important and matter. As suggested, different use cases, such as emerging contexts (e.g., artificial intelligence, social media systems, NoSQL databases, data lakes and traditional contexts (e.g., building a relational DBMS) could be examined across a variety of application domains (e.g., finance, healthcare, education).

Comparing Datish models against an accepted norm for each context and allowing practitioners to comment on the advantages and disadvantages of each would also provide valuable insights. In this context, it would be important to recruit individuals of different modeling abilities (reading and creating) to ensure maximal accessibility, resulting in evaluation of the language across tasks, contexts, domains, and backgrounds.

Finally, the flexibility of Datish (i.e., its rules are not strictly binding, and deviations are expected, if not encouraged) should be rigorously studied. While such flexibility opens Datish to a broad range of uses and makes it accessible to the widest range of audiences, a potential downside is ambiguity and confusion, when symbol use is unclear, ill-defined, and inconsistently used. Therefore, the limitations of such a language should be determined. In addition, studies should investigate how this can be mitigated in some cases by the kinds of uses of such a language, such as one-off models for specific analytics tasks (throwaway models, perhaps used by only one person or team). Research can also draw upon the open nature of human languages, and how ambiguity and confusion are minimized in natural communication [e.g., 48]. These new features of Datish create opportunities for theoretical, design and empirical research on conceptual modeling to explore the nature, benefits, and limitations of an evolving, living, and flexible universal conceptual modeling.

References

1. Atzeni, P., et al.: The relational model is dead, SQL is dead, and I don't feel so good myself. ACM SIGMOD Rec. **42**(1), 64–68 (2013)
2. Azevedo, C.L., et al.: Modeling resources and capabilities in enterprise architecture: a well-founded ontology-based proposal for ArchiMate. Inf. Syst. **54**, 235–262 (2015)
3. Bjørner, D.: Domain Science and Engineering: A Foundation for Software Development. Springer, Cham (2021). https://doi.org/10.1007/978-3-030-73484-8
4. Blaut, J.M., et al.: Mapping as a cultural and cognitive universal. Ann. Assoc. Am. Geogr. **93**(1), 165–185 (2003)
5. Bork, D.: Conceptual modeling and artificial intelligence: challenges and opportunities for enterprise engineering. In: Aveiro, D., Proper, H.A., Guerreiro, S., de Vries, M. (eds.) Enterprise Engineering Working Conference, pp. 3–9. Springer, Cham (2022). https://doi.org/10.1007/978-3-031-11520-2_1
6. Bugiotti, F., et al.: Database design for NoSQL systems. In: Yu, E., Dobbie, G., Jarke, M., Purao, S. (eds.) Conceptual Modeling, pp. 223–231. Springer, Cham (2014). https://doi.org/10.1007/978-3-319-12206-9_18
7. Burton-Jones, A., Weber, R.: Building conceptual modeling on the foundation of ontology. In: Computing Handbook: Information Systems and Information Technology, Boca Raton, FL, United States, pp. 15.1–15.24 (2014)
8. Castellanos, A., et al.: Basic classes in conceptual modeling: theory and practical guidelines. J. Assoc. Inf. Syst. **21**(4), 1001–1044 (2020)
9. Chatziantoniou, D., Kantere, V.: Data virtual machines: data-driven conceptual modeling of big data infrastructures. Presented at the EDBT/ICDT Workshops (2020)
10. Chatziantoniou, D., Kantere, V.: Data virtual machines: enabling data virtualization. In: Rezig, E.K., et al. (eds.) Heterogeneous Data Management, Polystores, and Analytics for Healthcare, pp. 3–13. Springer, Cham (2021). https://doi.org/10.1007/978-3-030-93663-1_1
11. Chomsky, N.: Knowledge of Language: Its Nature, Origin, and Use. Greenwood Publishing Group, Westport (1986)
12. Chua, C.E.H., et al.: Data management. MIS Q. 1–10 (2022)

13. Codd, E.F.: A relational model of data for large shared data banks. Commun. ACM **13**(6), 377–387 (1970)
14. Compagnucci, I., Corradini, F., Fornari, F., Re, B.: Trends on the usage of BPMN 2.0 from publicly available repositories. In: Buchmann, R.A., Polini, A., Johansson, B., Karagiannis, D. (eds.) BIR 2021. LNBIP, vol. 430, pp. 84–99. Springer, Cham (2021). https://doi.org/10. 1007/978-3-030-87205-2_6
15. De Carlo, G., et al.: Rethinking model representation-a taxonomy of advanced information visualization in conceptual modeling. In: Ralyté, J., Chakravarthy, S., Mohania, M., Jeusfeld, M.A., Karlapalem, K. (eds.) Conceptual Modeling, pp. 35–51. Springer, Cham (2022). https:// doi.org/10.1007/978-3-031-17995-2_3
16. Dehaene, S., et al.: Symbols and mental programs: a hypothesis about human singularity. Trends Cogn. Sci. (2022)
17. Dupré, J.: A process ontology for biology. Philos. Mag. **67**, 81–88 (2014)
18. Elahi, H., et al.: Pleasure or pain? An evaluation of the costs and utilities of bloatware applications in android smartphones. J. Netw. Comput. Appl. **157**, 102578 (2020)
19. Eriksson, O., et al.: The case for classes and instances-a response to representing instances: the case for reengineering conceptual modelling grammars. Eur. J. Inf. Syst. **28**(6), 681–693 (2019)
20. Fettke, P., Reisig, W.: Systems mining with heraklit: the next step. In: Di Ciccio, C., Dijkman, R., del Río Ortega, A., Rinderle-Ma, S. (eds.) BPM 2022 Forum, pp. 89–104. Springer, Cham (2022). https://doi.org/10.1007/978-3-031-16171-1_6
21. Germonprez, M., et al.: A theory of tailorable technology design. J. Assoc. Inf. Syst. **8**(6), 351–367 (2007)
22. Giebler, C., Gröger, C., Hoos, E., Schwarz, H., Mitschang, B.: Modeling data lakes with data vault: practical experiences, assessment, and lessons learned. In: Laender, A.H.F., Pernici, B., Lim, E.-P., de Oliveira, J.P.M. (eds.) ER 2019. LNCS, vol. 11788, pp. 63–77. Springer, Cham (2019). https://doi.org/10.1007/978-3-030-33223-5_7
23. Goddard, C.: Semantic theory and semantic universals. In: Semantic and Lexical Universals, pp. 7–29 (1994)
24. Gonzalez-Perez, C.: How ontologies can help in software engineering. In: Cunha, J., Fernandes, J.P., Lämmel, R., Saraiva, J., Zaytsev, V. (eds.) GTTSE 2015. LNCS, vol. 10223, pp. 26–44. Springer, Cham (2017). https://doi.org/10.1007/978-3-319-60074-1_2
25. Gregor, S., et al.: The anatomy of a design principle. J. Assoc. Inf. Syst. **21**(6), 1622–1652 (2020)
26. Guarino, N., Guizzardi, G.: In the defense of ontological foundations for conceptual modeling. Scand. J. Inf. Syst. **18**(1), 115–126 (2006)
27. Guizzardi, G.: Ontological foundations for structural conceptual models. Telematics Instituut Fundamental Research Series, Enschede, The Netherlands (2005)
28. Guizzardi, G., et al.: Towards ontological foundations for conceptual modeling: the unified foundational ontology (UFO) story. Appl. Ontol. **10**(3–4), 259–271 (2015)
29. Harman, G.: Object-Oriented Ontology: A New Theory of Everything. Penguin UK, London (2018)
30. Henderson-Sellers, B.: Why philosophize; why not just model? In: Johannesson, P., Lee, M.L., Liddle, S.W., Opdahl, A.L., López, Ó.P. (eds.) ER 2015. LNCS, vol. 9381, pp. 3–17. Springer, Cham (2015). https://doi.org/10.1007/978-3-319-25264-3_1
31. Hvalshagen, M., et al.: Empowering users with narratives: examining the efficacy of narratives for understanding data-oriented conceptual models. Inf. Syst. Res. 1–38 (2023)
32. Iacub, P.: Software ERP: El nuevo Gran Hermano de las organizaciones. Autores de Argentina, Buenos Aires (2015). https://bit.ly/3phEmbX
33. Kastrup, B.: An ontological solution to the mind-body problem. Philosophies **2**(2), 10 (2017)

34. Kaur, K., Rani, R.: Modeling and querying data in NoSQL databases. In: 2013 IEEE International Conference on Big Data, pp. 1–7 IEEE (2013)
35. Lima, L., et al.: An integrated semantics for reasoning about SysML design models using refinement. Softw. Syst. Model. **16**(3), 875–902 (2015). https://doi.org/10.1007/s10270-015-0492-y
36. Lorenzatti, A., Abel, M., Fiorini, S.R., Bernardes, A.K., dos Santos Scherer, C.M.: Ontological primitives for visual knowledge. In: da Rocha Costa, A.C., Vicari, R.M., Tonidandel, F. (eds.) SBIA 2010. LNCS (LNAI), vol. 6404, pp. 1–10. Springer, Heidelberg (2010). https://doi.org/10.1007/978-3-642-16138-4_1
37. Lukyanenko, R., et al.: Artifact sampling: using multiple information technology artifacts to increase research rigor. In: Proceedings of the 51st Hawaii International Conference on System Sciences (HICSS 2018), Big Island, Hawaii, pp. 1–12 (2018)
38. Lukyanenko, R., Storey, V.C., Pastor, O.: Foundations of information technology based on Bunge's systemist philosophy of reality. Softw. Syst. Model. **20**(4), 921–938 (2021). https://doi.org/10.1007/s10270-021-00862-5
39. Lukyanenko, R., et al.: Representing instances: the case for reengineering conceptual modeling grammars. Eur. J. Inf. Syst. **28**(1), 68–90 (2019)
40. Lukyanenko, R., et al.: System: a core conceptual modeling construct for capturing complexity. Data Knowl. Eng. **141**, 1–29 (2022)
41. Lukyanenko, R., Parsons, J.: Beyond micro-tasks: research opportunities in observational crowdsourcing. J. Database Manag. (JDM) **29**(1), 1–22 (2018)
42. Mayr, H.C., Thalheim, B.: The triptych of conceptual modeling. Softw. Syst. Model. **20**(1), 7–24 (2020). https://doi.org/10.1007/s10270-020-00836-z
43. Miller, G.: The magical number seven, plus or minus two: some limits on our capacity for processing information. Psychol. Rev. **63**, 81–97 (1956)
44. Moody, D.L.: The "physics" of notations: toward a scientific basis for constructing visual notations in software engineering. IEEE Trans. Softw. Eng. **35**(6), 756–779 (2009)
45. Muehlen, M., Recker, J.: How much language is enough? Theoretical and practical use of the business process modeling notation. In: Bubenko, J., Krogstie, J., Pastor, O., Pernici, B., Rolland, C., Sølvberg, A. (eds.) Seminal Contributions to Information Systems Engineering, pp. 429–443. Springer, Cham (2013). https://doi.org/10.1007/978-3-642-36926-1_35
46. Mylopoulos, J.: Information modeling in the time of the revolution. Inf. Syst. **23**(3–4), 127–155 (1998)
47. Norman, D.A.: The Design of Everyday Things. Bsic Books, New York, NY (2002)
48. Noth, W.: Handbook of Semiotics. Indiana University Press, Bloomington (1990)
49. Parsons, J., Wand, Y.: Emancipating instances from the tyranny of classes in information modeling. ACM Trans. Database Syst. **25**(2), 228–268 (2000)
50. Partridge, C., et al.: Are conceptual models concept models? Presented at the International Conference on Conceptual Modeling (2013)
51. Recker, J.: BPMN research: what we know and what we don't know. In: Mendling, J., Weidlich, M. (eds.) BPMN 2012. LNBIP, vol. 125, pp. 1–7. Springer, Heidelberg (2012). https://doi.org/10.1007/978-3-642-33155-8_1
52. Recker, J., et al.: From representation to mediation: a new agenda for conceptual modeling research in a digital world. MIS Q. **45**(1), 269–300 (2021)
53. Roberts, S.: Is Geometry a Language That Only Humans Know? (2022). https://www.nytimes.com/2022/03/22/science/geometry-math-brain-primates.html
54. Rosch, E., et al.: Basic objects in natural categories. Cogn. Psychol. **8**(3), 382–439 (1976)
55. Sablé-Meyer, M., et al.: A language of thought for the mental representation of geometric shapes. Cogn. Psychol. **139**, 101527 (2022)
56. Sablé-Meyer, M., et al.: Sensitivity to geometric shape regularity in humans and baboons: a putative signature of human singularity. Proc. Natl. Acad. Sci. **118**, 16, e2023123118 (2021)

57. Stea, D., et al.: Mapping as a cultural universal. In: Portugali, J. (ed.) The Construction of Cognitive Maps, pp. 345–360. Springer, Dordrecht (1996)
58. Storey, V.C., et al.: Conceptual modeling: topics, themes, and technology trends. ACM Comput. Surv. (2023)
59. Teigland, R., Power, D.: The immersive internet: reflections on the entangling of the virtual with society, politics and the economy. Palgrave Macmillan, New York (2013)
60. Wand, Y., Weber, R.: On the ontological expressiveness of information systems analysis and design grammars. Inf. Syst. J. **3**(4), 217–237 (1993)
61. Wand, Y., Weber, R.: Research commentary: Information systems and conceptual modeling - a research agenda. Inf. Syst. Res. **13**(4), 363–376 (2002)
62. Western, P.: Why the majority of data projects fail: the case for a Universal Data Language. https://snowplow.io/blog/project-failure-universal-data-language/. Accessed 09 Jan 2023
63. Wyssusek, B., Zaha, J.M.: Towards a pragmatic perspective on requirements for conceptual modeling methods. Presented at the EMMSAD (2007)
64. Zittrain, J.: The Future of the Internet–and How To Stop It. Yale University Press, New Haven (2008)

Supporting Method Creation, Adaptation and Execution with a Low-code Approach

Raquel Araújo de Oliveira[✉], Mario Cortes-Cornax, and Agnès Front

Univ. Grenoble Alpes, CNRS, Grenoble INP, LIG, 38000 Grenoble, France
{raquel.oliveira,mario.cortes-cornax,agnes.front}@univ-grenoble-alpes.fr

Abstract. Method Engineering emerged in the 90s as a discipline to design, construct and adapt methods, techniques and tools for the development of information systems. By executing a method step by step, users follow a systematic and well-defined way to attain the results which the method was created for. To support the creation of methods in a more guided and systematic way, a method framework can be used as a template, allowing one to benefit from the expertise of method engineers who regrouped their good practices in such frameworks. However, the creation and adoption of a method may be difficult if there is no tool to support these activities. In addition, method engineers may not have the programming skills to implement such a tool. In this context, we propose an approach inspired by the *low-code* paradigm for Method Engineering. The approach helps method engineers in creating new methods or adapting an already existing framework that integrates some construction rules for guidance. Our approach automatically provides tool support so that method experts can actually execute the method. This paper presents the approach through a proof of concept implementation, and a first empirical evaluation through semi-structured interviews.

Keywords: Method Engineering · Low-code · Framework of Methods

1 Introduction

In software engineering, development methods formalize the steps to follow in the software development life-cycle, looking for quality and client satisfaction. In [1] a method is defined as "*a process* for generating a set of models that describe various aspects of a software being built using some well-defined notation". Later on, this definition evolved to include not only the *process model* but also the *product meta-model*, to characterize the artifacts manipulated by the process.

Method Engineering is defined as the discipline to design, construct and adapt methods, techniques and tools for the development of information systems [2]. This engineering discipline promotes the adaptation of methods to particular contexts or projects. Particularly, our intent is to focus on one type of

---

Institute of Engineering Univ. Grenoble Alpes.

H. van der Aa et al. (Eds.): BPMDS 2023/EMMSAD 2023, LNBIP 479, pp. 184–198, 2023.
https://doi.org/10.1007/978-3-031-34241-7_13

methods, namely *methods for the continual evolution or improvement* of different types of systems such as *ecosystems, business processes, production processes,* etc. Indeed, nowadays, businesses are living in an ever-changing environment, supported by technological, environmental and societal breakthroughs. This dynamism demands organizations to continually evolve to provide faster, better or more innovative products and services to stay competitive in the market.

To create a new method, one should be well-aware of the application domain as well as the Method Engineering field. To facilitate this task, frameworks have been proposed to serve as a template from which a new method can be created. Method engineers can be in charge of creating such frameworks. However, this task is not well guided and requires considerable experience [4]. In addition, although such frameworks provide a huge help in terms of creating a new method, little support is found afterward [4], on the usage of the method.

Once a method is created for a specific need, an efficient execution of a method requires some tool support. Indeed, each step of the method's process can be handled using a variety of different techniques, and using different tools. For instance, in the Agile Methodology, in particular the Scrum Process, we can mention two steps needing different techniques: the definition of the product vision could be done using *brainstorming*, while following up the work could be done by *daily meetings*, and specific tools to support these techniques exist. While it is possible to execute the method step by step without a centralized control, and to somehow manually keep track of where we are and what was already done, it is more convenient to centralize this information. A tool to support method creation, adaptation and execution would therefore facilitate a method application. However, method engineers do not always have software development skills to create such a tool. A *low-code* approach (LCA) can help in achieving this goal, by automating the creation of a tool to support the execution of the created method. Indeed, the low-code paradigm promotes the development of applications with little coding, to rapidly deliver applications [20]. Our research question is therefore : *How can Method Engineering benefit from a low-code approach in order to create, adapt and execute methods ?*

In [17] we presented a preliminary work where low-code was applied to support method creation and execution. In this paper, we extend the previous one by integrating the possibility to create frameworks of methods (from which methods can be created by adaptation), thereby including a third profile of actors who can benefit from the approach: framework engineers (cf. Fig. 1). Hereafter, we present the approach and the implemented prototype, specially the method executor module, generated automatically through the *low-code* engine. We also report on preliminary user experiments performed on the prototype.

The outline of the paper is the following. First, Sect. 2 gives background and the state of the art relying on Method Engineering and low-code approaches. Section 3 overviews our low-code approach to support Method Engineering, followed by Sect. 4 which relies on an example to illustrate the implemented prototype. Section 5 presents the implementation as a proof of concept of the approach.

Section 6 presents the first steps of a user-centred validation. Finally, Sect. 7 concludes and highlights some future work.

2   Background and State of the Art

Approaches proposed in **Method Engineering** (ME) for the construction of a method are generally classified in [14,18]:

- *ad-hoc* approaches concerning the construction of a method "from scratch";
- *assembly-based* approaches proposing to reuse and compose method components (fragments, "method chunks", services, ...) to construct a specific method or a method family;
- *extension-based* approaches consisting of extending a method to produce a new one;
- *model-based* or *paradigm-based* approaches, where the construction of a new method is realized by instantiation or model adaptation [9].

We focus on a model-based approach by adaptation, where the construction of methods is based on the adaptation of methods of the same abstraction level. In this kind of approaches, methods are defined by both a *process model* and a *product meta-model*, relying on the OMG meta-layers of models [12]. The process model details the steps to follow to accomplish the goal of the method, while the product meta-model describes the artifacts manipulated by the process. Both the process model and the product meta-model are positioned in different meta-layers. The process model conforms to an existing language (i.e. *Maps*, presented in Sect. 4), while the product is positioned at the meta level.

Nowadays, method engineers must deal with vast and variable contexts when they are in charge of putting in place a method guiding the continual evolution of a system. Different examples of continual evolution methods can be found in the literature, each one proposing its own cycle of steps and ways to characterize the artifacts guiding the evolution, for example, PDCA (Plan, Do Check, Act) [8], DMAIC (Define, Measure, Analyze, Improve, Control) [7], and A3 [22]. Except for DMAIC [7], the aforementioned methods have not been formalized, which makes it challenging to integrate them in a framework of methods.

Different approaches [2,4,9,14,18] have been proposed in ME to deal with the construction of new methods by adapting existing ones. However, for the best of our knowledge there are no tools to support the creation of methods based on these approaches, and such adaptation is mainly paper-based. We formalized in previous works the As-Is/As-If framework [4] as a conceptual framework dedicated to the family [9] of continual evolution methods. This framework is composed of a process model and a product meta-model that method engineers can adapt when constructing a target method. The last one results in a method guiding the continual evolution of a system in a given context.

In our previous works, the use of this framework was simply guided by heuristics that method engineers could "manually" apply to adapt the process model and the product meta-model to their own domain. This paper presents a novel approach based on the low-code paradigm, to help method engineers to construct a new method, by adaptation of a framework of methods (such as As-Is/As-If), and to follow its execution.

Low-code development platforms (LCDP) enable rapid application delivery with a minimum of hand-coding, and quick setup and deployment [20]. The goal of such platforms is to ease the development of applications, by reducing drastically the coding efforts, or by eliminating coding all together. Although the term *low-code* first appeared in the literature in 2014 [20], some principles behind it are not completely new. There have been efforts to easy applications' development since a long time ago. Very popular in the 90s, Microsoft Office Access provides an easy way to create simple desktop applications with input forms to manage data in information systems. WordPress[1] has also been in the market since the 2000s providing a user-friendly way to create websites. The main difference with LCDP is that a bigger focus has been made on fast application delivery, beside the rapid application development (usually based on a visual and drag'n'drop way of development).

However, for the best of our knowledge, no LCDP had yet focused on ME. Most LCDP can be classified as *general purpose* platforms, while some are specific to *process modeling*. According to [19], general-purpose LCDPs target a wide range of applications with tools that address application creation, integration, deployment, life-cycle management, and distribution. Some general-purpose LCDP propose workflow automation, which to some extent relates with the method execution we propose to support in this paper. Examples of such LCDP are Mendix[2], OutSystems[3], and Simplicité[4]. However, the workflow automation in these LCDP helps in defining the business logic of applications behavior, which may be adapted to methods processes, but it is not their main focus.

On the other hand, LCDPs specific to process modeling focus on creating and configuring process flow logic and workflows, specially business processes. Some of those LCDPs are AgilePoint[5], Appian[6], Bonitasoft[7], Activiti[8], JBoss jBPM[9] or Intalio[10]. Most of these LCDPs support the Business Process Model and Notation (BPMN 2.0) language [11] to represent processes and also provide constrained ways to define a data model of the process (e.g. relational databases or java classes). The main difference with our approach is that ours allows method engineers to define data at the meta level (i.e. the product meta-model). This provides the possibility to benefit from a *Domain Specific Language*, to guide the creation of the product model, giving more flexibility when defining the artifacts

---

[1] https://wordpress.com/.

[2] https://www.mendix.com/.

[3] https://www.outsystems.com/.

[4] https://simplicite.fr.

[5] https://www.agilepoint.com.

[6] https://appian.com/.

[7] https://www.bonitasoft.com/.

[8] https://www.activiti.org/.

[9] https://www.jbpm.org/.

[10] https://www.intalio.com/.

that may be used in the method. Besides, our approach allows a larger range of profiles (namely framework engineers, method engineers and method experts, cf. Fig. 1) to benefit from the low-code paradigm. The next section introduces the approach and briefly presents the research methodology we followed.

3   Overview of a LCA to Support Method Engineering

This section provides an overview of a low code approach (LCA) focusing on the different users that can work together in the ME field. Based on our previous experience [4], we identified people with different profiles working together and playing different roles in the field of Method Engineering: (i) *framework engineers* know and can design different method frameworks from which methods can be created. These frameworks can be considered as method templates that may capitalize knowledge; (ii) *method engineers* are well aware of the Method Engineering discipline and can create a new method or adapt an existing framework or method for a specific purpose; finally (iii) *method experts* have deep knowledge in one (or more) specific method(s) and are able to lead its (or their) execution. The approach presented in this paper aims at supporting these three roles in achieving their goals.

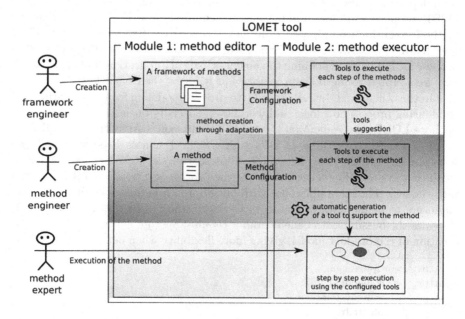

Fig. 1. A low-code approach to support Method Engineering.

Firstly, a framework engineer creates a framework of methods (Fig. 1), which facilitates further creation of a method. Such a framework would define a generic process model and product meta-model, adaptable to many application domains. It could include a set of heuristics, in order to restrict and guide the method construction rules. In the next step, framework engineers can configure the framework, by setting the most suitable tools to execute each step of the methods based on their framework.

Once a framework is created and configured, method engineers can create a method by adapting the latter, meaning that the process model and product meta-model of the framework can be extended to create a new method for a specific purpose, following the pre-defined framework heuristics. Alternatively, the method engineer can also create a method from scratch. The list of configured tools in the framework are then suggested to configure the new-created method (in case the latter was created based on a framework). In this step, a method engineer could also propose new tools.

Once a method is created and configured, the method expert can lead its execution step by step. Following the low-code paradigm, a supporting tool to execute the method is automatically generated and can be used by method experts in order to track the progression and the different artifacts resulting from each step.

In this work, we follow the THEDRE research methodology [16], a framework of scientific research in computer science. This method proposes guides to manage research, to correctly initiate the work, to experiment, to analyze data, and to write an article. This method is user-centred, therefore users are quickly put in the research cycle. In this research, the prototype we have developed to illustrate the approach was quickly evaluated by users, and the preliminary results are discussed in Sect. 6.

4   Running Example

This section presents the CEFOP [5] method as a running example which we will use to illustrate the approach presented in this paper, in Sect. 5. Figure 2 depicts the usage of the As-Is/As-If framework for the creation of the CEFOP method, a method dedicated to continual evolution of business processes within small and medium companies. The goal of the CEFOP method is to incite process participants empowerment and collective decision-making on the possible evolutions, by making participants' intervention more objective in particular through traces analysis and process mining techniques.

On the As-Is/As-If framework, the product meta-model is represented using UML class diagrams (depicted on the left part of Fig. 2), a well-known standard notation for representing conceptual data models, while the process model is represented using the Map [21] language (depicted on the right part of Fig. 2), a well-known notation to represent goal-oriented processes. Indeed, the As-Is/As-If framework adopts an *intentional-based* approach, in which the process model promotes a clear difference between *what* to achieve (the intentions, represented by ellipses) and the *ways* to achieve it (the strategies, arcs linking the ellipses) [21]. On the other hand, the product meta-model defines all the concepts

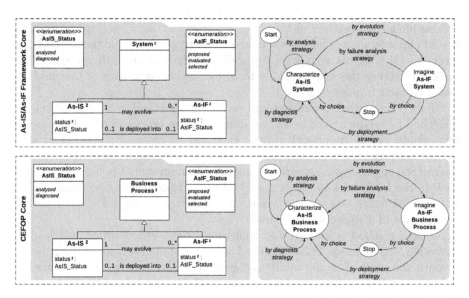

Fig. 2. As-Is/As-Is Core Package and its adaptation in CEFOP (on the left the product meta-models and on the right the process models).

(data artifacts) manipulated by the process model, as well as their relationships. For instance, in the CEFOP method, continual evolution of business processes is the main focus, so in the product meta-model, a class to characterize business processes can be found (cf. the bottom-left part of Fig. 2).

Figure 2 shows the adaptation of a fragment of the As-Is/As-If framework (the Core Package) to the CEFOP method. The top of Fig. 2 shows the template proposed by the As-Is/As-If framework for generic continual evolution methods, where we start from a current version of a system (As-Is) towards possible evolutions of it (As-If). The bottom of the image shows the CEFOP method adapted from the As-Is/As-IF template.

In this paper, we propose an approach to create frameworks of methods, allowing methods to be created or adapted in a more guided way. Furthermore, methods can be executed step by step. We use the As-Is/As-If framework to illustrate the creation of frameworks in our approach, nonetheless the approach is generic and can be used to create other frameworks of methods. The next section presents LOMET , a prototype that implements the approach.

5   Approach Implementation: The LOMET Tool

LOMET (for LOw-code Method Engineering Tool) is a web-based platform composed of two main modules: a *method editor* and a *method executor*. The method editor is a classic web diagram editor (dedicated to framework engineers and method engineers) allowing frameworks and methods to be created, while the method executor (dedicated to method experts) provides a supporting tool to execute a method, by applying the low-code paradigm (with user-friendly configurations and easy tool creation). Concerning the technologies, JointJS[11], HTML and CSS are used in the front-end, and Express[12] and MySQL in the back-end. Following, the aforementioned modules are described in more detail.

5.1   Creating a Framework of Methods (or a Method)

Figure 3 illustrates the framework of methods (and method) editor. At the top of the web editor, the method engineer or the framework engineer can choose to create a method or a framework. Several functionalities are available in both cases, accessible through a toolbar: *Save as* (both in a JSON file and in a database) and *Open* (from a JSON file), *Associate* chunks of the product meta-model with a part of the process model, and *Save* the method *as an image*. In case we want to create a method, through the button *From framework* we can select which framework our method is based on. There is also the possibility to skip this and create a method from scratch. Using the toolbar, we can also indicate that we want to apply the framework heuristics when creating our own method, or on the contrary if it is preferable to freely create our method using the framework as a template. Note that definition and use of the heuristics are out of the scope of this paper. The reader can refer to [4] for a deepen explanation. Other features available on the left and right sides of the user interface are the *Visual Zoom* and *Open a framework/method from the database* (a blue engine button). The Visual Zoom selector allows one to alternate the mouse scroll button function between visually zoom in/zoom out the diagrams and simply scroll the webpage.

The editor main zone contains two pages for creating the process model and the product meta-model (using Maps and UML class diagrams) of a method or a framework. A sticky toolbar available on each side of the pages allows one to drag'n'drop visual elements inside the models. We can connect elements by creating a link from a source to a target element. For instance, the "by evolution strategy" on the process model which connects the "Characterize As-Is Business Process" and "Imagine As-If B. Process" intentions (Fig. 3), or the associations between the "AS-IS" and "AS-IF" meta-classes on the product meta-model.

The process model includes an interesting feature called *Semantic Zoom* [10], a graphical technique to balance detail and context. While a physical zoom changes the size and visible details of objects, a semantic zoom changes the type and meaning of information displayed by the object, by using a semantic transition between detailed and general views of information. In LOMET, by clicking in a strategy, one can detail how it can be subdivided, in another sub-map below the previous one. For instance, in Fig. 3, the "by analysis" strategy (in dashed line) used to iteratively perform the intention "Characterize As-Is Business Process" can be further detailed in a sub-map, with extra intentions and strategies. Furthermore, the "by specification" strategy to go from the "start" to the "Identify Process Components" intentions is also detailed in a second sub-map below the previous one. Two levels of semantic zooms are available.

---

[11] https://www.jointjs.com/.
[12] https://expressjs.com/.

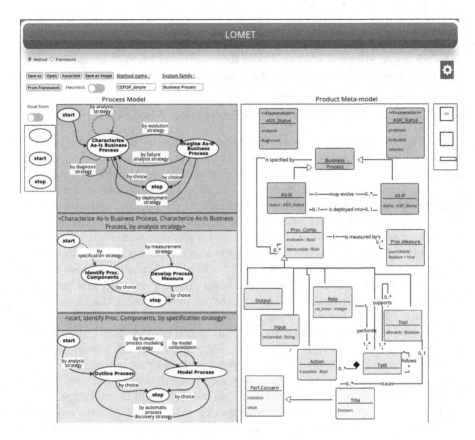

Fig. 3. User interface to create a framework of methods and a method in LOMET.

While the process model of a method is progressively created from a generic view (the main Map) to more detailed ones (the two sub-maps), the product meta-model is a single model containing all the elements manipulated by the process model in the context of the method. To identify more precisely which meta-classes are manipulated by a process model's fragment, we can associate them in LOMET using the *Associate* button in the toolbar. By linking a strategy to a set of meta-classes, LOMET colorizes them equally, resulting in the visual render illustrated in Fig. 3. Here, the "Process Component" (and its subtypes) and the "Process Measure" meta-classes are manipulated by the "by analysis" strategy in the process model (detailed in the two lower sub-maps).

5.2 Configuring a Framework of Methods (or a Method)

Once the framework of methods (or the method) is created, the framework engineer (or the method engineer) can configure it by indicating the most suitable tools to execute each step of the method (cf. Fig. 1). This is done at the process model level, and to do so, the method engineer selects each strategy of the

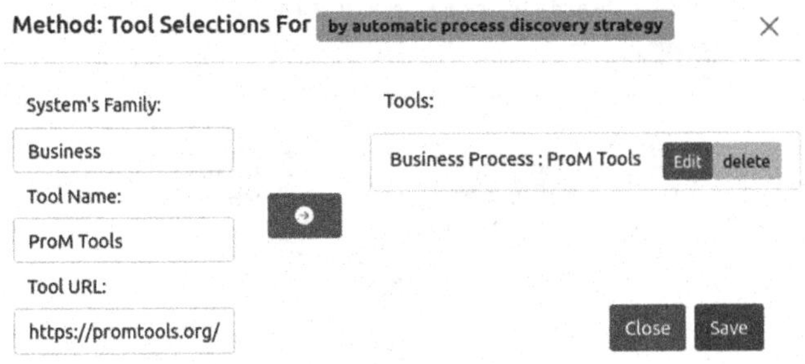

Fig. 4. User interface to configure a method in LOMET.

process model, and sets the URLs to the most suitable external tools to execute this part of the method. For instance, in Fig. 3, in order to "Identify the Process Components" at the CEFOP method (an *intention* in the second map), the first thing to do is to "Outline the Process", followed by "Model the Process" (in the third map), and one possible strategy to outline the process is "by automatic process discovery" (in the third map). This can be done using process mining tools such as ProM[13]. Therefore, the framework engineer (or the method engineer) can suggest this tool in LOMET (cf. Fig. 4), so that the method expert uses it when executing this step of the method.

In its current state, the method execution only takes into account the steps defined in the process model. The product meta-model is not yet exploited, so it is only informative. We already included a way to create product meta-models in the method editor in order to exploit them when the method is executed, as a future work. For instance, a product model could define the elements (process components) in which the business process improvement will focus on, such as inputs, outputs or tasks (cf. the product meta-model in Fig. 3), ignoring for instance activity execution flows. Therefore, when outlining a business process, only the elements identified in the product model will be considered in its continual evolution.

5.3 Executing a Method

Following the low-code paradigm, LOMET automatically generates a supporting tool for method experts to execute the method created and configured beforehand. The advantages of the supporting tool are threefold: firstly, method experts are provided with a visual indication of which steps of the method were already executed (in green), which one they are currently on (in yellow), and which ones are pending (in red), cf. Figure 5. Currently, method experts indicate manually in the tool the status of each step, by clicking on a strategy and changing its status. Secondly, method experts can execute the method step by step using the

---

[13] https://promtools.org/.

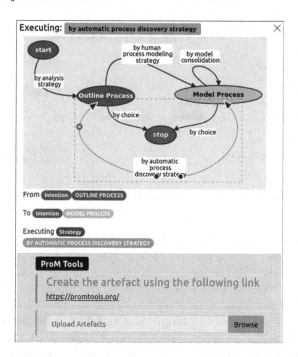

Fig. 5. User interface to execute a method in LOMET.

external tools configured by the method engineer. And lastly, they can keep in LOMET a repository of artifacts produced during the method execution.

To execute the method in the generated supporting tool, method experts: (i) click on each strategy of the process model (the top part of Fig. 5); (ii) click in the URL set by the method engineer (the bottom part of Fig. 5); (iii) are redirected to the external tool; (iv) where they can create an artifact in this external tool (for instance, a PDF containing the processes automatically discovered by process mining using the ProM tools); and (v) import this artifact back into LOMET (button *Browse* in Fig. 5). They can then follow these steps for each strategy of the process model in order to execute the method. If the method expert has already imported an artifact for a strategy before, she/he can visualize it in the same user interface (just below the *Browse* button in Fig. 5), allowing her/him to keep in LOMET a repository of artifacts produced by the method execution, for further access.

Our low-code prototype proposes a unique tool to execute the method step by step, helping method experts to handle the heterogeneity of existing tools suitable for each strategy of a method process model. Method experts may not be aware of these tools, and the method engineer expertise is necessary to configure the method with the most suitable tools. The low-code paradigm finds here an interesting application in the Method Engineering domain, allowing method engineers to provide a supporting tool for method experts to adopt the method without having to actually implement the tool.

6   Validation of the Functional Requirements of LOMET

This section presents an evaluation in progress of LOMET . The aim is to verify if the tool provides the adequate functional requirements for method engineers to build and provide support to their own methods. We also evaluate the tool usability. Non-functional requirements of LOMET are out of the scope of this paper. A user-centred experiment has been put in place within researchers that participated in the creation of their continual evolution methods without the help of any tool.

To carry out the evaluation, we choose a method recommended by sociologists and also by computer designers: semi-structured interviews [13]. The interviews are completed by observing the participants. We choose this method as it helps to identify ideas, opinions, or habits. These interviews are organized face to face with an interview schedule grid. For the moment, only three interviews have been realized, with research colleagues that lead projects where continuous evolution methods were produced (ADInnov [6], CEFOP [5] and CircusChain [15]).

We rely on our running example using the As-Is-As-If framework to provide to the subjects an incomplete adaptation of their own methods. After a video demonstration, the subjects had to complete a part of their methods through a protocol with different steps : 1) import the template; 2) manipulate the process model in order to complete a strategy using a semantic zoom; 2) manipulate the product meta-model in order to define the data model (product meta-model) manipulated by the process model; 3) configure the method to define the appropriate tools to execute the strategy; and finally 4) execute the defined strategy including the upload of a document representing the artifact of the aforementioned strategy execution using the pre-defined tool.

The validation had to produce some evidence regarding the following 3 usefulness/usability statements : 1) *"The LOMET tool is an appropriate way to monitor the execution of a method"*; 2) *"The LOMET tool is helpful to create a method compared to the creation without a tool"*; and 3) *"The LOMET tool is easy to use"*. The available material was: 1) the case study containing the exercise description; 2) two questionnaires explained below; 3) a 10-min video demo; and 4) the LOMET tool, accessible via a (for the moment) local URL.

The **first questionnaire** targeted the profile description of the subject. We question the subjects about what they consider to be their knowledge in the Method Engineering topic, what are their potential difficulties that they faced when building their methods without tool support, the functionalities that they may want to have in order to support their methods and how they currently follow up the method execution. Some interesting points follow. Firstly, none of the interviewed experts had a way to configure nor execute their methods, what they consider as drawbacks for the method adoption. Secondly, some desired functionalities were indicated: 1) the versioning possibility; 2) the possibility to use method fragments to build a new method; 3) a way to trace the method execution with artifacts on each step; 4) the possibility to highlight the coherence between the process model and the manipulated artifacts; 5) the possibility to highlight the impacts of a change in the method; and 6) the possibility to instantiate the method. As shown in the previous sections, all the mentioned desired functionalities are already considered in LOMET , apart from the impact analysis. The fragment composition is not yet well-developed but the possibility to define some fragments in the form of a framework, which can be then imported to create a new method, partly supports this feature.

After the video visualization and the exercises, the **second questionnaire** was used in order to ask the subjects about the advantages and disadvantages of the tool, as well as the difficulties that LOMET could have minimized when building their own methods. We also asked about the appropriateness of the proposed functionalities, and we rely on Brooke's System Usability Scale (SUS) [3] to evaluate the tool's usability.

The following **advantages** were put forward: 1) the tool was considered an appropriate way to enable knowledge capitalization; 2) the possibility to import a framework (template) accelerate the method construction; 3) the fact of using a specific and constrained language for modeling the method was also appreciated; 4) the process model was considered easy to manipulate. The semantic zooms helped to master the potential complexity; 5) the possibility to assign dedicated tools to the process strategies at the framework and method creation level was considered useful; 6) the use of colors and the possibility to associate process model elements with the product meta-model elements was also appreciated.

The following **disadvantages** were highlighted: 1) the method execution was considered limited (mainly status update and artifact uploads). Also, no automatic status update of the intention was proposed; 2) several usability problems were detected such as the need for clarification of the framework import and opening, the difficult way to add associations in the product meta-model, the non-intuitive image export, the lack of standardized way to interact with graphical elements, or the lack of a Ctrl+Z option. Nevertheless, considering the SUS questionnaire, the answers were mostly positive; 3) the product meta-model manipulation was sometimes hard, especially if there is a need to manipulate large models. There is no way to manage the complexity using semantic zooms as in the process model part; 4) there is no easy way to re-use method fragments. Indeed, even if the tool provides the possibility to reuse a framework as a template, there is no dedicated functionality to compose method fragments.

Considering the aforementioned problems, we plan to integrate the corresponding **improvements**. In a short term period, we aim at treating the execution limitations and enrich it with a specific forum so users can comment each uploaded artifact. In addition, the fact of adding a protocol that may be attached to the tool in order to guide its usage is also a priority. The prototype nature of the tool indeed induces some usability limitations that we also aim to treat rapidly. In a mid-term period, we want to explore the possible integration with a dedicated UML editor in the tool in order to facilitate the class diagram edition, for the product meta-model. Finally, the introduction of method fragments is considered to be a long-term objective that still has to be studied.

To conclude, it is still soon to consider that our three usefulness/usability statements have been validated, as we have only performed three interviews.

Still, as we show here, we have already received feedback that is useful to guide future improvements of the tool and the general approach. Indeed, the user-centred interviews are a valuable way to evaluate and improve the approach, with promising results.

7 Conclusion

We have presented in this paper an approach to support the creation of frameworks of methods, from which one can derive methods adapted to her/his domain. The approach benefits from the advantages of the low-code paradigm, allowing method engineers, who may not have programming skills, to produce and configure a tool to support method experts on the execution of methods. Therefore, we have tackled our research question presented in Sect. 1.

In our approach, a method is formalized by means of a process model (represented by Maps) and a product meta-model (represented by a UML class diagram). Any framework of methods using these formalisms can benefit from our approach. Once a method is created, the method engineer configures the most suitable tools to execute each step of the method, from which method experts can execute the method using a tool derived from this configuration, without having to write one single line of code.

As mentioned in Sect. 6, we plan at extending the tool by adding the possibility to include a set of guidelines (i.e. protocols) in the method. These protocols could be defined by the method engineer, in order to better guide the method expert when executing the method. Besides, we plan to extend the configurations' possibilities that method engineers do in the method, since for the moment they can set a list of tools allowing the method expert to execute each step of the method.

Acknowledgements. This work is funded by the Emergence Projects 2022 of the *Laboratoire d'Informatique de Grenoble* (LIG). We thank the work of Noe Choc, Junhao LI and Aymeric Surre in helping with the development of LOMET.

References

1. Booch, G.: Object oriented design with applications. Benjamin-Cummings Publishing Co., Inc., San Francisco (1990)
2. Brinkkemper, S.: Method engineering: engineering of information systems development methods and tools. Inf. Softw. Technol. **38**(4), 275–280 (1996)
3. Brooke, J., et al.: SUS-a quick and dirty usability scale. Usability Eval. Ind. **189**(194), 4–7 (1996)
4. Cela, O., Cortes-Cornax, M., Front, A., Rieu, D.: Methodological framework to guide the development of continual evolution methods. In: Giorgini, P., Weber, B. (eds.) CAiSE 2019. LNCS, vol. 11483, pp. 48–63. Springer, Cham (2019). https://doi.org/10.1007/978-3-030-21290-2_4
5. Çela, O., Front, A., Rieu, D.: Cefop: a method for the continual evolution of organisational processes. In: 2017 11th International Conference on Research Challenges in Information Science (RCIS), pp. 33–43. IEEE (2017)

6. Cortes-Cornax, M., Front, A., Rieu, D., Verdier, C., Forest, F.: ADInnov: an intentional method to instil innovation in socio-technical ecosystems. In: Nurcan, S., Soffer, P., Bajec, M., Eder, J. (eds.) CAiSE 2016. LNCS, vol. 9694, pp. 133–148. Springer, Cham (2016). https://doi.org/10.1007/978-3-319-39696-5_9
7. Deeb, S., Bril-El Haouzi, H., Aubry, A., Dassisti, M.: A generic framework to support the implementation of six sigma approach in SMEs. IFAC-PapersOnLine **51**(11), 921–926 (2018)
8. Deming, W.E.: Out of the Crisis, reissue. MIT Press, Cambridge (2018)
9. Deneckere, R., Kornyshova, E., Rolland, C.: Method family description and configuration. In: ICEIS, pp. 384–387 (2011)
10. Garcia, J., Theron, R., Garcia, F.: Semantic zoom: a details on demand visualisation technique for modelling owl ontologies. In: Highlights in Practical Applications of Agents and Multiagent Systems: 9th International Conference on Practical Applications of Agents and Multiagent Systems, pp. 85–92. Springer, Berlin (2011). https://doi.org/10.1007/978-3-642-19917-2_11
11. Group, O.M.: Business process model and notation - (bpmn 2.0) (2011). http://www.omg.org/spec/BPMN/2.0
12. Group, O.M.: Meta object facility (2016). https://www.omg.org/spec/MOF/About-MOF/
13. Hindus, D., Mainwaring, S.D., Leduc, N., Hagström, A.E., Bayley, O.: Casablanca: designing social communication devices for the home. In: Proceedings of the SIGCHI Conference on Human Factors in Computing Systems, pp. 325–332 (2001)
14. Hug, C., Front, A., Rieu, D., Henderson-Sellers, B.: A method to build information systems engineering process metamodels. J. Syst. Softw. **82**(10), 1730–1742 (2009)
15. Kurt, A.: Models and Tools for the Design, Assessment, and Evolution of Circular Supply Chains. Master's thesis, University of Grenoble, December 2021
16. Mandran, N.: THEDRE: langage et méthode de conduite de la recherche: Traceable Human Experiment Design Research. Ph.D. thesis, Université Grenoble Alpes (ComUE) (2017)
17. Oliveira, R., Cortes-Cornax, M., Front, A., Demeure, A.: A low-code approach to support method engineering. In: Proceedings of the 25th International Conference on Model Driven Engineering Languages and Systems: Companion Proceedings, pp. 793–797 (2022)
18. Ralyté, J., Rolland, C., Ayed, M.B.: An approach for evolution-driven method engineering. In: Information Modeling Methods and Methodologies: Advanced Topics in Database Research, pp. 80–101. IGI Global (2005)
19. Richardson, C., Rymer, J.R.: Vendor Landscape: The Fractured, Fertile Terrain of Low-Code Application Platforms. FORRESTER, Janeiro (2016)
20. Richardson, C., Rymer, J.R., Mines, C., Cullen, A., Whittaker, D.: New development platforms emerge for customer-facing applications. Forrester: Cambridge, MA, USA 15 (2014)
21. Rolland, C.: Capturing system intentionality with maps. In: Krogstie, J., Opdahl, A.L., Brinkkemper, S. (eds.) Conceptual Modelling in Information Systems Engineering. Springer, Berlin (2007). https://doi.org/10.1007/978-3-540-72677-7_9
22. Shook, J.: Managing to learn: using the A3 management process to solve problems, gain agreement, mentor and lead. Lean Enterprise Institute (2008)

IAT/ML: A Domain-Specific Approach for Discourse Analysis and Processing

Cesar Gonzalez-Perez[1]([☒]) [iD], Martín Pereira-Fariña[2] [iD],
and Patricia Martín-Rodilla[3] [iD]

[1] Incipit CSIC, Santiago de Compostela, Spain
cesar.gonzalez-perez@incipit.csic.es
[2] Universidade de Santiago de Compostela, Santiago de Compostela, Spain
martin.pereira@usc.gal
[3] Universidade de A Coruña, A Coruña, Spain
patricia.martin.rodilla@udc.es

Abstract. Language technologies are gaining momentum as textual information saturates social networks and media outlets, compounded by the growing role of fake news and disinformation. In this context, approaches to represent and analyse discourses are becoming crucial. Although there is a large body of literature on text-based machine learning, it tends to focus on lexical and syntactical issues rather than semantic or pragmatic. These advances cannot tackle the complex and highly context-dependent problems of discourse evaluation that society demands. In this paper, we present IAT/ML, a modelling approach to represent and analyse discourses. IAT/ML focus on semantic and pragmatic issues, thus tackling a little researched area in language technologies. It does so by combining three analysis approaches: ontological, which focuses on what the discourse talks about, argumentation, which deals with how the text justifies what it says, and critical, which provides insights into the speakers' beliefs and intentions, and is still being implemented. Together, these three modelling and analysis approaches make IAT/ML a comprehensive solution to represent and analyse complex discourses towards their evaluation and fact checking.

Keywords: domain-specific modelling · discourse · Argumentation · ontologies · IAT/ML

1 Introduction

When we use language to communicate, we are doing different things at the same time. We are transmitting certain information (e.g., "Fire!") to specific listeners, we are performing an action (e.g., warning someone that they might be in danger), and we are showing what we think to others (e.g., as a member of the health and safety team). Thus, the use of language is a practice, a "game" [39], which is guided by a set of implicit and explicit rules that determine who has acted appropriately and who has not, who is accepted in the group and who is not [10]. Discourse Analysis (DA) focuses on the study of language in use, unpacking the discourse structures or strategies used in the language to communicate something and understand how it is done.

© The Author(s), under exclusive license to Springer Nature Switzerland AG 2023
H. van der Aa et al. (Eds.): BPMDS 2023/EMMSAD 2023, LNBIP 479, pp. 199–213, 2023.
https://doi.org/10.1007/978-3-031-34241-7_14

However, DA is a hard task. DA is based on empirical analysis that goes beyond the automated application of quantitative measurements (such as word frequencies), as it requires a theoretically grounded qualitative analysis to unpack the subtle strategies and patterns that are used to deliver a specific message to the audience. Therefore, DA requires the combination of quantitative methods to collect a representative and reliable selection of fragments of text and qualitative ones to analyse the selected texts under the umbrella of a specific theory. Thus, we propose to adopt a domain-specific approach to support the process of discourse analysis. To achieve this, this paper presents a formalised approach for discourse analysis that combines quantitative and qualitative techniques. The proposed approach is called IAT/ML (Inference Anchoring Theory/Modelling Language) and it is built upon three pillars: ontological analysis, argumentation analysis and critical analysis.

The goal of ontological analysis is to develop a simplified model of the world that is referred to by the discourse that contains enough information as to apply conclusions inferred from the model to the real world [11]. The result of ontological analysis is an ontology or conceptual model.

The goal of argumentation analysis, in turn, is to unpack the argument structure of the discourse to determine the speakers' main claims and how they are justified or supported by other claims. The result of argumentation analysis is presented as a network of elements loosely based on Argument Interchange Format (AIF) [5].

Finally, the goal of critical analysis is to gain insights into the beliefs and intentions of the speakers in order to capture the social and political implications of the discourse and, potentially, intervene in order to remove any potential injustice or biased controversy [10]. Results of critical analysis are usually expressed in natural language, guided by a set of critical questions that are to be answered from the text being analysed.

Each of these three analysis approaches can be applied independently to a specific piece of text, obtaining a valuable result by itself. However, it is by combining the three together that we obtain the maximum potential of the proposed approach in terms of reproducibility and reliability, as many tasks of one type of analysis become easier and more reliable if we use the results of other types of analysis as input. IAT/ML offers such a capacity.

2 Previous Work

We can find different frameworks for ontological, argumentation and critical analysis in the literature. In every case, these frameworks have been developed without considering possible connections between them, with the exception of the Integrated Argumentation Model (IAM) [8], which is the only approach, to best of our knowledge, that combines ontological and argumentation analysis to some degree.

In the realm of ontological analysis, a vast body of literature exists on ontology engineering and conceptual modelling. Although these two strands of work come from different historical backgrounds and traditions, more recent works [12, 20] have shown that ontologies and conceptual models are very similar kinds of artefacts and, to most purposes, completely equivalent. Consequently, we will not make big differences between these two research traditions and jointly refer to them as "ontological analysis". Having said this, we must emphasise that "ontological analysis" in this paper refers to the development of human-oriented conceptual models rather than machine-oriented computational models. Products such as OntoUML [32] or ConML [23] are much closer to what we need than, for example, OWL [40] or RDF [41].

Argumentation analysis is also a field with a long research tradition. Here, we focus on approaches that emphasise its communicative dimension and have a computational development, such as those of Perelman & Olbrechts-Tyteca [27] or Toulmin [33]. The Argument Interchange Format (AIF) [5] constitutes a milestone in this regard. It defines an abstract language for the representation and exchange of argumentation data, and aims to be a standard in the argumentation community. Its core ontology defines three main categories: i) arguments and argument networks; ii) communication; and iii) context. Arguments are represented as directed graphs, where the nodes stand for information contents (such as a premise or a conclusion) or the application of an argumentation pattern or scheme. Communications capture how the production of utterances and dialogue evolves, representing them in terms of protocols and utterance sequences. Lastly, contexts capture the non-strictly linguistic elements that play a role in the elaboration of arguments, such as speaker backgrounds or personal commitments.

Several different contemporary theories of argumentation have adopted AIF as their underlying ontology. One of them, Inference Anchoring Theory (IAT) [29], aims to capture how propositional reasoning involved in argumentation is anchored in discourse. The Periodic Table of Arguments (PTA) [35, 36] focuses on natural discourse as well, defines a categorisation and a procedure for a systematic analysis and evaluation of arguments based on identifying some characteristics in every argument. The Comprehensive Assessment Procedure for Natural Argumentation (CAPNA) [22], another systematic method for argument analysis and evaluation, not only analyses argument structure but also its semantic content in order to offer a reliable evaluation.

Finally, the critical approach to discourse analysis can be characterised as an interdisciplinary field, which usually involves semiotics, anthropology, psychology, communication studies, and related fields. Gee [10] proposes a framework based on critical questions that address seven different aspects: significance, practices, identities, relationships, connections, sign systems and knowledge. Johnstone [25] follows a more linguistic approach, based on Speech Act Theory [2, 3] and Grice's theory of meaning [17]. Its main assumption is that meanings strongly depend on speaker's intentions, which are captured by the illocutionary forces and the conversational implicatures, so these become the focus of critical discourse analysis. Critical analysis is excluded from the approach proposed in this paper as it is still in development.

In summary, the practical totality of previous work in this field tackles one modelling perspective (ontological, argumentation or critical) at a time, neglecting the others for all practical purposes. In this regard, and while we recognise the immense value of the previous work described in this section, we can also claim that no comprehensive efforts have been made to date to integrate the three modelling perspectives so that a richer and more complete representation of discourse can be achieved.

3 Methodology

The research methodology that we employed was based on the hypothesis that a domain-specific approach is necessary to capture and support the process of discourse analysis, including the associated research questions. Although the issue of whether IAT/ML qualifies as a conventional DSML is not central to this paper, we decided that it would be a mistake not to consider guidance on DSML development for its creation.

We started off with the abstract research question of whether it is possible to develop a domain-specific approach to support the process of discourse analysis in an integral fashion, reconciling ontological, argumentation and critical analysis. In order to address this, some research sub-questions (RSQ) were raised:

1. a) What concepts and patterns are found in the discourse analysis process and its domain that are common to existing approaches? and b) Which ones we do not find in existing approaches, but are necessary after our experience analysing discourses?
2. Can we develop a domain-specific modelling language that fully describes and supports both the discourse analysis domain as well as the process for the three perspectives (ontological, argumentation and critical)?
3. Is it possible to implement this language in a modelling tool?
4. What degree of coverage does this language offer for the discourse analysis process, given a corpus to be analysed that is different from those used during development?

Following Design Science [21], our main research question (and the subsequent sub-questions) implies the construction of an artefact (namely, a DSML, or something like it). Technical Action Research (TAR, [38]) has been used to answer research questions through artefact construction in other domains such as smart cities or health [26, 30], so we adopted it, as it would allow us to integrate the construction of the DSML into ongoing research projects. In this sense, the initial versions of IAT/ML constituted an artefact at the service of practitioners in ongoing discourse analysis projects for experimentation and improvement. These projects, due to their very interdisciplinary nature (cultural heritage, feminist identities, and communication of the COVID-19 pandemic) brought together professionals of different backgrounds, including linguists, cultural heritage specialists, philosophers of language and software engineers, which broadened and generalised the domain of application of the approach and allowed its validation by different stakeholders in later phases. By applying TAR, it was possible to integrate the process of developing IAT/ML into our own research process, thus being able to respond to the SRQs listed above.

There is no single or optimal methodology for DSLM development, and approaches vary enormously, ranging from ad hoc proposals [7, 42], to those based on patterns [28], ontologies [18], or more oriented towards meeting the requirements of practitioners [9]. In our case, the empirical and incremental nature of the development of IAT/ML motivated the choice of an approach focused on meeting the needs of practitioners, in our case team members who were performing discourse analysis tasks. Taking Frank's method [9] as a reference, Fig. 1 illustrates the process followed for the design and development of IAT/ML.

Phase 1: Clarification of Scope and Purpose. In this phase, we defined the scope of IAT/ML [16] by working with language and discourse experts working in the above-mentioned ongoing projects. We performed some gap analysis in relation to existing discourse analysis techniques, mostly IAT [4].

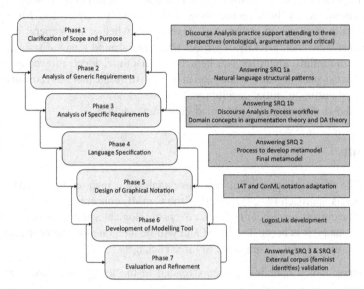

Fig. 1. IAT/ML design process, based on Frank's method. Grey shapes depict Frank's process, whereas red rectangles show IAT/ML development phases and specific results for each one.

Phase 2: Analysis of Generic Requirements. In this phase, we developed business-level requirements and a draft list of concepts that would be necessary to support discourse analysis from the described three perspectives.

Phase 3: Analysis of Specific Requirements. In this phase, we developed a sketch metamodel for IAT/ML as well as a list of functional requirements that should be supported by IAT/ML, such as computation of argumentation statistics or argument structure analysis.

Phase 4: Language Specification. In this phase, we defined the IAT/ML metamodel as described in Sect. 4 of this paper. We also cross-validated the concepts, relationships and implications of the metamodel with project team members in terms of the required linguistic and discursive concepts. For some of the concepts, such as that of ontological proxy [13], we needed to go back to phase 3 and revisit existing requirements for their refinement and adjustment.

Phase 5: Design of Graphical Notation. In this phase, we sketched some ideas for a graphical notation, mostly inspired by IAT [4] and ConML [23], and validated them with project team members for usability and acceptance.

Phase 6: Development of Modelling Tool. In this phase, we initiated the development of LogosLink, a software toolset that implements most of IAT/ML. This required achieving a moderately stable metamodel so that software development could proceed on solid grounds. Section 5.1 briefly describes LogosLink.

Phase 7: Evaluation and Refinement. The evaluation of a DSML and a corresponding modelling tool recommends checking them against the requirements building on the use scenarios created for requirements analysis. As Frank's method specifies, each use case serves to analyse whether and how corresponding requirements are satisfied by the DSML. In our case, the stable IAT/ML version was validated with respect to the initial requirements by the team members of the project for which IAT/ML was being experimentally used, as an initial way of verifying whether the general and specific requirements were met. Luckily, a project revolving around a new discourse analysis theme, that of feminist identities, was launched at that time, which allowed us to validate IAT/ML and LogosLink with a corpus and in relation to a topic that was radically different to those used during its initial development.

The IAT/ML metamodel is presented in the next section.

4   Results

IAT/ML, the proposed approach to discourse analysis, is inspired by the IAT argumentation analysis approach [4, 24] as well as the ConML conceptual modelling language [14, 23]. The current version of IAT/ML covers ontological and argumentation analysis, and critical analysis is being developed and will be integrated in the near future. Thus, the IAT/ML metamodel is composed of three packages:

- **Discourse**, which contains elements related to the locutions of speakers and the transitions between them.
- **Argumentation**, which contains elements related to the argumentative structure of the discourse, including its propositions and argumentation relations such as inferences, conflicts and rephrases. Argumentation elements are connected to discourse elements by illocutionary forces.
- **Ontology**, which contains elements related to the ontology being referred to by the discourse, including ontology elements such as entities, facets and features. Ontology elements are connected to argumentation elements through denotations.

The following sections provide additional details. Diagrams are expressed in ConML [14, 23].

4.1   Discourse

This package contains metamodel elements related to the literal discourse as spoken by speakers. Figure 2 depicts the major metamodel elements.

A Model is a container for a discourse, an argumentation, an ontology, and some additional elements such as speakers. A Speaker is an individual or group who participates in a discourse by speaking locutions and issuing propositions. A Discourse, in turn, is a portion of human speech that makes statements about the world and provides reasons to support, attack or comment on them. Two kinds of elements may exist in a discourse: locutions and transitions. A Locution is an utterance made by a speaker in the discourse, whereas a Transition is a discursive relationship between locutions. Transitions show discursive dependencies, and do not represent the chronological order of the discourse (which is given by timestamps of locutions) but must be compatible with it. Transitions provide the links that help the interpretation of a locution in relation to immediately related ones. For example, transitions of the Adding type indicate that a speaker adds something to what they said before; transitions of the TurnTaking type indicate that a speaker is talking after another speaker has finished.

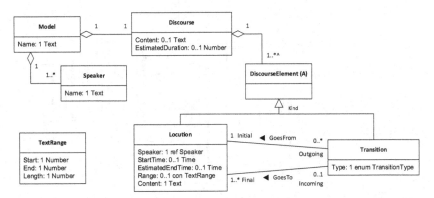

Fig. 2. Metamodel elements in the Discourse package.

By combining locutions and transitions, we can represent a discourse as a sequence of utterances connected in a linear fashion, with the occasional branch for embeddings (such as in appositions, e.g. "My sister, who lives in France, will be arriving tomorrow") or reportings (e.g. "Clinton said yesterday that she is not worried about the escalating tensions").

4.2 Argumentation

This package contains metamodel elements related to the argumentation as issued by speakers. Figure 3 depicts the major metamodel elements.

Within a model, an Argumentation is a collection of propositions and argument relations that work to make statements about the world and provides reasons to support, attack or comment on them. Two kinds of elements may exist in an argumentation: argumentation units and proposition groups. In turn, there are two kinds of argumentation units: propositions and argumentation relations. A Proposition is an argumentation unit corresponding to a state of affairs about the world. Propositions are self-contained and do not include unresolved references (such as anaphoric or deictic elements), so that their truth value is stable and as independent of the context as possible. Propositions can be characterised in a number of ways via attributes such as StatementType (fact or value), FactualAspect (existence, identity, predication, etc.), OntologicalAspect (logically necessary, physically possible, socially contingent, etc.), Modality (indicative, definitional, noetic, commissive, suggestive, etc.) and Tense (past, present, future or atemporal).

An Argumentation Relation, on the other hand, is an argumentation unit corresponding to a connection between two or more argumentation units so that some of them are argumentally dependent on others. There are three kinds: inferences, conflicts and

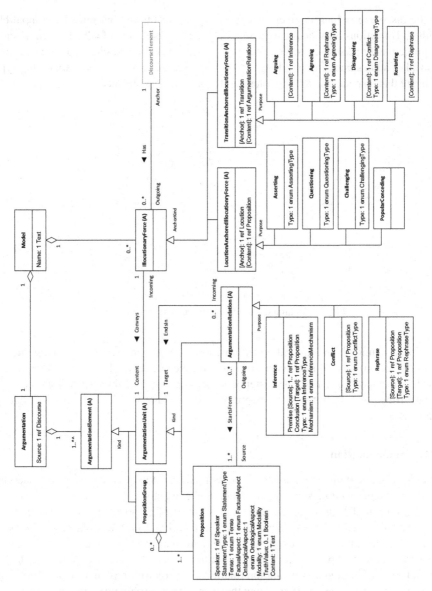

Fig. 3. Metamodel elements in the Argumentation package.

rephrasings. An Inference is an argumentation relation that indicates that one or more premise propositions are provided by a speaker to support a conclusion proposition. All the involved premise propositions are implicitly connected via conjunction. Inferences can be characterised through a Type attribute, which is based on the subtypes proposed by [34, 37]. A Conflict is an argumentation relation that indicates that a source proposition provided by a speaker is in any kind of conflict (logical or non-logical) with a target proposition. Finally, a Rephrase is an argumentation relation that indicates that a source proposition is provided by a speaker as a reformulation of a target proposition. Rephrases can be of multiple types, such as Abstraction (i.e. the speaker repeats the target proposition but raising the level of abstraction), Agreement (i.e. the speaker expresses agreement with the target proposition), or Reinterpretation (the speaker reinterprets the target proposition by changing its contents without frontally contradicting it, including mechanisms such as analogies, adding emotional nuance, straw man fallacies, etc.).

Finally, a Proposition Group is a collection of propositions within an argumentation that share some commonalities.

To connect argumentation to discourse, models contain illocutionary forces of different kinds. An Illocutionary Force is a connection between a discourse element and an argumentation unit in terms of speaker intent. They are taken from the ample literature on speech acts such as [3, 31]. There are different kinds of illocutionary forces; some of them are anchored on locutions, whereas others are anchored on transitions. Regarding locution-anchored illocutionary forces, an Asserting is an illocutionary force indicating that the speaker produces an anchor locution to communicate that they believe a content proposition, as in e.g. "Today is a beautiful day". A Questioning is an illocutionary force indicating that the speaker produces an anchor locution to obtain new information, as in e.g. "What's your name?". A Challenging is an illocutionary force indicating that the speaker produces an anchor locution to obtain a new proposition that works as a premise for a base proposition, as in e.g. Alice: "Today is a beautiful day"; Bob: "How so?". Finally, a Popular Conceding is an illocutionary force indicating that the speaker produces an anchor locution to communicate that they believe a well-known and commonly accepted content proposition, as in e.g. "Everybody knows that the Earth is round".

Regarding transition-anchored illocutionary forces, an Arguing is an illocutionary force indicating that the speaker produces an anchor transition to support a content inference, as in e.g. "Today is a beautiful day because it's sunny". An Agreeing is an illocutionary force indicating that the speaker produces an anchor transition to react affirmatively to a base proposition, as in e.g. "Yes, of course". Contrarily, a Disagreeing is an illocutionary force indicating that the speaker produces an anchor transition to react negatively to a base proposition through a conflict, as in e.g. "No way!". Finally, a Restating is an illocutionary force indicating that the speaker produces an anchor transition to recast a base proposition, as in e.g. "Most large cities are heavily polluted. In particular, Beijing's concentrations of nitrogen dioxide and PM10 concentrations are above national standards".

4.3 Ontology

This package contains metamodel elements related to the ontology referred to by the speakers. Ontologies in IAT/ML are multi-level, in the sense that multiple levels of instantiation are possible [1, 6]. Figure 4 depicts the major metamodel elements.

Within a model, an Ontology is a collection of elements that represent things in the world. There are three kinds of ontology elements: entities, features and facets. An Entity is an ontology element that represents an identity-bearing thing in the world. There are two kinds of entities: atoms and categories. An Atom is an entity that represents a non-instantiable thing in the world. Atoms correspond to urelements in set theory, or individuals in philosophy. A Category, in turn, is an entity that represents a class of things in the world. Categories correspond to sets in set theory or universals in philosophy. Categories work as types in relation to entities, so that atoms and categories can be instances of categories. Also, categories can be arranged in subtyping hierarchies, and multiple inheritance of features and facets is supported.

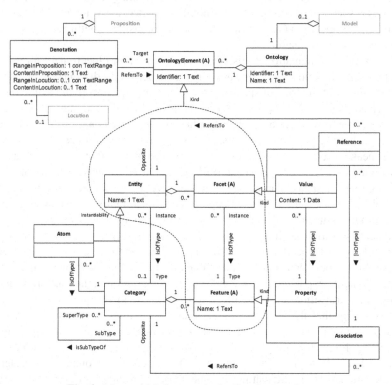

Fig. 4. Metamodel elements in the Ontology package.

A Feature is an ontology element that represents a type of predication on entities of a given category, that is, some shared property of all instances of a category. There are two kinds: properties and associations. A Property is a feature corresponding to quantities or qualities of the entities of the category, such as "Height". This is very similar to the concept of "attribute" in other modelling languages such as UML or ConML. An Association, in turn, is a feature corresponding to relationships of entities of the category to other entities, such as "IsLocatedIn".

Features work as types of facets. A Facet is an ontology element that represents a predication on an entity in the world, regardless of whether it is a category or an atom. There are two kinds of facets, corresponding to the two kinds of features: values and references. A Value is a facet corresponding to a quantity or quality of an entity, such as "Height = 135". A Reference, in turn, is a facet corresponding to a relationship of an entity to another entity, such as "IsLocatedIn = Rome".

To connect ontology elements to argumentation, denotations are used. A Denotation is a semiotic connection between a part of a proposition and a target ontology element. Denotations are based on the concept of ontological proxies [13, 15], which works to connect the argumentation and ontological aspects of discourse modelling in a single mesh of relationships so that connections can be captured and managed. Denotations are particularly useful as they allow us to connect multiple argumentation models to a common ontology so that the joint intertextual analysis becomes possible.

Additional details on IAT/ML, as well as a full technical specification, can be found on www.iatml.org.

5 Validation

IAT/ML has been validated through two parallel mechanisms. On the one hand, it has been implemented as the LogosLink toolset. On the other hand, it has been used to model the discourse, argumentation and ontologies of numerous texts in various projects.

5.1 Implementation in LogosLink

IAT/ML has been fully implemented in the LogosLink toolset, available from www. iatml.org/logoslink. LogosLink is a collection of libraries and user interface applications developed in C# on top of the Microsoft.NET Framework. It has a modular structure so that it can be used as an interactive stand-alone application or integrated in other projects.

The Discourse and Argumentation packages of IAT/ML have been implemented as part of the ArgumentationEngine library, which offers a complete object model for discourse and argumentation modelling together with the functionality to save and load models, obtain statistics, and other related functions. The Ontology package has been implemented in a separate library, OntologyEngine, which offers analogous features. A third library, Analysis, works on top of the previous two to carry out complex analytical techniques such as argument structure analysis or denotation analysis. Finally, the Desktop executable offers a desktop Windows-based user interface capable of diagramming argumentation models and offering full features for argumentation and ontological modelling of discourses. Documentation for LogosLink (both user's and developer's) can be found at www.iatml.org/logoslink.

5.2 Modelling in Various Projects

IAT/ML has been used to model discourses in a number of projects, using LogosLink as tooling support. One of these projects was "COVID19 en español: investigación interdisciplinar sobre terminología, temáticas y comunicación de la ciencia" [COVID-19 in Spanish: Interdisciplinary Research on the Terminology, Themes and Science Communication], funded by the Spanish National Research Council between 2020 and 2022. This project gathered a corpus of 877 COVID-related popular science articles published by The Conversation Spain [43] in 2020, amounting to 962,886 words, and analysed them to find out the main strategies and resources used to disseminate information about

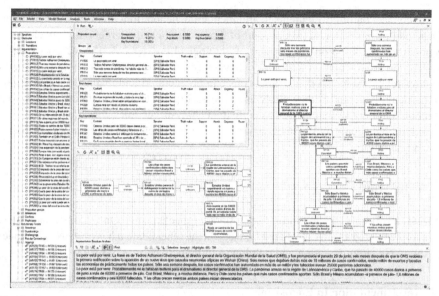

Fig. 5. Screenshot of LogosLink Desktop showing an argumentation model for an article on COVID-19. Black boxes represent locutions and transitions. Red boxes represent propositions and argument relations. Blue arrows represent illocutionary forces (Color figure online).

the pandemic within the Spanish-speaking world. Figure 5 shows a screenshot of an argumentation model developed during this project.

Another project where IAT/ML and LogosLink have been used is the ongoing doctoral work of Beatriz Calderón-Cerrato under two of the authors (Gonzalez-Perez and Pereira-Fariña). So far, this project has gathered a corpus of 68 documents, amounting to 53,256 words, related to cultural heritage and feminist identities, from sources such as legislation, press articles, transcribed interviews and social media posts. Although the corpus in this project is smaller than the previous one, this project is carrying out critical analysis as well as ontological and argumentation analysis. In particular, the incorporation of feminist identities as a theme at a later stage allowed us to validate the approach in relation to a corpus and topic other than those employed during development. This is one of the suggested approaches to validation offered by [19].

6 Conclusions

In this paper we have presented IAT/ML, a domain-specific approach for the modelling and representation of discourses based on the combination of three modelling perspectives: ontological, argumentation and critical. Ontological and argumentation analysis have been fully incorporated into IAT/ML and the LogosLink supporting tool, while critical analysis is still in development. In this regard, IAT/ML (and LogosLink) is the first of its kind, as no other approach, as far as we know, integrates different perspectives under a common and inter-connected modelling approach. This provides the ability, for example, to carry out intertextual argumentation analysis by connecting multiple argumentation models via a shared ontology; or to ground critical analysis on an underlying ontology and argumentation model to decrease its degree of subjectivity.

IAT/ML has been constructed empirically, by following a known method for DSML development at the same time that practitioners were using it. The same practitioners worked to validate and enrich the approach, both as part of the initial projects as well as under a new discourse theme that was added later.

IAT/ML is documented online on www.iatml.org, and LogosLink can be downloaded for free. We hope that this domain-specific approach, together with its tooling support, will contribute to better and more reliable discourse analysis projects and easier and more powerful discourse evaluation and fact-checking.

Acknowledgements. The authors thank Beatriz Calderón-Cerrato for her help and hard work during the development of IAT/ML and LogosLink. The authors also thank the AEI (Spanish National Research Agency) for the funding of project PID2020-114758RB-I00 through grant number MCIN/AEI/https://doi.org/10.13039/501100011033.

References

1. Almeida, J.P.A., Frank, U., Kühne, T.: Multi-Level Modelling (Dagstuhl Seminar 17492), Wadern, Germany (2018).https://doi.org/10.4230/DagRep.7.12.18
2. Austin, J.L.: How to do things with words: The William James lectures delivered at Harvard University in 1955, 2nd ed. University Press, Oxford (1989)
3. Austin, J.L.: How to Do Things with Words. Martino Fine Books, Reprint (2018)
4. Centre for Argument Technology, "A Quick Start Guide to Inference Anchoring Theory (IAT) (2017)
5. Chesñevar, C., et al.: Towards an argument interchange format. Knowl Eng Rev **21**(4), 293–316 (2006). https://doi.org/10.1017/S0269888906001044
6. Clark, T., Gonzalez-Perez, C., Henderson-Sellers, B.: A foundation for multi-level modelling. In: Atkinson, C., Grossmann, G., Kühne, T., de Lara, J. (eds.) Proceedings of the Workshop on Multi-Level Modelling co-located with ACM/IEEE 17th International Conference on Model Driven Engineering Languages & Systems (MoDELS 2014), vol. 1286, Regensburg, Germany: CEUR-WS.org, 2014, pp. 43–52
7. Craciunean, D.-C., Volovici, D.: Conceptualization of modelling methods in the context of categorical mechanisms. In: Karagiannis, D., Lee, M., Hinkelmann, K., Utz, W. (eds.) Domain-Specific Conceptual Modeling: Concepts, Methods and ADOxx Tools, pp. 543–565. Springer International Publishing, Cham (2022). https://doi.org/10.1007/978-3-030-93547-4_24
8. Doerr, M., Kritsotaki, A., Boutsika, K.: Factual argumentation—a core model for assertions making. J. Comput. Cult. Heritage **3**(3), 1–34 (2011). https://doi.org/10.1145/1921614.192 1615
9. Frank, U.: Some guidelines for the conception of domain-specific modelling languages. In: Enterprise modelling and information systems architectures (EMISA 2011) (2011)
10. Gee, J.P.: An Introduction to Discourse Analysis: Theory and Method. Routledge (2014)
11. GonzalezPerez, C.: Information Modelling for Archaeology and Anthropology. Springer International Publishing, Cham (2018). https://doi.org/10.1007/978-3-319-72652-6
12. GonzalezPerez, C.: How ontologies can help in software engineering. In: Cunha, J., Fernandes, J.P., Lämmel, R., Saraiva, J., Zaytsev, V. (eds.) Grand Timely Topics in Software Engineering. LNCS, vol. 10223, pp. 26–44. Springer, Cham (2017). https://doi.org/10.1007/978-3-319-600 74-1_2

13. Gonzalez-Perez, C.: Connecting discourse and domain models in discourse analysis through ontological proxies. Electronics (Basel) **9**(11), 1955 (2020). https://doi.org/10.3390/electronics9111955

14. Gonzalez-Perez, C.: a conceptual modelling language for the humanities and social sciences. In: Rolland, C., Castro, J., Pastor, O., (eds.) Sixth International Conference on Research Challenges in Information Science (RCIS), 2012, pp. 396–401. IEEE Computer Society (2012)

15. Gonzalez-Perez, C.: Ontological proxies to augment the expressiveness of discourse analysis. In: Gamallo, P., García, M., Martín-Rodilla, P., Pereira-Fariña, M., (eds.) Hybrid Intelligence for Natural Language Processing Tasks 2020, vol. 2693, pp. 1–3. CEUR-WS.org, 2020 (2020)

16. Gonzalez-Perez, C., Pereira-Fariña, M.: IAT/ML (2021). http://www.iatml.org/

17. Grice, H.P.: Logic and Conversation. In: Davidson, D., Harman, G. (eds.) The Logic of Grammar, pp. 64–75 (1975)

18. Guizzardi, G., Pires, L.F., van Sinderen, M.: An ontology-based approach for evaluating the domain appropriateness and comprehensibility appropriateness of modeling languages. In: Briand, L., Williams, C. (eds.) Model Driven Engineering Languages and Systems, pp. 691–705. Springer, Heidelberg (2005). https://doi.org/10.1007/11557432_51

19. Hamdaqa, M., Metz, L.A.P., Qasse, I.: icontractml: a domain-specific language for modeling and deploying smart contracts onto multiple blockchain platforms, pp. 34–43 (2020)

20. HendersonSellers, B.: Bridging metamodels and ontologies in software engineering. J. Syst. Softw. **84**(2), 301–313 (2011). https://doi.org/10.1016/j.jss.2010.10.025

21. Iivari, J.: Twelve theses on design science research in information systems. In: Hevner, A., Chatterjee, S. (eds.) Design Research in Information Systems, pp. 43–62. Springer, Boston (2010). https://doi.org/10.1007/978-1-4419-5653-8_5

22. Hinton, M., Wagemans, J.H.M.: Evaluating reasoning in natural arguments: a procedural approach. Argumentation **36**(1), 61–84 (2021). https://doi.org/10.1007/s10503-021-09555-1

23. Incipit CSIC: ConML Technical Specification, Incipit CSIC (2020). http://www.conml.org/Resources/TechSpec.aspx

24. Janier, M., Aakhus, M., Budzynska, K., Reed, C.: Modeling argumentative activity with inference anchoring theory. In: Mohhamed, D., Lewinski, M. (eds.) Argumentation and Reasoned Action. Volume I Proceedings of the 1st European Conference on Argumentation, vol. 1, no. 62, College Publications (2016)

25. Johnstone, B.: Discourse Analysis. Wiley (2018)

26. Krämer, M.: Controlling the processing of smart city data in the cloud with domain-specific languages, pp. 824–829 (2014)

27. Perelman, C., Olbrechts-Tyteca, L.: Traité de l'argumentation: La nouvelle rhétorique. Presses Universitaires de France (1958)

28. Pescador, A., Garmendia, A., Guerra, E., Cuadrado, J.S., de Lara, J.: Pattern-based development of domain-specific modelling languages, pp. 166–175 (2015)

29. Reed, C., Budzynska, K.: How dialogues create arguments. In: ISSA Proceedings 2010 (2010). http://rozenbergquarterly.com/issa-proceedings-2010-how-dialogues-create-arguments/

30. Fabián, José, et al.: Integration of clinical and genomic data to enhance precision medicine: a case of study applied to the retina-macula. Softw. Syst. Modeling **22**(1), 159–174 (2022). https://doi.org/10.1007/s10270-022-01039-4

31. Searle, J.R., Vanderveken, D.: Foundations of Illocutionary Logic. Cambridge University Press, Cambridge (1985)

32. Suchánek, M.: OntoUML Specification (2018). https://ontouml.readthedocs.io/. Accessed 09 Oct 2020

33. Toulmin, S.E.: The Uses of Argument. Cambridge University Press (2003). https://doi.org/10.1017/CBO9780511840005

34. Visser, J., Lawrence, J., Reed, C., Wagemans, J., Walton, D.: Annotating argument schemes. Argumentation **35**(1), 101–139 (2020). https://doi.org/10.1007/s10503-020-09519-x
35. Wagemans, J.: Period Table of Arguments (2020). https://periodic-table-of-arguments.org/. Accessed 16 Oct 2020
36. Wagemans, J.H.M.: Constructing a periodic table of arguments. SSRN Electron. J. (2016).https://doi.org/10.2139/ssrn.2769833
37. Walton, D., Reed, C., Macagno, F.: Argumentation Schemes. Cambridge University Press, Cambridge (2008)
38. Wieringa, R., Morali, A.: Technical action research as a validation method in information systems design science. In: Peffers, K., Rothenberger, M., Kuechler, B. (eds.) Design Science Research in Information Systems. Advances in Theory and Practice. LNCS, vol. 7286, pp. 220–238. Springer, Heidelberg (2012). https://doi.org/10.1007/978-3-642-29863-9_17
39. Wittgenstein, L.: Philosophical investigations, 3rd edn. Blackwell, Oxford (1989)
40. World Wide Web Consortium: OWL 2 Web Ontology Language. World Wide Web Consortium (2012). http://www.w3.org/TR/2012/REC-owl2-overview-20121211/
41. World Wide Web Consortium: RDF/XML Syntax Specification (Revised). World Wide Web Consortium (2004). http://www.w3.org/TR/2004/REC-rdf-syntax-grammar-20040210/
42. Zhou, S., Wang, N., Wang, L., Liu, H., Zhang, R.: CancerBERT: a cancer domain-specific language model for extracting breast cancer phenotypes from electronic health records. J. Am. Med. Inform. Assoc. **29**, 1208–1216 (2022)
43. "The Conversation, Spanish Edition (2020). https://theconversation.com/es. Accessed 16 Oct 2020

Enterprise Architecture and Transformation (EMMSAD)

A First Validation of the Enterprise Architecture Debts Concept

Simon Hacks[1] and Jürgen Jung[2](✉)

[1] Stockholm University, Stockholm, Sweden
simon.hacks@dsv.su.se
[2] Frankfurt University of Applied Sciences, Frankfurt am Main, Germany
jung.juergen@fb2.fra-uas.de

Abstract. The Enterprise Architecture (EA) discipline is now established in many companies. The architectures of these companies changed over time. They resulted from a long creation and maintenance process containing processes and services provided by legacy IT systems (e.g., systems, applications) that were reasonable when they were created but might now hamper the introduction of better solutions. To handle those legacies, we started researching on the notion of EA debts, which widens the scope of technical debts to organizational aspects. However, no studies have yet been conducted to validate if the concept of EA debts has a positive influence. Within this work, we have experimented with students of an EA course. Half of the students were taught the concept of EA debts, while the other half was taught about another topic simultaneously. Afterward, the students performed a modeling task graded by EA experts among the criteria of effectiveness, comprehensibility, minimality, and completeness. The analysis revealed no significant difference between the quality of the created models by the different student groups.

Keywords: Enterprise Architecture Debts · Concept Validation · Experiment

1 Introduction

The digital transformation does not only come with opportunities but also challenges such as business-IT alignment [32] (BITA). To cope with this challenge, a holistic view is required to drive digital innovations to fully understand the impact of products, employees, or business models [22]. One means to achieve this is Enterprise Architecture (EA) [18], which provides methods and tools to align business with IT, operationalize the business strategy, and can drive innovations [19]. EA provides transparency by business-related views and abstractions for describing application landscapes and information technology [18,36].

EA was introduced many years ago in many organizations, and related research produced a plethora of frameworks, methods, and tools [14,15]. Consequently, organizations' EAs often reflect this evolution through many artifacts

H. van der Aa et al. (Eds.): BPMDS 2023/EMMSAD 2023, LNBIP 479, pp. 217–226, 2023.
https://doi.org/10.1007/978-3-031-34241-7_15

and systems being implemented. At the same time, EA is often perceived as bureaucratic, document-centric, and hampering agility due to its focus on long-term effects [5,35]. However, there might be significant discrepancies between long-term EA objectives and individual projects. This may cause conflicts as the EA plans are not in line with business needs, and the EA gets disconnected from the business. Typical consequences are, for example: (1) Complex application landscapes with legacy systems and redundancies; (2) Outdated or incomplete EA artefacts and documentation; or (3) Procedures and organisational units in EA management that hamper IT innovations.

These consequences stem from past decisions that might have been justified at the corresponding time. However, the situation and context of an organization change, and these changes must also be reflected in the application landscape. But, existing legacy systems, historical procedures, and long-term planning processes slow the adoption of required changes.

To cope with this challenge, Hacks et al. proposed the term of EA Debts in order to describe those results from past decisions that hamper changes in IT [11]. Similar to the notion of technical debts, EA Debts represent blockers while moving from the current EA (as-is) towards a desired to-be-landscape. In contrast to technical debts, EA Debt encompasses technical systems, processes, organisational units, and regulations.

However, the beneficiary of EA Debts has been only confirmed anecdotally in personal conversations with practitioners. Yet, a more formal validation of the concept is missing. Within this work, we take the first step to closing this gap. Therefore, we designed an experiment with business informatics students in an EA course. The experiment aimed to answer the following research question:

RQ *Does knowledge about the concept of EA Debts improve the quality of to-be EA models?*

The idea of the experiment is to teach one-half of the students about the concept of EA Debts and not the other. Subsequently, the students need to solve a task in which they need to develop an improved EA given a certain scenario. The improved EA is documented in an EA model and evaluated by EA experts towards certain qualities.

The rest of this work is structured as follows. Next, we provide the background of the work, i.e., what is the concept of EA Debts about and what are related works. Then, we present the research method and the experiment in more detail before presenting the results. We conclude our work by discussing the results and giving further ideas on how to cope with the results and how to validate the concept of EA Debts further.

2   Background

2.1   Enterprise Architecture Debts

The increasing digitalization of organizations fosters agile methods, which creates new challenges for EA, as the EA conception phases to define proper target architectures become reduced [33]. One driver is the tendency of product owners to prefer short-term business value over solid architectural solutions, while means to propagate long-term architectural solutions are missing [10,34].

To address this challenge and to support enterprise architects in arguing for more sustainable solutions, Hacks et al. [11] extend the concept of Technical Debts, which describes past technical shortcuts that hamper IT developments [7, 20], to the EA domain by suggesting a more holistic view on the organization.

So far, Technical Debt has demonstrated its benefits in estimating deficits in software, being a tool for decision making, and increasing the awareness [16,30] However, it focused on the technical aspects of a single system, thus missing the opportunity to help the entire enterprise and every scenario [1,8,24].

Here the concept of EA Debts steps in, which Hacks et al. [11] define as "the deviation of the currently present state of an enterprise from a hypothetical ideal state." Such a deviation can be interpreted from two different perspectives: Firstly, it can result from decisions that are expedient in the short term but cause future changes to be more costly. Therefore, EA Debts might hamper the implementation of better solutions. In other words, it is related to the planning of the EA toward its evolution (ex-post). Secondly, the debt can describe a deviation in the actual EA that might have arisen due to changes in the valuation. In other words, when the decision was made, it was in line with the optimal EA, but over time, the strategic focus of the organization changed, leading to another optimal EA. Thus, the former decision is now causing a debt (ex-ante).

All previous research on EA Debts assumed the concept as beneficial. However, proof for this assumption beyond anecdotal confirmation in personal discussions is missing. Therefore, we take a first step in this direction here.

2.2 Related Work

Related research can be categorized into two categories. On the one hand, research is generally related to the concept of EA Debts. On the other hand, there is research trying to validate concepts and especially design patterns.

The main goal to be achieved with EA Debt is to provide means for analyzing and improving EAs, which is a continuous endeavor in EA-related research. In 2012, 37% of EA-related publications elaborated on analysis and 33% on planning efforts [31]. Barbosa et al. [3] pointed out that about 18% of EA analysis research focused on concerns about how the EA can be changed and around 15% on different aspects of alignment like BITA.

Besides EA Debt, different researchers developed analysis methods for EA. Considering structural aspects, Boufia and Molnár [6] apply hypergraphs to assess the alignment between the information system's architecture and business processes. Similarly, Mu and Kwong [23] develop a multi-objective optimization model to plan the integration of components, while Langermeier and Bauer [17] propose a model-based approach to ensure the compliance of projects with the overall planning. However, fewer formal approaches put the interaction with the stakeholders in focus. For example, Schilling, Aier and Winter [28] designed a label that communicates the sustainability of architectural decisions to EA's stakeholders, while Schlör and Jung [29] facilitate business support matrices to visualize the BITA. Other examples to achieve BITA are, for example, Mengmeng, Hunghui and Yi [21] proposing an approach to measure BITA in DoDAF or Öri and Szabó [38] proposing misalignment patterns.

Similar to our endeavor, Prechelt and Unger [25] were reasoning about a missing validation for the concept of design patterns in software engineering. To prove the assumption that design patterns are an effective means, they performed three controlled experiments. In another experiment, Prechelt et al. [27] researched if design patterns are always useful, especially if a simpler alternative might be better suited. Finally, Precht et al. [26] checked the hypothesis if it helps developers to document design patterns explicitly in the code.

Similarly, Alter and Wright [2] validated work system principles using questionnaires, which have been answered by MBA executive students. More concretely, the students were asked if their organizations should adhere to the principles and to what degree the organizations actually adhere. Additionally, the entire concept of Work System Theory has been validated by comparing it to accepted other concepts like UML, work practice theory, and practice theory.

3   Evaluating the Concept of *EA Debts*

3.1   Experiment as Research Method

An *experiment* has been chosen as a research method in order to evaluate the benefits of EA debts in a practical context. While doing so, a similar approach as presented in [26,27] has been followed as the research aims to validate the application of EA debts. Experiments have, as any research method, certain benefits and limitations [9]. They allow for some realism for the participants but lack of precision compared to an empirical study. However, they allow for validating a complex concept in a controlled environment [37].

The experiment has been conducted as a *controlled experiment* with two groups of participants on a pre-defined environment so that it can be reproduced [25]. A field study was not considered as we wanted all participants to be on the same level. According to the terminology provided by [4], the experiment was performed *in vitro*. We also did not conduct the experiment with practitioners in order to observe how newly trained people adapt to the concept of EA debts.

3.2   Generating the Artefacts

The experiment has been conducted with 35 students participating at a class on EAM on a post-graduate level. They were divided into 16 teams, consisting of two or three members. Each team was tasked to work on a case study[1] throughout the semester by defining the business architecture of a fictional company and deriving

---

[1] https://github.com/simonhacks/EADEvaluation/blob/main/
EMMSAD_Case_Description.pdf.

an ideal application landscape. This resulted in 16 enterprise architectures for the same imaginary company called *Hung Cha* (a specialist tea seller).

Before deriving the application landscape, student teams were randomly partitioned into two groups. One group of eight teams attended training on EA debts and got access to a catalog of typical EA debts. The other eight teams joined training on change management and were not introduced to the idea of EA debts. After the training, the teams started deriving their idea of an ideal application landscape for *Hung Cha* based on their respective business architecture.

Even though all teams used *ArchiMate* as a modeling language, the resulting artefacts varied. Team C defined the business capabilities together with associated software applications[2]. The capability map had to be defined on two levels and cover the whole company. The applications were identified by the students based on personal experience and market research. Any other models (e.g. *business motivation* and *business object model*) that were created as part of the case study have been omitted for the experiment as it would have increased the workload for the reviewers (cf. the following Sect. 3.3).

Team C's architecture looks quite minimalist as it only contains some applications and some capabilities are not supported by software systems. In contrast to this, team J's shows a slightly more elaborate architecture diagram[3]. The number of capabilities is quite similar but each level-2 capability is supported by a software system. However, it takes some more time in order to understand the underlying structure and the architecture seems to be tailored around *Oracle NetSuite* and its modules. Parts of it, however, seem to be developed in a hurry. The *Company overview* capability violates the naming convention and its sub-capabilities are not properly reflected. *BPMN* is a modeling language and, perhaps, was rather intended to be *BPM* for business process management. Furthermore, the associated tool might be good for process modeling but not for EAM. One of the sub-capabilities even has a German name[4].

Team F divided the capability map into *guiding*, *core* and *enabling* capabilities (cf. [12, p. 49])[5]. *Core* capabilities represent the core business or value-adding activities. *Enabling* capabilities support value creation and play a similar role as supporting activities. *Guiding* capabilities reflect a view on managing activities, like planning and monitoring operations. Team F only focuses on the core capabilities. Enabling and guiding capabilities were submitted in separate diagrams. It also contains unsupported capabilities (e.g. *Delivery Management* or *Quality Assurance*) which is a bit surprising in this case as the delivery was supposed to be done by an external service provider providing an API for shipping label creation. The diagram also shows an outdated system (*Stock Access DB*) that was supposed to be replaced.

---

[2] https://github.com/simonhacks/EADEvaluation/blob/main/C.png.

[3] https://github.com/simonhacks/EADEvaluation/blob/main/J.jpg.

[4] Teams were allowed to choose either German or English but they were not supposed to mix languages.

[5] https://github.com/simonhacks/EADEvaluation/blob/main/F_Core.jpg.

The experiment was coordinated and executed by two researchers. Researcher A was teaching the students and coordinating the creation of the application landscapes (i.e. the artefacts). He then anonymized the artefacts and handed them over to researcher B who then coordinated the evaluation. Researcher B was also not aware of the details and expectations of the case study but only of the result. Hence, no additional details were provided to the reviewers except the results as presented by the aforementioned examples.

3.3   Evaluating the Artefacts

The evaluation was done by seven practitioners having an EA background. Neither the practitioners nor researcher B were aware of whether the result was created by a team with EA debt knowledge or not. Only researcher A knew the relationship between the artifact and the corresponding student team. This approach has been chosen in order to reduce the risk of any influence or bias. Each practitioner was assigned to evaluate between five and nine different artefacts. They needed to assess them with respect to the following four-level Likert items:

- *Comprehensibility* describes how easy the model can be understood.
- *Effectiveness* relates to the capability of the model to achieve a good enterprise architecture in future.
- *Completeness* assesses if the model contains all relevant elements of the enterprise architecture.
- *Minimality* reflects if the model contains only necessary elements of the enterprise architecture.

The practitioners were provided with the case study description, the EA showing the applications, and corresponding business capabilities together with a short review guide. They then had to fill in an Excel sheet with numbers 1–4 for each application landscape and each Likert item. Only after the evaluation by the practitioners was finished, researcher B received the mapping of the application landscape to the student team and started summarising the results.

4   Results

After grading the different application landscapes, we united the different grading[6] leading to three grading per application landscape. First, we checked if there are fundamental differences in the perceptions of the application landscapes by comparing the maximum and minimum values given. We observed several times a difference of 2 between the ratings. However, this happened not in the majority of the cases (difference of 0 = 23%; 1 = 58%; 2 = 19%; 3 = 0%) and is also rather distributed among all application landscapes. Thus, we assume that the experts were mostly agreeing with each other on their rating.

Secondly, we calculated the standard deviation for all quality criteria to check if there are any anomalies along the different criteria (cf. Table 1). The standard

---

[6] https://github.com/simonhacks/EADEvaluation/blob/main/Results_Github.xlsx.

Table 1. Average (avg) and standard deviation (sd) of the experts' grading.

EA Debt taught	Comprehensibility	Effectiveness	Completeness	Minimality
no	avg: 2.83, sd: 0.50	avg: 2.63, sd: 0.45	avg: 2.88, sd: 0.41	avg: 3.25, sd: 0.49
yes	avg: 2.79, sd: 0.55	avg: 2.67, sd: 0.47	avg: 2.75, sd: 0.46	avg: 2.83, sd: 0.41

variation varies between 0.41 and 0.55 and, thus, we conclude that we cannot observe any anomalies here.

Lastly, we analyzed the graded quality criteria with respect to the concept of EA Debt being taught or not. Considering the results, we do not see a significant difference in the grading of the different application landscapes. The only bigger difference that we found is that teaching the concept of EA Debts led to larger models (minimality rated with 3.25 (no) vs. 2.83 (yes)). However, the difference is so small that we do not conclude a definitive influence here. Consequently, we cannot positively answer our research question.

5 Discussion and Conclusions

the results of the experiment show a clear answer to the research question *Does knowledge about the concept of EA Debts improve the quality of to-be EA models?*. The results of both groups have been assessed very similarly by the seven practitioners which implies that the knowledge of EA debts does not have any impact on the quality of the models. Even though the result might look disappointing, it only refers to the notion of *knowledge* as provided in the setup. It basically encompasses the knowledge of master students obtained during one semester in an EA class together with one training session on EA debts. During a retrospective, the researchers reflected on the results and the research method.

In fact, the selection of the participants should be reconsidered. Even though a controlled experiment with students can be conducted with a reasonable effort, it does not incorporate practical experience. The students did not have any exposure to EA before attending the class. Most of the concepts were quite new to them and they are lacking practical experience in a professional environment. Consequently, it is hard for students to assess the impact of an EA on the organisation. The case study also caused some ambiguities as it was no real-life case and some decisions on the design of the EA might seem arbitrary.

Moreover, we did not ensure that the students have grasped the concept of EA Debts. This could be ensured by testing the students on the topic after having received the lecture. This would separate the effectiveness of our teaching from the effectiveness of the concept itself.

Consequently, the benefits of applying best practices (like design patterns in software engineering or EA debts) are hard to grasp for novices. Applying design patterns does not happen mechanically, but, requires experience in software engineering and design. The reason for this is the additional level of abstraction while constructing a model. A model is supposed to represent a real-life situation but patterns relate to models and represent knowledge on good design decisions. In the same way, one needs experience in EA before understanding best practices on EA (like EA debts).

Even worse, many of the EA debts do not refer to the design of an artefact but to the organisation for creating and using those artefacts. For example, a *lack of documentation* can not be expressed by an artefact as it reflects the fact of not having the artefact. Also *unclear responsibilities* is usually not reflected in an EA but rather by a symptom showing that responsibilities should be clearly assigned. This might not be visible in the actual EA itself. Assessing such EA debts, even more, requires practical experience (i.e. experiencing the issues from a bad application architecture because there are no clear responsibilities). This experience cannot be provided by a single training session.

Another point for improvement is the fact that the students produced the artefacts over a longer span of time. Thus, it cannot be ensured that other parameters might have influenced the students. It would have been better to enforce the students to produce the artefacts in a closed environment to avoid pollution due to other parameters.

Concerning the evaluation, one can remark that a single evaluator did not evaluate all artefacts. We decided so to keep the effort for the evaluators on a manageable level while trying to address this shortcoming by randomly assigning the artefacts to the different evaluators. An alternative solution might be to ensure that the artefacts are of smaller size and that one evaluator is thus able to review all of them.

The conclusion of the authors is that further investigation into the benefits of EA debts is still necessary. Previous studies clearly show that people recognise the notion of EA debts as beneficial. Practitioners din not only reconfirm their relevance in previous research (e.g. [13]) but also provided a plethora of typical EA debts they perceive in their respective organisation. The following aspects will have to be considered for an upcoming evaluation:

- EA experience: Participants should be experienced in the enterprise architecture discipline
- Field study: A field study with professionals might be preferred over an in vitro experiment
- Training: Instead of a single training session, comprehensive training should be developed. Such training should not only show a catalogue of EA debts but also use practical examples and case studies for teaching their impact in a real-world environment.
- Focus: A follow-up experiment should rather focus on one aspect of an enterprise architecture rather than the four presented in the paper at hand.

Acknowledgements. We like to thank our experts for their voluntary work to assess the different models of our students.

References

1. Addicks, J.S., Appelrath, H.J.: A method for application evaluations in context of enterprise architecture. In: Proceedings of the 2010 ACM Symposium on Applied Computing, pp. 131–136. SAC 2010, ACM, New York, NY, USA (2010)
2. Alter, S., Wright, R.: Validating work system principles for use in systems analysis and design. In: ICIS 2010 Proceedings, No. 197 (2010)
3. Barbosa, A., Santana, A., Hacks, S., von Stein, N.: A taxonomy for enterprise architecture analysis research. In: 21st International Conference on Enterprise Information Systems, vol. 2, pp. 493–504. SciTePress (2019)
4. Basili, V.: The role of experimentation in software engineering: past, current, and future. In: Proceedings of IEEE 18th International Conference on Software Engineering, pp. 442–449 (1996)
5. Bente, S., Bombosch, U., Langade, S.: Collaborative Enterprise Architecture: Enriching EA with Lean, Agile, and Enterprise 2.0 Practices. Morgan Kaufmann (2012)
6. Bouafia, K., Molnár, B.: Analysis approach for enterprise information systems architecture based on hypergraph to aligned business process requirements. Proc. Comput. Sci. **164**, 19–24 (2019)
7. Cunningham, W.: The WyCash portfolio management system. ACM SIGPLAN OOPS Messenger **4**(2), 29–30 (1993)
8. Curtis, B., Sappidi, J., Szynkarski, A.: Estimating the principal of an application's technical debt. IEEE Softw. **29**(6), 34–42 (2012)
9. Dennis, A.: Conducting experimental research in information systems. Commun. Assoc. Inf. Syst. **7**(1), 5 (2001)
10. Gampfer, F., Jürgens, A., Müller, M., Buchkremer, R.: Past, current and future trends in enterprise architecture-a view beyond the horizon. Comput. Ind. **100**, 70–84 (2018)
11. Hacks, S., Hofert, H., Salentin, J., Yeong, Y.C., Lichter, H.: Towards the definition of enterprise architecture debts. In: 2019 IEEE 23rd EDOCW, pp. 9–16. IEEE, October 2019
12. Jung, J., Fraunholz, B.: Masterclass Enterprise Architecture Management. Springer, Cham (2021). https://doi.org/10.1007/978-3-030-78495-9
13. Jung, J., Hacks, S., De Gooijer, T., Kinnunen, M., Rehring, K.: revealing common enterprise architecture debts: conceptualization and critical reflection on a workshop format industry experience report. In: Proceedings - IEEE International Enterprise Distributed Object Computing Workshop, EDOCW, pp. 271–278 (2021)
14. Kaisler, S., Armour, F.: 15 Years of enterprise architecting at HICSS : revisiting the critical problems. In: Proceedings of the 50th Hawaii International Conference on System Sciences, vol. 2017, pp. 4807–4816 (2017)
15. Kotusev, S.: Enterprise Architecture: What Did We Study? Int. J. Coop. Inf. Syst. **26**(4), 1730002 (2017)
16. Kruchten, P., Nord, R.L., Ozkaya, I.: Technical debt: from metaphor to theory and practice. IEEE Softw. **29**(6), 18–21 (2012)
17. Langermeier, M., Bauer, B.: A model-based method for the evaluation of project proposal compliance within EA planning. In: 2018 IEEE 22nd EDOCW, pp. 97–106. IEEE, October 2018
18. Lankhorst, M.: Enterprise Architecture at Work. Springer, Berlin (2009). https://doi.org/10.1007/978-3-642-01310-2

19. Lapalme, J.: Three schools of thought on enterprise architecture. IT Prof. **14**(6), 37–43 (2012)
20. Li, Z., Avgeriou, P., Liang, P.: A systematic mapping study on technical debt and its management. J. Syst. Softw. **101**, 193–220 (2015)
21. Mengmeng, Z., Honghui, C., Yi, M., Aimin, L.: An approach to measuring business-IT alignment maturity via DoDAF2.0, pp. 95–108. IEEE JSEE, January 2020
22. Morakanyane, R., Grace, A., O'Reilly, P.: Conceptualizing digital transformation in business organizations: a systematic review of literature. In: 30th Bled eConference: Digital Transformation - From Connecting Things to Transforming our Lives, BLED 2017, pp. 427–444 (2017)
23. Mu, L., Kwong, C.: A multi-objective optimization model of component selection in enterprise information system integration. Comput. Ind. Eng. **115**, 278–289 (2018)
24. Nord, R.L., Ozkaya, I., Kruchten, P., Gonzalez-Rojas, M.: In search of a metric for managing architectural technical debt. In: 2012 Joint Working IEEE/IFIP Conference on Software Architecture and European Conference on Software Architecture, pp. 91–100 (2012)
25. Prechelt, L., Unger, B.: A series of controlled experiments on design patterns: Methodology and results. In: Proceedings Softwaretechnik 1998 GI Conference (Softwaretechnik-Trends), pp. 53–60. Paderborn (1998)
26. Prechelt, L., Unger, B., Philippsen, M., Tichy, W.F.: Two controlled experiments assessing the usefulness of design pattern documentation in program maintenance. IEEE Trans. Softw. Eng. **28**(6), 595–606 (2002)
27. Prechelt, L., Unger, B., Tichy, W.F., Brössler, P., Votta, L.G.: A controlled experiment in maintenance comparing design patterns to simpler solutions. IEEE Trans. Softw. Eng. **27**(12), 1134–1144 (2001)
28. Schilling, R., Aier, S., Winter, R.: Designing an Artifact for Informal Control in Enterprise Architecture Management. In: Fortieth ICIS 2019 (dec 2019)
29. Schlör, R., Jung, J.: Analysis using the business support matrix: elaborating potential for improving application landscapes in logistics. In: 2018 IEEE 22nd EDOCW, pp. 192–199. IEEE, October 2018
30. Seaman, C., Guo, Y.: Measuring and monitoring technical debt. Adv. Comput. **82**, 25–46 (2011)
31. Simon, D., Fischbach, K., Schoder, D.: An Exploration of Enterprise Architecture Research. Communications of the Association for Information Systems **32**(1), 1–72 (2013)
32. Tabrizi, B., Lam, E., Girard, K., Irvin, V.: Digital Transformation Is Not About Technology. Harvard Business Review, pp. 2–7 (2019). https://hbr.org/2019/03/digital-transformation-is-not-about-technology
33. Uludağ, Ö., Kleehaus, M., Xu, X., Matthes, F.: Investigating the role of architects in scaling agile frameworks. In: 2017 IEEE 21st International Enterprise Distributed Object Computing Conference (EDOC), pp. 123–132. IEEE (2017)
34. Uludag, Ö., Reiter, N., Matthes, F.: What to expect from enterprise architects in large-scale agile development? A multiple-case study. In: 25th AMCIS (2019)
35. Wierda, G.: Chess and the Art of Enterprise Architecure. R&A (2015)
36. Wierda, G.: Mastering ArchiMate. R&A, 2 edn. (2017)
37. Zelkowitz, M., Wallace, D.: Experimental models for validating technology. Computer **31**(5), 23–31 (1998)
38. Őri, D., Szabó, Z.: Analysing strategic misalignment in public administration. In: International Conference on Electronic Governance and Open Society, pp. 183–197 (2019)

Modeling Heterogeneous IT Infrastructures: A Collaborative Component-Oriented Approach

Benjamin Somers[1,2]([✉]) [ID], Fabien Dagnat[1] [ID], and Jean-Christophe Bach[1] [ID]

[1] IMT Atlantique, Lab-STICC, UMR 6285, 29238 Brest, France
benjamin.somers@imt-atlantique.fr
[2] Crédit Mutuel Arkéa, 29480 Le Relecq-Kerhuon, France

Abstract. The advent and growing sophistication of modern cloud-native architectures has brought into question the way we design IT infrastructures. As the architectures become more complex, modeling helps employees to better understand their environment and decision makers to better grasp the "big picture". As the levels of abstraction multiply, modeling these infrastructures is becoming more difficult. This leads to incomplete, heterogeneous views difficult to reconcile. In this article, we present a collaborative approach focused on improving the accuracy of IT infrastructure modeling through the involvement of all stakeholders in the process. Our approach, applied in an incremental manner, is meant to increase confidence, accountability and knowledge of the infrastructure, by assigning responsibilities early in the process and leveraging the expertise of each stakeholder. It is suited for both *a priori* and *a posteriori* modeling at a low adoption cost, through adaptation of existing workflows and model reuse. Building collaborative models in such a way aims at bridging the gap between different areas of business expertise. As a result, we believe that our approach allows to perform analyses and use formal methods on larger scale models and cover wider technical domains.

Keywords: IT infrastructure modeling · Collaborative infrastructure design · Heterogeneous models · Multi-viewpoint design · Model federation

1 Introduction

The evolution of IT infrastructures has followed a tendency towards abstraction. This has enabled the development and deployment of enterprise-wide systems with greater flexibility and scalability, in order to fulfill a wider variety of needs. These advances come however at the cost of increased architectural complexity [30]. In some domains such as banking, healthcare and defense, the lifetime of IT infrastructures can span over decades, combining the old and the new. Modern cloud-native IT infrastructures are therefore often built upon so-called *legacy* systems, with which they need to interact to perform business-critical operations.

H. van der Aa et al. (Eds.): BPMDS 2023/EMMSAD 2023, LNBIP 479, pp. 227–242, 2023.
https://doi.org/10.1007/978-3-031-34241-7_16

Yet, IT infrastructures do not depend exclusively on the proper operation of hardware and software: the human factor and the good performance of business processes must be taken into account. This is where Enterprise Modeling comes into the picture [32], with two major challenges. First, technical infrastructures tend to be stacked in technical layers (such as hardware, software, network...) while human organizations tend to be divided in business domains (financial, cloud operations, support...). These technical layers, however, do not necessarily match the business ones, and vice versa; this disalignment must be taken into account in the modeling. Second, all the stakeholders should be included in the modeling process [33], to properly capture the interactions within the infrastructure and the related responsibilities. The different stakeholders, however, have different skill sets, reflected in the use of different tools and a different jargon from other employees [3], making model alignment process even more complex.

It is important to gather this knowledge around a common model to have a good overview of IT infrastructures and to conduct analyses covering several technical and administrative domains. This article proposes a component-oriented metamodel that takes into account the various perspectives of such infrastructures. We argue that a complete and correct model is achieved by considering all of these viewpoints and better integrating the responsibilities of each stakeholder.

To this end, we present the theoretical background of our study in Sect. 2. Section 3 describes the metamodel we use. In Sect. 4, we propose a collaborative methodological framework to encode business processes and technical jobs in this metamodel. We present a case study in Sect. 5 to illustrate our approach by reasoning on a model. Finally, Sect. 6 concludes this article.

2 Related Work

Models convey domain-specific knowledge in a broad range of fields through abstraction of concepts. From technical to administrative areas, with various levels of granularity, they are an integral part of today's businesses [16]. IT infrastructure modeling combines the concepts of enterprise modeling and IT models, linked together to provide a complete picture.

2.1 Enterprise Modeling

Enterprise modeling has undergone major evolutions since its inception [32]. Models have become "active" [10], to manage the complexity of interactions across diverse business domains. Combined with formal methods, high-fidelity models can bring great value to companies adopting them [5]. However, due to the wide range of professions and tools used within these companies, such models are complex to produce and discrepancies occur [2].

Standards such as ISO 19439 [12] propose to model enterprises in (at least) four views (process, information, infrastructure and organization) on three modeling levels (requirements, design and implementation). Such a layered approach is found in many modeling frameworks, among which we can mention RM-ODP [1] and Archimate [29]. These frameworks provide a high-level way to model enterprises and allow to represent the infrastructures on which businesses lie. However, the large amount of concepts and the lack of precise semantics regarding IT infrastructures make the frameworks difficult to use in IT domains for people whose main job is not enterprise modeling [17]. Moreover, the matricial aspects of their approaches and their division into layers are not always suitable [14].

2.2 IT Models

Many languages and representations exist to describe IT infrastructures, from hardware to software, including networks and processes. A datacenter can be described by rack diagrams, illustrating the layout of servers and network components. A software can be represented using UML diagrams [23], to show its structure and the different interactions at work, or can be described by its code. A network topology can be seen as mathematical objects [24,27], described by switch configurations, or as code in *Software-Defined Networking* [18]. These areas also benefit from many contributions from the formal methods communities (*e.g.* Alloy [13] to verify specifications or Petri nets [20] to model complex behaviors).

However, most of these frameworks cannot interact with one another. This limit appears if we ask questions that cross several domains, such as "which services become non-operational if we unplug this cable?" [21] or "is my business domain impacted by this router vulnerability?".

2.3 Collaborative Modeling

Domain-specific languages are adapted to their respective domains [6] and can represent in detail things that holistic frameworks cannot. But these languages are sometimes not understandable by other parties. It leads to many metamodels [15], often sharing the same core concepts [4], being used to model enterprises.

The modeling process must come from a need and be undertaken by including all the professional disciplines concerned. However, due to a lack of modeling skills, some stakeholders are not able to participate in such a process [25]. Work in the model federation community [9] (where we maintain links between models expressed in different metamodels) is a step towards including the expertise of such stakeholders. Other approaches, such as composition [8] (where we build a common metamodel to align models) and unification [31] (where we build a single model) are described in the literature.

3   Our Proposal

In this article, we advocate a collaborative approach to IT infrastructure modeling. In this section, we present our metamodel (represented in Fig. 1) and detail its characteristics, before presenting its differentiating aspects.

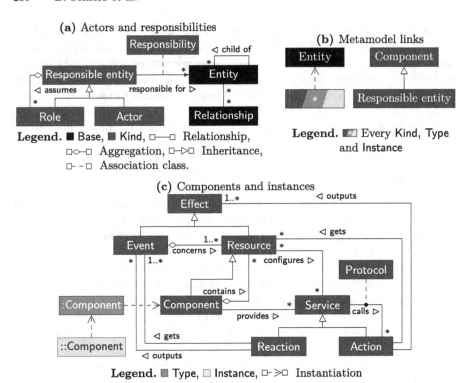

(a) Actors and responsibilities

Legend. ■ Base, ■ Kind, □—□ Relationship,
□◇—□ Aggregation, □–▷□ Inheritance,
□- -□ Association class.

(b) Metamodel links

Legend. ▨ Every Kind, Type
and Instance

(c) Components and instances

Legend. ■ Type, □ Instance, □–≫□ Instantiation

Fig. 1. Component-oriented metamodel

3.1 Presentation of the Metamodel

Our first contribution combines a responsibility-oriented metamodel (though simpler than what can be found in [7]) and a component-oriented metamodel, all within a reflexive unifying metamodel. Our metamodel is divided in three parts: the actors and their responsibilities (on Fig. 1a), the components and their instances (on Fig. 1c), and the additional links in the metamodel (on Fig. 1b).

Actors and Responsibilities. In our metamodel, *responsible entities* have *responsibilities* over *entities* and can assume *roles*. *Roles* represent generic sets of *responsibilities*. They can be used to encode access rights on an information system or positions in a company's organizational chart for example. *Actors* represent the actual *entities* which can assume *roles* and have *responsibilities*. They can be used for example to encode users, allowed to access specific servers because of their positions, or even a whole company, responsible for the proper functioning of the products it sells. *Relationships* represent all lines and arrows in models (and in the metamodel itself).

Components and Instances. Our metamodel is focused on *components*. They provide *services* (*actions* or *reactions* to *events*) that can in turn use other *components' actions* through *procotols*. They can also contain *resources*, that may be *entities* providing *services* (*components*, such as a web server) or not (such as configuration files, web resources, or even the models themselves). Both *resources* and *events* can be the result of an *action*, so we decided to unify them under the *effect* kind. Three layers appear here:

- The Kind layer (■), representing the core concepts of the metamodel;
- The Type layer (■), representing "types of" these concepts. For example, "physical server" is a type of *component*. To follow the UML notation, a *component* type is represented here as :Component.
- The Instance layer (□), representing "instances of" these concepts and types. For example, *a* physical server is an instance of "physical server" and "check webpage availability" is a *service* instance. In our work, we have not encountered the need for *service* types. An instance of :Component is represented here as ::Component.

Metamodel Links. Every Kind, Type and Instance of the metamodel is an instance of *entity*; it means that *responsible entities* can have *responsibilities* over them. For example, an *actor* can be responsible for the development of a software *component* (on the Type layer) and another can be responsible for its configuration and deployment (on the Instance layer).

A core feature of our metamodel is that *responsible entities* can be responsible of *responsibilities* themselves. It makes sense in a context of access management where a person may be responsible for the access right given to another person. As models can themselves be *resources* in the metamodel, it is easy to represent situations like an employee responsible for modeling a particular *component*. We think that both characteristics are distinctive features of our approach.

For consistency, *responsible entities* are also *components* and their behaviors can be encoded as *services*.

3.2 Collaborative Modeling

Our second contribution is a collaborative modeling framework using this metamodel relying on three principles: non-intrusiveness, refinability and correctness.

Non-intrusiveness. Most technical IT domain have their own sets of tools and representations to convey information and model systems [3]. Two persons in the same domain can understand one another thanks to this common jargon, but may struggle to interact with people in areas with which they are not familiar.

Working on small models whose boundaries are clearly defined enables experts to work collaboratively and still preserve the integrity and coherence of each model. Furthermore, these experts can take advantage of the most appropriate tools and techniques for their particular domains. Our metamodel intends to provide a framework adapted to linking these tools together, rather than replacing them. By allowing employees to work locally with their peers on models, we avoid the issues raised by [25] in the first phases of modeling.

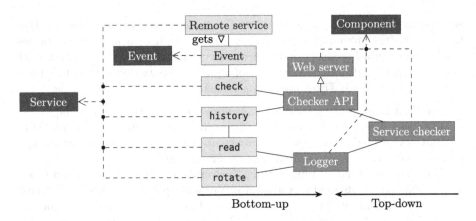

Fig. 2. Model for a generic service checker

Refinability. To reflect the actual design process of its components, people involved in infrastructure modeling should be able to gradually refine their models. This can be done either in a top-down (where one adds details) or bottom-up (where one abstracts them) approach, or a combination of both, as shown in Fig. 2. In this example, a top-down approach would describe what a "service checker" is, by dividing it into sub-components (Service checker, made of Checker API and Logger) and then refining their services (check, history...). A bottom-up approach would be to describe the services wanted for a "service checker" and combining them into components and super-components providing them.

Iterative conception goes through a succession of incomplete models. When working on a new piece of software, a common approach consists in letting the end-users describe their needs and iteratively producing code that meets these needs [26]. The initial need may be very imprecise and high-level and may require several refinement steps during the project's lifespan.

"Holes" in models can also arise from *blackbox* software or hardware, or even legacy components whose knowledge has been lost, for example due to employee turnover. Even though the knowledge of an IT infrastructure is partial, properties can still be deduced. By allowing imprecision, the benefit is threefold:

- Coherence: instead of making wrong assumptions, modelers can express their lack of knowledge, limiting the number of inconsistencies between models;
- Reconciliability: employees should not attempt to refine a component they are not responsible for, simplifying the reconciliation phase and ensuring that responsibilities are respected;
- "Fail-early"-ness: as properties can be proved early in a project modeling, safety and security issues can be addressed from the first stages of development.

Correctness. In order to get a detailed view of an IT infrastructure, it is crucial to involve all its stakeholders in the process. Indeed, the sum of local

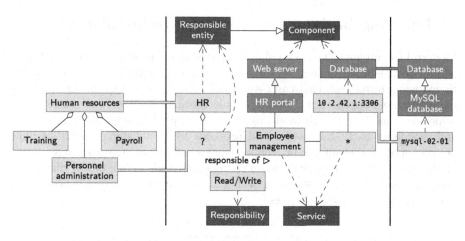

Fig. 3. Model reconciliation with three points of view
Legend. ▭◁▭ Reconciliation

viewpoints is not enough to produce an overall model: the reconciliation and the resulting links between models are essential. As the literature shows [22], model reconciliation is a complex task, this is why we advocate to start the collaborative modeling process as soon as possible.

If the modeling is done according to these principles, model reconciliation is mainly a matter of refining black boxes in other models and linking them together, as illustrated in Fig. 3. Here, we have three points of view, from three teams. On the left, the organizational structure of a human resources department is represented. In the middle, we have the design of a web application using a remote database (not modeled) allowing some HR people (unknown at modeling time) to manage employees. On the right, there is a simple model of said database.

During model reconciliation, the teams align their vocabularies (Human resources and HR), specify black boxes (? becomes Personnel administration) and combine knowledge (10.2.42.1:3306 refers to mysql-02-01). There is no universal method to solve modeling conflicts, but we think that modeling in incremental steps avoids solving them on larger models. The reconciliation process itself may be modeled using our metamodel, by assigning responsibilities to the employees performing the reconciliation. When a model is updated, it becomes easy to know who performed the reconciliation and notify them to review whether the change invalidates their work or not. This idea, which to our knowledge has not been explored, ensures that the overall model remains correct in the long term.

4   Encoding Business Processes and Technical Jobs

Modern IT companies have a combination of business processes, which are more administrative in nature, and very detailed technical workflows. Choosing a holistic modeling framework that can cover all these aspects in detail seems unrealistic. A federated approach [11] enables to take advantage of everyone's skills, while achieving a more thorough modeling. Such an approach keeps the metamodels and models of each stakeholder and proceeds by establishing semantics links between models. Yet, model interdependencies and inconsistencies can arise and hinder collaboration, especially when changes are made in one model that affect other models. As already stated in Sect. 3.2, our framework makes it possible to detect and react to these changes.

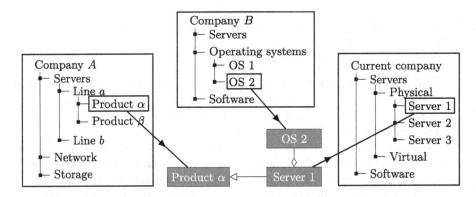

Fig. 4. An example of model reuse

In this section, we propose a methodological framework adaptable to concrete business processes, to build thorough yet accurate models using our metamodel.

4.1   Component Catalogs

Companies usually design their systems by using external components. For hardware systems, most of them include *commercially available off-the-shelf* components sold by other companies. In the software domain, third-party libraries and packages are an integral part of modern systems.

This decentralized aspect of system design can be applied to infrastructure modeling: manufacturers can produce models for their systems and users can integrate these models into their infrastructure models. Such models can be made available in catalogs available internally within companies and externally to clients or for public use. The benefit is twofold. First, responsibilities and knowledge are better distributed: the models are produced by system designers, not the users. Second, the modeling process is sped up: model reuse, as would code reuse in software development, allows designers to build systems faster.

The two modeling steps, design and use, are illustrated in Fig. 4, where a company's Server 1 is build from other companies' Product α and OS 2. One can then instantiate this Server 1 architecture in their models without redesigning it.

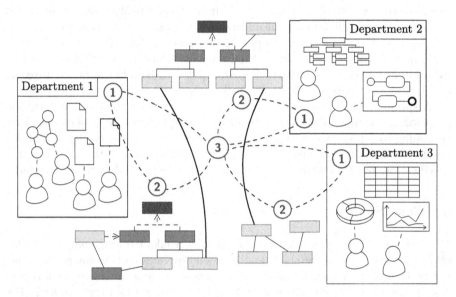

Fig. 5. *A posteriori* modeling. Step 1 corresponds to the inventory, step 2 is the modeling process and step 3 is the reconciliation.

4.2 *A Posteriori* modeling

Understanding the orchestration of a company's business processes can help optimize the existing, as well as build the new, in a better controlled way. In the banking industry for example, the use of legacy systems imposes technical choices that cannot be made without a good knowledge of existing architectures. Within the company's departments, this knowledge exists in diagrams, source code, configuration files... which first need to be identified (step 1 of Fig. 5). This step comes along with hardware inventories, if needed. Then, the identified elements are mapped onto our metamodel. Care must be taken to assign responsibilities to the model entities in the early stages of modeling (who *owns* which product, who develops which service, who is in charge of modeling which component...). Step 2 of Fig. 5 illustrates this process. In an iterative way, business processes interacting with the modeled elements must be identified. Agile collaboration frameworks should be used to implement this process, as they promote collaborative, quick and iterative changes. This is represented in step 3 of Fig. 5.

4.3   *A Priori* modeling

Accurate and complete models allow to better evaluate the financial and technical costs of projects, to optimize infrastructure dimensioning and to create *safe and secure by design* systems. Throughout the life of a project, it is important to ensure that a system does not deviate from its specification, for example due to a lack of communication, a misunderstanding or an urge to move too quickly. Verification of expert-defined properties on these models allows to ensure the conformity of such systems before their realization and helps to select a technical solution rather than another. For example, in a banking infrastructure, we could check that only certified personnel can access sensitive cardholder data.

A specification is seen in our approach as a model interface that technical proposals must implement. This extends the concepts from Object-Oriented Programming to infrastructure modeling. This concept of model typing is explored in [28]. Our metamodel ensures the syntactic conformance of the models to the specification, but the semantic conformance must be verified by domain experts.

5   Case Study

To illustrate our approach, let us now consider a fake banking company, called eBank. eBank provides banking and payment services to consumers and businesses. One of its flagship product, ePay, acts as a payment processor for companies and as an instant payment and expense sharing tool for consumers. The employees of the company want to have a better understanding of its overall processes and decided to use our approach to this end. In this section, we first make an inventory of the company's models. Then, we link these models together into our metamodel. Finally, we use the resulting big picture for a cross-model case study.

5.1   Heterogeneous Models

The company decided to start its modeling by focusing on ePay's environment, namely the company's organizational structure, the business processes around the product and the technical architecture. Each department uses domain-specific modeling tools, leading to different views of the overall infrastructure.

Organizational Structure. eBank is structured in two directions: Technical and Administrative, each subdivided into structures, divided themselves into departments. An organizational chart of the company is given in Fig. 6.

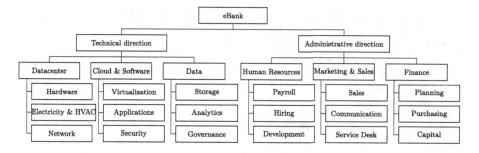

Fig. 6. eBank's organizational structure.

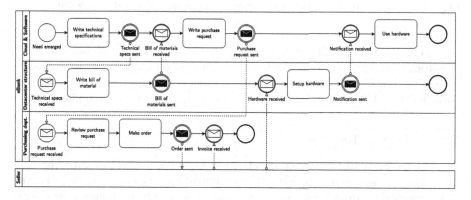

Fig. 7. BPMN diagram for purchasing new hardware. For clarity, we do not show the exclusive gateways and assume requests to be automatically accepted.

Business Processes. The company's activities are guided by various business processes. For the sake of brevity, we consider here only the equipment purchase process, represented in Fig. 7.

eBank has been using a task management solution for many years to track how many person-hours are needed for which projects. The solution is also used to know who is working on what at a given time. By reusing this software's database, employees created a catalog of common company tasks to predict their durations and help project planning. This catalog ranges from technical tasks, for example "commission a server", to administrative ones, for example "open a position". These two tasks are represented in Fig. 8.

Lastly, all financial transactions are managed by the finance department.

Technical Architecture. eBank manages a datacenter hosting the hardware necessary for its activities. Some services are hosted on dedicated machines and others are on an internal cloud infrastructure. Due to time constraints, ePay has not been migrated to a modern cloud infrastructure yet. The service follows an active/passive architecture, where only one node operates at a time.

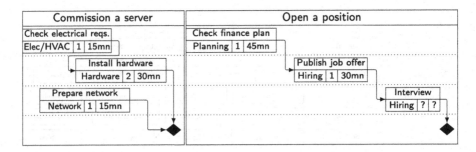

Fig. 8. Task catalog

Legend. □a□b□c□d Sub-task (*a*: title, *b*: department, *c*: people, *d*: duration), ◆ End

To check the proper functioning of its services in real time, the company has a monitoring infrastructure that measures availability and several key performance indicators. For business clients, ePay must process its requests within three seconds 99.9% of the time and must pay penalties in case of non-compliance.

5.2   ... Linked Together

After several rounds of modeling, eBank's employees came up with the representation shown in Fig. 9. First, the organizational structure (Fig. 6) is partially mapped to the eBank component and its four sub-components representing structures and departments. The BPMN diagram (Fig. 7) adds the Hardware component type, along with the Maintenance and Usage responsibilities that the Cloud & Software structure and Hardware department have on this Hardware. The task catalog (Fig. 8) adds knowledge about the Hiring department and its Hiring responsibility. The task management solution (Task manager) keeps track of the time spent on the Usage and Maintenance of the Hardware and on the Hiring process, highlighting the particular nature of responsibilities in our metamodel. Finally, the Finance department is responsible for employees' Wage payment, for the Invoice payment of Hardware and the company's Financial obligation regarding its Payment processing's SLAs.

5.3   Exploiting the Model

The company's real time monitoring has recently identified slowdowns in ePay on peak hours. Following our model, we can see that there is a potential impact on the Finance department because of its Financial obligations. Some employees have suggested scaling the infrastructure before such slowdowns violate SLAs. One way to do so is to setup new Physical servers and change the overall architecture of the services. This new architecture is expected to mobilize part of the Cloud & Software structure for several months. The Human Resources structure proposes to either ignore the potential problem or to assign its teams on the scaling project (by hiring new staff, outsourcing some of the work or reassigning staff without additional hiring or outsourcing).

In Fig. 10, we explore our model to trace the paths between the slowdown and the Finance department, to identify potential financial impacts. To make its decision, the company has to compare (a) the financial impact if nothing is done (resulting from the Financial obligation) to (b) the financial impact of the improved architecture (resulting from Invoice payments and the personnel cost). The company does not have an outsourcing process, so the analysis of the Outsource branch, represented by "?" in the figure, cannot be performed. We have not detailed the Reassign branch because it is outside the scope of this article. However, its analysis is valuable to the company since the reassignment of staff would change the time allocated in the Task manager. This would consequently have indirect impacts on the Finance department (for example, failure to deliver new features to clients due to a lack of time, leading to increased customer churn).

By calculating the cost of each decision branch, which is partly automatable, the company can make a decision regarding this particular problem.

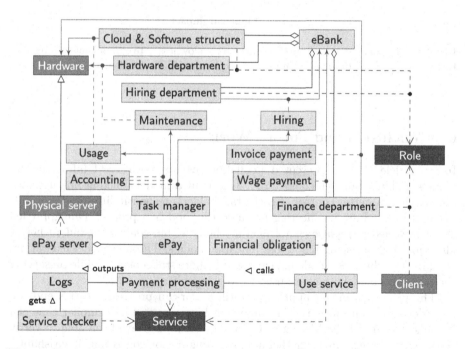

Fig. 9. ePay's big picture. To help the reader, instantiations are blue (□->□) and responsibility links and their association classes are red (□→□ and □- -□). (Color figure online)

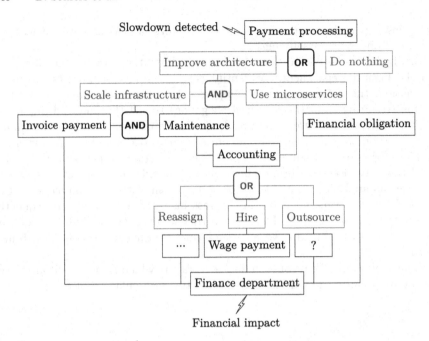

Fig. 10. Impact tree from application slowness to financial impact
Legend. ☐ Default branch, ☐ Employee suggestions, ☐ Model elements.

6   Conclusion and Future Work

In this article, we have presented a collaborative approach for IT infrastructure modeling. This approach consists of a generic metamodel aimed at linking models together, a better control of each stakeholder's responsibilities and methods inspired by software engineering to guide the modeling process. Our approach is not intended to replace established methods within companies, but rather to allow for analyses spanning across multiple models. Through model federation, we think that business modeling can include more stakeholders, while preserving the tools and models they are used to working with.

The validation of our approach is still a work in progress. To this end, we have developed an infrastructure modeling language and its compiler that can be linked to model checkers such as Z3 [19]. While we have been able to verify consistency (for example, whether a set of configuration constraints is satisfiable) and safety properties (for example, whether a system is fault-tolerant) on small models, we are now focusing on scaling our tool to larger models. An important step in the validation of our approach is an industrial experiment, covering broad business domains, that we are currently drafting.

References

1. Reference Model of Open Distributed Processing (RM-ODP). http://rm-odp.net/
2. van der Aalst, W.M.P.: Business process management: a comprehensive survey. ISRN Softw. Eng. (2013). https://doi.org/10.1155/2013/507984
3. Amaral, V., Hardebolle, C., Karsai, G., Lengyel, L., Levendovszky, T.: Recent advances in multi-paradigm modeling. In: Ghosh, S. (ed.) MODELS 2009. LNCS, vol. 6002, pp. 220–224. Springer, Heidelberg (2010). https://doi.org/10.1007/978-3-642-12261-3_21
4. Breton, E., Bézivin, J.: An overview of industrial process meta-models. In: International Conference on Software & Systems Engineering and their Applications (2000)
5. Cohn, D., Stolze, M.: The rise of the model-driven enterprise. In: IEEE International Conference on E-Commerce Technology for Dynamic E-Business, pp. 324–327 (2004). https://doi.org/10.1109/CEC-EAST.2004.65
6. van Deursen, A., Klint, P., Visser, J.: Domain-specific languages: an annotated bibliography. SIGPLAN Notices (2000). https://doi.org/10.1145/352029.352035
7. Feltus, C., Petit, M., Dubois, E.: ReMoLa: responsibility model language to align access rights with business process requirements. In: International Conference on Research Challenges in Information Science, pp. 1–6 (2011). https://doi.org/10.1109/RCIS.2011.6006828
8. Fleurey, F., Baudry, B., France, R., Ghosh, S.: A generic approach for automatic model composition. In: Giese, H. (ed.) MODELS 2007. LNCS, vol. 5002, pp. 7–15. Springer, Heidelberg (2008). https://doi.org/10.1007/978-3-540-69073-3_2
9. Golra, F.R., Beugnard, A., Dagnat, F., Guérin, S., Guychard, C.: Addressing modularity for heterogeneous multi-model systems using model federation. In: Companion Proceedings of the International Conference on Modularity (MoMo). ACM (2016). https://doi.org/10.1145/2892664.2892701
10. Greenwood, R.M., Robertson, I., Snowdon, R.A., Warboys, B.: Active models in business. In: Annual Conference on Business Information Technology (BIT) (1995)
11. International Organization for Standardization: ISO 14258:1998 – Industrial automation systems and integration - Concepts and rules for enterprise models (1998). https://www.iso.org/standard/24020.html
12. International Organization for Standardization: ISO 19439:2006 – Enterprise integration - Framework for enterprise modelling (2006). https://www.iso.org/standard/33833.html
13. Jackson, D.: Software Abstractions: Logic, Language, and Analysis, 2nd edn. The MIT Press, Cambridge (2011)
14. Jørgensen, H.D.: Enterprise modeling – what we have learned, and what we have not. In: Persson, A., Stirna, J. (eds.) PoEM 2009. LNBIP, vol. 39, pp. 3–7. Springer, Heidelberg (2009). https://doi.org/10.1007/978-3-642-05352-8_2
15. Kaczmarek, M.: Ontologies in the realm of enterprise modeling – a reality check. In: Cuel, R., Young, R. (eds.) FOMI 2015. LNBIP, vol. 225, pp. 39–50. Springer, Cham (2015). https://doi.org/10.1007/978-3-319-21545-7_4
16. Kulkarni., V., Roychoudhury., S., Sunkle., S., Clark., T., Barn., B.: Modelling and enterprises - the past, the present and the future. In: International Conference on Model-Driven Engineering and Software Development, pp. 95–100 (2013). https://doi.org/10.5220/0004310700950100

17. Lantow, B.: On the heterogeneity of enterprise models: ArchiMate and Troux semantics. In: IEEE International Enterprise Distributed Object Computing Conference Workshops and Demonstrations, pp. 67–71 (2014). https://doi.org/10.1109/EDOCW.2014.18

18. Masoudi, R., Ghaffari, A.: Software defined networks: a survey. J. Netw. Comput. Appl. (2016). https://doi.org/10.1016/j.jnca.2016.03.016

19. de Moura, L., Bjørner, N.: Z3: an efficient SMT solver. In: Ramakrishnan, C.R., Rehof, J. (eds.) TACAS 2008. LNCS, vol. 4963, pp. 337–340. Springer, Heidelberg (2008). https://doi.org/10.1007/978-3-540-78800-3_24

20. Murata, T.: Petri nets: properties, analysis and applications. Proc. IEEE **77**(4), 541–580 (1989). https://doi.org/10.1109/5.24143

21. Neville-Neil, G.: I unplugged what? Commun. ACM **65**(2) (2022). https://doi.org/10.1145/3506579

22. Nuseibeh, B., Kramer, J., Finkelstein, A.: ViewPoints: meaningful relationships are difficult! In: International Conference on Software Engineering, pp. 676–681 (2003). https://doi.org/10.1109/ICSE.2003.1201254

23. OMG: Unified Modeling Language (UML), Version 2.5.1, December 2017. https://www.omg.org/spec/UML/2.5.1

24. Park, K., Willinger, W.: Self-Similar Network Traffic: An Overview, chapter 1, pp. 1–38. John Wiley & Sons, Ltd., Hoboken (2000). https://doi.org/10.1002/047120644X.ch1

25. Renger, M., Kolfschoten, G.L., de Vreede, G.-J.: Challenges in collaborative modeling: a literature review. In: Dietz, J.L.G., Albani, A., Barjis, J. (eds.) CIAO!/EOMAS -2008. LNBIP, vol. 10, pp. 61–77. Springer, Heidelberg (2008). https://doi.org/10.1007/978-3-540-68644-6_5

26. Ruparelia, N.B.: Software development lifecycle models. SIGSOFT Softw. Eng. Notes **35**(3), 8–13 (2010). https://doi.org/10.1145/1764810.1764814

27. Salamatian, K., Vaton, S.: Hidden Markov modeling for network communication channels. SIGMETRICS Perform. Eval. Rev. **29**(1), 92–101 (2001). https://doi.org/10.1145/384268.378439

28. Steel, J., Jézéquel, J.M.: On model typing. Softw. Syst. Model. **6**(4), 401–413 (2007). https://doi.org/10.1007/s10270-006-0036-6

29. The Open Group: ArchiMate ® 3.1 Specification. https://publications.opengroup.org/c197

30. Urbach, N., Ahlemann, F.: Transformable IT landscapes: IT architectures are standardized, modular, flexible, ubiquitous, elastic, cost-effective, and secure. In: CSOC 2016. MP, pp. 93–99. Springer, Cham (2019). https://doi.org/10.1007/978-3-319-96187-3_10

31. Vernadat, F.: UEML: towards a unified enterprise modelling language. Int. J. Prod. Res. **40**(17), 4309–4321 (2002). https://doi.org/10.1080/00207540210159626

32. Vernadat, F.: Enterprise modelling: research review and outlook. Comput. Ind. **122**, 103265 (2020). https://doi.org/10.1016/j.compind.2020.103265

33. Voinov, A., Bousquet, F.: Modelling with stakeholders. Environ. Model. Softw. **25**, 1268–1281 (2010). https://doi.org/10.1016/j.envsoft.2010.03.007

Exploring Capability Mapping as a Tool for Digital Transformation: Insights from a Case Study

Jonas Van Riel[1]([✉]) [iD], Geert Poels[1,2] [iD], and Stijn Viaene[3,4] [iD]

[1] Faculty of Economics and Business Administration, Ghent University, Gent, Belgium
jonas.vanriel@ugent.be
[2] Flanders Make @UGent, CVAMO Core Lab, Gent, Belgium
[3] Faculty of Economics and Business, KU Leuven, Leuven, Belgium
[4] Vlerick Business School, Leuven, Belgium

Abstract. This study investigates how capability maps, an Enterprise Architecture artifact, can support digital transformation and for what purposes. Despite their potential, there is currently a lack of literature on the topic. The study uses the technique of a semi-structured interview in a case study to explore the role of capability mapping in planning and executing digital transformation. The results indicate that the practice of capability mapping can play a valuable role in different phases of digital transformation. The study also provides relevant insights for organizations looking to leverage capability maps as a tool for improving their digital transformation initiatives. This is realized by describing use cases derived from the case study.

Keywords: Capability Mapping · Digital Transformation · Business Capabilities · Enterprise Architecture

1 Introduction

One of the most considerable challenges organizations face is to remain relevant in a volatile, uncertain, complex, and ambiguous world where the pace of technological and economic change is high [1, 2]. The ensuing transformations of these organizations, required to overcome this challenge, can be complex for different reasons (e.g. overcoming organizational barriers and resistance to change, balancing stakeholder's needs and expectations, dealing with unclear or missing information). In addition, the focus of most of these organizational transformations has a significant digital component, further adding to the complexity [3, 4]. Viaene [5] indicates that a lack of perspective and a common language are primary reasons why so many people and organizations continue to struggle with Digital Transformation. Mushore and Kyobe [6] put an emphasis on (the lack of) coherence, important to adequately prepare an organization to better create business value in spite of industry disruptions that emerge from digital trends. As a result, achieving the desired outcomes of a digital transformation is a big challenge for many organizations [7].

© The Author(s), under exclusive license to Springer Nature Switzerland AG 2023
H. van der Aa et al. (Eds.): BPMDS 2023/EMMSAD 2023, LNBIP 479, pp. 243–255, 2023.
https://doi.org/10.1007/978-3-031-34241-7_17

Grave et al. [8] found evidence that capability maps can support digital transformation during the strategic planning process. A capability map is an Enterprise Architecture (EA) artifact that provides a structured overview of an organization's capabilities, represented as a diagram or in a textual format [9]. One of the purposes of the map is to support the execution of business strategy [10]. However, Grave et al. [11] indicate that they have not investigated which EA artifact should contain which particular EA information and further evidence or elaboration on what support capability maps can bring for digital transformation, is absent.

This paper reports on our exploratory qualitative research study that aims to comprehend what support capability mapping can offer for directing, designing, planning, and implementing digital transformation programs in organizations. Academic literature on the topic is scarce, even though capability maps are often used in practice and Kotusev [12] mentions them as one of the top five EA artifacts that actually proved useful in organizations. To investigate the role of capability mapping in Digital Transformation planning and execution, we analyzed a case study of an organization undergoing a digital transformation program. Insights from the iterative capability mapping process were triangulated with a key stakeholder interview and a review of additional documentation. The findings were documented in the form of use cases. This approach provided an initial contribution to the development of practical solutions for practitioners seeking to implement capability mapping in their digital transformation efforts. In addition, our study contributes to the domain of Enterprise Architecture by offering a preliminary understanding of how capability mapping might facilitate alignment of capabilities with digital strategies for successful digital transformation initiatives.

This paper is structured as follows: Sect. 2 provides background on digital transformation and capability mapping. Section 3 describes the research method of the study and presents the case study. Section 4 presents the results. Finally, Sect. 5 offers a conclusion.

2 Background

2.1 Digital Transformation

Different definitions of Digital Transformation exist [13, 14]. However, a recurring theme is that digital transformations trigger significant organizational change as they imply the introduction of digital products and services and significantly impact how organizations operate [3]. Transformation always involves a change from a current state to a future state but specific to Digital Transformation is that this change is enabled by the use of combinations of novel information, computing, communication and connectivity technologies, the so-called digital technologies [13, 15].

Vial [13] identified the building blocks of the digital transformation process (Table 1) in which digital technologies play a central role in both creating and reinforcing disruptions at the societal and industry levels, which then trigger strategic responses from organizations, a critical driver for success in digital transformation according to [16]. To remain competitive, organizations use digital technologies to modify their value creation paths. However, this requires structural changes and overcoming barriers that impede their transformation efforts. These changes can have both positive and negative impacts on organizations, individuals, and society.

Table 1. Building blocks of the digital transformation process [13]

Building block	Description	Relation to other blocks
Disruptions	Internal or external disruptions that trigger a strategic response. Examples: consumer behavior, competitive landscape or availability of data	This can be fueled by using digital technologies. Can be a trigger for a strategic response
Strategic Responses	This is the start of the digital transformation and focuses on creating both a digital business strategy and a digital transformation strategy	Can be triggered by disruptions, relies on the use of digital technologies
Use of Digital Technologies	The use of (or the desire to start using) digital technologies e.g., Analytics, Mobile technologies	Can fuel disruptions, enables changes in value creation paths
Changes in value creation paths	Changes in the way an organization creates value. E.g., through digital channels, (partially) digital processes or digital value propositions	The effectiveness of this is affected by structural changes and organizational barriers. Generates impacts
Structural changes	The structural changes implied by a digital transformation such as the organizational structure and culture, the roles and skills of employees, and the leadership	Affects the changes in value creation paths
Organizational barriers	Barriers that impact the realization of changes in value creation paths in a negative way. E.g. inertia and resistance (of employees)	Affects the changes in value creation paths
Impacts (positive and negative)	Impact of the digital transformation on the performance of the organization. Negative impact is related to (worsened) security and privacy. Positive impact is related to (an increased) efficiency and performance of the organization	Affected by the changes in value creation paths

2.2 Capability Maps

Capability-based planning employs capability maps to compare an organization's current situation (i.e., the baseline capability map) to a situation that is desired due to a strategic initiative (i.e., the target capability map). A capability map serves as base for capability-based management as it allows visualizing outcomes of different analytical exercises, for instance, heat mapping (e.g., highlighting the strategic importance of specific capabilities) and the allocation of resources (such as information, processes, and people) [9]. Through capability map analysis and comparison of baseline and target capability maps, shortcomings in capabilities can be identified, and a phased strategic plan can be developed to fill the gaps by so-called capability increments [17] that gradually improve and even extend the current capabilities to realize the strategy [9].

3   Research Method

3.1   Research Process

Our research process contained six phases, explained in Table 2.

Table 2. Research process overview

1	Study preparation • Through literature study, understand relevant concepts for this research (Digital Transformation, capability mapping) • Through literature study, understand the technique of use cases and how to describe use cases • Through literature study, understand the method of a semi-structured interview
2	Study design: Identify or create a template to describe use cases; define case study and participant selection criteria • In the absence of a use case template for EA artifacts, create a use case template useful for this study • Define criteria for the selection of a case study and interview participant(s)
3	Select case-study and participants (i.e., digital transformation stakeholders to interview) • Select an organization that matches the selection criteria • Contact key stakeholder in the digital transformation initiative and schedule interview
4	Create interview structure (for the semi-structured interview) • Develop an interview guide that can be used to structure the interview
5	Execute interview and follow-up • Provide information document upfront, containing the use case template and the interview guide • Collect data, including, if allowed by the case study organization, the used capability maps and any other available documentation regarding the use of capability mapping • Execute interview using the interview guide and discussing, where possible, the capability maps and other relevant documentation (for data triangulation) • Follow-up on interview(s) to clarify answers if they are not completely clear, if necessary

(continued)

Table 2. (*continued*)

6	Process and describe the results • Execute data analysis to describe the use cases by completing the template • Provide the interview(s) findings to each of the interviewed parties for final validation purposes • Synthesize the findings to answer the research question

3.2 Describing Use Cases

Khosroshahi et al. [18] identify multiple use cases of capability mapping, but the study lacks a structured way of documenting them and did not explore the relationship between capability mapping and Digital Transformation. We conducted a targeted literature review [19] to find use case documentation methods, searching Web of Science and Google Scholar databases with relevant terms ("documenting use cases" or "use case template") across multiple fields, without restricting the application field. Completed in October 2022, the search yielded a few relevant papers. We selected three notable sources. The first, discussed in Sect. 2.3 [20], offered valuable guidelines for use cases in organizational modeling. The second and third sources [21, 22] provided a template for describing a use case of an information system, which we partially employed as the foundation for our own template. To the best of our knowledge, a use case template for EA artifacts has not been published.

We did observe that the 5W1H (Why, Who, When, Where, What, and How) framework is often used for describing and organizing systems [23, 24]. "What?" and "Why?" questions are crucial for defining the use case scope and purpose. We refined the "What?" question for the different digital transformation process building blocks identified by Vial [13] (Table 1), determining the specific contribution of using and analyzing a capability map (Table 3). The "Who?" and "How?" questions address the actors involved and actions performed with capability maps, while the "Where?" and "When?" questions were deemed redundant since the "What?" question, related to Vial's model (Table 1), already reveals the phase in which capability mapping is used.

To document use cases of capability mapping in support of digital transformation, we devised a template (see Table 4 for a completed example) based on the 5W1H framework's relevant dimensions, using the questions from Table 3 for the "What?" and "Why?" dimensions. This template is a working tool for capturing use case information and considering important aspects in this study, rather than a final design artifact. We describe these use cases without intending to create an exhaustive catalog. By examining case study-related use cases, our aim is to better understand how capability mapping can effectively support digital transformation initiatives.

Table 3. Relationship between the building blocks of the digital transformation process [13] and the scope of the use case of capability mapping.

Building block	Questioning the scope of the use case of capability mapping (WHAT?)
Disruption	Does the use case support the capturing of the disruption and the possible effect on the organization?
Strategic responses	Does the use case support in defining the strategic responses?
Use of digital technologies	Does the use case support the selection and implementation of digital technologies?
Changes in value creation paths	Does the use case support in realizing changes in value creation paths?
Structural changes	Does the use case support in realizing the structural changes of the organization?
Organizational barriers	Does the use case support in mitigating the effects of organizational barriers?

3.3 Case Description

The "Belgian Insurance Company", BELINSUR for short, is a top 10 Belgian insurance broker. BELINSUR is undergoing a digital transformation despite a low level of enterprise architecture (EA) maturity within the organization. Prior to the digital transformation, the IT focus was primarily on operational aspects, and there was no real EA capability. The transformation was triggered in 2020 by two disruptions: changing customer expectations, such as faster and digital services, and a consolidation movement in the market that required the organization to stay competitive. The first digital business strategy was created during the second half of 2020 and the related digital transformation strategy during Q1 of 2021. The digital transformation at BELINSUR is phased, starting with structural changes and governance choices (e.g., what would be done centrally and what would be done locally in the branches), followed by establishing a structured approach to data management and governance and increasing the data quality in the organization. The next phase focuses on automating operational solutions and working towards introducing more customer-facing solutions and introducing predictive analysis. BELINSUR encountered some barriers, such as overwhelmed employees due to the pace of change in the organization, and the organization is highly focused on training and change management. Thus far, at the start of 2023, the ongoing transformation resulted in better management, improved analytics, and better financial results, demonstrating the positive impacts of digital transformation.

BELINSUR is considered particularly relevant for this explorative study, as all relevant building blocks of Vial's model (Table 1) are present and enabled the identification of multiple use cases, as presented in the results in Sect. 4. The study allowed for analysis during different stages of the transformation, providing a more comprehensive understanding of its value and the role of capability mapping.

Table 4. Completed template for documenting use cases

Use case name	UC 1 – Strategic emphasis	
Use case goals and contribution to Digital Transformations (What and Why)		**See Table 6**
Use case description (How)	Based on the organization's strategic goals and ambitions, a cause-effect relationship model is created. This model identifies the capabilities that are strategically important for realizing these ambitions. In other words, it highlights the primary focus capabilities that contribute to achieving the goals. The purpose is to align the leadership team on where to allocate the project budget (CAPEX) and provide focus for portfolio management. If the strategic goals and ambitions are unclear or misaligned, attempting to apply this use case will make it explicit. Without well-defined goals and ambitions, it is impossible to identify the most relevant capabilities needed to achieve them	
Producer (Who)	*Creator*	*Contribution*
	External consultant (facilitator) with input from key stakeholders (Leadership team, Senior IT manager, Enterprise Architects)	• Interviewing the stakeholders, facilitating workshops • Creating the goal derivation model • Indicating emphasis on the map
Consumer (Who)	*Consumer*	*Interest*
	Senior Management (C-level) Board of Directors	Aligning on what domains should be the focus of the project/program portfolio
Mapped information (How)	A 'status' is assigned to the capabilities, indicating whether a capability is essential for achieving strategic ambitions. The status is determined by using goal motivation techniques, such as Strategy Maps	
Reporting format (How)	Heat map: Capabilities are assigned a color to indicate their importance (white/blank for no specific focus, green for high strategic importance, and grey for out of scope or phase-out)	
Preconditions	A capability map should be present and accepted by the different parties. Strategic goals/ambitions should be clear and aligned	

3.4 Data Collection and Analysis

One author, an Enterprise Architecture practitioner, collaborated with a team of Enterprise Architects and key stakeholders at BELINSUR to create a capability map and explore its uses during the DT initiative. Additional data was collected through a semi-structured interview with the managing director of BELINSUR's two largest branches, who played a key role in the digital transformation. The case-study research was documented according to the guidelines of [25]. The interview was transcribed and coded [26,

27]. The interview guide was created based on [28]. Data triangulation was employed for credibility and validity by reviewing relevant documentation, such as the capability map and related information projected on the map, together with the interviewee. This was done to ensure proper alignment among all parties on the topics discussed and to capture as much relevant information as possible. The findings (Table 6) were validated by the interviewee, no additional follow-up interview was necessary.

Next, we used the collected data to fill in the use case template (for each use case). In the final step of our analysis, we examined the collected information on the use cases. This examination involved drawing insights from the use cases and synthesizing the results to offer a first understanding of the role of capability mapping in supporting digital transformations. Our findings are presented in the next section.

4   Results

In our case study, four use cases of using capability mapping to support digital transformation initiatives were identified based on the interview and the study of the relevant documentation. These use cases are briefly described in Table 5.

Table 5. Identified use cases of capability mapping at BELINSUR

Use Case (UC)	Short Description of use case
UC 1 - Strategic emphasis	After an analysis the capabilities that are deemed of strategic relevance for the next strategic planning horizon are indicated as such by the use of a color code
UC 2 - 'Target Operating Model' choices	Indication for each capability how it is to be organized (central of decentral), based on the four target operating models as defined by [29]
UC 3 - Gap analysis	Based on the strategic goals and ambitions of the organization, a gap analysis is done of each capability on four dimensions: Process, People, Information, Technology
UC 4 - Functional coverage of applications	A list/repository of all related IT solutions (applications) is created, and all IT solutions/applications are mapped to the relevant capabilities

The contribution of capability mapping to the different digital transformation building blocks is summarized in Table 6. If a cell in this table contains a positive answer ("yes"), then this provides an answer to the "What?" question (as presented in Table 3) and indicates what building block the use case contributes to. The additional information then provides the additional rationale (i.e., the "Why?" question) for the specific use case of capability mapping regarding that specific building block.

The use cases collected in this study demonstrate the practical applications of capability mapping in supporting the digital transformation building blocks (Table 6). One key finding is the role of capability mapping in improving alignment and coherence within this specific organization by offering a common view or language, facilitating communication. This was particularly relevant for building blocks related to structural changes,

Table 6. Contribution of capability mapping to the digital transformation building blocks

Building blocks	UC 1 - strategic emphasis	UC 2 - 'target operating model' choices	UC 3 - gap analysis	UC 4 - functional coverage of applications
Disruption	No evidence found	No evidence found	No evidence found	No evidence found
Strategic response	Yes. It helped to shape the digital transformation plan by providing insights on what capabilities were crucial for realizing the ambitions of the DT and facilitated alignment	Yes. It helped to shape the digital transformation plan, as it facilitated the choices that needed to be made on an organizational level to realize the ambitions of the DT	Yes. By presenting the outcome of a GAP analysis, the use case facilitated the creation of a phased DT plan	No evidence found
Digital technologies	Yes. No mention during the interview, but analyzing the additional artifacts related to the use case made clear that certain IT and Data capabilities were a prerequisite for leveraging digital technology, which is crucial to realize the ambitions of the DT	Yes. No mention during the interview, but analyzing the additional artifacts related to the use case made clear that how certain IT and Data capabilities would be organized, would have a great impact on how effective these capabilities would be in practice. As they were deemed a prerequisite for leveraging digital technology by UC1, this provided a relevant insight that facilitated alignment and decision making	Yes. No mention during the interview, but analyzing the additional artifacts related to the use case showed that the gap analysis included an assessment of technology, indicating which areas were underperforming opposed to the status required to realize the DT ambitions	Yes. No mention during the interview, but analyzing the additional artifacts related to the use case showed that the functional mapping was done and used to discuss technology
Value creation paths	No evidence found	Yes. No explicit mention during the interview, but analyzing the additional artifacts related to the use case showed that these choices on capability level also had implications for the process level and thus the value creation paths, enabling decision-making on that level	Yes. No explicit mention during the interview, but analyzing the additional artifacts related to the use case showed that to provide a GAP status on capability level, a GAP analysis of the underlying key processes was executed	Yes. No explicit mention during the interview, but analyzing the additional artifacts related to the use case showed that the functional mapping was done and used to discuss impact of technology on capabilities

(*continued*)

Table 6. (*continued*)

Building blocks	UC 1 - strategic emphasis	UC 2 - 'target operating model' choices	UC 3 - gap analysis	UC 4 - functional coverage of applications
Structural changes	Yes, it helped to make decisions on the organizational structures and culture, as well as skills and competencies needed to make the digital transformation a success	Yes, it helped to make decisions on the Organizational Structures (central vs decentral), which were an important prerequisite for the ensuing stages of the DT	Yes. No explicit mention during the interview, but analyzing the additional artifacts related to the use case showed that to provide a GAP status on capability level, a GAP analysis of the underlying people dimension was executed, providing insights related to competencies and availability of employees	No evidence found
Organizational barriers	Yes. It helped to start the discussions on what needed to change and create awareness with key stakeholders	Yes. It helped to start the discussions on what needed to change and create awareness with key stakeholders	Yes. It helped to start the discussions on what needed to change and create awareness with key stakeholders	No evidence found

such as value creation paths and governance choices. Capability mapping provides in this case a comprehensive overview of capabilities and interdependencies, enabling informed decisions and reducing ambiguity. As stated, a lack of common language and coherence is an important barrier to the success of a digital transformation. The use cases also emphasize the importance of capability mapping in supporting technological changes by clarifying technical capabilities and limitations. Overall, our findings suggest capability mapping can be a valuable tool for organizations implementing digital transformation programs, offering a structured approach to align capabilities with digital strategies.

5   Conclusion

In this paper, we explored the potential of capability mapping as a tool for supporting digital transformation programs through a single case study. Our study provided initial evidence of the practical application of capability mapping in the context of Digital Transformation, encouraging further research in this area. Specifically, our study suggested that capability mapping use cases might offer a comprehensive overview of an organization's capabilities and interdependencies, allowing for informed decisions related to digital transformation building blocks. This could reduce ambiguity and other barriers for successful digital transformation. By describing use cases identified in the case study and relating them to Vial's digital transformation model, we contributed to the development of practical solutions for practitioners considering capability mapping in their digital transformation efforts. Our main contribution to the domain of Enterprise Architecture is offering a preliminary understanding of how capability mapping might facilitate alignment of capabilities with digital strategies for successful digital transformation initiatives.

In the conclusion of our paper, it is essential to acknowledge the limitations of our study to provide a balanced and accurate perspective. Our research is based on a single case study, limiting generalizability. Including multiple case studies and diverse stakeholders would provide a more comprehensive understanding of capability mapping in digital transformation initiatives. Additionally, one of the authors was involved in the digital transformation initiative, which could potentially introduce bias in the interpretation of the findings. Future research could benefit from a more impartial approach, selecting case studies where none of the involved researchers were directly engaged in the digital transformation initiative, to ensure a more objective analysis of the data. Lastly, the use case template was developed as a pragmatic working tool. For future research, it would be beneficial to establish a more solid and well-argued foundation for the template.

Despite these limitations, our study contributes valuable insights into the role of capability mapping in digital transformation and offers a foundation for further research in this area, which will focus on expanding the catalogue of use cases and developing more formalized analysis and reporting methods. We plan to conduct larger-scale studies to examine the effectiveness of capability mapping in different phases of a digital transformation program, including the use of capability maps for implementation and monitoring of such programs. The broader goal of this research is to design and define methods that support organizations in realizing their digital transformation objectives, by aligning their capabilities with their digital strategies. We reckon that capability maps are a key element in such methods.

References

1. Bennett, N., Lemoine, G.J.: What a difference a word makes: understanding threats to performance in a VUCA world. Bus. Horiz. **57**, 311–317 (2014). https://doi.org/10.1016/j.bushor.2014.01.001
2. Tseng, Y.H., Lin, C.T.: Enhancing enterprise agility by deploying agile drivers, capabilities and providers. Inf. Sci. (Ny) **181** (2011). https://doi.org/10.1016/j.ins.2011.04.034
3. Verhoef, P.C., et al.: Digital transformation: a multidisciplinary reflection and research agenda. J. Bus. Res. **122**, 889–901 (2021). https://doi.org/10.1016/j.jbusres.2019.09.022
4. Wißotzki, M., Sandkuhl, K., Wichmann, J.: Digital innovation and transformation: approach and experiences. In: Zimmermann, A., Schmidt, R., Jain, L.C. (eds.) Architecting the Digital Transformation. ISRL, vol. 188, pp. 9–36. Springer, Cham (2021). https://doi.org/10.1007/978-3-030-49640-1_2
5. Viaene, S.: Digital Transformation Know How: Connecting Digital Transformation, Agility and Leadership. ACCO, Leuven (2020)
6. Mushore, R., Kyobe, M.: Optimizing the business value of digital transformation by aligning technology with strategy, work practices and stakeholder interests. In: 2019 IEEE 10th Annual Information Technology, Electronics and Mobile Communication Conference, IEMCON 2019 (2019). https://doi.org/10.1109/IEMCON.2019.8936263

7. Gurbaxani, V., Dunkle, D.: Gearing up for successful digital transformation. MIS Q. Exec. **18**, (2019). https://doi.org/10.17705/2msqe.00017

8. Grave, F., Van De Wetering, R., Kusters, R.: Enterprise architecture artifacts facilitating digital transformations' strategic planning process. In: 14th IADIS International Conference Information Systems 2021, IS 2021 (2021). https://doi.org/10.33965/is2021_202103l006

9. Van Riel, J., Poels, G.: A method for developing generic capability maps. Bus. Inf. Syst. Eng. **65**, (2023). https://doi.org/10.1007/s12599-023-00793-z

10. Bondel, G., Faber, A., Matthes, F.: Reporting from the implementation of a business capability map as business-IT alignment tool. In: Proceedings - IEEE International Enterprise Distributed Object Computing Workshop, EDOCW (2018). https://doi.org/10.1109/EDOCW. 2018.00027

11. Grave, F., Van De Wetering, R., Kusters, R.: How EA information drives digital transformation: a multiple case study and framework. In: Proceedings - 2022 IEEE 24th Conference on Business Informatics, CBI 2022, vol. 1, pp. 176–185 (2022). https://doi.org/10.1109/CBI 54897.2022.00026

12. Kotusev, S.: Enterprise architecture and enterprise architecture artifacts: questioning the old concept in light of new findings. J. Inf. Technol. **34**, (2019). https://doi.org/10.1177/026839 6218816273

13. Vial, G.: Understanding digital transformation: a review and a research agenda. J. Strat. Inf. Syst. **28**, 118–144 (2019). https://doi.org/10.1016/j.jsis.2019.01.003

14. Markus, M.L., Rowe, F., Markus, M.L., Rowe, F.: The digital transformation conundrum : labels , definitions , phenomena , and theories. J. Assoc. Inf. Syst. **24**, 328–335 (2023). https:// doi.org/10.17705/1jais.00809

15. Goerzig, D., Bauernhansl, T.: Enterprise architectures for the digital transformation in small and medium-sized enterprises. In: Procedia CIRP (2018). https://doi.org/10.1016/j.procir. 2017.12.257

16. Ross, J.W., Sebastian, I.M., Beath, C., Mocker, M., Moloney, K.G., Fonstad, N.O.: Designing and executing digital strategies. In: 2016 International Conference on Information Systems, ICIS 2016, pp. 1–17 (2016)

17. Aldea, A., Iacob, M.E., Van Hillegersberg, J., Quartel, D., Franken, H.: Capability-based planning with ArchiMate: linking motivation to implementation. In: ICEIS 2015 - 17th International Conference on Enterprise Information Systems, Proceedings, pp. 352–359 (2015). https://doi.org/10.5220/0005468103520359

18. Aleatrati Khosroshahi, P., et al.: Business capability maps: current practices and use cases for enterprise architecture management. In: Proceedings of the Annual Hawaii International Conference on System Sciences 2018-Janua, pp. 4603–4612 (2018). https://doi.org/10.24251/ hicss.2018.581

19. Vom Brocke, J., Simons, A., Niehaves, B., Riemer, K., Plattfaut, R., Cleven, A.: Reconstructing the giant: on the importance of rigour in documenting the literature search process. In: 17th European Conference on Information Systems, ECIS 2009 (2009)

20. Santander, V.F.A., Castro, J.F.B.: Deriving use cases from organizational modeling. In: Proceedings of IEEE International Conference on Requirements Engineering, 2002-Janua, pp. 32–39 (2002). https://doi.org/10.1109/ICRE.2002.1048503

21. Cockburn, A.: Basic use case template. Humans Technology Technical Report (1998)

22. Cockburn, A.: Writing Effective Use Cases. Pearson Education India (2001)

23. Chung, S., Won, D., Baeg, S.H., Park, S.: Service-oriented reverse reengineering: 5W1H model-driven re-documentation and candidate services identification. In: IEEE International Conference on Services Computing SOCA 2009, pp. 178–183 (2009). https://doi.org/10. 1109/SOCA.2009.5410445

24. Sowa, F., Zachman, J.A.: Extending and formalizing the framework for information systems architecture. IBM Syst. J. **31**, 590–616 (1992)

25. Yin, R.K.: Case Study Research and Applications (2018)
26. Saldaña, J.: Coding and analysis strategies. In: The Oxford Handbook of Qualitative Research (2014). https://doi.org/10.1093/oxfordhb/9780199811755.013.001
27. Saldaña, J.: The Coding Manual for Qualitative Researchers (No. 14). Sage (2016)
28. Savin-Baden, M., Howell-Major, C.: Qualititative Research: The Essential Guide to Theory and Practice. Routledge (2013)
29. Ross, J.W.: Forget Strategy : Focus It on Your Operating Model. Center for Information System Research. MIT. III (2005)

Model-Driven Engineering (EMMSAD 2023)

TEC-MAP: A Taxonomy of Evaluation Criteria for Multi-modelling Approaches

Charlotte Verbruggen$^{(\boxtimes)}$ ⓘ and Monique Snoeck ⓘ

Research Center for Information Systems Engineering, KU Leuven, Naamsestraat 69,
3000 Leuven, Belgium
{charlotte.verbruggen,monique.snoeck}@kuleuven.be

Abstract. Over the last fifteen years, various frameworks for data-aware process modelling have been proposed, several of which provide a set of evaluation criteria but which differ in their focus, the terminology used, the level of detail used to describe their criteria and how these are evaluated. In addition, there are well-established evaluation frameworks of a more general nature that can be applied to data-centric process modelling too. A comprehensive and unbiased evaluation framework for (multi-)modelling approaches that also caters for more general aspects such as understandability, ease of use, model quality, etc., does not yet exist and is therefore the research gap addressed in this paper. This paper addresses this gap by using existing evaluation frameworks and developing a taxonomy that is used to categorise all the criteria from existing evaluation frameworks. The results are then discussed and related to the challenges and concerns identified by practitioners.

Keywords: data-centric · process modelling · taxonomy · evaluation framework

1 Introduction

Multi-modelling approaches combine several modelling languages to address different aspects of a system under study. Over the past fifteen years, several prominent frameworks have been developed for integrating data and process modelling, including the BALSA framework [1], the PHILharmonicFlows framework [2], and the DALEC framework [3]. While these frameworks address the same perspectives (data and processes), each uses slightly different terminology and definitions. The DALEC framework is based on a systematic literature review, comparing several approaches, including BALSA and PHILharmonicFlows. DALEC uses the overarching term "*data*-centric" process modelling, while BALSA is a framework for *artifact*-centric business processes, and defines a business artifact as corresponding to "key business-relevant objects, their lifecycles, and how/when services (a.k.a. tasks) are invoked on them" [1]. PHILharmonicFlows is a framework for *object-aware* process management. According to the authors, process support must consider "object behaviour as well as object interactions" [2], and provide "data-driven process execution and integrated access to processes and data" [2], in order to be object-aware. While one might be tempted to consider the terms "data", "artifact"

H. van der Aa et al. (Eds.): BPMDS 2023/EMMSAD 2023, LNBIP 479, pp. 259–273, 2023.
https://doi.org/10.1007/978-3-031-34241-7_18

and "object" as synonyms, the definitions given by the authors make clear that each framework has its own particular perspective on data. A similar analysis can be made for the behavioural aspects: each framework has its own perspective on how behaviour is addressed.

Various evaluation frameworks have been proposed to demonstrate the value of proposals for data-aware process modelling approaches. They differ in a similar way in their use of terminology and definitions, but also in their focus, the level of detail used to describe their criteria and how these criteria should be evaluated. There are also well-established evaluation frameworks of a more general nature (e.g. Moody's Method Evaluation Model [4] and Krogstie's SEQUAL framework [5]). While these frameworks are not suitable for evaluating specific aspects related to combining data and process modelling, they do address other important aspects, such as utility, ease of use, model quality, etc. Such frameworks can also be applied to data-aware process modelling as well, and this would make it possible to address open problems in the field of data-aware process modelling [6].

Many aspects need to be considered when developing multi-modelling approaches. In addition to the ability to model the desired aspects, more general aspects such as understandability, ease of use, model quality, etc. need to be considered. Accordingly, an evaluation framework needs to address all relevant aspects. Such a comprehensive evaluation framework for (multi-)modelling approaches does not yet exist and is therefore the research gap addressed in this paper. We address this gap by making use of existing evaluation frameworks, as this offers the advantage of starting from proven and robust sets of criteria, while avoiding a bias towards specific solutions. At the same time, the diversity of frameworks allows for a good degree of comprehensiveness, while requiring the creation of a taxonomy to identify identical, similar or subsuming criteria. The resulting comprehensive taxonomy of criteria is useful for comparing existing approaches, identifying aspects of existing approaches that are underdeveloped, or validating the proposal of a new approach.

Section 2 first presents an overview of different prominent evaluation frameworks. In Sect. 3, we construct a new (meta-) taxonomy TEC-MAP (**T**axonomy of **E**valuation **C**riteria for a **M**ulti-modelling **AP**proach) that can be used to categorize all criteria from the frameworks discussed in Sect. 2. In Sect. 4, the criteria are classified in TEC-MAP. Finally, Sect. 5 discusses the populated TEC-MAP and relates the summarized evaluation criteria to challenges and concerns identified by practitioners.

2 Inventory of Frameworks

The compilation of a set of frameworks was approached from two angles. On the one hand, we looked for seminal evaluation frameworks from the domain of conceptual modelling and information systems engineering. On the other hand, we looked for the most prominent evaluation frameworks that are well-known in the data-aware process modelling community. The evaluation frameworks differ in their scope, the level of detail they provide and their grouping of criteria. Some frameworks focus on the user experience, while others focus on theoretical aspects. The frameworks with a more narrow scope also provide more detailed descriptions of their criteria and guidelines on how to measure the quality of an approach. Finally, each framework provides a different structure for grouping the criteria.

2.1 General Evaluation Frameworks

The Technology Acceptance Model (TAM). In 1985, Davis developed the Technology Acceptance Framework to evaluate the adoption of new technologies in the field of computer science [7]. This framework is very well adopted by the academic com-munity, as the dissertation has over 10.000 Google Scholar citations. Davis developed two scales (each consisting of six Likert-scale questions) to measure the perceived usefulness and perceived ease of use [8]. This paper has received over 70.000 Google Scholar citations. For both papers, the number of citations still increases every year, proving that the computer science community considers this to be an important evaluation framework. A major benefit of the model is that it can be applied to a wide variety of new technologies.

The Method Evaluation Model (MEM). As TAM can be applied to a wide variety of technologies, many derivatives have been developed [9]. In 2003, Moody developed the Method Evaluation Model specifically for the evaluation of IS design methods [4]. This publication has over 300 Google Scholar citations. Moody states that the success of a method consists of two dimensions: actual efficacy and adoption in practice. In order to measure both dimensions, Moody combined the TAM with Methodological Pragmatism. According to Methodological Pragmatism, the validity of a method is not based on its correctness, but on its pragmatic success. Moody defines pragmatic success as "the efficiency and effectiveness with which a method achieves its objectives". An efficiency improvement is defined as "reducing effort required to complete the task" and an effectiveness improvement is defined as "improving the quality of the result". Moody does not provide measures for actual efficiency and actual effectiveness, stating that these measures depend on the (class of) method(s) that is(are) being evaluated. As a general guideline, he suggests that efficiency should be measured in time, cost and cognitive effort and that effectiveness should be measured in the quantity and quality of the results of the methods. The other two factors (perceived ease of use and perceived usefulness) should be measured as described by Davis in [8].

SEQUAL. The SEQUAL framework is an extension of on the work of Lindland et al. (the LSS framework) [10], which was published in 1994. The LSS framework focusses on the assessment of the semiotic quality of models. The framework was then further developed in several different publications from 1996 until 2006 [5, 11, 12]. The last iteration ([5]) has over 400 citations. The SEQUAL framework considers a conceptual model as statements, and groups these statements into sets related to the modelling domain, the modeler's knowledge, the external model, etc. [5]. The quality levels 4 describe the coordination between sets [5]. Apart from suggesting set algebra definitions for the quality levels related to syntactic quality, the framework does not provide any metrics to measure the quality levels, as "the problem domain and the minds of the stakeholders are unavailable for formal inspection" [5].

The Conceptual Modelling Quality Framework (CMQF). The CMQF (2012) was developed based on the SEQUAL framework and the Bunge-Wand-Weber representation model (BWW) [13] which is an ontological theory published in 1990 that focusses on the modelling process [14]. CMQF has over 180 citations. It is a two-dimensional framework that integrates the SEQUAL framework and the BWW model into eight cornerstones. These cornerstones are divided vertically over the physical reality and the social reality and horizontally over the domain, the reference framework, the modelling language and the conceptual representation [13]. The framework then defines four layers of quality – the physical layer, the knowledge layer, the learning layer and the development layer – each with a number of quality types. The framework does not provide a way to objectively measure the quality types.

2.2   Frameworks for Data-Aware Process Modelling Approaches

BALSA. The BALSA framework (2008) specifies four dimensions of artifact-centric business process modelling – Business Artifacts, Macro Lifecycles, Services and Associations [1]. The authors describe Business Artifacts as business object, their data and their relationships to other artifacts. Macro Lifecycles are described as the lifecycle of a Business Artifact, and can be represented as a finite state machine. A Service is described as "a unit of work meaningful to the whole business process" [1]. Association are defined as a family of constraints on the changes that services make to artifacts. The BALSA framework can be used to construct an artifact-centric approach by selecting a set of model types that fit the four dimensions. However, the framework does not pro-vide a set of criteria to evaluate the resulting approach.

PHILharmonicFlows. PHILharmonicFlows (2011) is a framework that specifies a set of requirements for the modelling and execution of object-aware process management systems [2]. It has over 290 citations. The authors state that support for object-aware processes requires taking into account the integration of the different building blocks of such a process (Data, Processes, Functions and Users). The list of requirements in the PHILharmonicFlows framework was composed based on a set of case studies [15]. The requirements are grouped by the building block they correspond to, and can be fully supported, partially supported or not supported.

MMQEF. The Multiple Modelling language Quality Evaluation Framework (2018) provides a reference taxonomy of IS concepts, and a methodology to "evaluate the quality of a set of modelling languages used in combination within an MDE context" [16], The method does however not include a set of explicit evaluation criteria. The 5 reference taxonomy is based on the Zachman framework and consist of a Viewpoint dimension (Data, Function, Network, People, Time and Motivation) and an Abstractions dimension based on the Model-Driven Architecture (Computation-Independent Model, Platform-Independent Model, Platform-Specific Model, Physical Implementations).

DALEC. In 2019, Steinau et al. published a framework for the evaluation and comparison of data-centric process management approaches [3]. First, they conducted a systematic literature review resulting in an in-dept comparison of 17 process modelling approaches described in 38 publications, including the PHILharmonicFlows framework. Based on this SLR, they defined a set of 24 criteria grouped along the phases of the business process lifecycle. Similar to the PHILharmonicFlows framework, the criteria can be fully supported, partially supported or not supported, however, the DALEC framework also defines for each criterion the required conditions for the criterion to be considered partially or fully supported.

3   Methodology

3.1   Construction of the Taxonomy

In order to summarize the criteria from all the evaluation frameworks, we need to create a taxonomy. We followed the iterative method for taxonomy development (see Fig. 1) that was proposed by Nickerson et al. [17]. They define a taxonomy as "a set of dimensions each consisting of a set of characteristics that sufficiently describes the objects in a specific domain of interest" [17]. Below, we describe each step and Table 1 presents a summary of the process and the results. Detailed arguments and results are presented in Sect. 4.

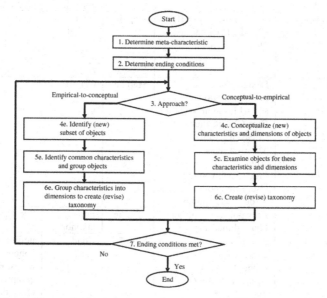

Fig. 1. The method for taxonomy development by Nickerson et al. [17]

Preliminary Steps. The **first step** of the method is to determine the meta-characteristic. Nickerson et al. describe the meta-characteristic as "the most comprehensive characteristic that will serve as the basis for the choice of characteristics in the taxonomy. Each characteristic should be a logical consequence of the meta-characteristic" [17]. Given that the purpose of our taxonomy is to provide an overview of evaluation criteria for data-aware process modelling approaches, we define the meta-characteristic as the characterization of evaluation criteria in the domain of multi-modelling.

The **second step** is to determine the ending conditions. Nickerson et al. define a minimal set of one objective and five subjective ending conditions: the taxonomy satisfies the definition of a taxonomy (objective), and the taxonomy is concise, robust, comprehensive, extendible and explanatory (subjective). We do not add any ending conditions to this set.

Table 1. A Summary of the taxonomy development

Step 1	Meta-character-istic	the positioning of evaluation criteria in the domain of data-aware process modelling			
Step 2	Ending conditions	the taxonomy satisfies the definition of a taxonomy the taxonomy is concise the taxonomy is robust the taxonomy is comprehensive the taxonomy is extendible the taxonomy is explanatory			
Iteration 1			**Iteration 2**		
Step 3	Chosen approach	Empirical-to-conceptual	Step 3	Chosen approach	Conceptual-to-empirical
Step 4e	Objects	All 72 criteria of MEM, CMQF, PHILharmonic-Flows and Dalec	Step 4c	Char. Added	Abstract syntax, Concrete syntax, Modelling guidelines, Tool support
				Dim.	Pillar dimension
Step 5e	Char.	Design phase Implementation phase Model Evolution phase Data Objects viewpoint Lifecycles viewpoint Microservices viewpoint Process viewpoint Users viewpoint 8 coord. viewpoints	Step 5c	Classification	
Step 6e	Dim.	Viewpoint dimension, Phase dimension	Step 6c	Full taxonomy	See Figure 5
Step 7	Cond. met?	definition ✓ concise ✓ robust ✗ comprehensive ✓ extendible ✓ explanatory ✓	Step 7	Cond. met?	definition ✓ concise ✓ robust ✓ comprehensive ✓ extendible ✓ explanatory ✓

First Iteration. The **third step** is to decide whether we follow the empirical-to-conceptual approach or the conceptual-to-empirical approach for the first iteration. The empirical-to-conceptual approach starts from available objects that need to be classified in the taxonomy, whereas the conceptual-to-empirical approach starts from the researcher's knowledge and understanding of the domain. In the first iteration, we will use the empirical-to-conceptual approach based on the evaluation frameworks discussed in Sect. 2.

In the empirical-to-conceptual approach, the **fourth step** is to identify a subset of objects. In this case, the subset of objects are the 72 evaluation criteria defined by the MEM, CMQF, PHILharmonicFlows and DALEC frameworks. Given that the criteria of TAM and the quality levels of SEQUAL are completely encompassed by the criteria of MEM and CMQF respectively, they were not included separately. When needed, criteria were split into sub-criteria so as to achieve similar granularity levels across the frameworks.

The **fifth step** is to identify the common characteristics and group the objects according to these characteristics and **the sixth step** is to group the characteristics into dimensions. The results of these steps are shown in Table 1.

At the end of each iteration, the **seventh step** is to evaluate the ending conditions. Given that the initial taxonomy satisfies the definition of a taxonomy by Nickerson et al., the objective ending condition is met. The initial taxonomy is also concise as the number of dimensions (2) and characteristics (18) are limited. It is comprehensive given that all objects from the sample can be classified. It is extendible and explanatory, given that more dimensions can be added and that the current dimensions explain the nature of the objects. However, the initial taxonomy is not yet robust since there are some groups of criteria (where criteria share the same characteristics for each dimension) that need further differentiation. Since not all ending conditions are met, a second iteration is required.

Second Iteration. In the second iteration, step 3–7 are repeated. In **step three**, we now decide to follow the conceptual-to-empirical approach so as to complement the insights obtained from studying the existing frameworks with insights from domain knowledge.

In the conceptual-to-empirical approach, **step four** is to develop characteristics and dimensions without considering actual objects, but by relying on the researcher's own knowledge and understanding of the domain. The additions are shown in Table 1.

In the conceptual-to-empirical approach, **step five** is to classify the existing objects according to the new dimensions and characteristics and **step six** is to add the new dimensions to the taxonomy. For example, criterion D02 of the Dalec framework (specification of data representation constructs) is classified under the Design phase characteristic in the Phase dimension, the Data Objects viewpoint characteristic in the Viewpoint dimension and the Abstract Syntax characteristic in the Pillar dimension. See Sect. 4.4 for the complete results.

In **step seven** the ending conditions are re-evaluated. Given that the taxonomy satisfies the definition of a taxonomy by Nickerson et al., the objective ending condition is met. The initial taxonomy is also concise as the number of dimensions (3) and characteristics (22) are limited. It is comprehensive given that all objects from the sample can be classified. It is extendible and explanatory, given that more dimensions can be added and that the current dimensions explain the nature of the objects. Finally, the taxonomy is now also robust since all criteria are well-grouped and do not require further differentiation. Since all ending conditions are met, the taxonomy is finished.

3.2 Analysis of the Criteria

Once the taxonomy has been constructed, we consider each group of criteria, meaning each set of criteria that falls under the same characteristics of each dimension. For each group, we determine which criteria are identical, subsuming or complementing each other. These criteria are accordingly adapted, resulting in the final taxonomy.

4 Results

4.1 The Phase Dimension

DALEC uses the phases of the process management lifecycle to group their criteria. The authors adopt and slightly modify the phases as defined in [18]. The resulting lifecycle consists of the Design phase, the Implementation & Execution phase and the Diagnosis & Optimization phase [3]. MMQEF uses the MDA abstraction levels [16] where the Computation-Independent Model and the Platform-Independent Model cover the Design phase, and the Platform-Specific Model and the Physical Implementation cover the Implementation & Execution phase. Given that the criteria for different models in the design phase are the same, we align the taxonomy to the phases of DALEC.

4.2 The Viewpoint Dimension

PHILharmonicFlows categorizes their requirements according the building blocks of an object-aware process (Data, Processes, Functions, Users) [2]. Similarly, BALSA defines 4 dimensions (Business Artifacts, Macro lifecycles, Services and Associations) [1]. Within the design phase, DALEC addresses data representation constructs (DRCs), object behaviour and object interaction [3]. Inspired by the ISO Architecture Description Standard [19], where each viewpoint is addressed by a different model kind, we define a set of 'viewpoints' based on these three frameworks – the Users viewpoint, the Data Objects viewpoint and three Behaviour viewpoints: the Lifecycles, Microservices and Process viewpoints. These dimensions also appear in MMQEF [16], albeit that MMQEF has just one behavioural viewpoint where all behavioural aspects are lumped together. Given that the Time and Network viewpoints of MMQEF are much less used in practice [20], and that Motivation is rather related to strategy, and that MMQEF does not provide any evaluation criteria, we leave these out here.

The User Viewpoint covers the criteria related to information about the users of the to-be-developed system. The Data Object viewpoint deals with criteria related to the data objects, their attributes and associations. Steinau et al. [3] provide an overview of different data-aware process modelling approaches and how they define their "Data Representation Constructs" (DRCs). While many approaches define lifecycles as part of their DRCs, we define lifecycles as defining the states an object can be in and that constrain the operations that can be performed on an object. Therefore, we consider this as a separate viewpoint related to behaviour. The Process Viewpoint covers criteria related to overall processes (either declarative or procedural processes) and the Microservices Viewpoint deals with criteria related to 'tasks' in the processes.

Given that the authors of both the PHILharmonicFlows framework and the BALSA framework emphasize the importance of considering the coordination between the building blocks and dimensions respectively [1, 2], we will add 'coordination viewpoints' to categorize requirements that deal with this coordination. In what follows, each of the coordination viewpoints will be defined, whereby a coordination viewpoint takes care of defining correspondences between two viewpoints [19]. Figure 2 presents the viewpoints and the coordination viewpoints. In some cases, the coordination between viewpoints is trivial and does not require an explicit evaluation (cfr. Green dashed arrows).

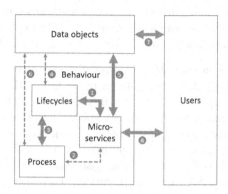

Fig. 2. The Viewpoints and Coordination Viewpoints (arrows)

- **Lifecycles – Microservices (1).** Coordination between the lifecycles and the Microservices is not trivial: the data-aware process modelling approach needs to define how lifecycles and microservices are related. For instance, if an exam is in the state *running*, the professor should not be able to grade the exam. Once the exam is *submitted*, the professor can execute the microservice *grade the exam*. This will trigger the transition from *submitted* to *graded* for the exam.
- **Microservices – Process (2).** Processes enforce sequence constraints on Microservices. The coordination is an inherent part of the definitions of the processes and is therefore trivial.
- **Lifecycles – Process (3).** The sequence constraints imposed by the lifecycles should be compatible with those imposed by the processes. For example, if a process requires *shipping* before *invoicing an order*, the lifecycle of the order object should allow shipping in the *unpaid* state.
- **Data objects – Lifecycles (4).** Each data object has at least a default lifecycle. Given that a lifecycle always belongs to one data object, coordination (i.e. correspondence between data and lifecycles) follows from the definitions of the lifecycles.
- **Data objects – Microservices (5).** This viewpoint deals with the direct coordination between Microservices and data objects. Microservices should be able to create, modify and/or end data objects.
- **Data objects – Process (6).** Data object instances can be created, modified or ended during a process through the invocation of microservices. This viewpoint is therefore trivial as it results from the combination of (2) and (5).

- **Data objects – Users (7).** This viewpoint considers how Read and/or Write permissions for (attributes of) instances of data objects are granted to users. For example, professors can only view and manipulate the grades for the courses they teach.
- **Microservices – Users (8).** This viewpoint considers how permissions for the execution of microservices are granted to users. For example, students can view but not update their grades.
- **Lifecycle – Users.** Coordination between Lifecycles and Users is not required, given that users don't interact directly with lifecycles but only via Microservices. This coordination thus results from combining (8) and (1).
- **Process – Users.** Coordination between Process and Users is not required, given that users don't interact directly with the process as a whole: they interact with the micro services. This coordination thus results from combining (8) and (2)

Figure 3 details how the TEC-MAP viewpoints cover the BALSA dimensions. For three of the four BALSA dimensions, the mapping to the TEC-MAP viewpoints is straightforward: the mapping of the BALSA Business Artifacts to the TEC-MAP Data Objects viewpoint, the mapping of the BALSA Macro Lifecycles to the TEC-MAP Lifecycles viewpoint, and the mapping of the BALSA Services to the TEC-MAP Microservices viewpoint. As stated in Sect. 2.2, the BALSA Associations can represent both associations between BALSA Services, and association between a BALSA Service and a transition in a BALSA Lifecycle. Therefore, the BALSA Associations dimension is mapped to the two corresponding coordination viewpoints in TEC-MAP: the Lifecycles – Microservices coordination viewpoint and the Microservices – Process coordination viewpoint.

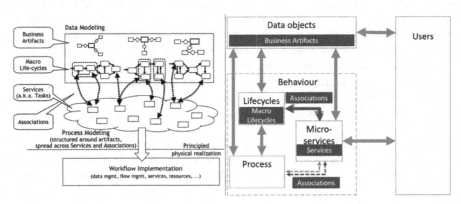

Fig. 3. The BALSA framework [1] (left) and the BALSA framework mapped onto the viewpoints of TEC-MAP (right)

Figure 4 details how the TEC-MAP viewpoints cover the PHILharmonicFlows building blocks. For three of the four PHILharmonicFlows Data building blocks, the mapping to the TEC-MAP viewpoints is straightforward: the mapping of the PHILharmonicFlows Data building block to the TEC-MAP Data Objects viewpoint, the mapping of the PHIL-harmonicFlows Users building block to the TEC-MAP Users viewpoint and the mapping of the PHILharmonicFlows Processes building block to the TEC-MAP Process view-point. As Künzle et al. state that the purpose of the PHILharmonicFlows Functions is separating the data logic and the process logic from the function logic by providing "for automatically creating end-user components, such as worklists, form-based activities, and overview tables containing relevant object instances" [2]. Therefore, the PHILhar-monicFlows Functions building block cannot be mapped on a TEC-MAP viewpoint. Mapping it on the TEC-MAP Implementation phase is a better fit.

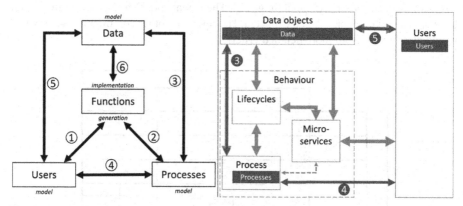

Fig. 4. PHILharmonicFlows building blocks, adapted from [2] (left) and the PHILharmonicFlows building blocks mapped onto the viewpoints of TEC-MAP (right)

Mapping DALEC onto the TEC-MAP viewpoints is straightforward – the DRCs are mapped onto the Data Objects viewpoint, object behaviour is mapped onto the three behaviour viewpoints and object interaction is mapped onto the coordination viewpoints related to the Data Objects viewpoint.

4.3 The Pillar Dimension

When considering modelling languages, the physical layer of CMQF distinguishes between the ontological constructs of a modelling language and its vocabulary and grammar. This corresponds to Kleppe's advice of complementing the abstract syntax of a modelling language (or its metamodel) with a concrete syntax and semantics [21]. Besides the language itself, also modelling tools and modelling guidelines are needed. The four pillars of a modelling approach are therefore the abstract and concrete syntax that make up the modelling language, the modelling guidelines that contain modelling rules and best practices, and tool support for all phases and viewpoints.

4.4 Final Taxonomy

Figure 5 provides a summary of the criteria grouped by characteristic within the tax-onomy. The final taxonomy can be found online[1] as interactive map of all criteria,

---

[1] https://merode.econ.kuleuven.be/TEC-MAP.html.

including different visualisation and filtering options. Clicking on a criterion displays some informative attributes: the origin, the original description and the proposed method of evaluation.

It immediately stands out that while the large majority of the cells have a minimum number of criteria, the design phase contains much more criteria than the two other phases, in particular for the Data Objects, Lifecycles, Microservices and Process viewpoints; There's a lack of criteria for the User viewpoint. To fill this gap, the modelling of the user viewpoint could benefit from investigating the field of User Interface design, which has a tradition of user modelling [22]. The trivial coordination viewpoints do not have any criteria, which is to be expected. However, the other coordination viewpoints would also benefit from more detailed criteria.

		Design		Implementation & Execution		Diagnosis and Optimisation	
Users		AS: 1	CS: 1	AS: 1	CS: 0	AS: 0	CS: 0
		MG: 2	T: 3	MG: 0	T: 2	MG: 0	T: 1
Data Objects		AS: 12	CS: 10	AS: 2	CS: 0	AS: 0	CS: 0
		MG: 8	T:3	MG: 0	T: 6	MG: 1	T: 1
Lifecycles		AS: 11	CS: 10	AS: 1	CS: 0	AS: 0	CS: 0
		MG: 7	T: 3	MG: 0	T: 2	MG: 1	T: 1
Microservices		AS: 9	CS:10	AS: 3	CS: 0	AS: 0	CS: 0
		MG: 8	T: 3	MG: 0	T: 3	MG: 1	T: 1
Process		AS: 10	CS: 10	AS: 1	CS: 0	AS: 0	CS: 0
		MG: 9	T:3	MG: 0	T: 7	MG: 1	T: 1
Microservices - Lifecycles		AS: 2	CS: 1	AS: 2	CS: 0	AS: 0	CS: 0
		MG: 2	T: 3	MG:0	T: 3	MG: 1	T: 1
Microservices - Process		AS: 0	CS: 0	AS: 0	CS: 0	AS: 0	CS: 0
		MG: 0	T: 0	MG:0	T: 0	MG: 0	T: 0
Lifecycles - Process		AS: 0	CS: 1	AS: 1	CS: 0	AS: 0	CS: 0
		MG: 2	T: 3	MG:0	T: 2	MG: 1	T: 1
Data objects - Lifecycles		AS: 0	CS: 0	AS: 0	CS: 0	AS: 0	CS: 0
		MG: 0	T: 0	MG:0	T: 0	MG: 0	T: 0
Data objects - Microservices		AS: 0	CS: 1	AS: 2	CS: 0	AS: 0	CS: 0
		MG: 2	T: 3	MG:1	T: 3	MG: 1	T: 1
Data objects - Process		AS: 0	CS: 0	AS: 0	CS: 0	AS: 0	CS: 0
		MG: 0	T: 0	MG: 0	T: 0	MG: 0	T: 0
Data objects - Users		AS: 4	CS: 1	AS: 4	CS: 0	AS: 0	CS: 0
		MG: 3	T: 3	MG: 0	T: 2	MG: 1	T: 1
Microservices - Users		AS: 3	CS: 1	AS: 3	CS: 0	AS: 0	CS: 0
		MG: 3	T: 3	MG: 0	T: 3	MG: 1	T: 1

Fig. 5. Summary of criteria groups in TEC-MAP. The table shows the number of criteria per Pillar for each Phase-Viewpoint combination. Groups with more than 5 criteria are indicated. AS = Abstract Syntax, CS = Concrete Syntax, MG = Modelling Guidelines, T = Tool support

5 Discussion

TEC-MAP represents a taxonomy of criteria for the evaluation of data-aware process modelling approaches. A first limitation is that the different levels of detail in original publications leads to room for interpretation. While the authors attempted to adhere as faithfully as possible to the intent of the original publications, the classification of certain criteria might be subject to discussion. Second, the majority of the criteria are theoretical. Only the TAM and MEM criteria cater for the practitioner's perspectives of ease of use, efficiency and effectiveness. A more in-depth evaluation of approaches and that potentially reveal other criteria can be achieved by interviewing practitioners. In a meta-review of surveys on MDE practitioners [23], some of the main challenges that practitioners face are the following: visual notations at odds with the principles of Physics of Notation [24], the organization's culture as an inhibitor of the adoption of modelling practices, missing tool functionalities and tools being difficult to use. TEC-MAP provides the required criteria for evaluating tool functionalities. However, for the other challenges, the criteria listed in TEC-MAP need further improvement. The Physics of Notation could be added as instrument to evaluate the Concrete Syntax. Complementing TEC-MAP with UTAUT2's "social norm" variable [9] could be used to analyse the cultural factors that might inhibit adoption, while also its "habit" variable could be relevant. Börstler et al. conducted a systematic literature review analysing thirty acceptance models and theories, and how they are applied in software development [25]. They discuss how each of these models and theories is evaluated within the individual context of a practitioner. One of the models that has been used more often and that is evaluated rationally instead of intuitively, is the Task-Technology Fit (TTF) model [25]. Complementing TEC-MAP with TTF would allow evaluating the tool usability and acceptance in more detail. Another interesting theory that they discuss is the Innovation Diffusion Theory which discusses the individual, organizational and external factors that impact the adoption of new technologies [25].

Finally, the evaluation of the ending conditions is (partially) subjective by design of the methodology, something that is inevitable according to [17].

6   Conclusion

This paper analysed and combined eight different frameworks in view of creating a more complete taxonomy of evaluation criteria for the evaluation of a multi-modelling approach to data and process modelling. The resulting taxonomy TEC-MAP collects 72 criteria arranged in four foundational viewpoints and six coordination viewpoints, 4 phases and 4 pillars. While the design phase has the largest number of criteria, many categories within the taxonomy have currently a limited number of criteria and the user viewpoints lack criteria. The taxonomy itself might thus benefit from further completion with additional criteria and may require extension with additional dimensions or characteristics in future. However, this is typical for a taxonomy according to [17]. Despite this room for further improvement and evolution, we believe that in its current state, the resulting taxonomy provides already a useful overview of evaluation criteria that can be adapted to the needs of researchers and a robust capstone for expanding it with additional sets of criteria. The next step of our research will be the application of the taxonomy for the evaluation of a concrete multi-modelling approach.

Acknowledgement. This research has been funded by the KU Leuven research fund, grant C17421017.

References

1. Hull, R.: Artifact-centric business process models: brief survey of research results and challenges. In: Meersman, R., Tari, Z. (eds.) OTM 2008. LNCS, vol. 5332, pp. 1152–1163. Springer, Heidelberg (2008). https://doi.org/10.1007/978-3-540-88873-4_17
2. Künzle, V., Reichert, M.: PHILharmonicFlows: towards a framework for object-aware process management. J. Softw. Maint. Evol. Res. Pract. 23(4), 205–244 (2011). https://doi.org/10.1002/smr.524
3. Steinau, S., Marrella, A., Andrews, K., Leotta, F., Mecella, M., Reichert, M.: DALEC: a framework for the systematic evaluation of data-centric approaches to process management software. Softw. Syst. Model. 18(4), 2679–2716 (2018). https://doi.org/10.1007/s10270-018-0695-0
4. Moody, D.L.: The method evaluation model: a theoretical model for validating information systems design methods. In: ECIS 2003 Proceedings, 2003, p. 79. [Online]. https://aisel.aisnet.org/ecis2003/79
5. Krogstie, J., Sindre, G., Jørgensen, H.: Process models representing knowledge for action: a revised quality framework. Eur. J. Inf. Syst. 15(1), 91–102 (2006). https://doi.org/10.1057/palgrave.ejis.3000598
6. Reijers, H.A., et al.: Evaluating data-centric process approaches: does the human factor factor in? Softw. Syst. Model. 16(3), 649–662 (2016). https://doi.org/10.1007/s10270-015-0491-z
7. Davis, F.D.: A technology Acceptance Model For Empirically Testing New End-User Information Systems: Theory and Results. Massachusetts Institute of Technology (1985)
8. Davis, F.D.: Perceived usefulness, perceived ease of use, and user acceptance of information technology. MIS Q. 18, 319–340 (1989)
9. Venkatesh, V., Thong, J.Y.L., Xu, X.: Consumer acceptance and use of information technology: extending the unified theory of acceptance and use of technology. MIS Q. 36(1), 157–178 (2012). https://doi.org/10.2307/41410412
10. Lindland, O.I., Sindre, G., Solvberg, A.: Understanding quality in conceptual modeling. IEEE Softw 11(2), 42–49 (1994). https://doi.org/10.1109/52.268955
11. Krogstie, J., Lindland, O.I., Sindre, G.: Defining quality aspects for conceptual models. In: Falkenberg, E.D., Hesse, W., Olivé, A. (eds.) Information System Concepts. IAICT, pp. 216–231. Springer, Boston, MA (1995). https://doi.org/10.1007/978-0-387-34870-4_22
12. Krogstie, J., Jørgensen, H.D.: Quality of interactive models. In: Olivé, A., Yoshikawa, M., Yu, E.S.K. (eds.), Advanced Conceptual Modeling Techniques, Berlin, Heidelberg: Springer Berlin Heidelberg, 2003, pp. 351–363 (2003). https://doi.org/10.1007/978-3-540-45275-1_31
13. Nelson, H.J., Poels, G., Genero, M., Piattini, M.: A conceptual modeling quality framework. Softw. Qual. J. 20(1), 201–228 (2012). https://doi.org/10.1007/s11219-011-9136-9
14. Wand, Y., Weber, R.: An ontological model of an information system. IEEE Trans. Softw. Eng. 16(11), 1282–1292 (1990). https://doi.org/10.1109/32.60316
15. Künzle, V., Weber, B., Reichert, M.: Object-aware business processes: properties, requirements, existing approaches. University of Ulm (2010)
16. Giraldo, F.D., España, S., Giraldo, W.J., Pastor, Ó.: Evaluating the quality of a set of modelling languages used in combination: a method and a tool. Inf Syst 77, 48–70 (2018). https://doi.org/10.1016/J.IS.2018.06.002
17. Nickerson, R.C., Varshney, U., Muntermann, J.: A method for taxonomy development and its application in information systems. Eur. J. Inf. Syst. 22(3), 336–359 (2013)
18. van der Aalst, W.M.P.: Business process management: a comprehensive survey. ISRN Softw. Eng. 2013, 507984 (2013). https://doi.org/10.1155/2013/507984
19. ISO: ISO/IEC/IEEE 42010:2011 Systems and software engineering — Architecture description. [Online]. https://www.iso.org/standard/50508.html. Accessed 9 Mar 2023

20. Bernaert, M., Poels, G., Snoeck, M., De Backer, M.: CHOOSE: towards a metamodel for enterprise architecture in small and medium-sized enterprises. Inf. Syst. Front. **18**(4), 781–818 (2015). https://doi.org/10.1007/s10796-015-9559-0

21. Kleppe, A.G.: A language description is more than a Metamodel. In: 4th International Workshop on Software Language Engineering, ATEM 2007 (2007)

22. Ruiz, J., Serral, E., Snoeck, M.: Evaluating user interface generation approaches: model-based versus model-driven development. Softw. Syst. Model. **18**(4), 2753–2776 (2018). https://doi.org/10.1007/s10270-018-0698-x

23. Verbruggen, C., Snoeck, M.: Practitioners' experiences with model-driven engineering: a meta-review. Softw. Syst. Model **22**(1), 111–129 (2023). https://doi.org/10.1007/s10270-022-01020-1

24. Moody, D.: The physics of notations: toward a scientific basis for constructing visual notations in software engineering. IEEE Trans. Softw. Eng. **35**(6), (2009). https://doi.org/10.1109/TSE.2009.67

25. Börstler, J., bin Ali, N., Svensson, M., Petersen, K.: Investigating acceptance behavior in software engineering—theoretical perspectives. J. Syst. Softw. **198**, 111592 (2023)

Integrating Physical, Digital, and Virtual Modeling Environments in a Collaborative Design Thinking Tool

Fabian Muff[(✉)] [iD], Nathalie Spicher [iD], and Hans-Georg Fill [iD]

University of Fribourg, Boulevard de Pérolles 90, 1700 Fribourg, Switzerland
{fabian.muff,nathalie.spicher,hans-georg.fill}@unifr.ch

Abstract. Design thinking is a creative process that requires brainstorming techniques that take place in a physical environment. However, such physical interactions are not possible in remote environments. In this paper, we propose a software tool for design thinking that bridges the gap between physical, digital, and virtual modeling environments. We describe and evaluate a virtual storyboarding application that enables remote collaborative design thinking in 3D and the conversion of these 3D models into 2D digital models. To evaluate the approach, we conducted an experiment with students and were able to derive directions for further research in this area.

Keywords: Design Thinking · 3D · Virtual · Modeling and Conceptual Modeling

1 Introduction

In times of fierce competition and ever-changing environments, companies must continually develop new and innovative solutions to survive on the market. One possibility to support innovation is the use of *Design Thinking* [10]. Design Thinking combines knowledge from design, social sciences, engineering, and management. It creates innovative ideas, systems, and services using multidisciplinary collaboration and iterative improvement techniques [12]. Traditionally, design thinking requires people to be in the same place, working with pen and paper and communicating in face-to-face conversations to share their knowledge [20]. However, as a result of the COVID-19 pandemic, more and more work is being done remotely. A recent Gartner survey[1] revealed that many enterprises will move considerable parts of their previously on-site workforce to a permanently remote work-model. This makes knowledge sharing in innovation processes more challenging. Remote working has been shown to reduce the process of tacit knowledge transfer between collaborators [4]. This is largely due to people working remotely and the lack of face-to-face interaction in shared work environments.

---

[1] Gartner study by Justin Lavelle – https://rb.gy/iwsmlf, last accessed: 13.03.2023.

© The Author(s), under exclusive license to Springer Nature Switzerland AG 2023
H. van der Aa et al. (Eds.): BPMDS 2023/EMMSAD 2023, LNBIP 479, pp. 274–284, 2023.
https://doi.org/10.1007/978-3-031-34241-7_19

Since Design Thinking is a highly creative process, the seamless exchange of information between physical, digital, and virtual modeling environments is desirable to keep up with new work demands.

Transferring physical Design Thinking models to digital formats, e.g. using whiteboards and storyboards, has been explored before [14,24]. In addition, approaches for Design Thinking using digital formats have been proposed [2], as well as ideas for working fully immersed in virtual 3D environments [22]. However, the integration of physical, digital, and virtual modeling environments for Design Thinking has so far not been achieved. The availability of such an approach would however facilitate the exchange of design information in hybrid work scenarios where some actors work remotely and others are physically present.

Therefore, we propose in the following a concept and prototypical implementation of a new modeling tool for the Design Thinking approach called "Storyboarding". Thereby, we aim to narrow the gap between traditional physical, digital, and virtual Design Thinking approaches. Three research questions guided our investigation, which are informed by design-science research (DSR) oriented methods, e.g. [17]. These are: **RQ1**: "What are the requirements for a software application that supports Design Thinking and that enables narrowing the gap between physical, digital, and virtual modeling environments?", **RQ2**: "What would a software tool look like that would meet these requirements?" and **RQ3**: "What are the results of evaluating the usefulness and usability of the implemented prototype?".

The remainder of this paper is structured as follows. Section 2 briefly discusses the foundations of Design Thinking and related prior work. Section 3 presents the research methodology, followed by the objectives of the solution and the requirements for the approach in Sect. 4. The realization of the prototype according to these requirements will be described in Sect. 5. After a demonstration and an initial evaluation in Sect. 6, the paper ends with the discussion and conclusion in Sect. 7.

2 Foundations and Related Work

In this section, we briefly present the foundations and the related work for *Design Thinking*, *Physical and Digital Design Thinking Approaches*, and *Design Thinking in virtual modeling environments*.

2.1 Design Thinking

According to Herbert Simon, the design process is a rational set of procedures that respond to a well-defined problem [19]. Design is thus an important activity as it creates solutions and appropriate structures for previously unsolved problems or new solutions to problems that were previously solved in other ways [1].

The user-centered method *Design Thinking* adopts this approach of design. *Design Thinking* typically reverts to an iterative five-step process, which systematizes the procedure of design until a solution is found. A commonly used scheme was developed at Stanford University and includes the following steps: 1. "(Re-)Design the Problem", 2. "Needfinding & Synthesis", 3. "Ideate", 4. "Prototype", and 5. "Test" [3]. Further, Design Thinking promotes the use of interdisciplinary teams for enhancing the overall creative performance and environment [20].

2.2   Physical and Digital Design Thinking Approaches

Design Thinking is traditionally conducted *physically* with people working together at the same location. Common techniques include *Mindmapping* with whiteboards, or *Storyboarding*, where scenes of future scenarios are visually or haptically depicted, e.g., using paper figures [20].

For enabling the transformation of these physical techniques to digital formats, several ideas have been proposed in the past. Wenzel et al. [24] presented an approach for transforming physical whiteboards into digital *Tele-Boards* by taking photos of the original whiteboards and transforming them with the help of a web-based procedure into digital replications. Miron et al. [14] presented the *Scene2Model* approach for the automatic transformation of haptic storyboards into diagrammatic models and their deployment in a computer-aided design environment. By tagging the storyboard figures with visual markers, the system is able to transform the arrangement of the physical figures into corresponding digital 2D models. In addition, there are several commercial collaborative whiteboard and Design Thinking tools available[2].

2.3   Design Thinking in Virtual Modeling Environments

We refer to digital Design Thinking approaches that use three-dimensional modeling environments as "Design Thinking in virtual modeling environments". Rive and Karmokar [18] presented a collaborative Design Thinking approach in virtual worlds by using *Second Life* [13]. Thereby, users can meet as avatars in a virtual world and work collaboratively on their ideas in different setups. Further, Vogel et al. [22] presented a virtual reality (VR) application that allows users to create Design Thinking storyboards of prototypes by collaboratively arranging virtual objects. Due to the high immersion through virtual reality, this approach aims to deliver an experience as close as possible to the traditional physical Design Thinking approach. However, this approach is based exclusively on virtual reality and does not provide an interface to digital or physical modeling.

In summary, several proposals for digital and virtual Design Thinking approaches have been made in the past. However, to the best of our knowledge, a virtual Design Thinking approach that bridges the gap between physical, digital, and virtual modeling environments has not yet been described in research or practice. Therefore, we will address this research gap through the design, development, and initial evaluation of a new virtual storyboarding modeling tool.

---

[2] See for example: Invision, SprintBase, Stormboard, Userforge, Smaply.

3 Methodology and Research Design

For the development of our approach, we revert to Design Science Research (DSR) and follow the procedure by Peffers et al. [17]. In the following, we outline the six steps of the design procedure.

The problem of the project has already been formulated in the introduction (Step 1). In *Objectives of a Solution*, we derive the requirements for our artifact by analyzing related work in the area of traditional, digital, and virtual Design Thinking (Step 2). The *Design & Development* phase (Step 3) includes decisions on the design of the artifact and a first implementation of a prototype to ensure the technical feasibility. In the *Demonstration* phase (Step 4) we describe the demonstration and evaluation of the artifact by reverting to a group of students. This includes a first quantitative evaluation of the usability by conducting a SUMI questionnaire [9] (Step 5). The *Communication* phase (Step 6) corresponds to the publication of the findings for the academic community and industry by means of this paper.

4 Objectives of a Solution

The objective of this work is to produce a new IT-artifact in the form of a software application for the problem domain [8,11] and contribute to the scientific knowledge base on how to solve upcoming problems in a remote working model [7,16]. Thereby, we aim to bridge the gap between traditional physical, digital, and virtual Design Thinking. To identify the different requirements for the design and functionality of the Design Thinking tool, we examined existing approaches in physical, digital, and virtual Design Thinking.

To develop the specific requirements for our artifact, we reviewed the literature on design thinking to first derive general Design Thinking requirements (DR) [1,19,20]. In a second step, we screened the literature for physical and digital Design Thinking modeling approaches [14,18,24]. In a third step, we reviewed the existing approaches in virtual Design Thinking [22], followed by the conception of a suitable state-of-the-art technology stack for implementing a storyboarding prototype.

Although there are tools for virtual collaborative Design Thinking [22], we have not found an approach that provides an interface between traditional physical, digital, as well as virtual Design Thinking. Based on the collected information, five design requirements were derived as mandatory requirements for our Design Thinking artifact. Thereby, we answer the first research question (RQ1).

DR 1: Know-How – Users can apply the same Design Thinking methodology in virtual modeling environments that they are familiar with in the physical and the digital worlds [14,24]. This refers to the re-use of existing Design Thinking methodologies to facilitate the interaction for users.

DR 2: Collaboration – Users can collaborate in real-time with others in the same environment as if they were in the same location [22,23].

DR 3: 3D-based – Users can understand spatial relationships by perceiving, and interacting with the environment in three dimensions [5].

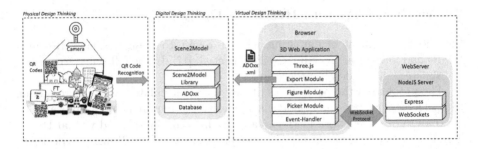

Fig. 1. Technical architecture of the modeling prototype.

DR 4: Browser-based environment – Users can run the application in a browser on different mobile and desktop devices [24].

DR 5: Interoperability – The models created in remote and virtual Design Thinking are compatible with physical models by using a digital information exchange interface.

5   Design and Development

In this section, we describe the development of our artifact in the form of a web-based modeling application according to the requirements listed above. Since our approach should enable the interoperability between physical, digital, and virtual systems, we decided to design a virtual *Storyboarding* tool that would be compatible with the Scene2Model modeling tool, which already bridges physical and digital storyboarding [14].

Our approach uses the graphics from SAP-Scenes[3]. Thereby, we meet the *Know-How* requirement, since the user does not have to learn a new methodology for using our modeling approach – see DR1.

According to the collaboration requirement (DR2), we foresee functionalities for sharing information about the scenes between different users. On a technical level, we added internal modules for handling the interaction with the Design Thinking figures – *Figure* and *Picker* module – see Fig. 1. These modules then propagate the changes made by a user to the back-end server and back to the connected users. With this functionality, we ensure that all connected users can manipulate the same scene simultaneously as if they were interacting with paper figures in physical space.

For enabling users to gain a spatial understanding of the environment, the 3D JavaScript framework Three.JS[4] is used for the front-end web client, thus meeting the requirement of three-dimensional perception (DR3). The storyboard figures can be moved and rotated in all three axes during modeling, allowing the user to perceive the spatial relationships between the various objects.

---

[3] https://apphaus.sap.com/resource/scenes.
[4] https://threejs.org/.

The prototype architecture has been designed to be platform-independent (DR4). This means that the application will work on any device with browser support. In regard to the interoperability of our prototype (DR5), we developed an *Export Module* (see Fig. 1) that allows the export of the virtually created models to the ADOxx-XML format [6]. This format is compatible with the 2D Design Thinking approach of *Scene2Model* [14]. This helps achieve the objective of easily sharing design information in hybrid work scenarios – see Fig. 1.

6   Demonstration and Initial Evaluation

For the demonstration and evaluation of our artifact, we chose an *Ex Post, naturalistic* evaluation strategy according to the *DSR Evaluation Strategy Selection Framework* by Venable et al. [21]. In the first step, we assessed the *technical feasibility* in terms of the fulfillment of the previously derived design requirements by implementing a prototype. Next, we evaluated the *usability* of the user interface through a lab experiment and a standardized usability questionnaire.

6.1   Technical Feasibility

As defined in the second research question (RQ2), the goal of this work is to investigate how an implementation of a software application that allows the collaborative, remote creation of 3D virtual Storyboard models and transformation of these scene models into 2D representations which are compatible with a traditional pen-and-paper approach. Regarding the design requirements DR1, DR3, and DR4, we were able to realize the prototype using the technology stack described in Sect. 4. The collaboration requirement of DR2 is currently implemented in a rudimentary manner, lacking synchronization of all element attributes. This is due to the high implementation effort required to develop this functionality to meet the expectations of today's users, especially when compared to advanced commercial collaboration tools.

The functionality required by DR5, i.e., the transformation of virtual models to the digital platform Scene2Model [14], is implemented in a module for the export of the 3D scenes to the ADOxx-XML file format. The models created with our artifact were successfully imported as 2D models into the Scene2Model tool, which is also capable of importing pen-and-paper models.

In summary, the evaluation of the technical feasibility shows that the software prototype meets all design requirements and that all intended functionalities could be implemented. The only limitation so far is the collaboration functionality, which does not yet allow full synchronization between all clients.

6.2   Usability of the Artifact

For a first usability evaluation, the software prototype has been tested with users as part of an introductory course in business informatics at the University of Fribourg. The goal of this study was to assess various dimensions of usability and receive feedback for potential improvements. 20 volunteer students, all studying either management, economics, or business informatics in their first semester received an introduction to *Design Thinking* and *Storytelling*. None of them had prior knowledge of Design Thinking. First, the participants were divided into three groups and were given the task of modeling a use case with the storytelling approach using SAP-Scenes paper figures[5]. The focus for this use case was to elaborate on the question: "How do you imagine a normal working day to be?". To familiarize participants with the storyboarding approach, traditional paper-and-pencil modeling was used.

The participants were then divided into groups of two. All had access to a special browser-based web application for modeling the digital *storyboard* in the 3D environment of the prototype application. The participants had to answer the question: "How do you imagine the digital University of Fribourg in the future?". The participants had about 30 min to model their *storyboard* with the 3D modeling prototype. Screenshots of the modeling environment, as well as an XML export of the scene, had to be submitted for evaluation. Some examples of the study's outcome for the virtual approach are depicted in Fig. 2.

Finally, the participants had to answer a standardized online SUMI questionnaire [9] for evaluating the prototype in terms of usability. We used the SUMI questionnaire because it is a well-accepted approach for evaluating the usability of a software prototype and freely available for academic purposes. In the following sections, we present the qualitative and quantitative results of the questionnaire.

6.3 Quantitative Results

In the quantitative part of the study, there were questions about *efficiency*, *affect*, *helpfulness*, *controlability*, and *learnability* of the artifact. From the 20 participants, there were 17 surveys that we could analyze. The mean value of the *efficiency* and the *affect* are with 46.59 and 46.29 respectively, clearly below 50 points. The *helpfulness*, *controllability* and *learnability* are 50.88, 50.18, and 50.94 points, each slightly above 50 points. With a *global usability score* of 47.94, the evaluation of the prototype is not extraordinary, since the usability is considered reasonable at an average of 50 out of 100 points.

However, the main focus of our user study was not the quantitative evaluation of our prototype. In the next section we will look at the qualitative part of the questionnaire.

6.4 Qualitative Results

The qualitative part of the questionnaire focused on the capabilities and limitations of the current prototype in order to identify potential drawbacks or problems and to improve these aspects in another DSR cycle.

---

[5] https://apphaus.sap.com/resource/scenes.

The SUMI questionnaire rates statements with "agree", "undecided", or "disagree" to evaluate software functionality. Participants generally agreed on the software's main functions but noted unexpected behavior and inadequate handling of failures. Although users generally had positive opinions, many would not recommend the software to colleagues. Furthermore, the questionnaire asked open questions for the evaluation of the given topic. We will focus here on the two questions "What do you think is the best aspect of this software, and why?" and What do you think needs the most improvement, and why?"

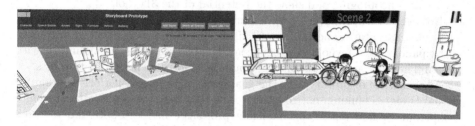

Fig. 2. Examples of the digital storyboards resulting from the case study. The storyboards have been created with the newly implemented modeling prototype.

Participants liked the prototype's simple interface, ability to have different views, faster arrangement of objects, and variety of objects with different attributes. However, some found interaction with the prototype challenging, including scrolling and keyboard events, cumbersome text entry, and difficulty scaling and moving objects. In addition, some users criticized the 3D environment because objects are simply 2D images placed on a plane, making it difficult to place them in relation to each other. Finally, some participants noted that the *Drag&Drop* functionality does not work in the *Safari browser*.

After the testing, we asked participants to indicate their preference between the traditional storytelling approach and the current prototype on a flip chart. Out of 17 answers, 13 participants preferred the traditional approach, citing reasons such as ease of use, collaboration, and interaction. Only three participants preferred the prototype, noting its eco-friendliness or personal preference for digital solutions.

By evaluating our prototype as described in this section, we addressed the last research question (RQ3).

7   Discussion and Conclusion

Although remote work and collaboration has received a tremendous boost from the pandemic, the design challenges it poses have not yet been addressed in research. Considering that an interface between traditional Design Thinking and virtual Design Thinking is needed to overcome the challenges of remote collaboration, our research aims to fill this research gap and encourage other researchers in this area. Therefore, we have developed a virtual *Storyboarding* modeling prototype that enables 3D collaborative remote design thinking, as well as the transformation of these 3D models into a digital 2D model. This was the first step towards bridging the gap between traditional physical, digital and virtual Design Thinking modeling approaches. By deriving the requirements for such a tool and implementing a first prototype, we answered the first two research questions – RQ1 and RQ2.

We evaluated technical compliance with the design requirements and conducted a user study with 20 participants to answer research question RQ3. The results are encouraging and show the potential of the 3D tool.

However, this prototype has some limitations as it is still in early development with missing features and incompatibilities. The evaluation involved university participants, most of whom were between 20 and 30 years old and unfamiliar with Design Thinking and storyboarding, potentially introducing evaluation bias.

At this stage of prototyping, the goal was not to have a perfect solution for virtual Design Thinking, nor to evaluate the tool based on a potential customer group, but to find out if the modeling prototype had the potential to bring virtual and traditional Design Thinking closer together.

The contribution of this research is manifold. Firstly, the prototype can serve as a guide for users interested in virtual collaborative Design Thinking to overcome the challenges of working remotely. Second, the use case of remote collaborative Design Thinking can inspire solutions in other virtual collaboration domains. Finally, our evaluation can encourage further research in business informatics to bridge traditional pen-and-paper and virtual models.

In the future we plan to verify the requirements by collaborative designers, extend the prototype by enabling virtual- and augmented reality (VR/AR) functionalities, and improve real-time collaboration. This would be possible, by using a metamodeling platform that already supports a VR/AR technology stack such as introduced by Muff and Fill [15]. This may open up new possibilities for even more immersive collaboration and natural interaction, as well as easier adaptability through metamodeling capabilities. We also plan to conduct an evaluation with a larger group of users to get more concrete feedback.

Acknowledgment. Financial support is gratefully acknowledged by the Smart Living Lab funding of the University of Fribourg (The Smart Living Lab is a joint project by EPFL, HEIA-FR, and UniFR.).

References

1. Blumrich, J.F.: Design. Am. Assoc. Adv. Sci. **168**, 1551–1554 (1970). https://doi.org/10.1126/science.168.3939.1551
2. Bork, D., Hawryszkiewycz, I., Karagiannis, D.: Supporting customized design thinking using a metamodel-based approach. In: AMCIS vol. 2017, p. 12 (2017)
3. Brenner, W., Uebernickel, F., Abrell, T.: Design thinking as mindset, process, and toolbox. In: Brenner, W., Uebernickel, F. (eds.) Design Thinking for Innovation, pp. 3–21. Springer, Cham (2016). https://doi.org/10.1007/978-3-319-26100-3_1

4. Crocitto, M., Arthur, M., Rousseau, D.: The boundaryless career: a new employment principle for a new organizational era. Acad. Manag. Rev. **23**, 176 (1998). https://doi.org/10.2307/259107

5. Feick, M., Tang, A., Bateman, S.: Mixed-reality for object-focused remote collaboration. In: The 31st Annual ACM Symposium on User Interface Software and Technology Adjunct Proceedings, UIST, pp. 63–65. ACM (2018). https://doi.org/10.1145/3266037.3266102

6. Fill, H., Karagiannis, D.: On the conceptualisation of modelling methods using the ADOxx meta modelling platform. Enterp. Model. Inf. Syst. Archit. Int. J. Concept. Model. **8**(1), 4–25 (2013). https://doi.org/10.18417/emisa.8.1.1

7. George, G., Lakhani, K.R., Puranam, P.: What has changed? The impact of COVID pandemic on the technology and innovation management research agenda. J. Manage. Stud. **57**(8), 1754–1758 (2020). https://doi.org/10.1111/joms.12634

8. Hevner, A.R., March, S.T., Park, J., Ram, S.: Design science in information systems research. MIS Q. **28**(1), 75–105 (2004)

9. Kirakowski, J., Corbett, M.: SUMI: the software usability measurement inventory. Br. J. Educ. Technol. **24**(3), 210–212 (1993). https://doi.org/10.1111/j.1467-8535.1993.tb00076.x

10. Lindberg, T., Meinel, C., Wagner, R.: Design thinking: a fruitful concept for IT development? In: Design Thinking: Understand - Improve - Apply, pp. 3–18. Springer, Berlin, Heidelberg (2011). https://doi.org/10.1007/978-3-642-13757-0_1

11. March, S.T., Smith, G.F.: Design and natural science research on information technology. Decis. Support Syst. **15**(4), 251–266 (1995). https://doi.org/10.1016/0167-9236(94)00041-2

12. Meinel, C., Leifer, L.: Front Matter: Design Thinking Research, pp. i–xxi. Springer, Berlin (2011). https://doi.org/10.1007/978-3-642-13757-0

13. Mennecke, B.E., et al.: Second life and other virtual worlds: a roadmap for research. In: Proceedings of the International Conference on Information Systems, ICIS 2007, Montreal, Quebec, Canada, 9–12 December 2007, p. 4. Association for Information Systems (2007)

14. Miron, E., Muck, C., Karagiannis, D.: Transforming haptic storyboards into diagrammatic models: the scene2model tool. In: 52nd Hawaii International Conference on System Sciences, HICSS, pp. 1–10. ScholarSpace (2019). https://hdl.handle.net/10125/59494

15. Muff, F., Fill, H.: Initial concepts for augmented and virtual reality-based enterprise modeling. In: Proceedings of the ER Demos and Posters 2021, St. John's, NL, Canada, 18–21 October 2021. CEUR Workshop Proceedings, vol. 2958, pp. 49–54. CEUR-WS.org (2021). https://ceur-ws.org/Vol-2958/paper9.pdf

16. Ozturk, P., Avci, C., Kaya, C.: The effect of remote collaborative work on design processes during the pandemic. Strateg. Des. Res. J. **14**(1), 114–123 (2021). https://doi.org/10.4013/sdrj.2021.141.10

17. Peffers, K., Tuunanen, T., Rothenberger, M.A., Chatterjee, S.: A design science research methodology for information systems research. J. Manag. Inf. Syst. **24**(3), 45–77 (2008). https://doi.org/10.2753/mis0742-1222240302

18. Rive, P., Karmokar, S.: Design thinking methods and creative technologies in virtual worlds. In: European Conference on Innovation and Entrepreneurship, p. 11 (2016)

19. Simon, H.A.: Sciences of the Artificial. MIT Press, Cambridge (1970)

20. Tschimmel, K.: Design thinking as an effective toolkit for innovation. In: Proceedings of the XXIII ISPIM Conference: Action for Innovation: Innovating from Experience, p. 1. The International Society for Professional Innovation Management (ISPIM) (2012)

21. Venable, J., Pries-Heje, J., Baskerville, R.: A comprehensive framework for evaluation in design science research. In: Peffers, K., Rothenberger, M., Kuechler, B. (eds.) DESRIST 2012. LNCS, vol. 7286, pp. 423–438. Springer, Heidelberg (2012). https://doi.org/10.1007/978-3-642-29863-9_31

22. Vogel, J., Schuir, J., Koßmann, C., Thomas, O., Teuteberg, F., Hamborg, K.: Let's do design thinking virtually: design and evaluation of a virtual reality application for collaborative prototyping. In: ECIS 2021 (2021)

23. Wang, P., et al.: AR/MR remote collaboration on physical tasks: a review. Robotics Comput. Integr. Manuf. **72**, 102071 (2021). https://doi.org/10.1016/j.rcim.2020.102071

24. Wenzel, M., Gericke, L., Thiele, C., Meinel, C.: Globalized design thinking: bridging the gap between analog and digital for browser-based remote collaboration. In: Plattner, H., Meinel, C., Leifer, L. (eds.) Design Thinking Research. UI, pp. 15–33. Springer, Cham (2016). https://doi.org/10.1007/978-3-319-19641-1_3

Opportunities in Robotic Process Automation by and for Model-Driven Software Engineering

Istvan David$^{(\boxtimes)}$ ⓘ, Vasco Sousa, and Eugene Syriani ⓘ

DIRO, Université de Montréal, Montreal, Canada
{istvan.david,vasco.sousa,eugene.syriani}@umontreal.ca

Abstract. Robotic Process Automation (RPA) offers a non-intrusive approach to workflow automation by defining and operationalizing automation rules through the graphical user interfaces of engineering and business tools. Thanks to its rapid development lifecycle, RPA has become a core enabler in many of nowadays' digital transformation efforts. In this paper, we briefly review how some of the critical success factors of RPA endeavors can be supported by the mature techniques of model-driven software engineering (MDSE); and how RPA can be used to improve the usability of MDSE tools. By that, we intend to shed light on the mutual benefits of RPA and MDSE and encourage researchers and practitioners to explore the synergies of the two fields. To organize such prospective efforts, we define a reference framework for integrating RPA and MDSE, and provide pointers to state-of-the-art RPA frameworks.

Keywords: RPA · MDSE · User Interfaces · Process automation · Automation

1 Introduction

Robotic Process Automation (RPA) aims to alleviate the human workload by automating workflows [1]. RPA offers a less intrusive alternative to traditional workflow automation: the integration of the automation technology is approached through the user interface of the software system. RPA bots emulate the user's behavior and interact with the information system through its user interface or by connecting to APIs to drive client servers, mainframes, or HTML code. Because the system subject to automation does not have to be altered, RPA offers a rapid development lifecycle and reduced development costs [2]. Often considered a core enabler of digital transformation with a high return on investment, RPA has been rapidly adopted by business-facing enterprises irrespective of their business sectors [3]. In recent years, numerous vendors have made substantial efforts to provide RPA platforms. Leading vendors like UiPath, Blue Prism, and Automation Anywhere offer enterprise-grade solutions in an integrated development and management platform. At the same time,

H. van der Aa et al. (Eds.): BPMDS 2023/EMMSAD 2023, LNBIP 479, pp. 285–293, 2023.
https://doi.org/10.1007/978-3-031-34241-7_20

large-scale business information system vendors, such as Microsoft, SAP, and IBM, have incorporated RPA into their portfolios by pivoting from traditional functionalities, e.g., BI and CRM [4].

Model-driven software engineering (MDSE) [5] is a paradigm in which software, including its processes (such as RPA processes), is modeled before it gets implemented. On the one hand, models provide means for formal analysis, something RPA processes could substantially benefit from. On the other hand, the success of MDSE heavily relies on the usability of engineering tools. The usability of MDSE tools, such as CAD tools and simulation software is far from efficient as complex engineering activities often rely on repetitive tasks [6]. RPA is a prime candidate to alleviate those issues. Despite these clear mutual benefits, synergies between RPA and MDSE have not been mapped yet. In this paper, we provide a brief overview of the relation between the two disciplines in both directions: RPA *by* and *for* MDE, and define a reference framework to organize future research and development on the topic.

State of the Practice RPA Frameworks. The latest (2022) Gartner Magic Quadrant report for RPA [7] lists four frameworks as clear market leaders. *UiPath*[1] offers features for governance, cloud-orchestrated RPA as a service, and intuitive UX for non-technical developers. Its main strength is the product strategy, centered around an integrated low-code platform. *Automation Anywhere*[2] is a leader in hyperautomation, i.e., combining RPA with machine learning (ML) capabilities. The Automation 360 platform offers RPA as a service, process discovery, analytics, and ML capabilities built on the TensorFlow framework that renders Automation Anywhere's screen capture accuracy superior to its competitors. *Microsoft Power Automate*[3] leverages the unparalleled ecosystem provided by the broader Microsoft Power Platform. Integration and orchestration capabilities with Power BI for analytics, Process Advisor for process mining, and Power Apps for low-code development are supported out-of-the-box. *Blue Prism*[4] offers cloud-based RPA solutions, governance tools, and advanced automation lifecycle management. With nearly 170,000 active RPA users, its customer ecosystem one of Blue Prism's strengths. Its industry-specific solutions and a wide array of enterprise application connectors make Blue Prism a leader in the RPA market.

2   Opportunities in RPA by MDSE

Recent in-depth surveys have identified key challenges and success factors of RPA endeavors [8,9]. Here, we outline three lines of research in MDSE (shown in Fig. 1) that could substantially contribute to the success of RPA.

---

[1] https://www.uipath.com/.

[2] https://www.automationanywhere.com/.

[3] https://powerautomate.microsoft.com/en-ca/robotic-process-automation.

[4] https://www.blueprism.com/.

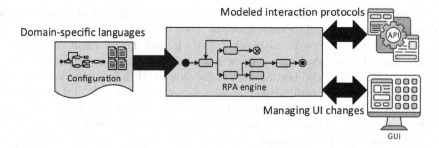

Fig. 1. Three potential contributions of MDSE to RPA.

2.1 Domain-Specific Languages for RPA Configuration

As reported by Plattfaut et al. [9], ensuring sufficient process knowledge as the basis for automation and allowing the process owner to be part of the development are critical success factors of sound RPA solutions. However, current RPA frameworks are shipped with mostly general-purpose process modeling languages that offer little-to-no customizability. This limits the involvement of process owners who typically possess highly domain-specific knowledge. In typical practical settings, however, RPA experts act as translators between the process owner and the RPA framework, and the success of capturing domain-specific workflows is entirely dependent on their understanding and interpretation, resulting in substantial accidental complexity. Domain-specific languages (DSLs) [10] could reduce this accidental complexity, narrow the cognitive gap between the domain expert and the RPA expert, and even allow expressing parts of the configuration, integration requirements, and test scenarios [9] by the domain expert. The modeling of multi-faceted RPA workflows might require an ensemble of modeling languages. While graphical notations for workflows are intuitive, their limitations are apparent when capturing complex structures. Multi-view Modeling [11] has been successfully employed in such scenarios and could provide foundations for modeling complex RPA configurations.

2.2 Explicitly Modeled Interaction Protocols with APIs

Ensuring compliance with IT and security policies is another critical success factor in RPA [9]. Establishing supporting tools that reach across organization silos challenges the organizational embeddedness and audit of RPA processes.

One important technical facet is the interaction between the RPA process and the various IT systems across the organization. Such orchestration tasks are typically approached at the source code level that the RPA engine can use during the execution of the main workflow. Relying on source code to integrate APIs is problematic for two reasons. First, such an approach gives rise to unwanted accidental complexity. Inefficient source code can lead to the limited performance of the RPA workflow, reduced quality, and bugs. The lack of proper exception handling is a known shortcoming of RPA [8]. Second, certification of the RPA workflow might be of particular interest in settings when critical infrastructure is involved in the overall orchestration; or when the RPA workflow has to carry out tasks in a mission-critical manner (e.g., in the development of a critical cyber-physical system). Relying on source code substantially complicates any analysis, verification, and certification of the overall RPA configuration. Explicit modeling of interaction protocols has been shown to be feasible and practical in developing complex engineering toolchains [12] and can translate well to RPA configurations. Statecharts and class diagrams have been suggested for modeling service interactions in engineering workflows [13], allowing the analysis and simulation of various behavioral properties, such as time-outs, exception handling, and parallelism. Finally, appropriately modeled interaction protocols enable the end-to-end simulation and optimization of the underlying workflow [14].

2.3   Managing Changes to User Interfaces

Flexibility and maintainability of RPA solutions, and support for their continuous evolution have been identified as additional success factors [8,9].

A severe shortcoming of RPA frameworks is their reliance on fixed user interfaces. Once an RPA configuration has been finalized, any change to the graphical user interface (GUI) might break it. This includes visible graphical elements that have been added, changed, or moved and HTML code not visualized on the GUI, such as changes to element identifiers or CSS classes. These limitations make RPA configurations brittle and could lead to substantial maintenance costs amidst unwanted vendor locking. Explicitly modeled GUI can significantly alleviate this problem [15]. Such approaches model the structure and behavior of the editor and generate the specific implementation from the models [16]. This enables associating RPA rules with the model itself instead of the specific GUI elements. Since models are manipulated through model transformations, the traceability of changes is explicit, enabling controlled evolution of RPA configurations based on the changes of the GUI.

3   Opportunities in RPA for MDSE

As much as RPA can benefit from MDSE, MDSE tools can benefit from RPA techniques as well. Complex modeling activities, such as developing model transformations and creating domain-specific languages, require repetitive tasks. Reusable and platform-specific workflow automation techniques, e.g., the Eclipse Modeling Workflow Environment, have been proposed to alleviate these problems. However, such approaches assume (i) the availability of advanced programming expertise and (ii) control over the business logic of the software tools at hand, e.g., open-source software. In such cases, the impact of RPA is moderate, as shown in Fig. 2. In the absence of programming skills and without control over the internals of tools, RPA becomes a viable and convenient alternative.

Here, we briefly discuss the primary and secondary candidates for RPA and provide example domains that rely heavily on model-driven techniques.

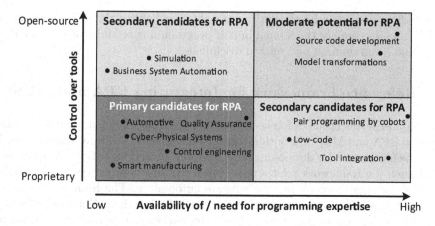

Fig. 2. Opportunities in using RPA for MDSE.

3.1 Primary Candidates for RPA

MDSE settings in which non-programmer experts are working with proprietary tools are the primary candidates for using RPA. Examples of such settings include traditional non-software engineering disciplines, such as control software and cyber-physical systems. While considered technical users, engineers in these domains do not necessarily possess the skills to automate their work using abstract process semantics. RPA can serve as a user-friendly alternative. Automotive and smart manufacturing engineering sectors are also reportedly lagging behind in digitalization [17], suggesting a high expected return on investment of digital improvement efforts, such as RPA. Screen capturing and workflow automation tools, such as Selenium [18], have been widely used for quality assurance purposes. However, these tools are limited to executing previously defined test cases on a graphical user interface. RPA-supported quality assurance opens up possibilities for automating the tester's tasks as well, including the selection, evaluation, and reporting of test cases, reconfiguring test cases, and improving test cases by incorporating historical data through machine learning.

3.2 Secondary Candidates for RPA

Shifting from proprietary to open-source tools (top-left quadrant) allows for more control over the internals of the engineering tools, and enables automation through the business logic or back-end. Such settings limit the potential of RPA. However, the potential lack of available programming expertise might justify using RPA. Such cases can be observed in simulation disciplines where experts often rely on open-source tools and algorithms and business systems automation with non-technical users. Settings with proprietary tools but featuring advanced programming expertise (bottom-right quadrant) are another group of secondary candidates for RPA. RPA can successfully automate activities in developing low-code platforms with proprietary components and provide a workflow-centric orchestration functionality for lightweight tools integration. RPA can also emulate the human in pair programming settings, as advocated in eXtreme Programming and related disciplines.

4   Reference Framework for Integrating RPA and MDSE

We propose a conceptual reference framework to realize the opportunities in integrating RPA and MDSE in both directions. As depicted in Fig. 3, the framework lays the foundation for developing RPA solutions by and for MDSE. At a conceptual level, the framework relates these two directions between RPA and MDSE; and relates them to conventional software automation. The framework aims to aid RPA developers and tool providers to contextualize their efforts in terms of a typical socio-technological modeling and simulation system (STMSS), in which human and organizational factors must be considered during the system's lifecycle as well [19]. Furthermore, it aids MDSE developers and tool providers to incorporate RPA into their continuous development efforts, possibly in a hybrid approach combined with conventional software automation techniques.

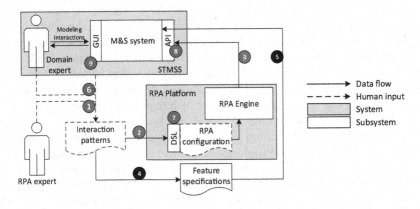

Fig. 3. Conceptual reference framework for integrating RPA and MDSE. ❶–❸ RPA for MDSE ❹–❺ Conventional Software Automation ❻–❾ RPA by MDSE.

RPA for MDSE. RPA endeavors start with eliciting interaction patterns between the human modeler (i.e., the Domain expert) and the technical interfaces. Typically, the RPA expert performs this activity, indicated ❶ in Fig. 3. These interaction patterns are subsequently translated into the RPA configuration ❷. This transformation spans the process definitions, API interactions, file I/O operations, etc. Then, the RPA engine executes the process by interacting with the API of the modeling tool and other tools in the tool chain ❸.

Conventional Software Automation. In a traditional software automation app-roach, the elicited interaction patterns serve as the inputs to Feature speci-fications ❹. These feature specifications are subsequently implemented in the STMSS to provide better automation ❺. RPA offers a non-intrusive and faster development cycle for the automation of modeling and simulation tasks. In con-trast, traditional software automation offers more robust solutions, thanks to the tighter integration with systems in the tool chain. The two approaches are best used in combination. For example, RPA-based automation can serve as a tem-porary patch until developments of conventional software automation catch up with the changing requirements, or as the scaffolding for user-facing acceptance testing before conventional software engineering developments commence.

RPA by MDSE. Through MDSE techniques and tools, the Domain expert can directly express interaction patterns ❻. Such tools are, e.g., DSLs ❼, which pro-vide high-level, concise mechanisms to specify RPA configurations. Both Domain experts and RPA experts can use syntax-directed editing and mixed textual-graphical editors for this purpose, possibly in a collaborative fashion [20]. State-of-the-art modeling and simulation systems often provide APIs for automation ❽, e.g., via scripting. RPA solutions might require more sophisticated API sup-port, e.g., RESTful web APIs with more complex interaction protocols between the RPA engine and the STMSS while preserving scalability and portability. Finally, to address the adaptability challenges of RPA, modeling and simulation tool vendors might develop GUIs with explicitly modeled capabilities to provide information to the RPA infrastructure for adaptation purposes ❾.

5   Conclusion

In this paper, we have outlined the opportunities in employing MDSE for the improvement of RPA practices and employing RPA for improving MDSE tools. We outlined three lines of research for prospective MDSE researchers in sup-port of improving the outlooks of RPA endeavors, especially in the areas of domain-specific languages, explicitly modeled interaction protocols, and mod-eled user interfaces. To assess opportunities in applying RPA in MDSE tools, we identified the openness of tools and the availability of programming exper-tise as the principal dimensions of MDSE settings that determine the potential impact of employing RPA. MDSE domains with proprietary tools or lacking advanced programming expertise are the primary candidates to leverage RPA. Such domains include automotive and CPS software engineering, various sim-ulation domains, and low-code application development. Finally, we proposed a reference framework that illustrates how domain-specific RPA configuration languages, explicitly modeled API interactions, and generative techniques for building robust GUIs, are elements of the MDSE toolbox that can contribute to RPA immediately and improve its reliability and performance.

Future research should focus on the details of the outlined research directions, and on conducting surveys to validate and detail the matrix of opportunities.

Adopters of RPA can use this paper as a guideline to better position their RPA efforts. Developers can use the pointers of this paper to make better choices when implementing new RPA features.

References

1. Aguirre, S., Rodriguez, A.: Automation of a business process using robotic process automation (RPA): a case study. In: Figueroa-García, J.C., López-Santana, E.R., Villa-Ramírez, J.L., Ferro-Escobar, R. (eds.) WEA 2017. CCIS, vol. 742, pp. 65–71. Springer, Cham (2017). https://doi.org/10.1007/978-3-319-66963-2_7
2. Asatiani, A., Penttinen, E.: Turning robotic process automation into commercial success - case OpusCapita. J. Inf. Technol. Teach. Cases **6**(2), 67–74 (2016)
3. Siderska, J.: Robotic process automation - a driver of digital transformation? Eng. Manag. Prod. Serv. **12**(2), 21–31 (2020)
4. Schaffrik, B.: The forrester wave^{TM}: robotic process automation, Q1 2021 - the 14 providers that matter most and how they stack up (2021)
5. Brambilla, M., Cabot, J., Wimmer, M.: Model-Driven Software Engineering in Practice, 2nd edn. Morgan & Claypool Publishers (2017)
6. Gamboa, M., Syriani, E.: Improving user productivity in modeling tools by explicitly modeling workflows. Softw. Syst. Model. **18**, 2441–2463 (2019)
7. Ray, S., et al.: Magic quadrant for robotic process automation. Von Gartner (2021). https://www.gartner.com/doc/reprints
8. Syed, R., et al.: Robotic process automation: contemporary themes and challenges. Comput. Ind. **115**, 103162 (2020)
9. Plattfaut, R., et al.: The critical success factors for robotic process automation. Comput. Ind. **138**, 103646 (2022)
10. Fowler, M.: Domain-Specific Languages. The Addison-Wesley Signature Series. Addison-Wesley (2011)
11. Verlage, M.: Multi-view modeling of software processes. In: Warboys, B.C. (ed.) EWSPT 1994. LNCS, vol. 772, pp. 123–126. Springer, Heidelberg (1994). https://doi.org/10.1007/3-540-57739-4_17
12. Biehl, M., El-khoury, J., Loiret, F., Törngren, M.: On the modeling and generation of service-oriented tool chains. Softw. Syst. Model. **13**(2), 461–480 (2014). https://doi.org/10.1007/s10270-012-0275-7
13. Van Mierlo, S., et al.: A multi-paradigm approach for modelling service interactions in model-driven engineering processes. In: Proceedings of the Model-Driven Approaches for Simulation Engineering Symposium, SpringSim 2018, Baltimore, MD, USA, 15–18 April 2018, pp. 6:1–6:12. ACM (2018)
14. David, I., Vangheluwe, H., Van Tendeloo, Y.: Translating engineering workflow models to DEVS for performance evaluation. In: Winter Simulation Conference, WSC 2018, Sweden, 9–12 December 2018, pp. 616–627. IEEE (2018)
15. Sousa, V., Syriani, E., Fall, K.: Operationalizing the integration of user interaction specifications in the synthesis of modeling editors. In: Proceedings of the 12th ACM SIGPLAN International Conference on Software Language Engineering, SLE 2019, Athens, Greece, 20–22 October 2019, pp. 42–54. ACM (2019)
16. Syriani, E., Riegelhaupt, D., Barroca, B., David, I.: Generation of custom textual model editors. Modelling **2**(4), 609–625 (2021)
17. Bughin, J., Manyika, J., Catlin, T.: Twenty-five years of digitization: ten insights into how to play it right. McKinsey Global Institute, Boston (2019)

18. Bruns, A., Kornstädt, A., Wichmann, D.: Web application tests with selenium. IEEE Softw. **26**(5), 88–91 (2009)
19. Baxter, G.D., Sommerville, I.: Socio-technical systems: from design methods to systems engineering. Interact. Comput. **23**(1), 4–17 (2011)
20. David, I., Syriani, E.: Real-time collaborative multi-level modeling by conflict-free replicated data types. Softw. Syst. Model. (2022). https://doi.org/10.1007/s10270-022-01054-5

Visualization and Process Modeling (EMMSAD 2023)

A Requirements-Driven Framework for Automatic Data Visualization

Tong Li[1(✉)], Xiang Wei[2], and Yiting Wang[1]

[1] Beijing University of Technology, Beijing, China
litong@bjut.edu.cn
[2] Institut Polytechnique de Paris, Palaiseau, France
xiang.wei@ip-paris.fr

Abstract. Data visualization is an essential method for analyzing big data. Regarding the increasing demands on data visualization generation and understanding, more professional knowledge and skills are required, which are difficult to meet in practice. In most cases, people visualize data using existing templates which might not fit their requirements. We believe that it is essential to establish the connections between users' visualization requirements and visualization solutions. In this paper, we propose a four-layer visualization framework to systematically and automatically map user requirements to data visualization solutions. Specifically, the framework is designed based on typical visual features and attributes and establishes mappings based on their semantics. Based on this framework, we have implemented a web-based prototype, which can automate the generation of visualization solutions from user visualization requirements. To evaluate the framework, we conducted a case study with one participant using the developed prototype and received positive feedback and suggestions.

Keywords: Data visualization · Visualization requirements · Visual variable · Prototype tool

1 Introduction

With the growth of science and the economy, we are entering an era where vast amounts of data are being generated at our fingertips. According to Domo[1], on average, each person creates at least 1.7 MB of data per second in 2020. The power of technology has penetrated deeply into our daily lives, allowing even ordinary users to access vast amounts of data. Big data analysis is increasingly influencing decision-making in various fields, such as economics and politics, and the conclusions drawn through this analysis have the potential to be game-changing [10]. Therefore, it is essential to know how to perform data analysis effectively. According to a scientific survey[2], the human brain processes images

---

[1] https://www.domo.com/.

[2] https://www.t-sciences.com/news/humans-process-visual-data-better.

H. van der Aa et al. (Eds.): BPMDS 2023/EMMSAD 2023, LNBIP 479, pp. 297–311, 2023.
https://doi.org/10.1007/978-3-031-34241-7_21

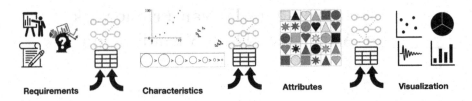

Fig. 1. Overview of the proposed four-layer framework.

60,000 times faster than text. Thus, data visualization is a popular method of processing and presenting data [12]. By presenting various features of data in the form of graphs and charts, data visualization provides a more intuitive and deeper understanding of the data compared to traditional data presentation methods. This is particularly useful for big data, where the visualization results can more effectively represent the information and patterns inherent in the data due to its volume and complexity.

Despite the proliferation of data visualization solutions, generating appropriate visualizations that match specific requirements remains challenging. Most visualization generation tools available today require users to have the expertise and make choices to obtain an appropriate visualization solution [2]. However, the multitude of choices and the lack of clarity on the goals of the requirements make it challenging for users to make effective connections between the two for data visualization. Even obtaining an explicit visualization requirement, such as comparing data, is still difficult to translate into a final visual presentation, such as using line or bar charts to show the comparison results.

In this paper, we propose a four-layer framework that aims to automate the data visualization process by establishing mappings between visualization requirements and visualization solutions. The proposed framework comprises a requirements layer, a visual characteristic layer, a visual attribute layer, and a visualization solution layer, as shown in Fig. 1. Specifically, the requirements layer presents typical visualization requirements, which we collect based on ten interviews targeted at studying users' understanding of data visualization. The visual characteristic layer and the visual attribute layer are defined based on Bertin's research [1]. The former is reasonably related to user requirements, while the latter guides the generation of visualization solutions. We have implemented a prototype tool that embodies our proposed framework and can automate the generation of visualization solutions based on users' specific requirements. We conducted a case study with one participant using our prototype tool to evaluate our proposal. The case study received positive feedback, demonstrating that our proposed framework and prototype tool are useful in practice.

2   Related Work

2.1   Data Visualization Techniques

Although visual charts can convey a great deal of information in a very compact manner, telling the story of big data in a logical way is still a difficult task. Bikakis et al. [2] focus on using modern visualization techniques to process larger and more dynamic data. Python is one of the best-known and most widely used languages for processing data. Furthermore, there are several libraries in Python, such as Seaborn [16], Matplotlib [9], and Plotnine (ggplot) [17], that provide rich templates and methods for data visualization, allowing users to have a standardized way to customize data visualization.

Apart from working with the native language, there are also many advanced studies that integrate data processing together with data visualization. Chuai and Yan [5] introduced methods from data collecting to analyzing. Ren et al. [14] is also an intelligent system that analyzes the data collected from multiple sources.

Although these tools and systems are powerful in data processing and can automatically generate visual charts from big data, they always require a high level of technical knowledge for the user to master them effectively.

2.2   Visualization Requirements Analysis

Many researchers have identified the problem of a lack of mapping between user requirements and data visualization in current automated data visualization systems. As a result, several studies have been conducted to address this issue.

One study by Buja et al. [3] categorizes high-dimensional data analytic tasks into three parts and matches them to three classes of interactive view manipulations. Wu et al. [18] define a set of common tasks in the Artificial Intelligence domain and propose visualizations that can be applied to these tasks. Additionally, a survey by Du and Yuan [6] provides an analysis of competitive sports data to help readers find appropriate visualization techniques for different data types and tasks. All these works provide good matching between user tasks and visual charts. Limited in a specific domain, users who build links are always more precise.

Besides, there are two ways to generalize these mappings. One approach is to collect and summarize mappings proposed by researchers in each domain. The other is to apply visualization on a more generalized dataset and abstract the mappings. Byrd and Dwenger [4] offer a data table that can automatically adjust to different tasks to help users practice and find the most appropriate visualization solution. Furthermore, Peña et al. [13] have proposed a more detailed classification of charts based on the analysis of the Linked Open Data (LOD) dataset. They suggest that this approach could help users to identify visualizations that best satisfy their goals.

Current studies aim to bridge the gap between requirements and data visualizations. However, the general mapping may only suit general user requirements, and specific visualizations are more precise for users working in a specific domain.

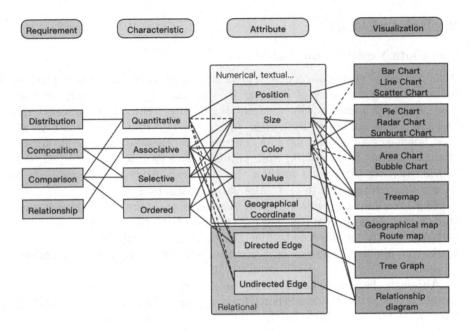

Fig. 2. Four-layer framework in detail.

3   A Four-Layer Framework for Automatically Generating Data Visualization Solutions

In this section, we will detail the design of our four-layer framework. The framework consists of four layers: requirement layer, characteristic layer, attribute layer, and visualization layer, as illustrated in Fig. 2. We will provide further explanation on why we selected these layers and how we built each mapping in the following subsections.

3.1   Understand and Collect User Visualization Requirements

To ensure our framework works automatically, we need to first understand users' requirements for data visualization. Conducting interviews is an effective empirical method for acquiring straightforward and inspired answers. By designing systematically structured questions, we can obtain as much information about user requirements as possible. The following questions were developed to understand why users need data visualization:

- *Q1:* In what scenarios do you need to create a data analysis diagram?
- *Q2:* What type of data have you worked with?
- *Q3:* What types of diagrams do you usually create?
- *Q4:* What kind of information do you obtain from the charts (shown in Fig. 3), and what tasks do you think they are designed for?

We designed *Question 1 (Q1)* to ask interviewees to describe the scenarios in which they require data visualization. Different types of visualizations have varying abilities to display source data, so we also included *Q2* and *Q3* in asking about the data types and visualization preferences of users. With these three questions, we can gain a general understanding of users' requirements for data visualization. As most current visualization tools require users to choose the appropriate visualization to represent their data, we expect that most users have developed their own approach to building this mapping and selecting the appropriate visualization. Therefore, we included *Q4* in asking users to describe the knowledge they have gained from existing visualization solutions.

We selected examples from six basic chart types (bar, line, area, network, map, and radial). For each chart type example, we hid the chart's title and legend, then encouraged participants to guess the purpose of the chart and the message it conveys. Based on users' responses, we can expect to find an inverse correspondence between the visualization scenarios and users' requirements.

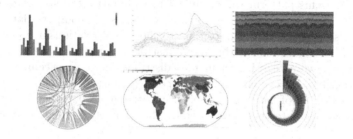

Fig. 3. Example charts provide in the interview.

Because we were conducting this interview to identify patterns from regular users and to gain inspiration from hearing them describe their work patterns, we looked for people who had previous experience with data visualization tools. This way, they could answer our questions more efficiently and clearly. Therefore, we invited 10 candidates to our interview, six of whom were female and four male. They were all aged between 20 and 40, had at least some basic computer skills, and had used data visualization tools more than twice.

After collecting and summarizing the answers we received, we found that they were generally focused, particularly for the first three questions. Although our candidates had different occupations, their answers were surprisingly focused on writing reports and giving presentations *(Answer 1)*. In response to the second question, their initial answers were all tables. Therefore, we had to guide them to recall the data types in tables before we received answers such as numerical type, descriptive type, and relational type *(Answer 2)*. With regards to the most frequently used charts, we summarized the top five types, which were the bar chart, line chart, scatter chart, pie chart, and geographical map *(Answer 3)*.

However, when summarizing the answers to the last question, we found that the responses were more diverse because establishing a connection between user requirements and visualization solutions is highly personalized. Participants' responses typically contained broad directions. For example, in the first bar graph response, a candidate suggested that they might use it to compare the amount of rainfall in different countries or to compare the sales of different brands of cell phones in different months. Even though the two answers given by this participant appeared to be in completely different areas, they both used the same verb, "compare". When we collated the answers we received for the first bar chart, we found that most responses used the verb "compare". For example, it was designed to compare the profits of different products of a company or the incidence of various accidents in the last six years. In fact, we went back to the origin of the graph and found that it was used to compare the distribution of people of different ages across continents in the United States. We, therefore, abstracted the many descriptive answers and used "comparison" as the explanation for the first chart.

Following this pattern, we continued to summarize the speculations of the other charts. We extracted five different purposes: to compare data, to show data trends, to show data composition, to show data relationships, and to show data distribution. Based on the verbs abstracted from the syntax of the user requirements, we categorize them into distribution, composition, comparison, and relationship. We exclude trends from our categorization, as trending is actually a presentation of data relationships. Additionally, we explain how these four requirements apply to the data, based on the complete context, as follows:

- *Distribution*: defines the relative or absolute position of data
- *Composition*: determines the category and hierarchy of data
- *Comparison*: compares the value of data
- *Relationship*: establishes the linkage between data

Based on the conclusions from the interviews, especially the last question, we found that most charts have an inherent meaning in the information they represent. People are surprisingly adept at guessing which type of information matches which type of chart. Moreover, people are also proficient at extracting information from a particular chart. In fact, a proper visualization can convey more information than we expect.

3.2 Mapping User Requirements to Characteristics of Visual Variables

By summarizing user requirements and examining the four extracted words, we found that they match some characteristics mentioned in Bertin's study [7]. One of Bertin's criteria for extracting visualization variables is the expressive power of these attributes in the visualization scheme, i.e., the visual characteristic. We selected the following four characteristics that can be matched to the requirements and adjusted their explanations:

Table 1. Requirements - Characteristics mapping.

Requirement	Characteristic
Distribution	Quantitative
Composition	Associative, Selective
Comparison	Ordered, Selective, Quantitative
Relationship	Associative

- *Quantitative*: a single or a group of visual symbols can present absolute value
- *Selective*: a single or a group of visual symbols can stand out from others
- *Ordered*: a series of visual symbols can be arranged in sequence
- *Associative*: a series of visual symbols can be grouped according to similarity

As mentioned above, we found similarities between the characteristics and requirements. However, during the selection of the characteristics, we found that they do not have a one-to-one relationship. Some requirements need to be expressed by multiple expression characteristics. Therefore, we defined a clear mapping between the requirements and characteristics of visual variables. For the *Distribution* goal, whether in the coordinate axis or the map, we can accurately read out the coordinate *quantitative* information. For *Composition*, there are differences between parts, so there is *selective*; each part can be combined into a whole, and there must be an *associative* between them. *Comparison* exists when there are differences among data values, so there is *selective*; values can be distinguished, so there is *quantitative*; if values can be sorted, there is *ordered*. *Relationship* matches the relational chart, so linked data can be grouped together, then there is an *associative*. When we draw a link, there is a weight on a different connection, so *quantitative* is involved. To show the mapping more clearly, we have put them into Table 1.

3.3 Mapping Between Characteristics and Attributes of Visual Variables

Next, we will focus on the attributes with different expressive characteristics and design mapping relations between the characteristics and attributes. Since each selected attribute has different characteristics, Table 2 shows the relationship among them. Specifically, in Table 2, Y indicates that the current attribute satisfies this property, X indicates that the current attribute does not have this property, and *?* indicates that the situation is not unique.

- *Position*: is a fundamental attribute commonly used in visualization. It refers to the X and Y coordinates, which respectively correspond to the horizontal and vertical addresses of a point in a two-dimensional (2D) space. Together, these coordinates provide precise location information for a point.
- *Size*: is selective because we can easily distinguish symbols with different sizes. Also, we can group symbols with similar sizes. We can order sizes either from small to large or vice versa. If the visualization variable is aligned with the

Table 2. Attributes-Characteristics Mapping.

Attributes/Characteristics	Selective	Associative	Quantitative	Ordered
Position	Y	Y	Y	Y
Size	Y	Y	?	Y
Value	Y	Y	X	Y
Color	Y	Y	X	X
Geographical	Y	Y	Y	Y
Directed edge	X	Y	?	Y
Undirected edge	X	Y	?	X

coordinate axis, we can quickly and directly obtain the area through simple and multi-calculation. But if not, it is difficult to see the value of the area directly. Therefore, the quantitative of the size is uncertain.

- *Value*: is mostly used to represent relative values. Given a group of visual variables with different gray scales, we can easily distinguish, categorize, and sort them. So it has "selective", "associative" and "ordered". Since it is a relative value and can't express the value directly, it does not contain "quantitative".
- *Color*: is an attribute that is often used to distinguish different variables or identify groups. Although it is very powerful in terms of identification, it is relatively weak in terms of expressing absolute values, and there is no accepted sorting order between different colors. So "color" has "selective" and "associative" but doesn't have "quantitative" and "ordered" attributes.
- *Geographical*: is an attribute that appears on the geographic map. It is similar to the "position" attribute on the coordinate axes and has four characteristics of expression. For example, the user can select a point on the map individually to get its geographic coordinates, sort it according to its latitude and longitude, or group it according to the pair of continental plates it belongs to.
- *Directed Edge* and *Undirected Edge*: are attributes that appears on a relationship map. Based on the connected node, we can easily select a connected link or group the links together. On edge, there is not always a weight on it. So the "quantitative" is uncertain. For the directed edge, there is a path to follow, so it contains "ordered", while the undirected edge doesn't.

According to Tamara [11], although some attributes share the same characteristics, their expressive abilities differ, and there is a hierarchy of these abilities. For instance, position, size, value, geography, and directed edges have ordered characteristics, with the position on a common scale having the best expressive ability. Position on an unaligned scale is slightly lower in the ranking than aligned position, followed by size, then color, and value. Although Tamara's study did not mention geographic coordinates, we believe there are similarities between geographic coordinates and position on unaligned scales, so we place them between position and size.

Furthermore, attributes with selective characteristics, such as position, size, value, color, and geography, also have different rankings. Ware [15] has proposed

Table 3. Attributes Characteristics Effectiveness Ranking.

Characteristics	Effectiveness Ranking	
	Non-Relational data	Relational data
Selective	Color > Value > Position > Geographical > Size	
Ordered	Size > Value > Position > Geographical	Directed edges
Associative	Color > Value > Position > Geographical > Size	Directed edges > Undirected edges
Quantitative	Position > Geographical	

a theory about the ability to combine variables, suggesting that human vision is more attracted to color, value, position, and size. We can thus create a ranking for each attribute based on its relevance, which is carried by all attributes. To determine the ranking, we can refer to selectivity. Although combination and selection work in opposite ways, the expressiveness of the attributes taken should be the same.

Finally, we consider the ranking between attributes that have quantitative characteristics. Since size does not necessarily express quantity, we do not put it in the hierarchy. The coordinate positions in the geographic map correspond to more information than the positions in the 2-dimensional axes. So in terms of the property of simply expressing a quantitative characteristic, it may be slightly inferior. In fact, when ranking, we find it difficult to compare directed edges and undirected edges with other attributes. While some attributes are reflected in many different charts, there are also some attributes that are specific to certain types of charts. The more long-used directed and undirected edges of relational diagrams clearly fall into the latter category. We wanted to find a rubric to classify these two attributes. Specifically, we ranked the expressiveness of different attributes separately and created a validity hierarchy table in Table 3.

3.4 Mapping Visual Variable's Attributes to Data Visualization Solutions

We have successfully established the mapping of user requirements to visual attributes. In the last mapping, we need to link the user requirements to the visualization solutions, i.e., the mapping between attributes and visualizations. Different visualization attributes have different differentiation capabilities among each other, as explained in Table 3. With this ranking in mind, we started analyzing how these attributes function in a complete visualization solution and how they combine with each other to convey different information ranges.

We extracted seven visualization variable attributes, and trying to traverse all the combination cases between them was impossible. On the other hand, detecting all the visual attributes contained in a visualization solution is a feasible way. This does the opposite of extracting visual variables from a complete visualization solution. To this end, we collected some existing cases of common visualization charts and grouped them into various chart types. In the process of finding all the matching attributes, we found that most attributes are usually expressed in a regular way, no matter what type of chart. In order to improve the efficiency of the analysis, we summarized the following guidelines for reference.

- *Position*: chart with axes of coordinates
- *Size*: chart involving the display of area
- *Value*: chart involving different light and dark variations of the same color
- *Color*: chart involving the display of multiple colors
- *Geographic location*: chart with map display
- *Undirected edges*: chart involving the display of undirected edges
- *Directed edges*: chart involving the display of directed edges

Table 4. Attribute - Visualization Mapping.

Attribute	Visualization
Position, (Color)	Bar, Line, Scatter Chart
Size, Color	Pie, Radar, Sunburst Chart
Position, Size, (Color)	Area, Bubble Chart
Color, Size, Value	Treemap
Geographical coordinates, (color)	Geographical, Route Map
Undirected edge, color, size	Relationship diagram
Directed edge	Tree graph

The mappings between attributes and visualization schemes are established and shown in Table 4. We illustrate the application of the mapping in detail with an example of an area chart.

Area Chart with Attributes. The example chart we have selected is an area chart that displays the unaudited revenue of Apple Inc. The chart presents revenue values of the United States, Europe, China, Japan, and other Asia-Pacific regions for different quarters between 2014 and 2016. Users can easily compare the total revenue amounts in different quarters within a given region or compare the percentage of the total share of different regions at the same time.

To identify the visual variable attributes in this chart, we apply the summary rule described above. First, the chart includes two axes - the x and y axes - which allow users to find individual data and track their values. Therefore, the area chart includes the location attribute. Second, the chart represents the values of the data not only by the y-axis coordinates but also by the area of a region enclosed by the x and y axes. The areas are stacked in the ascending direction of the y-axis to show the total values and percentages in combination. Thus, the area chart includes the area attribute. The colors in the chart are used to distinguish different independent variables. However, when the data has only one independent variable, the color attribute is not meaningful. We also found examples of area charts that use a single color. Therefore, the color attribute is optional. Finally, numerical values, geographic maps, undirected edges, and directed edges are not addressed in the area chart.

In summary, area charts always include the location and area attributes and may include the color attribute at some point.

Bubble Chart with Attributes. The second example we chose is the bubble chart. The main purpose of this chart is to compare the life expectancy of different countries on different continents using the Gross Domestic Product (GDP) as a measurement factor. Additionally, the population of each country is also shown on the chart.

In the same way, we apply the general guidelines used to analyze the area chart to the bubble chart. We first focus on the two axes. The x and y coordinates determine the location of each bubble containing its data, so the bubble chart includes the location attribute. Then, the population is represented by the area of the bubble, making it include the area attribute. Countries in different continents are marked with different colors, providing a small visual grouping that is easy to read and understand. However, the grouping does not affect the presentation of the underlying data, so the color is an optional attribute. Finally, values, geographic maps, undirected edges, and directed edges are not addressed in the bubble chart. Therefore, we can conclude that the bubble chart also contains location, area attributes, and color attributes (optional).

Comparing the area chart and the bubble chart horizontally, we find that both share the same attributes. Furthermore, comparing the service purposes of both charts, we find that both are also used for "comparisons". This further validates that our mapping relationship is potentially valid.

4   Prototype Tool

Our approach is implemented as a tool that automatically generating a series of visualization solutions. The tool follows the four-layer framework and prompts users to input their data and select their requirements. Once the user inputs their data, the tool generates all the matching charts by applying the three mappings.

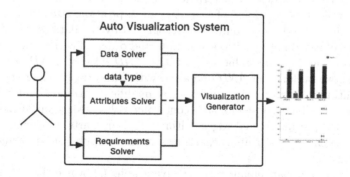

Fig. 4. System architecture.

The tool is a web-based application that runs on Python and Flask. The system architecture is shown in Fig. 4. To run the tool locally, the user can open and run the project in PyCharm, and install the Flask package. After that, the user can open their browser and go to port 5000 to access the tool's homepage, which prompts the user to upload their data and proceed to the next page. The data solver is fully implemented in Python, allowing users to specify the data source and apply selection filters. Some interactive elements, such as HTML components and JavaScript, are used to guide users in entering their requirements. All visualization solutions templates are imported from the Plotly library [8].

5   Evaluation

After thoroughly reviewing related research in this domain, we realized that no other approaches provide the same functionalities as our proposed tool. As such, we cannot compare our approach to any baseline, but we can evaluate it through a suitable case study. To evaluate the effectiveness of our approach, we invited a participant to simulate a practical application of our system and conduct a practical case study. The participant had a clear goal of creating the most suitable visualization scheme.

This participant is a sports events enthusiast who, during his vacation, watched many games of the 2021 Tokyo Olympics. He wanted to create a poster to display the performance of each country in the Olympic Games, and he realized that using a chart would be a condensed and suitable representation for a poster. He searched for a dataset and found one with four columns: the country name, total number of medals, number of gold medals, and number of silver and bronze medals.

The participant uploaded the data and then selected the page, guided by the comparison hint to check the difference and size of the data, which is ideally suited for datasets with two or three groups of numerical data.

Based on the mapping shown in Fig. 2, the comparison matched quantitative, selective, and order characteristics. As mentioned in the previous section, we only consider the mapping of four attributes: position, size, color, and value, based on the non-relational data type recognized by the data solver. Therefore, quantitative mapping to position, selection, and order all correspond to size and value. Since the comparison has quantitative *AND* selective *AND* ordered characteristics, we perform an *AND* operation with the corresponding attributes as well, resulting in position, size, and value as qualified attributes. In the last layer of mapping, we don't consider charts containing color, geographical coordinates, directed edges, or undirected edges. Ultimately, Bar charts, Line charts, Scatter charts, Area charts, and Bubble charts are chosen to apply user data and present it to the users.

This time, our participant received five graphs (shown in Fig. 5). From the bar chart, this participant can directly compare the number of medals. Also, to compare the number of gold, silver, and bronze medals. However, our participant

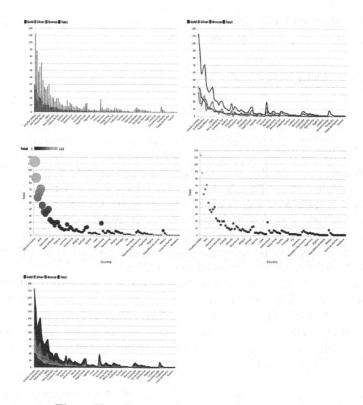

Fig. 5. Visualization solutions on the case study.

thinks it is not clear since there are too many countries, and each of them takes four column bars, making the x-axis too long. While in the line chart, he does not like the lines going through all the points because it makes the value of the points vague. Then in the scatter chart and bubble chart, he received similar results. The only difference between them is that there is one more dimension: "size", used to present the value on top of "color". Yet, in these two charts, only the total medal number is presented. Based on these two charts, our participant suggests using a different color to represent different medals. So we can have all the information separately shown in the charts. The reason why our system did not generate this chart is that it does not contain a color attribute. Lastly, the area chart uses a 2-dimensional visual symbol to present the number, so it expands the comparison value. The user commented that with the help of the stacked area, we greatly decreased the length of the x-axis. But ideally, in the area chart, we do not need to separately show the total number because the stacked area from all medals already reveals the value.

In the end, the participant put the area chart onto his poster. He preferred it because all the information is covered in the chart, and it suited better to the poster size. He left high praise for the system because it helped him to get the most suitable visualization solution quickly.

6 Conclusion

In this paper, we propose an approach based on user requirements for generating visualization models to assist non-expert users in clarifying their data analysis goals and deriving the most appropriate visualizations to facilitate data analysis. Compared to other approaches, our framework covers the entire process, from defining and modeling user requirements to implementing visualizations. The greatest advantage of our framework is that it effectively links user requirements with visualization solutions, making it easier for non-technical users to obtain appropriate visualization solutions without requiring in-depth knowledge of visualization techniques or data source descriptions. Additionally, we list all visualization solutions that meet the requirements, giving the user flexibility in selecting the best solution that meets their needs.

Based on the insights gained from user interviews, we plan to address additional user requirements in our future work, such as predicting future trends in the data. Additionally, we can expand the visualization scheme by including more visualizations and establishing mapping relationships. Moreover, we intend to conduct more large-scale empirical evaluations of our approach to further assess its validity and usability.

Acknowledgement. This work is partially supported by the Project of Beijing Municipal Education Commission (No. KM202110005025), the National Natural Science Foundation of China (No. 62162051), and the Beijing Natural Science Foundation Project (No. Z200002).

References

1. Bertin, J.: Semiology of Graphics. University of Wisconsin Press (1983)
2. Bikakis, N.: Big data visualization tools. arXiv preprint arXiv:1801.08336 (2018)
3. Buja, A., Cook, D., Swayne, D.F.: Interactive high-dimensional data visualization. J. Comput. Graph. Stat. 5(1), 78–99 (1996)
4. Byrd, V.L., Dwenger, N.: Activity worksheets for teaching and learning data visualization. IEEE Comput. Graph. Appl. 41(6), 25–36 (2021). https://doi.org/10.1109/MCG.2021.3115396
5. Chuai, Y., Yan, H.: Achieving the success of sustainability systemic design through data visualization approach. In: Trzcielinski, S., Mrugalska, B., Karwowski, W., Rossi, E., Di Nicolantonio, M. (eds.) AHFE 2021. LNNS, vol. 274, pp. 215–222. Springer, Cham (2021). https://doi.org/10.1007/978-3-030-80462-6_27
6. Du, M., Yuan, X.: A survey of competitive sports data visualization and visual analysis. J. Vis. 24, 47–67 (2021). https://doi.org/10.1007/s12650-020-00687-2
7. Griffin, T.: Semiology of graphics: diagrams, networks, maps. Bertin, Jacques (trans. W. j. Berg). The University of Wisconsin Press, Madison, 1983. 416 pages. ISBN 0 299 09060 4. US$75.00, cloth. Cartography 16(1), 81–82 (1987). https://doi.org/10.1080/00690805.1987.10438353

8. Hossain, S.: Visualization of bioinformatics data with dash bio. In: Calloway, C., Lippa, D., Niederhut, D., Shupe, D. (eds.) Proceedings of the 18th Python in Science Conference, pp. 126–133 (2019). https://doi.org/10.25080/Majora-7ddc1dd1-012

9. Hunter, J.D.: Matplotlib: a 2D graphics environment. Comput. Sci. Eng. **9**(03), 90–95 (2007)

10. Manyika, J., et al.: Big Data: The Next Frontier for Innovation, Competition, and Productivity. McKinsey Global Institute (2011)

11. Munzner, T.: Visualization Analysis and Design. CRC Press, Boca Raton (2014)

12. Ou, X., Zhu, Z., Chen, J., Xiao, W.: A study of data visualization of the neocoronary pneumonia epidemic. In: 2020 IEEE Eurasia Conference on IOT, Communication and Engineering (ECICE), pp. 315–317 (2020). https://doi.org/10.1109/ECICE50847.2020.9301964

13. Peña, O., Aguilera, U., López-de Ipiña, D.: Exploring LOD through metadata extraction and data-driven visualizations. Program **50**(3), 270–287 (2016)

14. Ren, P., et al.: Intelligent visualization system for big multi-source medical data based on data lake. In: Xing, C., Fu, X., Zhang, Y., Zhang, G., Borjigin, C. (eds.) WISA 2021. LNCS, vol. 12999, pp. 706–717. Springer, Cham (2021). https://doi.org/10.1007/978-3-030-87571-8_61

15. Ware, C.: Information Visualization: Perception for Design. Morgan Kaufmann, Cambridge (2019)

16. Waskom, M.L.: Seaborn: statistical data visualization. J. Open Source Softw. **6**(60), 3021 (2021)

17. Wickham, H.: ggplot2. Wiley Interdisc. Rev. Comput. Stat. **3**(2), 180–185 (2011)

18. Wu, A., et al.: AI4VIS: survey on artificial intelligence approaches for data visualization. IEEE Trans. Vis. Comput. Graph. **28**(12), 5049–5070 (2022). https://doi.org/10.1109/TVCG.2021.3099002

Comparing Different Visualizations for Feedback on Test Execution in a Model-Driven Engineering Environment

Felix Cammaerts[✉][iD] and Monique Snoeck[iD]

Research Center for Information System Engineering, KU Leuven, Leuven, Belgium
{felix.cammaerts,monique.snoeck}@kuleuven.be

Abstract. In Model-Driven Engineering (MDE), source code can be automatically generated from models such as a class diagram and statecharts. However, even under the assumption that a model is correctly translated into executable code, there is no guarantee that the models correctly capture the user requirements. The validity of a model can be asserted by means of model execution or testing the (prototype) application generated from the model. The completeness of such validation effort can be expressed in terms of model coverage of the executed scenarios. TesCaV is a Model-Based Testing (MBT) tool that provides users feedback by visualizing which test cases have been performed and which ones not yet. This allows TesCaV to be used in an educational setting as its feedback about the manual test cases can be alleviated to let students understand how to adequately test a software system. However, it remains unclear what the best way is to provide this feedback in terms of providing the user maximal information with minimal cognitive load. This research evaluates several proposed visualizations created according to information visualization principles, and makes a ranking based on a questionnaire distributed to 45 participants.

Keywords: Visual feedback · UI design · MBT · MDE

1 Introduction

Software testing is an important, however often neglected part of the software development lifecycle. A report has estimated the cost of poor software quality at \$2.08 trillion for the year 2020 in the US alone [12]. A large portion of this, namely \$1.56 trillion, has been attributed to operational failures. This means that deployed software systems contain unmitigated failures that go unreported.

An important reason for this is that little attention in education is dedicated to the topic of software testing due to the teachers often being at odds with the larger number of topics to teach. This is because a lot of time is spent on other topics, such as requirements analysis and system design [8]. This leads to graduate students not being able to live up to industry standards when it comes to software testing [16]. In fact, it has been reported that senior-level computer science students are unable to adequately test a small piece of software [4].

H. van der Aa et al. (Eds.): BPMDS 2023/EMMSAD 2023, LNBIP 479, pp. 312–326, 2023.
https://doi.org/10.1007/978-3-031-34241-7_22

Providing testing education tools allows teachers to introduce the topic of software testing to their students without losing lecture time on other topics. Such tools can also ensure that students are prepared to meet industry standards for software testing. In order to achieve this, it is important that software testing is introduced into the classroom taking into account the cognitive learning process of students [16].

An example of such an educational software testing tool is TesCaV (TESt CoverAge Visualization) which provides users with feedback on the manual tests they have performed on a software system [14]. TesCaV is a module of MERODE, a MDE approach in which a software system can be developed based on a class diagram and statecharts. Users can generate a prototype application from the models and execute scenarios to validate the models. While doing so, TesCaV provides the users with feedback on the adequacy of their testing.

Previous research has already provided evidence that TesCaV is perceived as useful for the student's learning process as well as easy to use [14] and that the use of TesCaV leads students to perform more elaborate tests on the software system [2]. Despite this positive evaluation, the use of TesCaV also evidenced room for improvement: students seem to experience testing fatigue supposedly due to the cognitive overload induced by the provided feedback. In particular, the specific aspect of the visual design of the provided feedback has not yet been evaluated. This raises the question of reconsidering the User Interface (UI) design of the tool. Previous research has pointed out that a poorly designed UI will lead to students not being intrinsically motivated, while interfaces that motivate students are realistic, easy-to-use, challenging and engaging [13]. Furthermore, other research also highlights the importance of interface consistency [18]. An inconsistent UI for web-based e-learning systems led to skilled students making more errors, while also reducing their learning satisfaction. The continued usage intention of self-paced learning tools has been reported to be impacted by two major factors [5]. These factors are the perceived functionality and perceived system support, which in turn impact the perceived usefulness and perceived ease of use respectively.

Validation and verification aim to ensure that a system meets the specified requirements. In the context of MDE, verification is the process of ensuring that the models are consistent, complete, and conform to the specifications and standards. This can involve checking the syntax and semantics of the models, as well as verifying that they adhere to the requirements and constraints of the system. Validation in MDE is the process of evaluating the models to ensure that they meet the user's requirements and expectations. This can involve simulating the models to test their behavior, as well as testing the generated code or other artifacts produced from the models.

To check the validity of a software model, feedback on the set of test scenarios used to test the model can be structured according to a number of criteria. These model validation test criteria can be broadly grouped into four main categories [15,17]: class-based criteria, transition-based criteria, state-based criteria and method-based criteria. The class-based criteria are: Class Attributes (CA),

Associations end multiplicity (AEM) and Generalization (GEN). The transition-based criteria are: All-transitions (AT), All-Loop-Free-Paths (ALFP), All-One-Loop-Paths (AOLP) and All-Loops (AL). All-States (AS) is the only state-based criterion and All-Methods (AM) is the only method-based criterion.

To the best of our knowledge, no previous research has been conducted to understand the optimal way to present the visual feedback on the level to which a set of test scenarios meets these criteria. This research will thus focus on the following research question: *Which type of visual feedback yields students with the highest perceived understanding and lowest perceived cognitive load for each of the criteria in Model-Based Testing?* To answer the research question, several possible ways of providing visual feedback for the same underlying information were investigated. These *visualizations* are presented to users for a comparative evaluation to understand which type of feedback is preferred. The results of the research will make it possible to propose visualizations that will help students to gain a better understanding of adequate software testing and, in particular, coverage. As the visualizations are based on UML Class diagrams and state-charts, even though the proposed visualizations have been designed specifically for TesCaV, similar visualizations could be proposed for other educational software testing tools.

The remainder of this paper is structured as follows: Sect. 2 gives an overview of related work on teaching of software testing. Section 3 provides an overview of the research method: how the proposed visualizations were designed and how they were evaluated. Section 4 shows the results of the evaluation, which are then discussed in Sect. 5. Finally, Sect. 6 discusses the contributions and possible future research possibilities.

2   Related Work

A wide array of software testing tools aimed at providing educational support already exists. Most of these tools are based on white-box testing, in which the internal implementation of the code is taken into consideration.

Using test-driven development, Edwards [10] has introduced an approach to teach software testing. The students are tasked to first write the tests for the software system. It has been reported that per 1000 lines of code, students had 45% less bugs. This was implemented using Web-CAT, an open-source system that allows for automatic grading [21].

CodeDefenders is a gamification approach that helps students to learn software testing based on mutation testing [19]. A student can either be an attacker or a defender. An attacker aims to find bugs in a program that were not found by the tests. A defender aims to write tests for the code snippets, so that all bugs are found, and the attacker ideally is not able to find any other bugs. An experience report, using CodeDefenders in class, has reported that students actively engage with CodeDefenders when it is offered to them and they also improve their testing skills [11].

Testing Tutor is a web-based assignment submission platform that supports different types of feedback that facilitate different levels of testing pedagogy. This is done via a customizable feedback engine [7]. Different types of feedback were evaluated during a study. The researchers concluded that students who were given conceptual feedback achieved a higher code coverage, and less redundant test cases than students who received detailed feedback [7].

Marmoset is an automated submission and testing system [22]. Marmoset can be used to provide both instructors and students feedback. To ensure that students start testing early, tokens are used to gain access to the instructor's private test cases. When students start early, it becomes possible for instructors to understand difficulties that students face and help them overcome those. Students have been reported to have a positive experience using Marmoset [22].

A tool for acceptance testing, which is a black-box testing tool, has been introduced by Sarkar and Bell [20]. Final year high school students provided feedback for possible improvements of the tool.

Model-Based testing (MBT) is a testing approach in which test cases are automatically generated from a given software model [9]. In general, MBT follows five distinct steps [24]:

1. Create a test model: a test model is designed based on the requirements of the system
2. Generate abstract test cases: abstract test cases are generated based on different criteria
3. Concretize the abstract test cases: executable testing scripts are generated from the abstract test cases
4. Execute generated test cases
5. Analyse the results of the executed test cases

TesCaV is a tool that has been introduced to provide feedback about test coverage while testing the validity of models [14]. TesCaV can be considered a MBT tool as well as -under the hood- it automatically generates test cases from a software model to calculate the coverage that has been achieved by manual testing. The test cases used by TesCaV are based on TCGen [17], which is based on a subset of the testing criteria used in [15] and [17].

The process differs however from the above steps. With TesCaV, the user usually performs the following steps:

1. Create a model (class diagram (EDG) and statecharts (FSMs)) based on the requirements.
2. Generate runnable code from the model.
3. Validate the model by means of manual execution of test scenarios with the prototype application.
4. Receive feedback on test coverage and on sequence constraints.

It is in this fourth step that TesCaV is used to provide the user with feedback on test coverage. After having received feedback about the model, the user might have to either change the model in case the requirements are not met or do more manual testing in case the coverage is too low.

What makes TesCaV different from most model-based testing tools, is that the generated test cases are not executed automatically, but are instead used to provide the user with feedback on the manual testing that has been done so far. This means that TesCaV can be used by students who are unfamiliar with software testing: they can use TesCaV's feedback to gain a better understanding of how to adequately test a software system.

3   Research Method

3.1   Visualizations Design

For each of the testing criteria of TesCaV, several visualizations are proposed. The proposed visualizations can be subdivided into three categories, namely: statechart-based (SC) visualizations, class diagram based (CD) visualizations and table-based visualizations.

The proposed visualizations depend on the nature of the testing criterion. For example, providing a statechart for providing feedback about a class-based criterion or providing a class diagram for feedback about a state-based or transition-based criterion would yield little value. For each criterion it is possible to provide feedback based on either a class diagram or statechart depending on the nature of the criterion and also to provide table-based feedback. The only exception to this is the class attribute criterion for which a class diagram according to the MERODE notation would yield too little information as it would only provide feedback about the classes, rather than about the attributes of these classes.

For each visualization, color is used as a main encoding mechanism for the information that has to be conveyed to the user. Red is used to indicate test cases that have not been covered, while orange is used for test cases that are partially covered and green is used for fully covered test cases. Examples can be found in Fig. 1 (both table-based), Fig. 3 (left: table-based, right: statechart-based) and Fig. 4 (left: class diagram based, right: table-based).

Although, as researched by Cleveland and McGill [6], the use of color ranks low in terms of the relative difficulty in assessing quantitative value, this is not an issue for us as users are familiar with these colors from traffic lights. Similarly, Spence [23, p. 60–61] mentions that color is often used for elevation maps, because it is familiar to people. Furthermore, Card also said that the purpose of information visualization is to amplify cognitive performance, not just creating interesting pictures [3]. Using the same color scheme as a traffic light, allows for a good match with the user's cognitive model and thus color can still be effective even though being placed low on the ranking of Cleveland and McGill [6].

The visualizations also make use of position. The class diagram based visualizations make use of position by highlighting different object types in the class diagram. statechart-based visualizations do something similar for the states and transitions. The table-based visualizations do not make use of position, however, they do provide a compact way to represent two-dimensional data.

Depending on the layout of the table, different types of table-based feedback can be proposed. For example, for the Class-Attribute criterion, the coverage of an object type can be highlighted in the relevant row of the table (see Fig. 1, left visualization), or instead placed in a separate column (right visualization). Similarly, Fig. 2 shows both proposed tables for the ALFP criterion. Figure 2 is also representative for the AOLP, AL and AEM criteria. The only transition-based criterion with merely one proposed table is the AT criterion. Only one table is proposed for the AT criterion because the test cases of this criterion consist of only one transition and this can be represented with only one cell in a table, without having to combine several cells to understand whether the test case has been covered. Similarly, only one table is proposed, instead of two different types of table, for the AM criterion as one cell in the table represents one test case. Nonetheless, a statechart can still be used for the AM criterion in which different transitions labels (methods) can be highlighted.

A combined visualization is also proposed for the ALFP, AOLP and AL criteria, which are transition-based criteria where test cases consist of more than one transition. The visualization uses a combination of both a statechart and a table. The statechart and the table are placed side by side as they provide different levels of detail. In a statechart it is only possible to give a transition a single color, and as a transition may be part of several test cases for these criteria, it becomes difficult to give feedback about it. The table can therefore provide more detail to the user if required. For example, consider the AOLP table + statechart visualization shown in Fig. 3. The table gives an overview of each individual path of the criterion and which transitions of these paths have already been traversed. In the statechart, it is not possible to distinguish between the different test cases, but it is possible to show better how the states and their transitions are related.

	Object type	Attribute	Tested
Covered	Job	Name	✓
Partially covered		StartDate	✗
Uncovered	Application	Name	✓
✓ tested		Date	✓
✗ not tested	Review	Date	✗

Object type	Attribute	Tested	Covered
Job	Name	✓	✗
	StartDate	✗	
Application	Name	✓	✓
	Date	✓	
Review	Date	✗	✗

✓ tested
✗ not tested

Fig. 1. Table 1 (left) and 2 (right) for the Class-Attribute criterion.

3.2 Visualizations Evaluation

In order to determine the best way to provide visual feedback for each of the different testing criteria, users will be asked to rank the proposed visualizations per criterion based on which visualization helps the user understand the criterion the most and provides the most appropriate amount of information. The visualizations were evaluated using mockups, instead of actually being

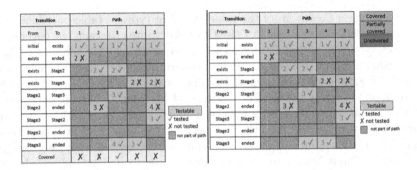

Fig. 2. Table 1 (left) and 2 (right) for the All-Loop-Free-Paths criterion.

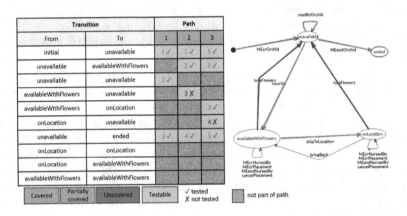

Fig. 3. Table 2 + statechart visualization for the All-One-Loop-Paths criterion.

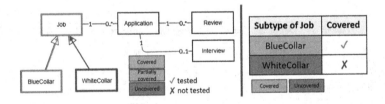

Fig. 4. Class diagram 1 (left) and Table 1 (right) visualization for the Generalization criterion.

implemented into TesCaV. This allows to incorporate feedback that is gathered about the visualizations in a less time-consuming manner.

Looking at the proposed visualizations for the ALFP, AOLP and AL criteria, there is an imbalance in the information being displayed in the components of the visualizations. Since a transition can have at most one color, the statechart component is unable to show the possible different test cases that a transition can be part of. This problem does not exist for a table, as each column in a table can be used to represent a test case of a criterion, and it can be indicated whether a transition is part of that test case or not. Assuming that users prefer to receive more information, we hypothesize that the visualizations that provide more information (statechart + table), will be preferred to the visualizations that provide less information (table only). The first hypothesis is therefore:

Hypothesis 1 (H1). *When more information is provided in a visualization it will be preferred over a visualization with less information.*

The main difference between the two types of table that are proposed for different visualizations, is the way the status (fully, partially or not covered) of a test case is displayed. For example, looking at Fig. 2, the first ALFP test case is partially covered. In the left table, this is indicated by placing a red cross in the last column, while in the right table this is indicated by the orange color of the header cell for that test case. We believe that the use of the cross and tick icons is preferable over the color coding, as this is consistent with the way that the separate elements of the test cases are represented and thus reduces the cognitive load of having to understand additional colors in a visualization. Henceforth, our second hypothesis becomes:

Hypothesis 2 (H2). *Tables in which the coverage of a test case is summarized in an extra row using crosses and ticks are preferred over tables in which the coverage of a test case is shown using a three-valued color coding.*

A questionnaire was used to evaluate these visualizations[1]. For each criterion the different visualizations were placed next to each other and the participant was asked to indicate his preference based on the question *Which visualization helps you understand the* `criterionName` *criterion best and shows you the most appropriate amount of information?* In this way, for each criterion, we can determine which type of visualization is the most intuitive (the least cognitive load and the most informative). For the criteria with only two proposed visualizations, just one comparison was requested. For the AEM criterion, three comparisons were made (Table 1 vs Table 2, class diagram vs Table 1 and class diagram vs Table 2). Four comparisons were requested for the ALFP, AOLP and AL criteria, namely: Table 1 vs Table 2, Table 1 vs Table 1 + state chart, Table 2 vs Table 2 + state chart and Table 1 + state chart vs Table 2 + state chart.

For the criteria with only one comparison, the responses to the questionnaires can be considered as votes for a visualization. However, when more than one comparison was made for a criterion, the Bradley-Terry model was used [1, pp. 436–439]. The Bradley-Terry model allows pairwise comparisons to be made and provides a ranking of the individuals in a population. The Bradley-Terry model can be used when not all individuals have been ranked against each other. In this case for example, there was no direct comparison between Table 1 vs Table 2 + statechart, for any of the criteria.

---

[1] The approval for the distribution of this questionnaire can be found under SMEC number G-2023-6238-R2(MIN).

Only visualizations for the same criterion are compared, as the intention of this research is to understand which visualization is best for each criterion separately. Given the large number of comparisons to be made, the questionnaire included an attention question in two places, so as to be able to identify respondents who were not concentrating.

The questionnaire was administered to two cohorts. The first cohort is familiar with class diagrams, statecharts and the MERODE approach. The second cohort is only familiar with class diagrams, but not with the MERODE approach or statecharts.

4   Results

A total of 45 participants have filled the questionnaire. Of these 36 were valid, meaning all questions were answered and the attention questions have been answered correctly. For the first cohort, 8 responses were received, with 6 valid submissions. These are master students who have followed a course on conceptual modelling. Their average age is 24.3 years. For the second cohort, 37 responses were received, with 30 valid submissions. These are master students who have followed a course on information system design. Their average age is 24.3 years. Participants of both cohorts are studying for a degree at the business and economics faculty. For the Bradley-Terry model 5 iterations were used to calculate the scores, as this was sufficient to obtain a clear ranking. For the single comparisons, the ranking is based on the amount of preferential votes. The results are given in Table 1. This table shows per criterion the obtained score for each visualization and a ranking of these visualizations based on those scores. The scores are given per cohort, as well as all results together. An overview of the preferred visualizations is given in Fig. 5 in the Appendix.

5   Discussion

5.1   General Discussion

For the AEM and GEN (class-based) criteria a class diagram-based visualization is the preferred visualization for both cohorts. For the AT (transition-based) and AS (state-based) criteria, the statechart is the preferred visualization for both cohorts. For the AM (method-based) criterion, the preferred visualization is the table for the two cohorts together. However, for the first cohort the preference went to the statechart, possibly due to the small sample size and/or the students being familiar with statechart.

For the ALFP, AOLP and AL (transition-based) criteria, the combination of a table and statechart is preferred over just a table. Providing evidence for H1. The table that shows the coverage of the test cases as tick marks and crosses (Fig. 2, left) is preferred over the table that shows this coverage with color coding (Fig. 2, right), thus providing evidence for H2. However, for the CA criterion, the table using the color coding is preferred over the table that does not use

Table 1. Resulting scores and rankings for the visualizations per criterion and per cohort.

Criterion	Visualization	Comparison	Coh. 1	Coh. 1 rank	Coh. 2	Coh. 2 rank	Comb. rank	Figure	Evidences
AT	SC 1	Direct	5	1	19	1	1	5b	
AT	Table 1	Direct	1	2	11	2	2		
AS	SC 1	Direct	6	1	18	1	1	5a	
AS	Table 1	Direct	0	2	12	2	2		
GEN	CD 1	Direct	6	1	25	1	1	5c	
GEN	Table 1	Direct	0	2	5	2	2	4 (right)	
AEM	CD 1	BT	3.37	1	2.84	1	1	5d	
AEM	Table 1	BT	0.14	3	0.24	3	3		H2
AEM	Table 2	BT	0.28	2	0.39	2	2		
CA	**Table 1**	Direct	5	1	26	1	1	5e	H2
CA	Table 2	Direct	1	2	4	2	2	1 (right)	
ALFP	Table 1	BT	0.16	4	0.24	4	4	2 (left)	H2
ALFP	Table 2	BT	0.35	3	0.41	3	3	2 (right)	
ALFP	**Table 1 + SC**	BT	3.27	1	2.41	1	1	5f	H1 H2
ALFP	Table 2 + SC	BT	1.11	2	1.47	2	2		H1
AOLP	Table 1	BT	0.00	4	0.28	4	4		H2
AOLP	Table 2	BT	0.31	3	0.46	3	3		
AOLP	**Table 1 + SC**	BT	3.90	1	2.38	1	1	5g	H1 H2
AOLP	Table 2 + SC	BT	1.18	2	1.32	2	2	3	H1
AL	Table 1	BT	0.08	4	0.18	4	4		H2
AL	Table 2	BT	0.44	3	0.59	3	3		
AL	**Table 1 + SC**	BT	3.06	1	2.11	1	1	5h	H1 H2
AL	Table 2 + SC	BT	1.20	2	1.49	2	2		H1
AM	**Table 1**	Direct	2	2	17	1	1	5i	
AM	SC 1	Direct	4	1	13	2	2		

color coding. Looking at the totality of preferred visualizations, it seems that the color coding is only preferred for class diagrams. These findings seem to contradict H1 to a certain extent: the three valued-color coding provides more detailed information than the (binary) ticks and crosses. On the other hand, the ticks and crosses are given in a separate summary row, whereas the colors are applied to the header row. A possible explanation for the preferences is that too much information may also lead to cognitive overload. It thus seems important to strike the correct balance between too little and too much information. Further research with eye tracking could reveal whether or not students make use of the summary information in the table-based visualizations.

These results show that for the AEM, GEN, AT, AS and AM criteria, the visualization that is currently implemented in TesCaV is preferred over the newly proposed visualizations. For the ALFP, AOLP and AL criteria, which are also the more complicated criteria, visualizations that provide a more detailed explanation to the user are preferred. In fact, the provision of a table combined with a statechart is always preferred over the provision of a table alone. This may be due to the fact that for these criteria multiple transitions need to be covered in a single statechart to cover one test case. The statechart visualizes the relations between the different states via lines and arrows, while the table provides a more detailed explanation of how the different transitions are part of one or more test cases.

5.2 Internal Validity

When interpreting the aforementioned results, it is important to consider various factors that may affect their validity. To ensure the internal validity of the questionnaire, several measures have been taken. Firstly, a pre-test was conducted with eight participants who are familiar with the MERODE approach. They filled out the same questionnaire as the analyzed participants, and their responses were used to check whether the questionnaire's questions were clear and free of technical errors. However, their responses were not included in the analyzed results. Secondly, a section of the questionnaire was dedicated to providing a brief explanation about statecharts to mitigate the impact of participants' unfamiliarity with them. Thirdly, measures were taken to prevent a learning effect that could result from showing participants the visualizations in a specific order. The visualizations were shown in a random order to each participant, and they were created for three separate, unrelated models. Fourthly, to ensure that each participant evaluated each visualization fairly, each question included a link to the full-sized image of the visualization, reducing the chance of bias occurring due to resizing. Lastly, to ensure participants' truthful responses, two attention questions were used. If at least one of these questions was answered incorrectly, the participant's responses were discarded.

Unfortunately, it was not possible to randomize the order of the visualizations within one comparison. For example, for the comparison of the All-Transitions statechart against the All-Transitions table-based visualization, the All-Transitions statechart visualization was always shown on the left due to technical constraints. Nonetheless, this is unlikely to have had a significant impact on the results as the questionnaire specifically asked participants to compare the visualizations that were shown side-by-side. Additionally, the visualizations were still placed in a different order for comparisons between a statechart and table-based visualization for a different criterion.

5.3 External Validity

To ensure that the experiment's findings can be applied to a wider population, the questionnaire was distributed to two cohorts. The first cohort had knowledge of the MERODE approach and statecharts, while the second cohort only had knowledge of class diagrams. Results from the study can be relevant to students at large who have some background knowledge on class diagrams. Furthermore, since the visualizations in the study used standard UML notations, the results can be applied to any software that uses UML class diagrams and statecharts.

6 Conclusion

6.1 Contributions

This research has proposed different visualizations for providing feedback on model coverage test criteria. A questionnaire was used to rank preferred visualizations for each test criterion. These preferred visualizations can be used in testing education software to provide better feedback on the manual testing a user has performed on a software system.

For most criteria, the currently implemented visualization in TesCaV is the preferred visualization. However, for the ALFP, AOLP and AL criteria, newly proposed visualizations were preferred over the TesCaV visualizations. From the proposed visualizations we were able to determine that for test criteria that require multiple transitions in a statechart per test scenario (ALFP, AOLP and AL), there is a preference for providing both a table and a statechart in the visualization. More generally speaking, this shows that a visualization that provides more information is preferred. However, when comparing different layouts for a table, it was found that the preference was for tables with a lower cognitive load. In this research these were tables that used ticks and crosses instead of a color coding to show the status of a test case. An overview of the preferred visualizations is given in Fig. 5 in the Appendix.

Further Research. Further research can aim to implement the proposed visualizations into TesCaV and measure the effect on learning of software testing by novice users. A possible method is using A/B testing for comparing the effect of the new visualizations to the old visualizations. With A/B testing, one group of students is given the current visualizations, while the other group is given the newly proposed best ranked visualizations. This will allow to understand which visualizations yield the highest increase in test coverage. Furthermore, the current visualizations can be further improved upon. For instance, the color codings do not take into account the needs of color blind users. A dual coding could be used as another visual variable to ensure that color blind users are also able to use the visualizations accordingly.

The visualizations themselves can also be further extended by making them interactive. For example, when considering an All-One-Loop-Paths test case, the user could hover over a transition, after which TesCaV can highlight the test cases that particular transition is part of. This would partially solve the issue of a statechart not being able to differentiate between the different test cases that one single transition might be part of in a transition-based criterion. Furthermore, the entire interface that TesCaV uses can also be improved. The visualizations proposed here merely represent one aspect of TesCaV, namely how the feedback is visualized. However, TesCaV as a complete module can be improved in terms of the user experience. For example, currently TesCaV does not recalculate the visualizations and scores if further testing is done: the user has to close and re-open the module to obtain updated feedback.

Even though previous research has provided evidence that TesCaV leads users to do more elaborate testing on a software system [2], at this point it remains unclear whether this effect persists after the usage of TesCaV. A new experimental design could be proposed to specifically evaluate the long-term effect of training with TesCaV: do user still perform better when no longer using TesCaV?

Acknowledgment. This paper has been funded by the ENACTEST Erasmus+ project number 101055874.

Appendix

(a) Preferred visualization for the AS criterion.

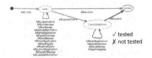

(b) Preferred visualization for the AT criterion.

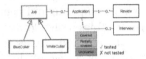

(c) Preferred visualization for the GEN criterion.

(d) Preferred visualization for the AEM criterion.

	Object type	Attribute	Tested
	Job	Name	✓
		StartDate	✗
	Application	Name	✓
		Date	✓
	Review	Date	✗

(e) Preferred visualization for the CA criterion.

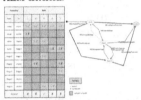

(f) Preferred visualization for the ALFP criterion.

(g) Preferred visualization for the AOLP criterion.

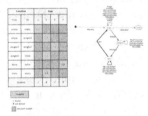

(h) Preferred visualization for the AL criterion.

(i) Preferred visualization for the AM criterion.

Fig. 5. The preferred visualization for each criterion.

References

1. Agresti, A.: Categorical Data Analysis, vol. 792. Wiley, Hoboken (2012)
2. Cammaerts, F., Verbruggen, C., Snoeck, M.: Investigating the effectiveness of model-based testing on testing skill acquisition. In: Barn, B.S., Sandkuhl, K. (eds.) PoEM 2022, pp. 3–17. Springer, Cham (2022). https://doi.org/10.1007/978-3-031-21488-2_1
3. Card, S.: Information visualization. In: Human-Computer Interaction, pp. 199–234. CRC Press (2009)
4. Carver, J.C., Kraft, N.A.: Evaluating the testing ability of senior-level computer science students. In: 2011 24th IEEE-CS Conference on Software Engineering Education and Training (CSEE&T), pp. 169–178. IEEE (2011)
5. Cho, V., Cheng, T.E., Lai, W.J.: The role of perceived user-interface design in continued usage intention of self-paced e-learning tools. Comput. Educ. **53**(2), 216–227 (2009)
6. Cleveland, W.S., McGill, R.: Graphical perception: theory, experimentation, and application to the development of graphical methods. J. Am. Stat. Assoc. **79**(387), 531–554 (1984)
7. Cordova, L., Carver, J., Gershmel, N., Walia, G.: A comparison of inquiry-based conceptual feedback vs. traditional detailed feedback mechanisms in software testing education: an empirical investigation. In: Proceedings of the 52nd ACM Technical Symposium on Computer Science Education, pp. 87–93 (2021)
8. Cowling, T.: Stages in teaching software testing. In: 2012 34th International Conference on Software Engineering (ICSE), pp. 1185–1194. IEEE (2012)
9. Dalal, S.R., et al.: Model-based testing in practice. In: Proceedings of the 21st International Conference on Software Engineering, pp. 285–294 (1999)
10. Edwards, S.H.: Teaching software testing: automatic grading meets test-first coding. In: Companion of the 18th Annual ACM SIGPLAN Conference on Object-Oriented Programming, Systems, Languages, and Applications, pp. 318–319 (2003)
11. Fraser, G., Gambi, A., Kreis, M., Rojas, J.M.: Gamifying a software testing course with code defenders. In: Proceedings of the 50th ACM Technical Symposium on Computer Science Education, pp. 571–577 (2019)
12. Krasner, H.: The cost of poor software quality in the US: a 2020 report. In: Proceedings of Consortium Information and Software, QualityTM (CISQTM) (2021)
13. Lewis, R., Stoney, S., Wild, M.: Motivation and interface design: maximising learning opportunities. J. Comput. Assist. Learn. **14**(1), 40–50 (1998)
14. Marín, B., Alarcón, S., Giachetti, G., Snoeck, M.: TesCaV: an approach for learning model-based testing and coverage in practice. In: Dalpiaz, F., Zdravkovic, J., Loucopoulos, P. (eds.) RCIS 2020. LNBIP, vol. 385, pp. 302–317. Springer, Cham (2020). https://doi.org/10.1007/978-3-030-50316-1_18
15. Marín, B., Gallardo, C., Quiroga, D., Giachetti, G., Serral, E.: Testing of model-driven development applications. Softw. Qual. J. **25**, 407–435 (2017)
16. Marín, B., Vos, T.E., Paiva, A.C., Fasolino, A.R., Snoeck, M.: ENACTEST-European innovation alliance for testing education. In: RCIS Workshops (2022)
17. Pérez, C., Marín, B.: Automatic generation of test cases from UML models. CLEI Electron. J **21**(1) (2018)
18. Rhee, C., Moon, J., Choe, Y.: Web interface consistency in e-learning. Online Inf. Rev. **30**(1), 53–69 (2006)
19. Rojas, J.M., Fraser, G.: Code defenders: a mutation testing game. In: 2016 IEEE Ninth International Conference on Software Testing, Verification and Validation Workshops (ICSTW), pp. 162–167. IEEE (2016)

20. Sarkar, A., Bell, T.: Teaching black-box testing to high school students. In: Proceedings of the 8th Workshop in Primary and Secondary Computing Education, pp. 75–78 (2013)
21. Shah, A.R.: Web-cat: a web-based center for automated testing. Ph.D. thesis, Virginia Tech (2003)
22. Spacco, J., Hovemeyer, D., Pugh, W., Emad, F., Hollingsworth, J.K., Padua-Perez, N.: Experiences with marmoset: designing and using an advanced submission and testing system for programming courses. ACM SIGCSE Bull. **38**(3), 13–17 (2006)
23. Spence, R.: Information Visualization, vol. 1. Springer, Heidelberg (2001)
24. Utting, M., Legeard, B.: Practical Model-Based Testing: A Tools Approach. Elsevier, Amsterdam (2010)

Unblocking Inductive Miner
While Preserving Desirable Properties

Tsung-Hao Huang(✉) and Wil M. P. van der Aalst

Process and Data Science (PADS), RWTH Aachen University, Aachen, Germany
{tsunghao.huang,wvdaalst}@pads.rwth-aachen.de

Abstract. Process discovery aims to discover models to explain the behaviors of information systems. The Inductive Miner (IM) discovery algorithm is able to discover process models with desirable properties: free-choiceness and soundness. Moreover, a family of variations makes IM practical for real-life applications. Due to the advantages, IM is regarded as the state of the art and has been implemented in commercial process mining software. However, IM can only discover block-structured process models that tend to have high fitness but low precision. To improve the quality of process models discovered by IM while preserving desirable properties, we propose an approach that applies property-preserving (free-choiceness and soundness) reduction/synthesis rules to iteratively modify the process model. The experimental results show that the models discovered by our approach have a more flexible representation while preserving desirable properties. Moreover, the model quality, as measured by the F1-score, is improved compared to the original models.

Keywords: Process Discovery · Free-choice Net · Synthesis Rules

1 Introduction

Process mining provides a wide variety of techniques for stakeholders to gain data-driven insights. To name just a few, process discovery, conformance checking, performance analysis, predictive monitoring, and process enhancement are examples that process mining can offer [1]. Process discovery aims to discover process models that can reflect the behavior of information systems. As a prerequisite for many other techniques, process discovery plays an essential role in a process mining project. Once a process model is discovered from the event log (generated during the process execution in the corresponding information systems), the stakeholders can apply further process mining techniques to generate insights for optimization.

Generally, a discovery algorithm is evaluated by analyzing the process models it discovered. Four dimensions are usually considered: fitness, precision, generalization, and simplicity [1]. Moreover, process models with properties such as free-choiceness and soundness are preferable. On the one hand, a sound process model ensures the absence of apparent anomalies such as dead components

© The Author(s), under exclusive license to Springer Nature Switzerland AG 2023
H. van der Aa et al. (Eds.): BPMDS 2023/EMMSAD 2023, LNBIP 479, pp. 327–342, 2023.
https://doi.org/10.1007/978-3-031-34241-7_23

(e.g., transitions that can never be executed) in a model [1]. On the other hand, a free-choice process model has separated constructs for choice and synchronization. Such constructs are naturally embedded in other widely-used and high-level notations such as BPMN (split and join connectors). Consequently, it is straightforward to convert free-choice nets to other notations. Last but not least, an abundance of analysis techniques from theory [12] are available for free-choice models.

The state-of-the-art process discovery algorithm - the Inductive Miner (IM) - can discover process models with the properties mentioned above by exploiting the representation of process trees. By design, the converted Petri net from a process tree is always sound and free-choice. However, a process tree has limited expressive power as the resulting models can only be block-structured, i.e., process models that can be separated into parts with a single entry and exit [20]. As a result, when applying IM to discover models with non-block structures, the quality of the discovered models is often compromised. Specifically, the discovered models usually have high fitness but low precision.

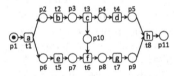

(a) A process model W_{out} with non-block structures. The behaviors cannot be modeled by a process tree without duplicate activity labels.

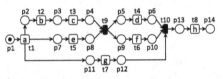

(b) A model W_{in} discovered by the IMf (with default value 0.2 for the noise threshold) using the log generated by W_{out}.

Fig. 1. An example showing the problem when applying the Inductive Miner to discover a process model with non-block structures. W_{in} allows much more behaviors (low precision) that are not possible in W_{out} as activity g is concurrent to many other activities. At the same time, W_{in} introduces additional constraints that are not in W_{out}, e.g., activity d can only be executed after activity e.

Figure 1 shows an example that motivates the proposed approach. Figure 1a is a process model W_{out} with non-block structures. In model W_{out}, there are two concurrent branches after activity a but at the same time, there exists a dependency between them. Using one of the most used IM variants: Inductive Miner - infrequent (IMf) to discover a process model from a log generated by W_{out}, the discovered model would be W_{in} in Fig. 1b. One can see that the behaviors of the two models (W_{out} and W_{in}) are different. Using process trees as the internal representations, no variations of IM can ever discover a model with the same behavior expressed by W_{out} without duplicate activities. Nevertheless, its scalability and guarantees of desirable properties still make it an attractive option for real-life applications.

To improve the quality of the models discovered by the IM while preserving desirable properties, we propose an approach to iteratively modify a model discovered by the IM. Taking a log and the corresponding model (discovered by

IM) as input, the approach iteratively modifies the model by applying the reduction/synthesis rules. Both reduction and synthesis rules are property-preserving (free-choiceness and soundness). Experiments using publicly available real-life event logs show that the quality (w.r.t. F1-score) of the models discovered by IM is indeed improved by our approach. Moreover, the modified models are always sound and free-choice thanks to the property-preserving reduction rules [12,19].

The remainder of the paper is organized as follows. We review the related work in Sect. 2 and define necessary concepts in Sect. 3. Sect. 4 introduces the approach. Section 5 presents the experiment and Sect. 6 concludes the paper.

2   Related Work

A comprehensive overview of process discovery approaches can be found in [8, 15]. While various process discovery algorithms have been proposed, only a few ensure both soundness and free-choiceness. The Inductive Miner (IM) exploits process trees to guarantee both properties. However, the resulting models are confined to be block-structured. Using process trees to model a process with non-block structures often results in process models with compromised quality. Several approaches [7,9,11] can discover non-block structured models but cannot ensure both properties.

Another group of approaches ensures the desirable properties by applying synthesis rules from free-choice net theory [12]. Dixit et al. [14] were among the first to use synthesis rules for process discovery. The focus was on enabling the interactive setting of process discovery, which requires constant feedback from users with domain knowledge. Nevertheless, the ideal models often cannot be discovered without going back and forth by a combination of reduction and synthesis rules [14]. Furthermore, to recommend to the user the most prominent modifications, the approach needs to evaluate all the possibilities. To address the problems, [18,19] introduces the Synthesis Miner to automate the discovery by introducing predefined patterns using synthesis rules and a search space pruning mechanism.

A closely related field to our proposed approach is process model repair where an existing process model is modified for the purpose of enhancement. Given an existing model and a log containing the behaviors that cannot be replayed by the model, an approach is proposed in [16] to add behaviors to the model locally such that the resulting model can incorporate all the behaviors in the log while staying as similar as possible to the existing model. Instead of fixing all the identified problems (misalignments) as in [16], the approach in [22] prioritizes the changes with the highest impact on fitness. The model repair approaches mentioned so far [16,22] have a tendency toward fitness (being able to replay all the traces) while ignoring other quality dimensions, which often leads to over-generalized models. To avoid the over-generalization pitfall, an interactive repair approach is proposed in [6], where users are expected to provide feedback after viewing the visualization of the mismatches between the event log and the process model. Nevertheless, all the approaches discussed above [6,16,22] do not guarantee sound and free-choice process models.

3   Preliminaries

In this section, we introduce the concepts used throughout this paper. For some set A, $\mathcal{B}(A)$ is the set of all multisets over A. For some multiset $b \in \mathcal{B}(A)$, $b(a)$ denotes the number of times element $a \in A$ appears in b. For example, if $A = \{x, y, z\}$, then $b = [x, y^6, z^8] \in \mathcal{B}(A)$ is a multiset consisting of 15 elements. $b(z) = 8$ as z appears eight times in b. $\sigma = \langle a_1, a_2, ..., a_n \rangle \in A^*$ denotes a sequence over A with length $|\sigma| = n$. For $1 \leq i \leq |\sigma|$, $\sigma(i) = a_i$ denotes the i-th element of σ. For instance, $\sigma_s = \langle x, y, x, z \rangle \in A^*$, $|\sigma_s| = 4$, and $\sigma_s(3) = x$. $\langle \rangle$ is the empty sequence. Given two sequences σ and σ', $\sigma \cdot \sigma'$ is the concatenation, e.g., $\langle b \rangle \cdot \langle a, c \rangle = \langle b, a, c \rangle$.

Definition 1 (Sequence Projection). *Let A be a set and $X \subseteq A$ be a subset of A. For $\sigma \in A^*$ and $a \in A$, $\lceil_X \in A^* \to X^*$ is a projection function defined recursively with (1) $\langle \rangle \lceil_X = \langle \rangle$ and (2)*

$$(\langle a \rangle \cdot \sigma) \lceil_X = \begin{cases} \langle a \rangle \cdot \sigma \lceil_X, & \textit{if } a \in X \\ \sigma \lceil_X, & \textit{otherwise} \end{cases}$$

For example, $\langle a, b, a \rangle \lceil_{\{a,c\}} = \langle a, a \rangle$. Projection can also be applied to multisets of sequences, e.g., $[\langle a, b, c \rangle^6, \langle a, b, b \rangle^6, \langle b, a, c \rangle^2] \lceil_{\{b,c\}} = [\langle b, c \rangle^8, \langle b, b \rangle^6]$.

Definition 2 (Activities, Trace, and Log). *$\mathcal{U}_A$ is the universe of activities. A trace $\sigma \in \mathcal{U}_A^*$ is a sequence of activities. A log is a multiset of traces, i.e., $L \in \mathcal{B}(\mathcal{U}_A^*)$.*

Definition 3 (Petri Net & Labeled Petri Net). *A Petri net is a tuple $N = (P, T, F)$, where P is the set of places, T is the set of transitions, $P \cap T = \emptyset$, $F \subseteq (P \times T) \cup (T \times P)$ is the set of arcs. A labeled Petri net $N = (P, T, F, l)$ is a Petri net with a labeling function $l \in T \nrightarrow \mathcal{U}_A$ mapping transitions to activities. For any $x \in P \cup T$, $\bullet x = \{y | (y, x) \in F\}$ denotes the set of input nodes and $x \bullet = \{y | (x, y) \in F\}$ denotes the set of output nodes.*

Note that the labeling function could be partial. If a transition $t \in T$ is not in the domain of l, i.e., $t \notin dom(l)$, it has no label. In such a case, we also write $l(t) = \tau$ to indicate that the transition is silent or invisible. In the labeled Petri net W_{in} of Fig. 1b, transition $t9 \notin dom(l)$ so we say that $t9$ is a silent transition. In this paper, we assume the visible transitions of a labeled Petri net have unique labels, i.e., $\forall_{t_1, t_2 \in T \wedge l(t_1), l(t_2) \in dom(l)} (l(t_1) = l(t_2) \Rightarrow t_1 = t_2)$.

Definition 4 (Free-choice Net). *Let $N = (P, T, F)$ be a Petri Net. N is a free-choice net if for any $t_1, t_2 \in T : \bullet t_1 = \bullet t_2$ or $\bullet t_1 \cap \bullet t_2 = \emptyset$.*

Observe that both nets in Fig. 1 are free-choice nets.

Definition 5 (Path, Elementary Path, Strongly Connected Petri net). *A path of a Petri net $N = (P, T, F)$ is a non-empty sequence of nodes $\rho = \langle x_1, x_2, ..., x_n \rangle$ such that $(x_i, x_{i+1}) \in F$ for $1 \leq i < n$. ρ is an elementary path if*

$x_i \neq x_j$ for $1 \leq i < j \leq n$. For $X, X' \in P \cup T$, $elemPaths(X, X', N) \subseteq (P \cup T)^*$ is the set of all elementary paths from some $x \in X$ to some $x' \in X'$. N is strongly connected if for any two nodes x and y, there is a path from x to y.

Definition 6 (Marking). *Let $N = (P, T, F)$ be a Petri Net. A marking $M \in \mathcal{B}(P)$ is a multiset of places. (N, M) is a marked Petri net.*

A transition t is *enabled* in marking M if each of its input places has a token, i.e., $\forall_{p \in \bullet t} M(p) > 0$. Tokens are graphically represented as black dots. An enabled transition can fire. Firing a transition consumes a token from each of its input places and produces a token for each output place. A transition is dead in marking M if no reachable marking enables t.

Definition 7 (Workflow Net (WF-net)). *Let $N = (P, T, F, l)$ be a labeled Petri net, $M_{init}, M_{final} \in \mathcal{B}(P)$ be the initial and final marking respectively. A workflow net (WF-net) is a triplet (N, M_{init}, M_{final}) such that (1) there exists a source place $i \in P : \bullet i = \emptyset$ and a sink place $o \in P : o\bullet = \emptyset$. (2) $M_{init} = [i]$ and $M_{final} = [o]$ (3) the net $N' = (P, T', F', l)$ is strongly connected, where $t' \notin T$, $T' = \{t'\} \cup T$ and $F' = F \cup (o, t') \cup (t', i)$.*

In Fig. 1b, W_{in} is a WF-net with $M_{init} = [p1]$ and $M_{final} = [p14]$. An important property of WF-net is soundness. Three properties [1] need to be held for a WF-net to be sound (1) safeness: places cannot have multiple tokens in any reachable marking (2) option to complete: it is always possible to reach the marking in which only the sink place is marked (3) no dead transitions. Both W_{out} and W_{in} in Fig. 1 fulfill the three properties.

Definition 8 (Reachable Markings & Complete Firing Sequences [2]). *Let $W = (N, M_{init}, M_{final})$ be a WF-net with $N = (P, T, F, l)$ a labeled Petri net. $M[t\rangle M'$ denotes that t is enabled in marking M and the resulting marking M' of firing t is $M' = (M \setminus \bullet t) \cup t\bullet$. Let $\sigma \in T^*$ be a sequence of transitions. $M[\sigma\rangle M'$ denotes that there exists a set of marking $M_1, M_2, ..., M_{n+1}$ such that $M_1 = M, M_{n+1} = M'$, and $M[\sigma(i)\rangle M'$ for $1 \leq i \leq n$, i.e., σ is an enabled firing sequence leading from M to M'. M' is a reachable marking from M if $\exists_{\sigma \in T^*} M[\sigma\rangle M'$. $cfs(W) = \{\sigma \in T^* | M_{init}[\sigma\rangle M_{final}\}$ is the set of complete firing sequences of the WF-net W, i.e., all enabled firing sequence leading from the initial marking M_{init} to the final marking M_{final}.*

For W_{in} in Fig. 1a, $\sigma_1 = \langle t1, t2, t3, t5, t7, t9, t4, t6, t10, t8 \rangle \in cfs(W_{in})$ is a complete firing sequence. Firing a transition t in a WF-net is equivalent to executing an activity $l(t)$ if $t \in dom(l)$. Applying the labeling function to a sequence, we get the corresponding trace of the WF-net, e.g., $l(\sigma_1) = \langle a, b, c, e, g, d, f, h \rangle$. Note that, if a transition of a complete firing sequence has no label, it is simply skipped in the corresponding trace.

Definition 9 (Traces of a WF-net [2]). *Let $W = (N, M_{init}, M_{final})$ be a WF-net. $lang(W) = \{l(\sigma) | \sigma \in cfs(W)\}$ is the set of traces possible in W. $act^b(W) = \{\sigma(i) | \sigma \in lang(W) \wedge 1 \leq i \leq |\sigma|\}$ is the set of activities possible in W.*

Definition 10 (Adding Artificial Start & End Activities [2]). ▶ $\notin \mathcal{U}_A$ *and* ■ $\notin \mathcal{U}_A$ *are two special activities indicating the start and end of a trace. For any log* $L \in \mathcal{B}(\mathcal{U}_A^*)$, $\hat{L} = [\langle ▶ \rangle \cdot \sigma \cdot \langle ■ \rangle | \sigma \in L]$. *For any* $S \subseteq \mathcal{U}_A^*$, $\hat{S} = \{\langle ▶ \rangle \cdot \sigma \cdot \langle ■ \rangle | \sigma \in S\}$.

Definition 11 (Directly-Follows Relations of a Log and a WF-net [2]). *Let* $L \in \mathcal{B}(\mathcal{U}_A^*)$ *be a log and* $W = (N, M_{init}, M_{final})$ *be a WF-net.*

- $act(L) = [a \in \sigma | \sigma \in L]$ *is the multiset of activities in log* L.
- $df(L) = [(\sigma(i), \sigma(i+1)) | \sigma \in \hat{L} \wedge 1 \leq i < |\sigma|]$ *is the multiset of directly-follows relations in the log.*
- $df^p(W) = \{(\sigma(i), \sigma(i+1)) | \sigma \in \hat{S} \wedge 1 \leq i < |\sigma|\}$ *(where* $S = lang(W)$*) is the set of possible directly-follows relations according to* W.

Note that the special start and end activities have been added (Definition 10) to the traces in $\hat{L}$ and $\hat{S}$. For a log $L = [\langle b, c \rangle^8, \langle b, a \rangle^6]$, the log after adding the start/end activities would be $\hat{L} = [\langle ▶, b, c, ■ \rangle^8, \langle ▶, b, a, ■ \rangle^6]$ and the multiset of directly-follows relations is $df(L) = [(▶, b)^{14}, (b, c)^8, (c, ■)^8, (b, a)^6, (a, ■)^6]$.

4   Approach

In this section, we present the proposed approach. As shown in Fig. 2, the approach takes a log L and a WF-net W discovered by the IM as inputs. Internally,

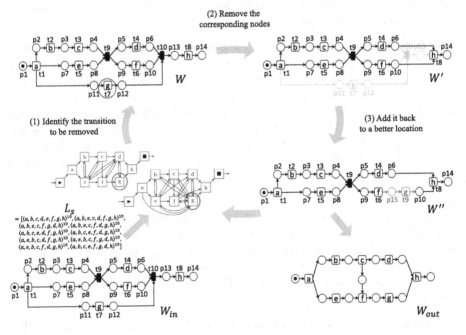

Fig. 2. An example showing a single iteration of our approach.

the input WF-net is iteratively modified in order to produce a better model w.r.t. F1-score[1], which is the harmonic mean of the fitness and precision measures.

The general procedure of each iteration is to (1) identify the transition to be removed, (2) remove the corresponding nodes (transitions and possibly also places) from the WF-net, and (3) add it back to a better location w.r.t. F1-score. In the following subsections, we introduce each step more precisely. We use the following log L_s and the corresponding WF-net W_{in} (in Fig. 1b) discovered by the IM and as the running example.

$$L_s = [\langle a, b, c, d, e, f, g, h\rangle^{10}, \langle a, b, e, c, d, f, g, h\rangle^{10}, \langle a, b, e, c, f, g, d, h\rangle^{10},$$
$$\langle a, b, e, c, f, d, g, h\rangle^{10}, \langle a, b, c, e, d, f, g, h\rangle^{10}, \langle a, b, c, e, f, d, g, h\rangle^{10},$$
$$\langle a, e, b, c, d, f, g, h\rangle^{10}, \langle a, e, b, c, f, g, d, h\rangle^{10}, \langle a, e, b, c, f, d, g, h\rangle^{10},$$
$$\langle a, b, c, e, f, g, d, h\rangle^{10}]$$

4.1   Identification of the Transition to Be Removed

In each iteration, we start by identifying the transition to be removed. We compare the directly-follows relations from the input log L and WF-net W to identify the target transition. The basic idea is to find the activity $a^\times$ with the most different directly-follows relations in L and W. Subsequently, the corresponding transition $t^\times$ can be identified using the activity label $a^\times$.

As noise or infrequent behaviors can pose additional challenges for process discovery algorithms, we filter out the infrequent behaviors in the set of directly-follows relations to make the proposed approach noise-tolerant.

Definition 12 (Filtered Directly-Follows Relations [20]). *Let $L \in \mathcal{B}(\mathcal{U}_A^*)$ be a log and $a \in act(L) \cup \{\blacktriangleright, \blacksquare\}$.*

- *$maxOut(a, L) = max(\{df(L)(a, b)|(a, b) \in df(L)\})$ is the weight of the most frequent directly-follows relations with activity a being the preceding activity.*
- *$dff(L, \omega) = \{(x, y)|((x, y) \in df(L)) \wedge (df(L)(x, y) \geq maxOut(x, L) \times \omega)\}$ is the set of filtered directly-follows relations with $0 \leq \omega \leq 1$ as the noise threshold.*

One can think of this as filtering the edges on the corresponding Directly-Follows Graph (DFG). For every activity a, the outgoing edges are filtered out if they occur less than ω times the most frequent outgoing edges of a. The default value for ω is 0.2 [20]. Next, we define the pre- and post-set of activity in a log and a model based on the (filtered) directly-follows relations. Then, the similarity score of an activity is defined based on the differences of its (filtered) directly-follows relations in the log and the model.

Definition 13 (Preset, Postset, and Similarity Score). *Let $L \in \mathcal{B}(\mathcal{U}_A^*)$ be a log, $a \in \mathcal{U}_A^*$ be an activity, and $W = (N, M_{init}, M_{final})$ be a WF-net.*

- *$pre(a, L, \omega) = \{b|(b, a) \in dff(L, \omega)\}$ is the set of activities that activity a directly-follows according to the filtered directly-follows relations $dff(L, \omega)$.*

---

[1] We use the following formula for the F1-score: $2 \cdot \frac{precision \cdot fitness}{precision + fitness}$.

- $post(a, L, \omega) = \{b | (a, b) \in dff(L, \omega)\}$. *is the set of activities that directly-follow activity a according to the filtered directly-follows relations $dff(L, \omega)$.*
- $pre^b(a, W) = \{b | (b, a) \in df^b(W)\}$ *is the set of activities that activity a directly-follows in the traces possible according to W.*
- $post^b(a, W) = \{b | (a, b) \in df^b(W)\}$ *is the set of activities that directly-follow activity a in the traces possible according to W.*
- $sim(a, W, L, \omega) = \frac{1}{2} \times \frac{|pre(a,L,\omega) \cap pre^b(a,W)|}{|pre(a,L,\omega) \cup pre^b(a,W)|} + \frac{1}{2} \times \frac{|post(a,L,\omega) \cap post^b(a,W)|}{|post(a,L,\omega) \cup post^b(a,W)|}$ *is the similarity score of the activity a based on the difference of its directly-follows relations in L and W.*
- $simMin(W, L, \omega) = \{a \in A | \forall_{b \in A} sim(a, W, L, \omega) \leq sim(b, W, L, \omega)\}$ *(where $A = act(L) \cap act^b(W))$ is the set of activities with the lowest similarity score.*

With DFGs, Fig. 3 shows the filtered[2] directly-follows relations of the running example, log L_s (Fig. 3a) and model W_{in} (Fig. 3b). Taking activity h as an example, $pre(h, L_s, 0.2) = \{d, g\}$, $pre^b(h, W_{in}) = \{d, f, g\}$, and $post(h, L_s, 0.2) = post^b(h, W_{in}) = \{\blacksquare\}$. Hence, the similarity score is $sim(h, W_{in}, L_s) = \frac{1}{2} \times \frac{2}{3} + \frac{1}{2} \times 1 = \frac{5}{6}$. The function $simMin(W_{in}, L_s, 0.2) = \{g\}$ calculates the similarity score of all the activities and returns the one(s)[3] with the lowest score, which is activity g in this case. One can also observe that from the two DFGs in Fig. 3, as g is concurrent to all the other activities except for a and h in W_{in}, which results in very different directly-follows relations in the two graphs.

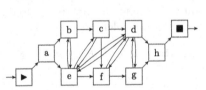

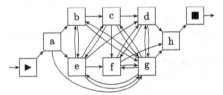

(a) The DFG showing the directly-follows relations of L_s.

(b) The DFG showing the directly-follows relations of W_{in}.

Fig. 3. Two directly-follows graphs (DFGs) showing the directly-follows relations of the running example, log L_s and model W_{in}.

Once we get the target activity $a^\times$, the next step is to remove the corresponding transition $t^\times$ from the WF-net. As has been seen in Fig. 2, for our running example, $a^\times = g$ and $t^\times = t7$.

4.2   Removal of the Corresponding Nodes

Since we are only interested in the WF-nets with desirable properties: soundness and free-choiceness, we need to ensure the removal of the corresponding transition $t^\times$ from the WF-net can keep the properties. Additionally, we would like

---

[2] Note that none of the directly-follows relations are filtered out using the default noise threshold for our running example L_s as most of the relations are frequent.

[3] There can be multiple activities with the same lowest similarity score. In such a case, we randomly choose one from the set.

to make sure that the language of the resulting WF-net W' is the same as the original WF-net W if we only consider the activities that exist in both nets, i.e., $lang(W)\lceil_{act^b(W')} = lang(W')$ (see Definition 1 and 9).

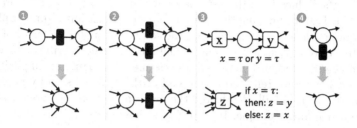

Fig. 4. Behavior preserving reduction rules based on [4,21].

To achieve all the conditions mentioned above, a straightforward and naive approach is to relabel $t^{\times}$ to silent transition τ. However, such a naive solution would potentially leave a lot of silent transitions in the final WF-net. Therefore, after relabeling $t^{\times}$ to be silent, we apply the behavior-preserving reduction rules [4] based on Murata [21] to remove the redundant silent transitions. Figure 4 shows the reduction rules that are used in this paper.

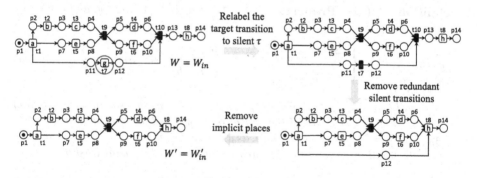

Fig. 5. Applying the reduction step to the running example.

The reduction rules are able to preserve soundness and behaviors but not necessarily free-choiceness. The rule of question is the third one in Fig. 4. For example, let the transition labeled by x be t. Imagine there exists a transition t' with the same input place as t, i.e., $\bullet t' = \bullet t$. After the reduction, the free-choice property can be violated. The reason is that the transition labeled by z and transition t' should have the same set of input places (by Definition 4) but this may not be the case. Thus, we check the free-choice property of the resulting net and only accept the change if it is also a free-choice net.

Removing the silent transitions using the rules specified above can also leave redundant (also called implicit) places in the resulting net. As implicit places have been well-studied and a formal definition is out of the scope, we refer to [10,17] for more details. In general, a place is implicit if removing it does not change the behavior of the net. As shown in Fig. 5, place $p12$ is an implicit place obtained after removing the redundant silent transitions. Implicit places are often not desirable as they can increase the computational complexity of analysis algorithms. Moreover, simplicity and readability are crucial criteria for a process model. Having redundant places in a process model impairs its simplicity. Thus, the implicit places are removed at the end of the removal step by applying the technique specified in [10]. We denote the resulting net after the removal step as W'. For our running example, $W' = W'_{in}$, as shown in Fig. 5.

4.3   Relocation

In the last step of the iteration, we try to find a better location on the WF-net W' w.r.t. F1-score to add a transition (hereafter denoted as t^+) labeled by $a^\times$. In general, the suitable location to add t^+ should be located between the transitions labeled by the preceding and following (in terms of the causal relations) activities of activity $a^\times$. Thus, we use the causal relationship among activities in the log to identify the preceding and following activities. In the following, we formally define a few log properties to illustrate the idea.

Definition 14 (Log Properties [19]). *Let $L \in \mathcal{B}(\mathcal{U}_A^*)$ be a log and $a, b \in \mathcal{U}_A$ be two activities.*

- $caus(a, b, L) = \begin{cases} \frac{df(L)(a,b)-df(L)(b,a)}{df(L)(a,b)+df(L)(b,a)+1} & \text{if } a \neq b \\ \frac{df(L)(a,b)}{df(L)(a,b)+1} & \text{if } a = b \end{cases}$ *is the strength of causal relation (a, b).*

- $A_\theta^{pre}(a, L) = \{a_{pre} \in \mathcal{U}_A | caus(a_{pre}, a, L) \geq \theta\}$ *is the set of a's preceding activities with a strength of the causal relationship that is at least θ.*

- $A_\theta^{fol}(a, L) = \{a_{fol} \in \mathcal{U}_A | caus(a, a_{fol}, L) \geq \theta\}$ *is the set of a's following activities with a strength of the causal relationship that is at least θ.*

For the running example, we would like to find the preceding and following activities for activity $a^\times = g$ by applying the last two functions in Definition 14. Using the default threshold value for θ (0.9) [19], we get the set of preceding activities as $A_\theta^{pre}(g, L_s) = \{f\}$ and the set of following activities as $A_\theta^{fol}(g, L_s) = \{h\}$. Afterward, we consider every node on the elementary path (Definition 5) between the sets of preceding and following activities as the suitable location. As shown in Fig. 6, the suitable location would be $\{t6, p10, t8\}$.

Same to the removal step, we also want the resulting net W'' of the relocation step to be free-choice and sound after adding transition t^+ to the suitable location. Accordingly, we apply the patterns defined in [19] to modify the WF-net W' from the removal step. The patterns (including skipping and looping, etc.) are defined based on the synthesis rules introduced in the free-choice net

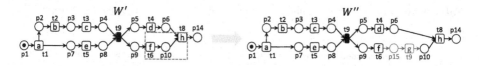

Fig. 6. Adding a transition labeled by activity g back to the WF-net.

theory [12]. Following the synthesis rules ensures that the two properties can be preserved [13,19]. For the formal definitions of the patterns and rules, we refer to [12,19].

Applying the patterns results in a set of candidates (WF-nets). The candidates are then evaluated based on the alignment-based precision [5] and fitness [3] scores. After that, the candidate with the highest F1-score is selected for the next iteration. As shown in Fig. 6, W'' is the resulting WF-net after adding transition t^+. The loop continues until no further improvements are made w.r.t. the F1-score for three consecutive iterations, which can be set by the users as well.

5 Evaluation

In this section, we evaluate our approach and discuss the experimental results. The approach is implemented[4] in Python using PM4Py[5].

5.1 Experimental Setup

For the experiment, we would like to compare the quality of the WF-nets before and after using our approach. The inputs are an event log L and the corresponding WF-net W discovered by the Inductive Miner. We apply the most widely used IM variation: Inductive Miner-Infrequent (IMf). Two publicly available real-life event logs are used, which are BPI2017[6] and Road Traffic Fine Management[7] (hereafter traffic) respectively. Using the event prefixes, BPI2017 is split into two sub-logs, BPI2017A and BPI2017O. For each log, we apply IMf using six different values (0.0, 0.1, 0.2, 0.3, 0.4, and 0.5) for the noise filter threshold and choose two models with the highest F1-scores. In total, we have six different model-log pairs that will be used as input for our approach.

5.2 Results

Table 1 shows the results of the experiment. The left-hand side of the table records the quality of the input models w.r.t. precision, fitness, and F1-score while the right-hand side of the table records the same for the output models after using our approach.

---

[4] https://git.rwth-aachen.de/tsunghao.huang/unblockIM.

[5] https://pm4py.fit.fraunhofer.de/.

[6] https://doi.org/10.4121/uuid:3926db30-f712-4394-aebc-75976070e91f.

[7] https://doi.org/10.4121/uuid:270fd440-1057-4fb9-89a9-b699b47990f5.

Table 1. Results showing the changes in model quality before/after using our approach.

	before					after			
	IMf-filter	model-id	precision	fitness	F1-score	model-id	precision	fitness	F1-score
BPI2017A	0.2	1	0.936	0.999	0.967	7	0.936	0.999	0.967
	0.4	2	0.999	0.948	0.973	8	0.996	0.960	0.978
BPI2017O	0.2	3	0.907	0.997	0.945	9	0.956	0.997	0.998
	0.5	4	1.000	0.957	0.978	10	1.000	0.989	0.995
traffic	0.2	5	0.555	0.958	0.703	11	0.734	0.961	0.832
	0.4	6	0.752	0.862	0.803	12	0.901	0.865	0.883

Except for model 1 (whose resulting model (model 7) is essentially the same), the F1-scores of all other models increase. Moreover, almost all of the output models show improvements in both precision and fitness. The only exception appears in models 2 and 8, where there is a trade-off between precision and

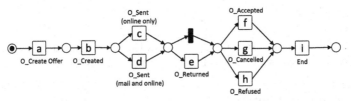

(a) Before (model-id:3): activity f ($O\_Accepted$) does not have to follow activity e ($O\_Returned$). However, the behaviors in the log suggest such a restriction.

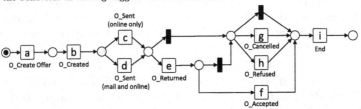

(b) After (model-id:9): activity f ($O\_Accepted$) can only be preceded by activity e ($O\_Returned$). Also, activities c, d, and e can now be directly followed by activity i.

Before (model-id: 3)

	a	b	c	d	e	f	g	h	i
a	#	>	#	#	#	#	#	#	#
b	<	#	>	>	#	#	#	#	#
c	#	<	#	>	>	>	>	>	#
d	#	<	#	#	>	>	>	>	#
e	#	#	<	<	#	>	>	>	#
f	#	#	<	<	<	#	#	#	>
g	#	#	<	<	<	#	#	#	>
h	#	#	<	<	<	#	#	#	>
i	#	#	#	#	#	<	<	<	#

Log (BPI2017O)

	a	b	c	d	e	f	g	h	i
a	#	>	#	#	#	#	#	#	#
b	<	#	>	>	#	#	>	>	#
c	#	<	#	>	>	#	>	>	>
d	#	<	#	#	>	#	>	>	>
e	#	#	<	<	#	>	>	>	>
f	#	#	#	#	<	#	#	#	>
g	#	<	<	<	<	#	#	#	>
h	#	<	<	<	<	#	#	#	>
i	#	#	<	<	<	<	<	<	#

After (model-id: 8)

	a	b	c	d	e	f	g	h	i
a	#	>	#	#	#	#	#	#	#
b	<	#	>	>	#	#	#	#	#
c	#	<	#	>	>	#	>	>	>
d	#	<	#	#	>	#	>	>	>
e	#	#	<	<	#	>	>	>	>
f	#	#	#	#	<	#	#	#	>
g	#	#	<	<	<	#	#	#	>
h	#	#	<	<	<	#	#	#	>
i	#	#	<	<	<	<	<	<	#

(c) The footprint matrices of the BPI2017O log and the before/after models (id: 3 and 8). The number of different cells is reduced from 14 to 4. The different four cells stem from the fact that it is possible in the log to skip activity c or d to directly execute g or h after activity b.

Fig. 7. A comparison of the before/after models for the BPI2017O log.

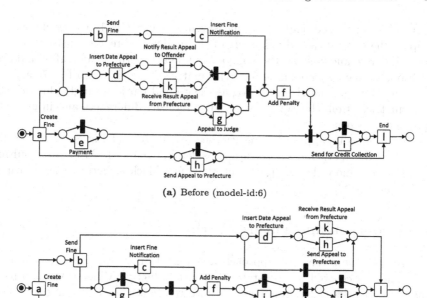

(a) Before (model-id:6)

(b) After (model-id:12): The modified model has quite some changes except for a few activities such as the start and end activities. First, activity b (*Send Fine*) is placed as the start of two parallel branches. Also, the activities related to "Prefecture" (d,h,k) are now placed closely together as one of the branches after activity b. The self-loop behavior of activity e (*Payment*) is not captured by both models. We assume there is a trade-off between precision and fitness here as allowing self-loop for activity e would probably increase fitness slightly but decrease precision significantly.

Before (model-id: 6)

	a	b	c	d	e	f	g	h	i	j	k	l
a	#	>	#	>	>	>	>	#	#	#	#	#
b	<	#	>	#	>	‖	#	‖	#	#	#	#
c	#	<	#	#	‖	>	#	‖	#	#	#	#
d	<	#	#	#	‖	#	#	>	>	>	#	#
e	<	‖	‖	‖	#	‖	‖	‖	‖	>	‖	‖
f	<	#	<	#	‖	#	<	‖	>	<	<	>
g	<	#	‖	‖	‖	>	#	‖	‖	‖	‖	>
h	<	‖	‖	‖	‖	‖	‖	#	‖	‖	‖	>
i	#	#	#	#	<	<	#	‖	#	#	#	>
j	#	#	#	<	‖	>	‖	‖	#	#	‖	#
k	#	#	#	<	‖	>	‖	‖	#	#	#	#
l	#	#	#	#	<	<	#	<	#	#	#	#

Log (traffic)

	a	b	c	d	e	f	g	h	i	j	k	l
a	#	>	#	>	>	#	>	#	#	#	#	#
b	<	#	>	‖	‖	#	‖	‖	#	#	#	>
c	#	<	#	‖	‖	>	>	‖	#	#	>	#
d	<	‖	‖	#	‖	‖	‖	‖	‖	‖	>	‖
e	<	‖	‖	‖	#	‖	‖	‖	>	‖	‖	‖
f	#	#	<	‖	‖	#	‖	‖	>	‖	‖	#
g	<	‖	<	‖	‖	‖	#	‖	>	‖	‖	>
h	#	‖	‖	‖	‖	‖	‖	#	‖	‖	‖	>
i	#	#	#	<	<	<	<	‖	#	<	<	>
j	#	#	#	‖	‖	>	‖	‖	>	#	‖	>
k	#	#	#	<	‖	‖	‖	‖	>	‖	#	>
l	#	<	#	<	<	#	<	<	<	<	<	#

After (model-id: 12)

	a	b	c	d	e	f	g	h	i	j	k	l
a	#	>	#	#	>	#	>	#	#	#	#	#
b	<	#	>	>	‖	>	>	#	#	#	#	#
c	#	<	#	‖	‖	>	#	‖	#	#	‖	#
d	#	<	‖	#	‖	‖	#	>	‖	‖	>	>
e	<	‖	‖	‖	#	‖	‖	‖	‖	>	‖	‖
f	#	<	<	‖	‖	#	<	‖	>	>	‖	>
g	<	<	#	‖	‖	>	#	‖	‖	‖	‖	>
h	#	#	‖	<	‖	‖	‖	#	‖	‖	‖	>
i	#	#	#	‖	<	<	#	‖	#	#	‖	>
j	#	#	#	<	‖	<	‖	‖	#	#	‖	>
k	#	#	#	<	‖	‖	‖	‖	#	#	#	>
l	#	#	#	<	<	<	#	<	<	<	<	#

(c) The footprint matrices of the traffic log and the before/after models (id:6 and 12). In total, the number of different cells is reduced from 47 to 39. For most of the activities, the differences either decrease or at least remain except for activities b,g, and h.

Fig. 8. A comparison of the before/after models for the traffic log.

fitness for a better F1-score. One can observe that the quality of the output models depends on the input model. For the same log, our approach produces a different model depending on the existing model. Such a dependency is expected as the applications of reduction/synthesis rules depend on the existing structure of the original model [13, 19].

In addition to the aggregated measurements in Table 1, we would like to compare the structures and behaviors of the models before/after using our approach. Figure 7 and 8 show the comparisons between the before/after models. Additionally, the corresponding footprint matrices[8] are shown in Fig. 7c and 8c. Using the footprint matrix of the log as the ground truth, we highlight the cells of the matrices from the WF-nets in red to indicate differences and in green to represent consensuses.

After using our approach, one can see in Fig. 7c and Fig. 8c that the differences in the footprint matrix are considerably reduced. Also, the resulting models have a more flexible representation (non-block structures) as shown in Fig. 7b and Fig. 8b.

6   Conclusion and Future Work

In this paper, we present an approach that aims to improve the quality of process models discovered by the state-of-the-art Inductive Miner (IM) algorithm while retaining desirable properties, such as free-choiceness and soundness. Our approach iteratively modifies the model by removing problematic transitions (using reduction rules) and adding them back (using synthesis rules) to a better location on the model based on F1-score. By applying rules developed from free-choice net theory [12], we ensure that any modification to the net preserves these desirable properties. Moreover, our approach results in a process model that is not restricted to block-structured, allowing for a more flexible representation and potentially higher quality. We implemented the approach in Python and evaluated it using real-life event logs, with experimental results demonstrating improved quality (measured by F1-score) compared to models discovered by IM alone. Additionally, several resulting process models exhibit non-block structured behaviors, and the directly-follows behaviors of the resulting models are more in line with those from the corresponding log.

There are several possible directions for future work. As the evaluation is limited to two real-life event logs, the restricted experiment post a potential threat to the validity of the approach. Moreover, the experimental results show that it is possible to produce a model without any changes. An open question is whether the approach can improve quality in general. Thus, we plan to conduct a more comprehensive evaluation with more real-life event logs and compare it with existing works. The extended experiment can help to further understand when and how well the approach works. Another direction is to take the similarity between the existing and the modified models into consideration so that the resulting model stays as close as possible to the original one.

---

[8] The cells in the matrix represent the relations between the corresponding two activities. For two activities $x, y \in \mathcal{B}(\mathcal{U}_A^*)$, $x > y$ means that x is directly followed by y but not the other way round. $x \# y$ represents that the two activities never follow each other while $x \| y$ means x and y both directly follows each other. For more details and a formal definition of the footprint matrix, we refer to [23].

Acknowledgements. We thank the Alexander von Humboldt (AvH) Stiftung for supporting our research.

References

1. van der Aalst, W.M.P.: Process Mining - Data Science in Action, 2nd edn. Springer, Heidelberg (2016). https://doi.org/10.1007/978-3-662-49851-4
2. van der Aalst, W.M.P.: Discovering directly-follows complete Petri nets from event data. In: Jansen, N., Stoelinga, M., van den Bos, P. (eds.) A Journey from Process Algebra via Timed Automata to Model Learning. LNCS, vol. 13560, pp. 539–558. Springer, Cham (2022). https://doi.org/10.1007/978-3-031-15629-8_29
3. van der Aalst, W.M.P., Adriansyah, A., van Dongen, B.F.: Replaying history on process models for conformance checking and performance analysis. WIREs Data Mining Knowl. Discov. **2**(2), 182–192 (2012)
4. van der Aalst, W.M.P., Dumas, M., Ouyang, C., Rozinat, A., Verbeek, H.M.W.: Choreography conformance checking: an approach based on BPEL and petri nets. In: The Role of Business Processes in Service Oriented Architectures. Dagstuhl Seminar Proceedings, vol. 06291. Internationales Begegnungs- und Forschungszentrum fuer Informatik (IBFI), Schloss Dagstuhl, Germany (2006)
5. Adriansyah, A., Munoz-Gama, J., Carmona, J., van Dongen, B.F., van der Aalst, W.M.P.: Measuring precision of modeled behavior. Inf. Syst. E Bus. Manag. **13**(1), 37–67 (2015)
6. Armas Cervantes, A., van Beest, N.R.T.P., La Rosa, M., Dumas, M., García-Bañuelos, L.: Interactive and incremental business process model repair. In: Panetto, H., et al. (eds.) OTM 2017. LNCS, vol. 10573, pp. 53–74. Springer, Cham (2017). https://doi.org/10.1007/978-3-319-69462-7_5
7. Augusto, A., Conforti, R., Dumas, M., Rosa, M.L., Bruno, G.: Automated discovery of structured process models from event logs: the discover-and-structure approach. Data Knowl. Eng. **117**, 373–392 (2018)
8. Augusto, A., et al.: Automated discovery of process models from event logs: review and benchmark. IEEE Trans. Knowl. Data Eng. **31**(4), 686–705 (2019)
9. Augusto, A., Conforti, R., Dumas, M., Rosa, M.L., Polyvyanyy, A.: Split miner: automated discovery of accurate and simple business process models from event logs. Knowl. Inf. Syst. **59**(2), 251–284 (2019)
10. Berthelot, G.: Transformations and decompositions of nets. In: Brauer, W., Reisig, W., Rozenberg, G. (eds.) Advances in Petri Nets. LNCS, vol. 254, pp. 359–376. Springer, Heidelberg (1986). https://doi.org/10.1007/BFb0046845
11. Carmona, J., Cortadella, J., Kishinevsky, M.: A region-based algorithm for discovering petri nets from event logs. In: Dumas, M., Reichert, M., Shan, M.-C. (eds.) BPM 2008. LNCS, vol. 5240, pp. 358–373. Springer, Heidelberg (2008). https://doi.org/10.1007/978-3-540-85758-7_26
12. Desel, J., Esparza, J.: Free Choice Petri Nets. No. 40, Cambridge University Press, Cambridge (1995)
13. Dixit, P.M.: Interactive process mining. Ph.D. thesis, Technische Universiteit Eindhoven (2019)
14. Dixit, P.M., Verbeek, H.M.W., Buijs, J.C.A.M., van der Aalst, W.M.P.: Interactive data-driven process model construction. In: Trujillo, J.C., et al. (eds.) ER 2018. LNCS, vol. 11157, pp. 251–265. Springer, Cham (2018). https://doi.org/10.1007/978-3-030-00847-5_19

15. van Dongen, B.F., de Medeiros, A.K.A., Wen, L.: Process mining: overview and outlook of Petri net discovery algorithms. Trans. Petri Nets Other Model. Concurr. **2**, 225–242 (2009)
16. Fahland, D., van der Aalst, W.M.P.: Model repair - aligning process models to reality. Inf. Syst. **47**, 220–243 (2015)
17. García-Vallés, F., Colom, J.M.: Implicit places in net systems. In: PNPM, pp. 104–113. IEEE Computer Society (1999)
18. Huang, T., van der Aalst, W.M.P.: Comparing ordering strategies for process discovery using synthesis rules. In: Troya, J., et al. (eds.) ICSOC 2022. LNCS, vol. 13821, pp. 40–52. Springer, Cham (2022). https://doi.org/10.1007/978-3-031-26507-5_4
19. Huang, T., van der Aalst, W.M.P.: Discovering sound free-choice workflow nets with non-block structures. In: Almeida, J.P.A., Karastoyanova, D., Guizzardi, G., Montali, M., Maggi, F.M., Fonseca, C.M. (eds.) EDOC 2022. LNCS, vol. 13585, pp. 200–216. Springer, Cham (2022). https://doi.org/10.1007/978-3-031-17604-3_12
20. Leemans, S.J.J., Fahland, D., van der Aalst, W.M.P.: Scalable process discovery and conformance checking. Softw. Syst. Model. **17**(2), 599–631 (2018)
21. Murata, T.: Petri nets: properties, analysis and applications. Proc. IEEE **77**(4), 541–580 (1989)
22. Polyvyanyy, A., van der Aalst, W.M.P., ter Hofstede, A.H.M., Wynn, M.T.: Impact-driven process model repair. ACM Trans. Softw. Eng. Methodol. **25**(4), 28:1–28:60 (2017)
23. Rozinat, A., van der Aalst, W.M.P.: Conformance testing: measuring the fit and appropriateness of event logs and process models. In: Business Process Management Workshops, vol. 3812, pp. 163–176 (2005)

Author Index

H. van der Aa et al. (Eds.): BPMDS 2023/EMMSAD 2023, LNBIP 479, pp. 343–344, 2023.
https://doi.org/10.1007/978-3-031-34241-7

Printed in the United States
by Baker & Taylor Publisher Services